Alexander Bethune, John Bethune

**Tales of the Scottish Peasantry**

Alexander Bethune, John Bethune

**Tales of the Scottish Peasantry**

ISBN/EAN: 9783337074814

Printed in Europe, USA, Canada, Australia, Japan

Cover: Foto ©ninafisch / pixelio.de

More available books at **www.hansebooks.com**

# TALES

OF THE

# SCOTTISH PEASANTRY

# TALES of the SCOTTISH PEASANTRY

### *By* ALEX. AND JOHN BETHUNE.

**COLLECTED EDITION.**

*Extracts from the Literary Notices of the earlier editions:—*

"The reader who shall purchase this book,—and he may safely purchase it for its intrinsic powers of amusement,—will be surprised at the tone of thought and general elegance of style. Alexander Bethune, had he published anonymously, might have passed for a regular *littérateur.*"—*Spectator.*

"It is the perfect propriety of his taste, no less than the thorough intimacy with the unobtrusive subjects he treats of, which gives Mr. Bethune's little book a great charm in our eyes."—*Athenæum.*

"These tales are written by a man who has spent his life among the sort of people and amidst the scenes he has described. They will be popular, not only with the peasantry of Scotland, but those who know and love their character and ways."—*Tait's Magazine.*

"The author is an excellent example of the sturdy indomitable race of Scottish peasants. The tales, for the most part, pertain to the class to which the writer belongs, and with which he is, of course, most familiar. They display a minute acquaintance with Scottish character, and convey an admirable delineation of the scenes of humble life."—*Glasgow Argus.*

"The pictures of rural life and character appear to us remarkably true, as well as pleasing."—*Chambers' Journal.*

"Mr. Bethune's manner of writing is pure and unaffected, and beautifully adapted to the spirit of his narratives."—*Fife Herald.*

"Of these productions we can speak in terms of unqualified praise."—*Edinburgh Evening Post.*

"The style and composition, both in prose and poetry, are of a superior order, and the tales are interesting."—*Edinburgh Observer.*

"The work is quite a literary phenomenon."—*Fifeshire Journal.*

"The author has taken the best way to rivet the attention, and to interest the heart, of his readers. His unvarnished tales unfold the life and character of the Scottish peasantry; tales drawn from his own observation and from truth, devoid of all improbability, of mawkish sentimentalism, and over-wrought character or incident."—*Edinburgh Weekly Chronicle.*

"These tales do credit alike to the head and heart of their author."—*Aberdeen Herald.*

"We were quite struck with the superiority of thought and style in these tales. As a painter of Scottish manners, he may claim a place in the same niche with the authors of Halloween and Glenburnie."—*Edinburgh Advertiser.*

BY

*ALEX<sup>R</sup> AND JOHN BETHUNE*

*With Biography of the Authors
By John Ingram, F.S.A. Scot.*

LONDON: HAMILTON, ADAMS, & CO.
GLASGOW: THOMAS D. MORISON
1884.

# EDITORIAL PREFACE.

No apology is required for the republication of these tales. Their own merit is sufficient justification for their reappearance in the present handy form. They were originally published in two volumes in 1838 and 1843, and, at the time, excited great interest in the literary world from the highly characteristic and original features they contained, and from the general interest felt in the noble-minded and highly-gifted authors. Copies of the original volumes are now rarely to be met with, and when they do turn up, it is at a price which practically puts them beyond the reach of the ordinary reader. This has been so for many years, and the wonder is that they have not been reproduced ere now in a suitable form, and at a moderate cost. Most of the tales are written by Alexander, a few by John, whom, however, we associate with his elder brother in the biographical sketch, as their life-pursuits, tastes, and interests, were so interwoven as almost to be identical. They were also authors of much miscellaneous literature, including poetry and biography, which appeared in the periodical literature of the day. These contributions, however, the publisher does not consider as coming within the scope of the present volume.

Regarding the tales, they are not only good in themselves, but they assist in preserving and illustrating in a popular form the manners, habits, and local customs of the Scottish peasantry during the first quarter of the present century. And in addition, they possess to an unusually high degree the more excellent and nobler qualities of simplicity, and of being true to nature, with a distinct and ever present, but not obtrusive tendency to teach some high moral purpose, or to give expression to some healthy, soul-touching sentiment, which the heart loves to cherish

# CONTENTS.

|  | PAGE |
|---|---|
| PREFACE . . . . . | 5 |
| BIOGRAPHICAL SKETCH OF THE BROTHERS BETHUNE . . . . . . . . | 9 |
| THE DEFORMED . . . . | 31 |
| THE FATE OF THE FAIREST . . . . | 61 |
| THE DECLINE AND FALL OF THE GHOST . | 80 |
| THREE HANSELMONDAYS . | 98 |
| MARGARET CLINTON . | 118 |
| THE COVENANTER'S GRAVE | 130 |
| THE STRANGER . | 169 |
| DISINTERESTEDNESS . . | 178 |

## CONTENTS.

|  | PAGE |
|---|---|
| THE DRUNKARD | 184 |
| THE ILLEGITIMATE | 243 |
| THINGS AND THOUGHTS | 271 |

JONATHAN MOUDIWORT:

    Chapter I.—Indications of Character—Small Beginnings . . . . . 278

    Chapter II.—Ways and means indispensable to rising in the World . . . . . . 288

    Chapter III.—Important discovery concerning the keeping of the Sabbath, and other matters, ending with a marriage . . . . . 298

    Chapter IV.—Poetical Justice—Untoward Accidents, and the Conclusion . . . . 308

THE COUSINS . . . . . . 314

AULD PETER AND HIS FOSTER SON . . . 327

# BIOGRAPHICAL SKETCH

#### OF THE

# BROTHERS BETHUNE.

---

It has almost become proverbial that Scotland has supplied from her peasantry, the names of more men eminent in Science, Art, Literature, and especially in Song, than that furnished by the same class in any other country. Perhaps this may be accounted for variously. Some men have risen on the strength of their own inherent genius, if not to fortune in their lifetimes, at least to their names having become famous and immortal, and their works successful, after their death. To this class might be said to belong Burns, and, in a lesser degree Hogg, and a host of other minor celebrities. Some attribute the reason of the Scotsman's prominence on the long bead-roll of fame to his national characteristic, untiring industry and perseverance, which, with a fair share of education and common-sense, is bound, they say, in the long run to end in success. Such examples have generally risen from the peasantry, that class which has long proved the worthiest and most virtuous of our rural population, a class accounted the mainstay and backbone of our nationality before the days of Highland depopulation and political centralisation.

From parents possessed of superior mental and moral endowments belonging to this class, have sprung such types as Allan Cunninghame, the Messrs. Chambers, and, along with the highest personal genius, inherent and partially inherited, that almost crown of Scotland's literary glory, Thomas Carlyle, the greatness of whose life and work will only be seen and appreciated as time rolls on. Other two men more humble in their origin and less gifted in their genius, but equally great in the purity, nobility, and unspotted nature of their lives, and whose works are sufficiently meritorious to deserve a permanent record in the history of their country's literature, are Alexander and John Bethune, the authors of the following tales, whose names have become inseparably associated, and long familiarly known, as the Brothers Bethune.

Regarding their literary efforts, while some of it might have been due to the promptings of poverty, very much also was the result of their large-hearted benevolence, and real human interest they took in their fellow-beings, and in their laudable ambition to produce something that would be of more than a mere passing interest in the literary world. This interest we find to be an intelligent one. Their whole previous career, their training and education, or rather the want of it, was most unfavourable to the proper expression of their thoughts and ideas. But this did not lessen their value; they were familiar with the manners and customs of the class to which they belonged, and could trace the workings of their minds on a given subject from their earliest dawnings to full fruition; they knew their likes and dislikes, their prejudices, their virtues and their failings, and, knowing all this, could pourtray with graphic power, the result of long and laboured experience, the scene or idea they had conceived. What they wished to teach, above everything else, was truth, morality, and that self-dependence which was so very characteristic of their own lives. But they did not begin by prating to the people empty pious platitudes; they knew human nature too well to think they would swallow the pill unless it was gilded, so they first endeavoured to interest the people in their tales and stories, and allowed the lesson they meant to teach through them, to sink unconsciously into their minds. They believed it better to write a tale which would have the elements of some great truth or moral virtue in it, and which might be read by thousands, than to write a book full of valuable instruction, which might lie unlooked at on the bookseller's shelves. This was well illustrated in their own experience, for, while their tales were very popular, and gained them a little money, their volume on "Practical Economy," the joint labours of both, while equally meritorious, was by no means so much sought after.

Alexander, the elder brother, was born at Upper Rankeillour, in the parish of Letham, Fifeshire, in the month of July, 1804, and John, the younger, in August, 1811, in the same county, and in the parish of Moniemail, at a place called The Mount, once famous as the residence of Sir David Lyndsay. Both their parents were servants, and though they had always a severe struggle with poverty, they were noted for their general excellence of character, especially the mother, Alison Christie, who seems to have been a woman of superior mind and great independence of spirit, qualities inherited in a still stronger degree by her two sons. One who knew her well says: "She was altogether a rare character, auld Aily!—pious, but not austere; devout, but not bigoted; beneficent without ostentation, hospitable, kind-hearted, and generous even to a fault. She deserved (if ever woman on earth deserved it) the title of a 'Mother in Israel.' What a wonderful fund of humour she had too! had her lot been cast in a higher sphere of life, and her education been like her abilities, she would doubtless have been admired as an ornament of her sex. From her, if genius be hereditary, the poets must have derived the singular talent which they possessed." Of the father the same authority says that he was a worthy patriarch with the snows of eighty or ninety winters on his venerable head, and that from his precepts and example the sons derived much of that unbending integrity and noble independence which uniformly distinguished them.

In consequence of the poverty of the parents, the education of the sons was almost entirely of the home or domestic sort, and chiefly devolved upon the mother, who was henceforth to be responsible for their mental and moral training. Alexander was never more than four or five months at a school till he was about three-and-twenty, when he attended evening-classes for a short time, while John was but one day.

As the father was a servant, the family had to endure the inconvenience of frequent removals from place to place during the first seven or eight years of Alexander's life, but after the birth of the younger brother, John, they came to Woodmill, in the parish of Abdie. In 1813 they again removed to a place called Lochend, about a quarter of a mile distant, and here they continued to reside for the next twenty-four years. Alexander tells us that it was in consequence of his parents being, from ill-health and other causes, unable to apprentice him to any trade that he betook himself, at the age of fourteen, to the humble occupation of a labourer. No doubt digging drains and ditches is a prosaic as well as a toilsome occupation for a young literary genius, aspiring to climb Parnassus' heights; yet, through it all, he never flinched from the oneness of his purpose, but "still bore up and steer'd right onwards."

Several years were thus spent in struggles to relieve the circumstances of his parents, while those hours of leisure he could command were employed in reading such books as he could borrow in the neighbourhood, and in otherwise endeavouring to improve his mental faculties. Such were some of the hard and cruel toils of his early life, that he says, more than a year afterwards, his joints, on first attempting to move in the morning, creaked like machinery wanting oil.

Meanwhile, John, whom we formerly stated had only been one day at school, was sent when about eight years of age to herd two cows, which their father, as forester on the Woodmill estate, was then allowed to keep. This herding by the margin of "the waveless lake," as he loved to call the little Loch of Lindores, was little to his taste. But worse was to follow. During the winter of 1823-4, to assist in supporting himself, he broke stones, along with his brother Alexander, on the road between Lindores and Newburgh. He was still under thirteen years of age—in fact, quite a boy, and from the lack of motion necessary in such work, his legs and feet were sometimes almost frozen. But he had caught the spirit of independence, and would have suffered or encountered anything, so that he might enable them to get quit of some debt which had been incurred in consequence of their father's illness.

In March, 1824, he apprenticed himself for two years to a weaver in the village of Collessie, about three miles distant from his home. At this business he very soon could earn as much as one-and-tenpence a-day, while Alexander could make little more than half that amount at stone-breaking. In order to make a provision for his aged father, Alexander determined to learn the business also. By an agreement with his master, John's engagement terminated sooner than the stipulated time. They then took a house as a work-shop, and with about ten pounds, that had been saved by the most "desperate economy," purchased looms and other articles appropriate to weaving; and at Martinmas, 1825, John commenced that business on his own account, with Alexander as an apprentice. But the commercial crash which immediately followed—1825-26—so utterly disappointed all their calculations, that they were again glad to resume their occupations as out-door labourers, the one at a shilling and the other at one shilling and twopence a-day. Some time after this, when trade recovered a little, their weaving-shop was required by the landlord for other purposes, and their weaving utensils, which had cost, what to them was quite a little fortune, was so much useless lumber.

In addition to the many hardships of boyhood and youth, John had to struggle with all the evils of an enfeebled constitution. From 1827 till his death, he was more or less troubled with dyspepsia, which in time developed into a complication of diseases, ending in consumption. Alexander attributes the commencement of his disorders to his remaining too long in the fresh water while bathing, and by over-exertion in the potato-harvest, taxing his bodily powers too severely before he had attained the full strength of manhood. In the winter of 1827, by working in wet drains, up to the knees in water and exposure to severe frost, the seeds of his future illness were sown. During the early months of 1828 he was laid up with a bad cold, upon recovering from which he was visibly much paler than before, and was ever after very subject to periodical attacks of hard, dry cough, which lasted for weeks and sometimes for months. Add to this the facts contained in the following extract from a letter of Alexander's, written during his last illness, and we will probably see the true origin of that disease which terminated fatally in the case of both brothers:— "From 1814," he says, "to 1837 we, with the exception of one year, lived in a house which, for the greater part of that period was in such bad repair, that when it rained we had to place the most of the dishes that we possessed upon the top of the beds to intercept the water that oozed through the roof; and when the rain began to fall after we were sleeping, it was no uncommon thing for us to awake in the morning with the bed-clothes partially wet about us. In winter, too, during a thaw, or a protracted fall of rain, the water came in under the foundation of the back wall, and flowed in a stream through the floor, nearly the whole length of the house, till it made its escape by the door. Nor was this the worst of it; in some places it formed pools of such extent, that my brother and myself, who slept at the further end of the house, were frequently obliged to lay stones and pieces of wood on them to enable us to reach our bed. We did not seem to suffer anything at the time, but I am now convinced that to the damp air with which we were so often surrounded, he (John) owed a part of that delicacy of the chest which at last consigned him to an early grave, while I am, perhaps, indebted to the same cause for a something of the same kind."

In October, 1829, John was engaged as a day labourer in the gardens and plantations on the estate of Inchrye. The following month Alexander, while blasting rock in a quarry was, by an explosion of gunpowder, carried a distance of nine or ten yards, and pitched into a cairn of stones, where he was so severely mangled, that recovery was doubtful. John now became, for the next four months, the sole bread-winner of the family, in addition to carefully nursing his brother at night till the danger was passed. Three years after, Alexander was a second time "subjected to nearly the same sort of discipline." On this occasion there were two of them employed about the blast when it exploded. The other man was killed, while he, though more fortunate, was found, when taken up, to be quite insensible, and sadly scorched and cut about the hands, head, and face.

During the periods of convalescence after these disasters, he amused himself with various efforts of literary composition, chiefly in verse. Alexander mentions a circumstance which tended greatly to quicken their taste for literature, and stimulate their ambition for literary pursuits, since which, both he and his brother had been unceasing in their efforts of self-improvement. When about the age of twenty-one, he made the acquaintance of a St. Andrews student, who, in order to procure the means of prosecuting his studies, had opened an evening school in one of the houses at Lochend. He was an excellent reciter of poetry, and had his mind well stored with a number of the best pieces from the best authors. With these he amused and delighted his hearers in his leisure time, the greater part of which was spent with the Bethunes. Alexander's first serious attempt to write a book, he attributes to the following incident, which we give in his own words.

"As it is sometimes curious to see what a trifling incident will give an impulse to the human mind, I may here be permitted to tell you what it was that first set me seriously to the task of writing a book. A young lady, the daughter of a neighbouring laird, who farmed his own property, of about eighty acres, himself, had been in the habit of sometimes calling to inquire for my mother, who had been a servant in the family of her grandmother. From her she had learned that myself and my brother were much given to reading, and that we sometimes went a little farther, and made attempts at writing. We were accordingly favoured with the loan of a book called 'The Amethyst,' a sort of religious annual. . . . We were forthwith requested to furnish some verses for the succeeding number, which were to be forwarded by the said young lady to its editor. Without being greatly taken with the proposal, the verses were forwarded to our supposed patroness. About three weeks thereafter, being then employed breaking stones upon the public road, I was saluted by the young lady, who, after enquiring after the health of my father and mother, proceeded, with some embarrassment, to tell me that, after a great deal of consideration, she had come to the conclusion that it would be for my advantage to suppress the verses; but that she really felt vexed, as I might possibly feel vexed, at their not being sent, etc., etc. To this I replied that the thing had excited no expectations, and therefore could occasion no disappointment; and that I should be truly sorry for myself if I could be 'hurt' at such trifles. But while I said this to her, I said, or rather thought, to myself,—All very right, and only what might have been expected; but, in time, we shall see if a smooth-faced girl is to have the power of determining whether I am to appear in print or not; and from that hour I never lost sight of my purpose for a moment till the MS. of 'Tales and Sketches of the Scottish Peasantry' was complete."

Discouragements like these, however, instead of proving obstacles in the path of genius, act rather as an incentive to more determined perseverance, and, in the end, leads to greater success.

In 1833 it was agreed by the brothers that they should conjointly produce a small volume of Scriptural pieces, which was to have been entitled, "The Poetical Preacher," but owing to the repeated illness of the younger brother, and various other causes, the design was abandoned. John's contributions towards it were afterwards included in the volume of poems, with life prefixed, published after his death.

It may be observed that many of Alexander's first literary efforts, like those of his brother's, took the form of verse; but though endowed with a fair share of the poetical faculty, he never by any means excelled in this line of composition to the same degree as he did in prose.

Up till this time both brothers had subjected themselves to a severe and continued course of self-culture, in which they resorted to some curious expedients. Of course this could only be done in the brief intervals snatched from their duties as bread-winners, in the walks to and from their work, or, while eating their humble meals. By sitting up late, and rising early, they had contrived to write a good deal, both in poetry and prose, but in such a secret manner that the fact was scarcely known beyond the family circle.

Holding the views of practical and social economy they did, it was quite natural they should wish to make a little money by their writings, as well as to have their ideas given to the world through some organ of the press that was seen and read by the public. They had hitherto been unable to accomplish this, and to overcome the difficulty, Alexander, in the month of May, 1835, addressed a long and very characteristic letter to one of the Messrs. Chambers, in which he gives many interesting particulars regarding himself, his position and education, his ideas of men and things in general, and his attempts at authorship, asking his influence and advice as to the best method of bringing them before the public. At this time he says he had as many verses—which he did not call poetry—as would make a small volume; prose essays, etc., that would fill another; while he could easily furnish a third, composed of tales or little novels. He confesses that, like Burns, he had early "some stirrings of ambition," chiefly to make his fellowmen at least less miserable. "But," he says, "in me those risings of the heart had no outlet. What could a labourer do with seven shillings, or seven-and-sixpence a week? My efforts I found were but a mockery of benevolence, and showed rather the will than the ability to relieve. I might indeed," he continues, "have wriggled myself into some sort of notice and earned higher wages—I might have got myself promoted to be foreman over a few ditchers and dykers, and by 'damning them to get on,' as is customary with such officials, I might have procured a little favour with their masters and a little money for myself." But he disdained to be a slave-driver. He could not learn a trade, as he saw no means of support during the apprenticeship. There was no prospect of ever being able to earn more than the very barest means of subsistence for himself and two parents, whose support depended wholly upon him and his brother John. It can scarcely be wondered at then, that he should turn his thoughts to writing. It appeared the only open door to him. Others had succeeded in the same way, and why not he? Hence this appeal to Mr. Chambers, and his anxiety to submit to him "a few of these unquenched snuffings of the midnight taper," that he might pass an opinion as to their merit, and the propriety of giving them to the public. He goes on to confess he is ambitious, but not merely of "getting on in the world." . . . "I never looked," he says, "upon a fine coat as the alpha and omega of a man's ambition." He is quite aware the opinions he holds regarding society are heretical; he thinks them (the rich) "in many respects as ignorant as himself, and in most respects as selfish as one could well wish them to be." He "cannot imagine how roast beef and plum-pudding should make a man either clearer-headed or better-hearted than porridge and potatoes. The last, with the addition of some milk and much water, has been exclusively the fare of the present writer, and he has no wish to change it." . . . He adds, "There is nothing which I would not attempt, nor any difficulty from which I would shrink, with the prospect of being ultimately successful before me. I would not, however, travel the dirty road to public notice and fame which some have waddled over. I would prefer poverty and an obscure death, with an honest independence of thought and principle, to wealth and eminence procured by fawning upon the rich and flattering lordly patrons." The principle expressed in these two sentences was rigidly adhered to by both brothers throughout their brief career.

About three months after the date of this letter, "The Harvest Day," a tale of humble life, appeared in *Chambers's Journal*, No. 185. This is one of Alexander's finest compositions. It was quickly followed in No. 188 by "Hazleburn: A Story of Scottish Rural Life." These two were probably the first of his stories which appeared in print. Previous to this, however, he had sent through a friend some pieces to Blackwood, but there is no reason to suppose they were ever inserted. Afterwards the two brothers contributed poetical and other productions of a varied nature to various periodicals.

In July, 1836, the MS. of "Tales and Sketches of the Scottish Peasantry" was taken to Edinburgh, and early in 1837 was published by Messrs. Fraser & Co. For the absolute copyright of this the author was to be allowed the price of fifty copies. Five of the pieces contained in this volume were written by John. Shortly after the appearance of "Tales and Sketches," very favourable notices appeared in the leading literary journals, and, among others, the *Athenæum* and *Spectator* speak of them in terms of the most unqualified praise. Some of the critics, considering that the author was humbly born, self-educated, nursed in poverty, and struggling with adversity, termed the work a literary phenomenon.

In 1835, the year preceding that in which the MS. of their "Tales and Sketches" was sent to Edinburgh, it almost seemed as if the sun of prosperity was for once to shine upon the fates of these remarkable brothers. John obtained the situation of overseer at Inchrye, and an assistant also being required, Alexander accompanied his brother in that capacity. John's income during this period was £26 yearly, with some trifling perquisite—a larger sum than he ever earned at any former or later period of his life. At the end of six months, however, the estate passed into other hands, and it was at once intimated to the overseer that his services would not be required longer than the year for which he was engaged. Thus soon were their brightening fortunes clouded. The house, also, at Lochend, in which they had lived for so many years, was situated on this property, and they soon received notice from the new proprietor that they must leave it. The brothers considered they were very harshly dealt with on this occasion, and determined to provide a home for their aged parents where they would not be subject to the whim or caprice of any landlord. For this purpose they selected about a quarter of an acre of ground on the Back-hill of Ormiston, better known as Mount Pleasant, immediately above the town of Newburgh. Having settled as to the amount of feu duty to be paid for the ground, a sufficient quantity of stones was procured, and then the brothers, with their own hands, commenced to build on the 26th July, 1837. Alexander tells us how they left home every morning before five o'clock, travelled three miles, and wrought till nearly half-past seven in the evening, with no more rest than was absolutely necessary to swallow their breakfast and dinner, said dinner consisting exclusively of bread, which they often ate from their pockets, working all the time. After the day's work was done they had to perform the return journey of three miles. This dreary task was repeated day after day, except during the space of less than a week, when they had the assistance of a regular mason. To ordinary mortals this self-imposed task would seem a cheerless one; but the vision of seeing their parents provided for in comfort during their declining years was sufficient to cheer them in their extraordinary exertions, and warm their hearts as they trudged wearily homewards after each day's toil. When they commenced the house they had only £30 in money, and two bolls of oatmeal. By the time it was finished, on the last day of September,—a little over two months—this was all expended, and they were glad again to engage in such work as they could find, in order to procure the daily necessaries of life for themselves and the family, and to provide a little money to defray the expenses of removing to their new home. This house which they had reared by such "desperate exertion and economy," is a substantial stone structure of two stories in height, and thirty-six feet in length by twenty in breadth; a sufficiently tangible monument to the filial affection and personal worth, as well as of the arduous toil of two poor peasant sons of genius, whose humble virtues and manly character ought to be their country's pride.

To this house they removed on the 9th November, 1837, and, during the following winter, which was so severe as to partly prevent them from engaging in their ordinary labour, they busied themselves with a revision of the MS. of their "Lectures on Practical Economy," which had been returned to them from Edinburgh for that purpose.

This little book is probably one of the most interesting productions of the Brothers Bethune. The lectures were written chiefly with the intention to benefit the homes and habits of the poor. To the usual charm and simplicity of their style, in this case was added, at least from the practical point of view, perfect knowledge of, and familiarity with their subject—a knowledge gained by dearly-bought experience extending from the cradle to the grave. Even the method of its production might aptly be considered as an illustration of the subject, as well as a literary curiosity. The lectures were first written upon brown paper bags ripped open, shreds of paper which had come to the house with tea, sugar, tobacco, etc.—in short, anything that would carry ink, while the authors had no better writing-desk than their knees. The whole of the writing, too, was done with two quills, which were more than half used-up to commence with. They had no books or authorities to consult on the subject save the one article on "Accumulation" in the *Penny Cyclopædia*. Though a failure financially, it was very favourably spoken of by men eminent in the literature of the subject on which it treated; among others Dr. Thomas Murray, the lecturer on Political Economy, Maculloch, and George and Andrew Combe.

Another instance may be given here of their practical economy in the frugality of their habits. Alexander says, in his letter to Mr. Chambers, 1835, before quoted:—"As an evidence of how little I require for myself, it may be mentioned that the coat in which I now write has actually served me since the year 1827. During the whole of that time it has been on service every day, with the exception of about eight months, for which period, between accidents, smallpox, and other diseases, I was mostly confined to bed, or at least unable to wear it much."

Their little volume was well received by the press in general. The *Edinburgh Chronicle* says of it:—"The work is not only right in the main, but it is right in all its details. It embodies a system of practical philosophy. It does not profess to be a system of Political Economy, though, so far as it goes, its Political Economy is sound; but it is a system of social, domestic, personal, and practical economy. It unfolds the general framework and mechanism of society, particularly as respects the industrial classes. It explains the nature of social life and civil society; shows on what principles these depend, and how they may be improved; and how the great objects of human life—health, happiness, and independence—may be best promoted. And the task is performed in a manner so logical, in language so vigorous yet perspicuous, and in a spirit so bland and philanthropic, that while the work cannot but please the scholar, it is equally calculated not merely to please, but to interest and instruct the uneducated reader."

Their intention regarding this work was first to deliver the series of lectures in the surrounding towns and villages, and then when they had acquired, by this means, a certain amount of popularity, to sell the copy-right to a publisher. But they found the labour and irksomeness of committing them to memory intolerable, and were unable to overcome their natural diffidence sufficiently to enable them to appear as public teachers. The idea was reluctantly abandoned, and the MS. sent to Edinburgh, from which it was returned, as stated above, during the winter of 1838, shortly after they had entered their new home.

The authors had already taken considerable pains with their subject, and they now made such alterations and amendments as had been suggested to them by the friendly critics to whom it had been submitted, and again returned it to Edinburgh in the month of March.

In the meantime they had experienced their first family bereavement, by the death of their father, which took place, after a few days illness, on the 8th February. This was a great blow to both, especially to John, whose health for some time had been gradually getting more precarious. Nor is it astonishing that such was the case. His trifling savings were required to defray the funeral expenses of his father, and he was living through the severity of this severe winter, on oatmeal and potatoes, without any addition whatever, not even that of milk. So says Alexander, whose fare was doubtless as primitive and scanty. This pinching poverty and lack of generous nourishment, succeeded by a summer of drudgery must have told on even a stronger constitution than that of John Bethune's. In November he gave up all outdoor labour, and rather rashly resolved to trust to his pen for support in the future. For months he scarcely ever went out, so eager was he to succeed in his now undivided profession. But one evening at the end of January, 1839, he went to a meeting of the Newburgh Temperance Society, for which he had some time acted as Secretary. After sitting for two or three hours in a strongly heated room, he felt, on coming out to the open air, a tendency to shivering. It was a night of intense cold;

he had three miles to walk, and before he reached home, he had caught that fatal cold which paved the way for his dismission from the world.

In getting publishers for his writings, he was only partially successful. One disappointment succeeded another, till on the 8th May, 1839, they received a letter, announcing the publication at last, of their lectures on Practical Economy, and stating that it was no favourite with the trade, as not one of the Edinburgh booksellers had subscribed for a single copy, and that it was not likely to sell in haste. Deeply mortified at the failure of a work, regarding which he was so sanguine of success, his health, which had been very indifferent for some months, now gave way, and, after an illness with many fitful intervals of improvement and relapse, he breathed his last on the 1st of September, 1839. Through all this illness, he was attended by Alexander, with a care and tenderness that could scarcely be surpassed, even by the love or self-devotion of woman. He left all his own labours that he might attend on his wants. He went with him to various places for change of air, supported him in his extreme weakness, and even put on his clothes in the morning to warm them for him ere he got out of bed. Alexander was inconsolable at the loss of his brother, part of his very existence seemed to have been wrenched from him. So great was his grief, that it cast a gloom over the whole remaining portion of his life, that nothing could altogether dispel. We find him in a letter to a friend thus lamenting his loss—"Seven months since he was laid to sleep in the dust, never again to be awakened, by spring, or summer, or any returning season, till the mighty angel shall come forth, and swear that time shall be no longer. . . . Every morning when I awake, every night when I lie down, everything with which I am surrounded, and every moment which passes, brings him freshly to my remembrance. To me the rising sun shines on loneliness, and his setting beam writes in shadows the deep and sad conviction that my most valued, and almost my last friend, is gone."

He commenced to write a sketch of his brother's life, without any view to its future publication, and this served in a measure to wean him from the melancholy which threatened to overwhelm him. He says if he himself were dead, there lives not one who could tell aught concerning his brother, "save that he lived poor, toiled hard, and died early," and further adds, "that our feelings and pursuits were almost the very same, that we never knew what it was to have separate interests for a single moment, that we had buffeted, or rather been buffeted, by fortune together from boyhood, that we had supped from the same table, sat by the same fire, and slept in the same bed, with very few interruptions, from the period of infancy, and that we were nearly the last of the name and the race to which we belonged." At the request of some friends, he agreed to prepare for publication, together with this life, a selection of John's poems. To him it was indeed a labour of love. He entered upon it with great zeal, spared no pains, working at it both night and day, excepting such times as enabled him to procure the necessaries of life, either by the drudgery of his ordinary toil, or by his literary labours. The principal object in making this attempt was to raise a few pounds, wherewith to place a stone over his brother's grave in Abdie churchyard.

When the "Life and Poems" was ready, it was sent for revision to a literary friend, who had performed the same kind office for the former works published by the Brothers Bethune. Five or six hundred copies of the book were subscribed for, and the remainder of the issue of seven hundred almost immediately sold on publication. *The Athenæum*, *The Witness*, and other papers spoke very favourably of it, while its reception by the public must have been highly gratifying to Alexander. Had a larger edition been printed, the result, from a pecuniary point of view, might have been pretty considerable. It passed into a second edition the following year, 1841, published by Wright and Albright, Bristol. As an introduction, a very appreciative extract is given of a letter from James Montgomery the poet. A good number of new poetical pieces have been added, and, had it not been that the publishers were dissuaded from it, by Mr. Montgomery in this same letter, they would have willingly enlarged the second edition to two volumes without the least scruple. This memoir of his brother secured for its author much sympathy and attention from many who were utter strangers to him, along with offers of assistance, all of which he firmly and consistently refused. When money was sent him he invariably returned it, and, while thanking his would-be benefactors, told them at the same time that he considered it the duty of every man to provide for his own necessity, as far as his ability would go.

He once received an anonymous letter containing fifteen pounds, which he was merely to acknowledge receipt of through his publishers; he did so, but informed his unknown friend that the money was lodged in the bank subject to his order. Mr. Bethune was never able to ascertain the name of this kind and generous friend, but we believe it was Mr. H. F. Chorley, the author of "Music and Manners" and other works, who, with the assistance of some friends, contributed the money and transmitted it through the publishers, Messrs. A. & C. Black. Those who became interested in him, and wished to befriend him in any way, were obliged to confine their efforts to promoting the sale of his books, a means of relief which he evidently considered did not infringe the stern principle of his independence. So jealous was he of this feeling of independence and self-respect, that he was sometimes afraid his friends were *making a demand* for his books, as a pretext for bestowing their own benevolence upon an author, who had too much of the "pride of poverty" in his disposition to accept it in any other form.

The following is an instance of his almost Quixotic honesty in money matters. A friend who had succeeded in disposing among his acquaintances of about 100 copies of his brother's "Life and Poems" at four shillings each, sent him the money, which he at the time accepted, partly to relieve the wants of his mother, who was now so ill as to require almost his whole care and attention night and day. The price mentioned in the prospectus, and for which the book usually sold, was three shillings, at which rate the 100 copies would have realised fifteen pounds. The difference between this and twenty-two pounds, the sum sent by his friend, he afterwards returned, determined not to use one farthing of what he considered did not exclusively belong to him.

Notwithstanding the painful minuteness of the narrative of John's long and tedious illness, this affectionate memoir is full of interest. It presents to us a vivid picture of the peasant class of Scotland, and of peasant life at that time. It traces their own early education, or rather the want of it, their efforts of self-improvement under the most unpromising circumstances, learning to read, write, and spell almost when they had reached manhood, then making their acquaintance with such volumes as may be considered heirlooms in the family of every Scottish peasant, such as the "Cloud of Witnesses," "The Scots Worthies," "The History of Bruce and Wallace," and the "Poems of Burns." Subsequently it details all the difficulties, struggles, latent and secretly cherished ambitions, and wonderful efforts of self-denial practised through years of grinding poverty and toil. The marvel is that so much industry, good sense, sobriety, and other virtues that adorn their spotless lives had no more seeming result from a worldly point of view. They were born poor, and poverty and misfortune haunted them through life. None of their undertakings seemed to prosper, accident, disease, and death again and again interfered with the execution of their plans, and at last carried them both off, partly victims to the injudicious over-exertions of their early life, and partly to the continued, and perhaps unavoidable hardships of their maturer years, just as their case was beginning to attract the universal sympathy and respect of the public.

The favourable reception accorded to Alexander's life of his brother was marred by another melancholy bereavement, the death of his mother, which occurred on the 21st December. During the whole of her illness, her son attended and watched over her with the most affectionate and self-denying care, and he states that for nearly five months his clothes had never been off except to change his shirt. After repeatedly taxing his powers to such an extreme, it is little wonder that he died early.

The successive deaths, at short intervals, of so many near relations, united with the other hardships of his lot, left him very dejected in spirit. He says his mother's death was the annihilation of the last shred of that little world of domestic affection, in the midst of which he was once happy, and among the remaining ruins of which he still wished to dwell. But all was now over, the last green spot around which memory, imagination and fancy were alike fain to linger, had for ever disappeared, and an unvariegated desert remained behind. Though poverty and sorrow had almost broken his spirit, still he laboured on with the usual unflagging industry, and there were even seasons in his life when he could reflect upon his departed friends with a melancholy interest which had more in it of pleasure than of pain. But we find that while formerly he wrote with greater hopefulness regarding his prospects in the future, now hope had ceased to gild that future for him, and he shrank from the very idea of making any change in his situation, even when it appeared to be for the better. One such change he did make about this time, 1841, but it was unsatisfactory, and he never ventured another. Mrs. Hill, the wife of the Inspector of Prisons in Scotland, having read his brother's "Life and Poems," became interested in the author, and procured for him what she conceived would be a comfortable situation in the Glasgow Bridewell. He accepted it without having any very sanguine expectations regarding it, but on getting there he learned he would have to officiate for a year or two as a turnkey in order to master the science of "prison discipline," after which he might have a chance of promotion by being appointed a jailor in some county town with a salary of forty or fifty pounds a year. He was disappointed when he found the duties he was expected to perform were those of a turnkey, and with that consideration for others which characterised all his actions, he resolved, for the sake of his patroness, to remain for a few months, and then beg to be allowed to retire from a situation for which he considered himself unqualified. But little over a week had passed, after entering upon his duties, when he caught a bad cold, and, fearing the effects would be similar as in his brother's case two years previously, he wrote a note resigning his situation, and returned home, most of the way on foot. From the effects of this wild goose chase, as he called it, he did not recover for three or four months. Of all conceivable occupations, it was the least adapted to a man of the habits and character of Alexander Bethune.

Mrs. Hill, however, still continued to interest herself in his behalf, and next endeavoured to procure for him a post as teacher or librarian in the Perth Penitentiary. A long and interesting correspondence passed between them in which he embodies some of his views in regard to prison discipline. Nothing ever came out of the Perth affair, so that his ambition to become a moral teacher of some sort or other was still ungratified.

In 1842 he published a memoir of his grandmother, Annie Macdonald, the sale of which fully answered his expectations, and brought him about twenty pounds. In the month of July of the same year he paid a visit of eight or ten days to Aberdeenshire, to see his friend and future biographer, Mr. William M'Combie, a kindred spirit with himself, and the author of "Hours of Thought" and "Moral Agency." He walked on foot the greater part of the way, going and returning. This same year, at the end of the harvest, he paid another visit to Edinburgh to make arrangements for the publication of the "Scottish Peasant's Fireside." This volume appeared in February, 1843, and was published by Adam and Charles Black, who took the whole risk, and allowed the author half of the clear profits that might arise from the sale. While it was passing through the press in the end of 1842, he was attacked by fever, from which he never properly recovered. By a gradual transition, the disease developed into that of pulmonary consumption. He removed to the little village of Kennoway for change of air, but derived no advantage from it.

In one of the periods of his partial convalescence, an offer was made to him, which he conditionally accepted, of the editorship of the *Dumfries Standard*, a paper about to be started in the Non-intrusion interest in Dumfries. This was almost the only flash of fortune's lamp that had brightened his worldly path, and seemed as if it was the one gleam of comfort, specially sent to cheer the struggling spirit in its journey to the great beyond. The salary was to have been £100 a year, not a large one, certainly, for an editor, but vast indeed to one whose former resources were so limited, and whose habits and mode of life were so economical. But alas! it never was destined to be more than a prospect. It is questionable, even had he recovered sufficiently, whether he would have found the employment so congenial to one of his temperament as he anticipated. Even poor Hugh Miller himself, upon whose recommendation he was selected, found the self-same task a hard one indeed, and in the end sank under it.

After his return from Kennoway, he became gradually weaker, and soon ceased all attempts at writing. He had, during this period, relaxed a little his principles of independence, and allowed some English friends and others to minister to his comfort. He only permitted this in one or two cases, and from those whose friendship he highly valued, and accompanied by the proviso that he would either repay the money, or devote it to the relief of others, if ever he should be able to resume his labours. One of those friends was a Quaker lady in England, who had formerly sought to assist him, and who had since been one of his most regular and welcome correspondents. Several medical gentlemen, also, belonging to Bristol, through one of their number, tendered him their professional advice, offered to supply him with money, and even undertook the whole responsibility of having him removed to enjoy the benefits of some milder and more equable climate—such as that of Bute—which it was supposed would be favourable to the recovery of his health. His rapidly increasing weakness, however, prevented this from being carried into effect. There is thus some slight satisfaction in the reflection that during his last illness, he lacked no comfort, and was nursed with great care and tenderness by his surviving aunt, Mrs. Ferguson. After a few months lingering illness, he died on Tuesday, the 13th June, and was buried on the following Saturday.

He had expressed his desire to be laid in the same grave as his brother, but owing to some carelessness, another had been opened, into which the body was placed. But this so dissatisfied his aunt, that she had it disinterred, and put, according to his desire, into his brother's grave. The monument erected by Alexander to his brother John, is a square stone pillar about seven feet high, with a cornice surmounted by a vase. On the north side has been put the following inscription :—

IN THE SAME GRAVE
WITH JOHN, REST THE REMAINS OF
HIS BROTHER,
ALEXANDER BETHUNE,
THE LAST MEMBER OF A WORTHY FAMILY,
WHO DIED, JUNE 13TH, 1843,
AGED 38.

WITH SCARCELY ANY SCHOOL EDUCATION,
AND UNDER THE PRESSURE OF POVERTY, AND
THE SEVEREST TOIL, HE PRODUCED SEVERAL
WORKS OF MUCH MERIT, ILLUSTRATIVE OF THE
CHARACTER AND MANNERS, AND CONDUCIVE TO THE
IMPROVEMENT, OF HIS OWN CLASS OF SOCIETY;
AND WAS AS REMARKABLE FOR HIS INDEPEN-
DENCE OF SPIRIT AND PRIVATE VIRTUES,
AS FOR HIS LITERARY ATTAINMENTS.

This monument now marks the burial place of the whole family, and may with truth be said to be "the graves of an household." Charles Kingsley, himself a nobleman among men, says—"This spot and the house they built, will become a pilgrim's station, only second to Burns's grave, whenever the meaning of worth and worship shall become rightly understood among us." Many may learn a lesson of great usefulness to themselves, and those around them, from the simple story of the lives of John and Alexander Bethune.

J. I.

# TALES

OF

# THE SCOTTISH PEASANTRY.

## THE DEFORMED.

> Deformity is daring.
> It is its essence to o'ertake mankind
> By heart and soul, and make itself the equal—
> Ay, the superior of the rest. There is
> A spur in its halt movements, to become
> All that the others cannot, in such things
> As still are free to both, to compensate
> For stepdame Nature's avarice at first.
> BYRON.

It has been observed, that deformed people are often envious and vindictive, and that few of them are remarkable for those social qualities which are the constituents of domestic happiness. The mind may sometimes be influenced by the formation of the body, but the extraordinary development of evil passions, and the comparative want of kindly feeling, in the victims of deformity, may more frequently be traced to other causes. The scoffs and ridicule to which they are too often subjected in youth are in themselves sufficient to dry up the sources of affection, or convert them into bitter springs from which no waters of sympathy can afterwards flow.

If the boy should be so fortunate as to experience the effects of kindness, without being pampered into arrogance or spoiled by improper indulgence, he will naturally acquire the qualities and imitate the example of his guardians and protectors, and as he grows up he may become the ornament of his kind. The fountains of his heart, by being imbued with kindly feeling at their very opening, may pour forth the stream of universal benevolence; and by comforting the distressed, ministering to the wants of the poor, and conferring happiness on all with whom he is concerned, he may prove, to those who would darken futurity with sceptical doubts, that so much excellence cannot end with "darkness and the worm." But if, on the contrary, the boy, from deformity or any other cause, should be made the subject of ridicule and scorn among his play-fellows, and treated with contempt or left to wither in neglect by older people—should he be condemned to suffer insults and injuries without pity or protection, his heart will naturally yearn to be revenged, and as he grows up he will grasp at every opportunity for gratifying this passion. Marked out as a fit subject for ridicule when *young*, he insensibly imbibes the desire to inflict on others what he has himself suffered. The lesson of malevolence is easily learned, and he soon becomes an adept in that which it should be the care of all to avoid—the art of making others unhappy.

What the effect of such treatment may be, even upon a powerful and, naturally, a benevolent mind, the following story is intended to illustrate.

Hugh M'Arthur was one of those children who, though born without any apparent defect, became afterwards deformed, no one can tell how. At three years of age, when he should have been all life and motion, his legs were so feeble that he was seldom out of his mother's arms; and when set down, he could only tumble about on the floor, assuming attitudes so grotesque, that he appeared more than half an idiot. For the next five or six years, little alteration in his habits or constitution ensued: his growth was stunted, and the weakness in his legs still continued. But as it was impossible for his parents, who were very poor, to provide him with a nurse, he was left to his own instincts, which led him to crawl forth and mingle with the other children as he best could. Here a new source of vexation awaited him. His mis-shapen body and awkward motions made him a common object of sport. They mimicked his uncouth figure, and waddled along on their hands and knees, in mockery of his painful mode of progression; and when, in this way, they had chafed him into a rage, he vented his wrath in unavailing efforts to take vengeance, which but increased the merriment of his tormentors, whose superior agility gave them the most perfect security. They would continue thus to tease him with perverse ingenuity, till the overwrought passions of the wretched boy, after having exhausted themselves in fruitless efforts to punish the aggressors, sunk into moody silence; and then, as a last refuge from insults which he had neither patience to bear nor power to repel, he would crawl home, there to sit in a corner, and sob bitterly for hours together.

To add to his other causes of discomfort and discontent, his little tormentors now began to bestow on him a number of opprobrious names, such as "Hirplin' Hugh," "Hugh the hobbler," "Humphy Hugh," etc.; and the elder boys, improving upon the hints which these afforded, soon formed them into alliterative rhymes, which were for ever rung in his ears. Of these the following may serve as a specimen :—

"Hobblin' Hugh !
A hairy worm crawls like you."

"Hirplin' Hugh 'ill never grow strang,
But creep like a puddock, his hale life lang."

"Humphy M'Arter—hirplin' Hugh,
Gets gutters to hobble in the hale year through."

To these, and many more of the same kind, which were calculated to keep him in remembrance of his weakness and deformity, he was compelled daily to listen. It is true, his parents might have done something to prevent the annoyance to which the unfortunate child was in this manner exposed; but they were exactly of that class of persons who never trouble themselves about any thing, so long as they are not personally affected. They had other children, moreover, who, with the thoughtlessness of youth, sometimes joined in tormenting their brother abroad; and then, to save themselves from that chastisement with which otherwise they might have been visited, combined in misrepresenting him at home. Hugh was, besides, no favourite with his mother. His own account was seldom believed; and a kick, or a cuff, accompanied with—"Haud yer tongue, ye dour little scoundrel!" or, "Gae to the door, ye ill-lookin' vagabond!" was the only redress he got when he ventured to complain. Thus he passed his years of infancy and boyhood,—a creature, as it appeared, destined to receive none of the benefits of parental tenderness, and an utter stranger to "the milk of human kindness."

About this time, however, he experienced some alleviation of his sufferings, by being put to school. The school was kept by a female—the wife of an artisan—who, having had a better education than usually falls to her class, conceived she might turn it to some account, by teaching a few children to read. This individual felt for the unfortunate boy; and, by interposing her authority, succeeded for a time in rescuing him from that contempt, with which his heart had hitherto been crushed. Under her care he took to reading with extraordinary diligence; and, as a reward for his assiduity and good conduct, he was permitted to be the playmate of her little daughter—an only child—during the intervals of school hours. To this humble pair he looked up with the most deferential respect, and his infant companion engaged a large share of his boyish attention.

When about fifteen years of age, a remarkable change began to manifest itself in his frame. Nature, curbed, as it appeared, in his lower extremities, began to operate, with increased power, in the upper part of his body. His chest became capacious; his shoulders swelled out to an uncommon breadth; and, by the time he attained to years of maturity, but for his legs, which were still feeble and disproportionably short, his hands, arms, and the whole upper part of his body, might have passed for those of a giant. His hands and arms, in particular, gave him a decided superiority over ordinary men,—the latter being long to deformity; while, in the former, he possessed such power, that it was almost impossible to loose his hold. People now became cautious of maltreating him. He was known to be a dangerous enemy; and thus he commanded a certain kind of respect, which, however, he attributed solely to fear. He never forgot the ill treatment he had experienced in infancy and boyhood: and this, together with the conviction that, were he again to become the helpless being he had been before, his reception would still be the same, gave an unsocial turn to his thoughts, and a coldness to his manner, which effectually repelled all attempts at kindness on the part of others, and kept him in a sort of isolation from his fellows. His countenance, however, was manly; and, when silent, a close observer would have said there was in it an expression of benevolence, or generosity, or some good feeling, at least; but, when he spoke, there was often biting irony in his very look. He never forgot his own deformity, nor seemed to wish that others should forget it; but in his conversation he took satirical vengeance upon the mental weaknesses of others. For this his early training had given him uncommon abilities. Despised and scorned when young, he had been accustomed, from the dawn of reason, to search into the characters of men; and when he there found scope for the exercise of his satirical vein, he used it less for the purpose of retaliation, than for the gratification of that proud sense of mental superiority, which in some degree compensated him for what he considered the partiality of Nature to those who were better formed, and more fortunate, than himself. From this habit of mind, all the weak and inconsistent points of men's characters became familiar to him: all hearts seemed to be laid bare before him. He saw through hypocrisy, and detected lurking fraud at a glance: and his remarks often fell, with fearful effect, on those who least expected it. The consequence of all this was, that he became exceedingly unpopular among his neighbours, who would have treated him with less ceremony, had it not been that no one cared for being the first to give him offence. Still it must not be forgotten, that this morbid state of mind, and the position in society in which it placed him, originated rather in the combination of circumstances already noticed, than in any natural defect in his disposition, as his subsequent career may, perhaps, serve to show.

When young, Hugh had been considered incapable of learning any trade, and he was therefore allowed to loiter about, doing occasionally little jobs, though much oftener idle. But, when about seventeen, both his parents died. As this event threw him utterly destitute upon the world, it became indispensable that he should do something for his own support. In this many supposed he would utterly fail, and that he would ultimately settle down into a wandering beggar; but here they were mistaken; there was a latent energy in his character, upon which they had not calculated.

He now became a doer of all sorts of drudgery; sometimes feeding cattle for the neighbouring farmers; at others, thrashing with the flail, when he could procure such employment—any thing by which he could command a livelihood, no matter how coarse or mean the labour. Not choosing to become a lodger in the houses of others, he hired a house of his own, which he supplied with some rude articles of furniture, such as a bed, a chair, and a few culinary utensils. Here he lived a sort of hermit; no one intruded upon his privacy, and for a time he showed no disposition to intrude upon that of others. But the most unsociable being on earth can seldom live long in a state of perfect loneliness. It is natural for the heart of man to seek the support of some human sympathy—the intercourse of some kindred spirit,—in short, a refuge from itself; nor was even Hugh M'Arthur altogether without this relief. With his early friends, the schoolmistress and her husband, he was brought once more in contact. With them were associated no bitter recollections. They both possessed feeling dispositions; and, as his helplessness had formerly induced them to afford him all the protection they could, the loneliness in which he now lived elicited their sympathy, and made them treat him with even more than ordinary kindness. It was here he found all the friendship he sought, and, perhaps, all he could enjoy.

The schoolmistress, who had discontinued teaching, now took an interest in some of his domestic arrangements; and the attentions he received were to his heart like the "spring of the desert," which gives a freshness to the arid soil around it. They came mingled with no alloy of bitterness; the recollection that he had experienced the same treatment in his feeble and defenceless boyhood enhanced their value, and he regarded those who bestowed them with an affection only the deeper for its being thus concentrated. The better part of his nature was thus brought to light; and his humble friends, in their turn, manifested a growing esteem for him. But like the water of the desert, which vivifies and fertilises that portion only of the wide waste which lies nearest to it, the new feelings thus awakened in M'Arthur's breast were only local in their operation. His heart overflowed with grateful affection to his generous friends, but to the rest of the world he was still the same. Thus, without any visible alteration in his manners, he reached his twenty-sixth year, hated by some, feared by others, and treated with the mere semblance of respect by all save the members of one little circle.

It was now his misfortune to lose both his friends, who died, leaving an only daughter to the protection of a world, which too often cares but little for such wards.

Lilias, at the time of her bereavement, was about seventeen —a slender, brown haired, blue eyed lass; and though many have been left destitute at an earlier period of life, yet her prospects were sufficiently dreary. Infancy may look upon the death of the nearest and dearest without fully comprehending the extent of its loss; and riper age, with blunted feelings, accumulated interests, and gathered experience, may better bear it; but Lilias was exactly at that time of life when the feelings are keenest, when the counteracting influence of time is unfelt, and the lessons of experience are scarcely begun.

Thus situated, Hugh M'Arthur felt for her as if he had been a brother: not only did he sympathise with her in her sorrow, but, for several days, he laboured incessantly to devise some means by which he might assist her in providing for herself. This, however, was no easy task. Delicacy prevented him from taking a young female under his own protection, because he knew the world would not be tardy in making its own uses of the circumstance; and the habits of thought which his early ill-treatment had produced, deterred him from making any application to others in her behalf. The only scheme he could think of was to pay the rent of the house in which her father and mother had died, if she would consent to remain in it; and, by lessening his own expenses, to assist her in supporting herself there, until marriage, or some other honourable means of subsistence, should render farther aid unnecessary. This alternative he determined to adopt; but he had himself a stern regard for independence, and a horror at the bare idea of incurring an obligation. He sometimes made his own heart a key to the hearts of others—ascertaining their feelings through the medium of his own; and here a voice within made him pause and ponder over the most delicate way of offering his services. While he thus hesitated between an ardent desire to befriend this deserted orphan, and an almost unnecessary caution as to the manner in which it should be done, a kind lady came forward, and proposed to engage her as a servant to her son, who was then establishing himself, for the first time, upon a farm. He was a young unmarried man; an experienced female had been already procured to manage the affairs of his household, and Lilias was to be her assistant. The situation seemed exactly fitted to her years and capacity; and, in her destitute state, it was an easy matter to prevail upon her to accept of it.

Her master's farm was at a distance of several miles, and Hugh now saw her but seldom, though she still continued to occupy a place in his thoughts. He would have kept up a more friendly intercourse; for the respect which he entertained for her parents, now that they were no more, had been transferred to her, and he regarded her with an affection which would have been *love*, had it not been for the idea of his own deformity, which never ceased to haunt him. But he knew that were he to appear on terms of intimacy with her, his most disinterested attentions would be attributed by others to a different motive than mere friendship; and many scornful jests at her expense, and witty allusions to her mis-shapen lover, would be the certain result. For these reasons, he locked up his feelings in his own breast, and forebore all exhibition of kindness; reserving his friendship till she should stand in need of such assistance as he could bestow.

The reader must now suppose that an interval of nearly two years has been passed over.

Early in the month of November, an annual fair was held in the principal town of the district in which the subject of our narrative had settled himself: and to this fair the peasantry, for many miles round, dressed in their holiday apparel, had long been accustomed to go indiscriminately. The men went, some to be in the way of procuring masters, others to purchase articles of clothing, and many merely "to see and be seen." The young women, on their part, rarely failed to frame some excuse for going, the real object being that they might have an opportunity of seeing old sweethearts, or, where these were wanting, be in the way of making new ones. The presence of the matrons was also necessary to see that their husbands did not indulge in too much spirituous liquor, and to direct them in buying clothes for the children, or their own winter dresses. Thus, all went, and most were happy in the anticipation, if not in the actual enjoyment, of *Martinmas Market*. It was, moreover, considered a point of etiquette among the unmarried men, that each should have his lass to come home with; and when two or more became rivals for the smiles of some rural beauty, animosities, and petty brawls, and cuffs, and sometimes broken heads, were the consequence. But this seems to be a cause which operates in the same way everywhere, however its effects may be restrained or modified by fashion or education. Nor does it appear that the rich and the learned possess the slightest advantage over the poor and the ignorant in these matters; for very rich and very learned men have frequently been known to forge an excuse out of such an affair for shooting a fellow-creature, or standing up themselves to be shot, when their poor and unlearned brethren, in all probability, would have only exchanged a few bad names, or, at worst, taken a bout at fisticuffs. But both systems are moral evils, the existence of which in society is the more to be deplored, that there is little likelihood of their ever being eradicated.

In the proceedings thus imperfectly sketched, Hugh M'Arthur had no share. An event which involved the interests of many —which was a source of mirth and enjoyment to thousands— and which would afford abundant topic for future gossip to all —possessed no interest for him. No one thought of the poor deformed recluse, and he cared not for them. On that day he toiled as usual; and when night set in clear and frosty, he retired to his solitary abode by the road-side, and betook himself to his book, after closing his door, that he might not be disturbed by the groups of people who were now returning from the market,—some sober and silent, some half tipsy and noisy, and others in such a plight that they could not walk without the assistance of their more temperate companions. It was now nine o'clock, and Hugh, having laid aside his book, was preparing to extinguish his light and go to bed, when he was alarmed by an impatient knocking at his door. He arose and approached it, with what haste he could, to drive away the disturbers of his peace; but on removing the bolt, what was his surprise to see Lilias stand before him, with her hair dishevelled, her dress partially torn, and her whole manner and appearance betokening a state of the greatest agitation and alarm. In the middle of the road two men were staggering to and fro, quarrelling, and occasionally exchanging blows. To see the being for whose welfare he was most warmly interested so situated, was enough for Hugh. Lilias was kindly welcomed in; but before he could inquire the cause of her distress, the belligerent parties on the road had cemented their quarrel, and united in demanding her back. "They would have her," they said. "She had promised to go along with them; and Humpy M'Arter had better give her up, or they would beat his bones for him." To this Hugh made no reply; but laying hold of them, one in each hand, he led them to the middle of the road, as easily as if they had been children, and then pushing them as far apart as the length of his arms would admit, he brought them suddenly together, as if he intended to make their heads clash; but, by another effort, checking them as suddenly before they met, he let them go, and asked, in a calm, but stern voice, "What more they wanted?"

The touch of his hand, like the spell of a magician, dissipated the fumes of the liquor, and restored them to their sober senses. They felt that farther resistance would only be provoking an enemy with whom they had no power to contend; and without a word they walked off, glad, as it seemed, to be thus permitted to depart.

Lilias explained that she had been at the fair. The fellow-servant who accompanied her deserted her in the early part of the day; and when about to return home, she was compelled to accept the escort of another. But her first companion overtook them on the road, and claimed her as his charge. Both being excited with liquor, a violent altercation ensued, which, but for Hugh's timely interference, might have terminated seriously to her.

Hugh, with all his eccentricities, and in the midst of that misanthropy which circumstances had conspired to infuse into him, was still a man, and liable to be affected by all that affects others. He felt proud of being thus trusted by a woman in the bloom of youth and beauty. He would have been proud of the distinction, trifling as it was, though conferred by a stranger; but when it was bestowed by the sole-surviving stem of the only two individuals for whom he had ever cherished the glow of friendship, its value was increased a thousand fold.

That Lilias might not again be exposed to insult or ill treatment, he offered to accompany her home, and the readiness with which his offer was accepted, awakened feelings of gratification he had never known before. There is no heart so callous as not to exult in the consciousness of having done a virtuous or a generous deed. Mortals are so constituted, that they can enjoy little but in communion with their kind—to give is to receive; and a trifling service bestowed may return, either at the time or long afterwards, in a host of pleasing recollections, worth ten times the labour which it cost: nor does it at all invalidate the truth of this, that there are men who will not allow themselves to be beguiled into the purest pleasure which man can enjoy—that of increasing the happiness of another.

On the road to her master's farm, the girl's gratitude for the protection and kindness she had met, gave a warm frankness to her voice and manner, which would have gratified any one not wholly dead to the charms of female society. Her words, indeed, were only such as might have been used by another in the same situation; but to the discriminating ear of her deformed guide, the tone in which they were uttered told that they came from her heart. And on him, accustomed as he was to the show rather than the reality of feeling, their effect was scarcely to be calculated. He felt as if he could have sacrificed life, and all he held dear, to be of the slightest service to one who could repay with gratitude so deep the trifling effort he had made in her behalf. He strove, however, to conceal his emotions, lest their expression should alarm her; and for a time he succeeded. But when they were about to part, as he took her hand to bid her "good night," his pent-up feelings rushed to his lips, and forced a vent for themselves in words.

"Lilias," said he, "I know that I am deformed; but I loved your parents for the respect and kindness which they extended towards me when I was scorned and rejected by every one else; I shall cherish their memories while life remains; and now, I cannot tell the pleasure I have derived from being thus honoured by you, their only daughter! Yes," he continued, his enthusiasm increasing, "I know that I am deformed and ugly—that scorn and contempt, in the garb of respect, is all I must look for; but I have a heart to feel like other men; and though the feelings of that heart have been seared, and its sympathies recklessly trampled down, it has ever scorned a dishonest deed; nor has it once stooped to the meanness of deceit!"

"I know your worth," said the girl, half timidly.

"Till this heart ceases to beat," continued he, placing her hand, which he still held in his, upon that part of his breast where the strong pulsations of his heart gave an undulating motion to its surface—she felt alarmed at the unwonted emotion which he betrayed, and made a gentle effort to withdraw her hand; but he pressed it so close, in a tumult of feeling, that the circumstance escaped his notice, and he proceeded, "Till this heart ceases to beat, continue to think you have a friend; and whatever your wants or distresses may be, scruple not to make them known to him, and trust to his affection for every assistance. I have always looked upon *you* with a fond regard. When you were a child, to lead you forth to play was my greatest happiness; and now, had I been younger, and richer, and fairer, I should have been proud"——He paused abruptly, and in a dejected tone of voice continued, "but I am older than you, and deformed, and poor, and I must keep my affection for you within the bounds of a brother's for a sister."

Here he paused, as though he expected a reply; but Lilias had no powers to speak. Young, and susceptible of gratitude for the slightest kindness, her feelings were at that moment too much for utterance, and she could not articulate a single word during the short interval which he allowed her. He, however, did her wrong in supposing that she could not return his affection; she knew and appreciated his worth, and there wanted but a more explicit declaration of a warm attachment on his part to call forth a corresponding sentiment on hers. Indeed, it was difficult to say, friendless as she was, but she might even wish for some such declaration, some word which would give her the prospect of a permanent claim upon that heart which now beat beneath her hand; and the tumult of these wishes, not altogether unmingled with hopes, might contribute materially to her agitation. But upon this subject he said nothing more, and her extreme sensibility prevented her from making any reply. A vain or selfish mind might have been piqued at her silence,—not so her poor mis-shapen friend. He slowly drew her hand from his bosom, as if loath to lose the grateful feeling which it imparted, and pressing it gently and even tenderly in his own,—"Farewell," said he, "I was not made for woman's love; you cannot look upon me with affection, but if ever your sunshiny friends should forsake you, come to me, and I will cleave to you in the storm! Farewell, Lilias. Do not forget what I have said—farewell!"

The sensitive girl faintly returned his parting salute; and when he was gone, she wept like a child bereft of its nurse. The sense of safety and protection—the new and conflicting emotions—which his presence and impassioned language had awakened, gave place to feelings of loneliness and dejection, rendered the more bitter by the recollection of her desolate condition.

The lapse of nearly another year found Hugh in every respect unaltered. His days were spent in the severest drudgery, and his evenings in the solitary seclusion of his home. One evening in the latter end of Autumn he had returned from the labours of a wet and stormy day. The twilight had faded to that faint glimmer which ushers in the night. He had been drenched by the storm, and, as he sat by a cheerful fire drying his wet clothes, Lilias once more stood before him. She had not knocked at the door, nor asked admittance, but opening it herself, came in, and stood, with a bewildered air, in the middle of the floor. She was so changed since he last saw her that for a moment he doubted his senses. The bloom had forsaken her cheeks; she seemed exhausted; there was an unspeakable wildness in her air; her eyes were inflamed, and their lashes were still wet with tears.

Hugh rose from his seat, re-assured himself of her identity, and, observing that she was shivering with cold, placed his own chair close by the fire, and then almost forced her into it. Remarking her visible distress he insisted on knowing the cause of it, or at least what he could do to assuage it. But not a word could she speak; every attempt at utterance ended only in tears and sobs. Anxious and perplexed he bent over her in silence for a few minutes, while her bosom seemed to heave with a convulsive motion, and she covered her eyes with her hands. At last he caught the contagion of her sorrow; and, while his voice trembled, and a tear stood in his eye, he entreated her, for God's sake, if the power of utterance remained, to keep him no longer in suspense. His growing agitation overcame her scruples, and with a desperate effort she began the story of her misfortunes.

The lovers of high-wrought character and unmixed fiction, where all is immaculately good or extravagantly bad, may perhaps find fault with what follows. But these should be reminded that perfection is not to be found in man or in woman: the best may *fall;* and those who have watched their own hearts most narrowly will seldom be the most forward to boast of their stability.

Lilias, who was with child by her master, had been turned out of his house on the forenoon of the day on which she sought the shelter of Hugh M'Arthur's roof; and it would be impossible to imagine a state more miserable and forlorn than that to which she was now reduced. For a young woman, in any circumstances, to have her fair fame, and prospects of an honourable marriage, thus blasted is distressing enough; but when the case is that of a friendless orphan it is much worse. In the present instance, it was supposed, that on the part of her seducer there existed a disposition to acknowledge his fault, and make some provision for her and her unborn babe; but he wanted resolution to avow his guilt at once, and a combination of circumstances soon put it out of his power.

For more than a year back his friends, and particularly his mother, had been looking forward to what was considered an excellent match for him, in the hand of a young lady who was sole heiress to a considerable property; and when poor Lilias's state could no longer be concealed, these friends poured in upon him, some with hopes that he was not guilty, others with representations of the ruin which it would bring upon his prospects if he were but suspected; and, among the rest, his mother, who was a well-meaning woman, but too partial to the *so called* honour of her son, declared, that if he should confess himself the father of the child, she would have him disowned and disinherited. Overborne by the fear of shame and poverty, the young man, naturally facile, though by no means reprobate, resolved on sacrificing justice to expediency; and, by so doing, exposed the deluded victim of his passion and folly to be branded as a strumpet and a cheat by his mother and her female friends, and, ultimately, turned out of doors to beg, or starve, if she could not do better.

Among her few acquaintances there were some who pitied her destitute condition, and would have afforded her shelter; but to take her in was to give countenance to her story, and certain offence to the many friends of her seducer. The labouring population in rural districts are ever fearful of offending those above them. Thinly scattered, and often but indifferently educated, they have no organisation among themselves; their living, in many instances, seems to depend upon the good-will of their employers. And thus it was with these poor people: they allowed the fear of future evil to overpower their sense of humanity. All wished to shift the responsibility from themselves, and each advised the poor outcast to try some other; declaring, at the same time, that had it not been for their dependence on Mr. This or Mrs. That, who was an uncle, or an aunt, or a cousin to her former master, they would have befriended her. Thus disappointed, heartbroken, and on the point of sinking under the influence of fatigue, shame, and despair, she at last recollected the words of her kind-hearted, though uncouth, friend. Her "sunshiny friends" had indeed "forsaken her," but he had promised to "cleave to her in the storm." His remembered words served somewhat to revive her; and though the day, wet and stormy, was wearing to its close, she bent her weary steps toward his dwelling. But, as she approached the house, a bewildering sense of her shame and guilt again overwhelmed her, and she stood irresolute before the door. What if he too should refuse her admittance? And then the stormy night—a hedge for shelter, and the bare ground for a bed, presented themselves to her imagination. She felt her brain reel beneath the weight of these accumulated terrors; her mind wandered, and, in a state of temporary insanity, she lifted the latch and entered.

The kind reception she met with gradually recalled her scattered senses, and strengthened her in the delicate task of telling her melancholy tale. Nor did she tell it in vain. To be poor, friendless, homeless, and denied the common privilege of society, were to the poor deformed peasant sufficient motives to befriend her; nay, to be disowned by the whole human race would only have stimulated his generosity, for he even longed for opportunities to show how light the opinions of others weighed with him. But he needed not this motive to awaken his benevolence. On that night, he warmed, and fed, and laboured to cheer her with the words of consolation. No harsh upbraiding of her weakness, or coarse allusion to "her innocence and honour lost;" no reflection on the past, or admonition for the future, did he suffer to escape him—but with courtesy and kindness, he endeavoured to reconcile the disconsolate girl to her forlorn condition.

As soon as it was day, he left her, and taking with him all the ready money he could collect, proceeded to the next village. Here, by dint of entreaties, promises, and pledges of indemnification for all expenses, he succeeded in procuring her lodgings in the house of a respectable tradesman, whither she removed without loss of time. After this, he administered the means of her support till she became the mother of a boy, and then assisted her in taking a house for herself—still continuing to contribute such sums of money as he could spare, to enable her to maintain herself and her child. To make these contributions, he was often obliged to subject himself to the severest privations. He had never exhibited a wish to hoard money; and his employers, aware of this, and thinking that he had no one but himself to provide for, uniformly took advantage of him, by allotting him an undue proportion of labour, and a very meagre remuneration. But Hugh murmured not at their dishonesty; nor, amid the embarrassments to which it subjected him, did he ever regret or grudge to implement the obligation he had voluntarily imposed on himself. On the contrary, he seemed to consider Lilias as much entitled to his care as if she had a legal claim on him for support; and it is probable this relation might have lasted during their lives, had her state continued to require it. But the same Providence—if we may so far presume to trace the ways of Omnipotence—which had punished her for her transgression, by the hopeless despair which seemed to close around her after her ejectment, had also a train of effects ready to bring into operation for her future support. The extraordinary beauty of her infant son soon drew the general attention of their humble neighbours. This led to an intimacy with the mother, whose story they listened to with commiseration, acknowledging her own comparative innocence, and the injustice with which she had been treated. This kind of intercourse gradually became more familiar, till she ultimately attained a place of permanent respect in the estimation of all. Thus a favourable change was produced in her circumstances. The feelings and responsibility of a mother roused her to extreme diligence; and, with the native independence of poverty, she soon found assistance in providing for herself unnecessary. Still, however, her first benefactor continued to watch over her, and to lend his help when any unforeseen contingency occurred. His last act of benevolence was to appropriate a small sum of money for the child's education, who had now grown a fine active boy, and promised soon to be able to earn his own subsistence, by herding cattle or sheep for some of the neighbouring farmers.

When he had performed these beneficent deeds, actuated by a desire to see more of the world, M'Arthur left his native county, and went northward to A———shire. Here he again settled, and betook himself regularly to the feeding of cattle. In this occupation many years passed over him. Meanwhile his character instead of altering as his life advanced, only became more confirmed. Flashes of eccentric benevolence, or generosity, at times would burst from the cloud of gloom and mystery which hung over him; but the common tone of his conversation was as sarcastic and ironical as before; always managed in such a way, however, that for any one to take offence, would have been to acknowledge that he deserved personally the censure which was couched in general terms.

He now became attached to wandering about, seldom remaining more than a year in one place; and, in that short period, though those with whom he was associated could easily perceive his extraordinary personal strength, and forbidding temper, no one had time to discover his better qualities; and he was generally regarded, all over the country, as a misanthrope—one whose hatred of mankind would certainly drive him, sooner or later, to commit some crime which would bring him to punishment. His only redeeming features were an independent spirit and strict honesty, and these were acknowledged by all. He was now in the decline of life; but a robust constitution, strict habits of temperance, and constant exercise, warded off decay; so that he still possessed his animal functions unimpaired, and in the full vigour of health.

Circumstances about this time compelled him to attend the great *hiring* market of the district. Here, after wandering about in the crowded streets for the greater part of the day, and hearing his ungainly appearance made the subject of several ludicrous remarks, towards evening an upland farmer asked him, between jest and earnest, if he wanted a master; and the question being answered in the affirmative, they set about making an agreement.

The farmer, not altogether certain if he would answer his purpose, and thinking, moreover, that he would be easily satisfied, offered him the merest trifle as wages. Hugh had never been accustomed to great rewards, but here the matter was carried rather too far: his temper had been previously ruffled, and he rejected the offer with marked disdain. The other, who was a humorist in his own way, supposing him a fit subject for sport, began to jeer him on his uncouth appearance: "I'm thinkin' I've offered ye owr muckle, man," said he; "thae shanks o' yours wadna carry your maut-seck o' a body atween the barn an' the byre in a hale half day."

"They've carried me farrer, in less time," was the reply.

"But if your hands be like your feet," rejoined the other, "I'm sure ye wad be, at best, but a guid-for-naething kind o' creatur about a farm town!"

"Whatever my hands may be," retorted the peasant, "hitherto they've aye provided for my head."

"Troth, I wadna wonder but fat ye're right," said the farmer: "hands an' head o' ye look no that oonlike things made for making ither fok's pouches an pantries licht an toom, an' keeping yer ain aye moderately foo an heavy."

"And for *teaching* fools," interrupted Hugh, "that their owner may not be insulted with impunity!"

"Weel, man, that's wonderfu'," said the farmer in a sneering tone; "but if they hae ta'en up the trade o' *teachers*, I'm thinking they'll no want scholars; for I'm far cheated, if they haena had, at least, ae fool no far bye since *that* day your mother bore you."

"And, perhaps, *this* day they have another near enough to be made wiser," retorted Hugh, no longer able to control his passion; and with these words he lifted his giant arm to fell him to the earth.

The farmer's wit, such as it was, had attracted a number of listeners, who now interposed in his behalf, and by their efforts prevented the parties from coming to blows.

"The filthy creatur!" said the farmer, as he was leaving the place of contention, "wha wad hae thought *it* wad hae the face to offer to strike a man?"

"When we next meet," said the other, whose thoughts were still occupied with the insulting taunts with which he had been greeted—"when we next meet, maybe we'll hae fewer onlookers, an' then you may learn at your ain expense, whether *it has the face* ——." Here he checked himself, and leaving the sentence unfinished, moved away in a contrary direction; and as he walked off, those who had witnessed the scene indulged each his own conjecture as to what might be the purport of the unfinished threat, while all agreed that it *was* a threat, and "something no fit to be *spoken out.*"

After being thus baffled in his attempt to take vengeance for what he considered a gross insult, Hugh's next care was to steal out of the town, and, by an unfrequented road, return home.

Those who have been exposed to any particular kind of obloquy, and accustomed to guard against it, are often ready to make their minds "suspicion's sanctuary." The farmer's remarks might be dictated by mere thoughtlessness, or a natural turn for dry humour; but as Hugh proceeded on his solitary route, pondering on the imputations of dishonesty and folly which had thus wantonly, as he conceived, and without the shadow of a foundation, been cast in his face, and when he reflected on the hollow respect with which he had often been treated, when insolence could not be safely offered, it appeared to him that mankind were in league against him. Such is the effect of a partial view. He even questioned the justness of the Creator's laws, in having made him a thing to be hooted and scorned. Dissatisfaction with himself, and disgust at others, grew upon his mind. He avoided every house and place, where he had a chance of meeting any one, with as much care as if it had been contamination to look on a human face; and when by footpaths and byeways he reached his *bothie*, he entered it unperceived, and shut himself in.

On that night, Mr. Oakfield, the farmer with whom he had the discord, was missing; and the next morning his body was found at a solitary part of the road, where he had been murdered, and afterwards robbed, as it appeared, of a large sum of money in bank notes, his watch, and every thing valuable which could be found about his person.

At whose door the murder was laid need hardly be told: a general suspicion prevailed, that Hugh M'Arthur was the guilty person; and, on the forenoon of the same day he was taken from his employment by the executive of the district, and conveyed to prison.

A precognition was immediately entered into. Several witnesses were examined, all of whom declared that they had been witness to the quarrel, and heard the half-uttered threat; others had observed him in the market; but, of those present, no one could be found to say, that they had seen him on the way home, or that he had arrived there early. A boy was examined, who slept in the *bothie* with him; but he had been late in leaving the market, and stopped over night with his mother, who resided in the outskirts of the town. Against this, it was in vain that the prisoner urged his having quitted the market early, taken an unfrequented road, and gone immediately to bed after his return. Nothing positively exculpatory appeared; the circumstantial evidence went far to criminate him; and he was finally committed for trial.

In the present instance, the tide of popular opinion was decidedly against the prisoner. His solitary habits were talked of in every circle, and invariably attributed to a mind brooding on desperate deeds. His former sayings were dragged from the oblivion into which they had fallen, and bandied about from mouth to mouth with unceasing diligence; his cutting sarcasms, and the manner in which he had been accustomed to speak of the conduct of others, were carefully commented on; and all concurred in believing that they proceeded from a heart imbued with bitterness to mankind, and a total want of all fellow-feeling and natural affection. Those who had suffered, no matter how justly, from the dissecting criticism of his remarks, or the heart-searching glance of his eye, were now the most busy in disseminating bad reports concerning his conduct and character. The murder, which gave birth to the discussion, gave it also a fearful interest; and thus distorted accounts and exaggerated stories continued to multiply and spread, till the indignation of the country against the supposed murderer was wrought up to the highest pitch. Time would have moderated this fever of excitement; but unfortunately, in the plenitude of the frenzy, his trial came on.

Without friend or relation, or any one to comfort or speak a kind word to him in this trying juncture, he bore all with a magnanimity and firmness which might have done honour to the greatest stoic of the Grecian school; but this, so far from securing admiration, was construed into obduracy of heart, and only served to strengthen the general impression of his guilt.

In the midst of these malignant influences, all of which were against him, he found a powerful friend in one who was, to appearance, a perfect stranger. A young gentleman, by name Mr. Stevenson, who was fast rising to eminence at the Scottish bar, and at the time residing with his mother in Edinburgh, happening to read his name and commitment in the newspapers, immediately left his other business, and hurried northward to procure the necessary information for enabling him to conduct the defence. On arriving in the vicinity, his first care was to examine narrowly what character the prisoner had borne previous to the commission of the alleged crime. In the excited state of the country, it was difficult to come at any thing like the truth; but he gleaned enough to satisfy him that the temper and general habits of Hugh M'Arthur were not such as to warrant the belief that he would engage in a secret murder to gratify a momentary feeling of revenge several hours after the offence had been given. This, taken in conjunction with the circumstance that neither the money, watch, nor any of the other articles abstracted from the pockets of the deceased, had been found upon the supposed culprit, though his seizure was almost immediate, convinced him that the murderer must be sought somewhere else. But for a time nothing transpired which could fix even suspicion on any other.

The prisoner himself was the first to give the hint. He

recollected having seen two *thimble-rig men* in the market, who had endeavoured to inveigle him into their game, and though he had eluded them, he set them down at the time, in his own mind, for pick-pockets. One of them was present during the altercation, and when it was ended Hugh heard him say, with reference to himself: "That old blackguard would murder a man for his money!"

A pedlar boy was next discovered, who had been favoured with a night's lodging in Mr. Oakfield's barn, and knew him perfectly. On the day of the fair he had been enticed into a game by the thimble men; and, having lost the whole of his ready-money, remained late in the streets, trying to sell as much as would enable him to pay for his bed and supper. He recollected seeing Mr. Oakfield enter a tavern, after it was dusk, and also encountering one of the thimble men several times in passing and re-passing the street where it stood. The circumstance caused him some alarm, for he *jaloused* they were desperate villains. When Mr. Oakfield left the house, he saw the fellow set off with a hasty step, in the same direction, and pass him on the other side of the street. This was exactly what Mr. Stevenson wanted, and he now began to entertain hopes, that, if one or both of these individuals could be found, some circumstance might be elicited which would give a different aspect to the whole affair. On making farther inquiry, it was discovered that the thimble men had never been seen since the night in which the murder and robbery were committed. Suspicion in his mind now amounted to conviction; and, though the county magistrates were so prepossessed with the idea that the murderer was already in custody, as to refuse all assistance, he, at his own risk, brought Mr. Samuel Sleuth, at the time one of the most eminent thief-catchers in Europe, to the place, to ascertain the marks of the fugitives; and, after having procured the necessary warrants, he dismissed him, with instructions only to make despatch, and spare no expense in tracking his prey. So far all was well; but still it was to be feared, unless these men should be found, or strong reasons appear for transferring the charge to some other, the unfavourable circumstances in which the prisoner was placed would of themselves condemn him.

The trial came on, and the last accounts from Mr. Sleuth, received only three days previous, were, that though he had been able to track one of the fugitives for a time with tolerable accuracy, at a place which he named, he had there lost all trace of him; and that he was now in pursuit of a person bearing some of the marks, but so few and faint, that his hopes of success were by no means sanguine.

When placed at the bar, to be tried for his life, the prisoner showed no sign of sorrow or dejection. He was pale from confinement, but his manner was firm and collected. The indictment, which had been framed with all the circumlocution of the law, charged him with the crimes of *murder and robbery.* After it was read, the evidence was produced, and a number of witnesses examined, none of whom had any thing directly criminatory to allege, though they proved a great deal about the solitary habits, and strange disposition, of the prisoner, at which a smile occasionally played on his strongly marked features. The quarrel at the fair, and the subsequent murder and robbery of Mr. Oakfield, were also clearly proved; and, from the connection which appeared to exist between the two, the guilt of the individual at the bar seemed to be strangely made out.

Mr. Stevenson, the counsel for the prisoner, who had hitherto laboured, by cross-examination, to shake the testimony of the witnesses, now endeavoured to avail himself of the exculpatory evidence which had been summoned in. But, as matters stood, this was to little purpose; for the very witnesses whom he had selected with the greatest care, though they told what they considered the truth, were so imbued with the popular prejudice against the prisoner, that their evidence did not essentially differ from what was already adduced, and tended only to produce signs of impatience in the jury; nor was it till Mr. Winterface, the public prosecutor, rose to address them, that they seemed to resume their attention.

It would be tiresome to the reader, and could serve little purpose, to give the address at full length. But an extract from it, and another from that of Mr. Stevenson, may serve to show the different lights in which the same subject may be exhibited, and the conflicting deductions which may be drawn from the same occurrences.

Mr. Winterface, in addressing the jury, said, "that the crime of murder had been committed on the person of an unoffending and respectable subject. No one had seen the horrid deed; but an individual was now placed before them, whom, from all the circumstances which had been adduced, and so clearly proven, they were warranted to look on as the murderer. That individual was known to have been a man of a gloomy disposition, and retired habits. He had never shown the slightest trait of kindness for his fellow creatures, or kept up a community of sentiment with them. He had wandered from place to place, and lived in loneliness—the companion of his own dark thoughts, and a prey to misanthropic musings. No pity had softened his nature—no friendly intercourse had humanised his heart—no sympathy with man, or fear of God, could be found in the tenor of his conduct. His manner of life had been well calculated to harden the heart, and prepare it for crime. In such an individual the dark passions of envy, malice, revenge, were likely to predominate; and these circumstances were of themselves sufficient to fix suspicion upon him. But when the dark tissue of events, which preceded the murder, were brought together, in an unbroken chain of evidence, this suspicion of guilt rose to a certainty of crime. When a man of such habits and temper had been heard quarrelling with the deceased in the streets of a populous town, and seen to lift his hand, in direct violation of the laws of his country, to strike a fellow-subject in a public market, almost without provocation; and, when prevented from offering violence on the spot, indulging in muttered threats, and half finished sentences, the meaning of which evidently was, that he would wait a fitting opportunity to avenge the supposed insult; when, after all this, the unfortunate man, who had unwittingly been the cause of ruffling his gloomy temper, and stirring his worst passions, is found—murdered! without any assignable cause, and without even a suspicion attaching itself to any other,—where were they to look for the murderer?" &c.

Mr. Stevenson, after going over the whole of the evidence, and noticing its inconsistencies and assailable points in the most forcible and eloquent manner, said, " Gentlemen of the jury, I have thus endeavoured to show the inconclusiveness of the evidence upon which you are called to decide; permit me now to remind you of the awful nature of the trust reposed in you. It is not to settle a disputed point of property—it is not to decide who shall be the heir of an estate—it is not to award damages and repel slander propagated by one party to the injury of another. These, and similar matters of civil discord, are of every-day occurrence; and although justice ought always to be sacred, however petty the cause which calls for its exercise, the very familiarity of such cases may render jurymen indifferent to the consequences of their judgment—and men who have been ruined by a judicial verdict may live to attain higher honours and greater possessions than those of which they were deprived, or to recover, by future probity, that reputation which the law denied. But it is none of these matters which awaits your decision on the present occasion. The case before you is one, the vital importance of which demands the most calm and profound deliberation. You are to decide whether a fellow-creature, possessing the same feelings and sympathies, and the same love of life, as yourselves—whether he shall live to participate in the enjoyments of that existence which God hath conferred on us all, or, on the mere suspicion which an accidental coincidence seems to have woven around him, be condemned to ignominy, and death, and the execration of all who hear his name spoken. Yes, the life of one, to whom life is as sweet as to any or all of you, hangs quivering on the balance of your thoughts. Pause, therefore, and consider, that life is a gift which God alone can give, and which, if man take away without a sufficient reason, instead of doing justice, he becomes a murderer; nor will his crime be lessened, in the eyes of his Maker, for its being cloaked by the sanction of law. It is a light thing that one guilty man may escape, but it is truly awful to condemn the innocent to death. Gentlemen, the character of the prisoner has already been sufficiently darkened by that inexplicable train of accidents which has brought him here. You have heard peculiarities, in themselves innocent, with strange ingenuity tortured into an evidence of guilt; and seen his solitary habits, by being viewed through the uncertain medium of suspicion, made to witness against him, as if it were a virtue to steep his character and name in the very dregs of infamy, wrung from a crime of which there is no proof that he has been guilty. It is a maxim, that wherever there is an effect, there must be a cause. Let us trace these peculiarities to their source; and, when we have discovered the cause from which they sprung, perhaps they may cease to be received as evidence against him. Let any of you suppose an exchange of condition with the prisoner, and then, what an alteration in your feelings and social affections this exchange would make! Suppose that you were thrown upon the world with all the ardent feelings and warm-heartedness of youth, but, by some mischance, less elegantly formed than others; and, in consequence of a defect which you could not remedy, treated by your play-fellows and companions as a being made only for their sport—persecuted with malicious jests and bitter mockery—made a mark for contumely and coarse wit—loaded with nick-names and low abuse—the laughing-stock and scorn of all; nor even allowed to enjoy a quiet hour of pleasing reflection, till Nature, as if repenting of her former partiality, had endowed you with extraordinary strength of both body and mind. Would your relish for society have improved, or your sympathies been stirred and expanded in such a waste, and under the care of such cultivators? Suppose, then, that those who before had scorned and abused you, finding that they could no longer do so with safety, should turn and crouch before you, and, with servile submission, and fawning artifices, seek your favour. To an individual with little knowledge of man, a weak memory, and feeble reflecting powers, *this* might be happiness; but with a mind constituted like that of the prisoner, and all the insults you had endured bearing bitter fruit in your bosom, I ask you, would you not attribute the change to some motive not differing materially from fear? and would not its natural consequence be, to make you withdraw from that society where you could expect no return for affections wasted—no genuine sympathy—and no reciprocity of feeling? Such, gentlemen, is the history of the prisoner, and the origin of his solitary habits. Yet, for all this, where he was treated with only common kindness, his affections were warm, and his gratitude unbounded. And, did the forms of the Court permit, it could easily be proved that he has exhibited traits of character, and shown himself possessed of a fund of benevolence which might shame the pretensions of the greatest philanthropists.

"Though the tide of prejudice and popular indignation, which has set so strongly in against him, has had a most unfavourable influence, and tended materially to make the proof less clear than otherwise it would have been, still it has been proved, that his previous life, up to the unfortunate night which consigned him to a prison, has been one not only of strict honesty, but abhorrence of crime—this has been proved, while not a shadow of proof exists that he is a robber. Had he been of an inconsiderate or nervous temperament, it might have been argued, that after taking a fatal revenge remorse had seized him, and he had fled from the scene of his guilt, leaving the body to enrich some future passenger. But who among the praised, or the proudly innocent, ever bore himself with more dignified calmness, or showed less of perturbation under the trial of misfortune, than he has done since he was placed at the bar? In the midst of every thing to appal, and nothing to support the guilty heart, no nerve of his has been shaken, and he has noticed the grievous accusations which have been brought against him with a smile. Is this evidence of mental imbecility? or could he have done so, had an atrocious murder been weighing on his conscience? And, besides, let it never be forgotten, that the crime, if perpetrated by him, must have been the offspring, not of a sudden burst of passion, but of a resolution deliberately formed. And who, I now ask, after he had contemplated such a deed, and determined to do it, would have hesitated to avail himself of the only advantage which it offered? It may be said, that he has secreted the money; but the thing, if it were not impossible, is altogether improbable. He had not time to carry it to a distance, nor did he make the attempt; he could not conceal it in the fields with the prospect of deriving any advantage from it, for it consisted wholly of paper; he entered no house, save that in which he slept, and there, after the most careful search, nothing was found. Gentlemen, I mention not these things as mere flashes of rhetoric, or because it is my business to declaim; but from a strong conviction that the prisoner at the bar has been brought there without a just cause. And I feel confident, that time will yet unravel this mystery, and bring to light the secret murderer. For these reasons, I do hope that you will consider this case well before you come to a decision; and that you will not, upon the slender evidence which has been produced, consign a fellow-creature to infamy and an ignominious death."

A suppressed murmur of applause ran through the court as Mr. Stevenson concluded. The spectators had never before heard one word said in defence of the prisoner; they now felt their minds wander in uncertainty as to his guilt, and many of them wished that he might yet escape. The conviction of the jurymen was also shaken: upon them the efforts of the counsel for the prisoner had produced their full effect; but the judge, who was himself fully satisfied as to the guilt of the individual in question, foresaw the turn which this was likely to give to their decision; and in his *charge* stated the case in such a manner that his own opinion of it could not be misunderstood.

It is quite possible, even at the present day, for a jury to degrade themselves into becoming the mouthpiece of a judge; and in this instance, a few men, little accustomed to think for themselves in aught save the matter of fortune-making, summoned from the obscurity of their daily employments, and trusting implicitly to the superior learning and discrimination of a presiding power, easily fell into the error of adopting the judge's ideas, and echoing back his sentiments.

The jury retired, and after a few minutes' deliberation, were "unanimously of opinion that the prisoner was guilty of the crime of murder, as libelled."

The awful sentence of death was then pronounced in due

form, and with the usual exhortation to the prisoner, "to listen attentively to such spiritual guides as might be provided for him—to repent of his former transgressions—and, in particular, of that most aggravated crime which had called down the vengeance of his country—and to seek mercy while it might be found."

During this awfully imposing part of the ceremony, he stood with the most perfect composure; and, while the hearts of the spectators scarcely beat, so intense was their feeling, he noticed its conclusion with a smile. With him all hopes of escape, if such had been, were now over, and the officers in attendance were preparing to convey him back to prison; but while they were endeavouring to open a passage, he requested permission to speak a few words. The court, thinking he might intend to thank them for the manner in which his trial had been conducted, granted his request, and he proceeded. He had anticipated the issue of the trial; his thoughts had been previously arranged, his words selected, and his sentences formed; and he spoke without embarrassment or hesitation.

"Gentlemen of the jury," said he, "I should perhaps thank you for your good and patient conduct; but as condemning an innocent man to death is no very fit subject for congratulation, I cannot presume to praise, and to censure would serve no end. I have read your thoughts throughout; your minds were open to conviction; and had you been left unawed by imposing forms, and unswayed by popular prejudice, you would have done me justice. To those on the bench I have nothing to say; they have done for me in their vocation what they would have done for another in my place. But there is one here, whose conduct should call forth other expressions—I mean the man who has voluntarily come forward to plead the cause of one, against whom the imputation of the most horrid crime, and the cry of causeless indignation, has gone abroad. His exertions have been great; and for the sake of his fame, I am almost sorry that they have been unsuccessful. For myself, I have no such feeling. I have been a thing only not made the subject of mockery every hour of my life, because I had the power of inflicting pain; not openly ridiculed by every one I chanced to meet, because I could hurl back their weapons with a keener edge than they came; and not trodden into mire, because my frame was not among the substances which yield easily to the foot of the passenger. I have no dishonest deed with which to accuse myself; no friend to sympathise with what I suffer, or mourn my fate; and no infamy can penetrate the grave, or disturb the repose of the dead—that repose which awaits alike the king and the beggar, the sage, so called, who is supposed to die in peace, and the man who makes his exit amid the execrations of assembled thousands. For me, it is a light thing to leave the world. My history has been truly narrated; but, if it were not too much, I should be fain to know how, at this distance of time and space, from the day and the place of my nativity, the narrator became so well acquainted with it."

Here the speaker was interrupted, by the attendants of the court endeavouring to enforce silence among the spectators. For some minutes past, a faint whispering had prevailed near the door, and this was now beginning to spread, in spite of the efforts which were making to suppress it. The last words of the condemned man had been addressed to Mr. Stevenson; but he either did not hear them, or was too deeply engaged to make any answer. The whispering was occasioned by a man on horseback galloping up to the place: some words which he had dropped at the door had been eagerly caught up by the crowd, and communicated from man to man, in an under tone, till the noise began to disturb the solemnity of the scene within. The horseman was the bearer of a letter for Mr. Stevenson; it had the word "*express*" written in very large characters, and underlined, above the address. He pressed through the crowd, and without ceremony delivered it to that gentleman in the court, who immediately broke the seal, and seemed to forget every thing else in perusing it. Having caught its import, almost without reading, as soon as comparative silence was procured, he rose, with the excitement of hope portrayed in his countenance, to request that the prisoner might not be removed for at least half-an-hour, as he had strong reasons for believing that some circumstances, to him of the very greatest importance, would be brought before the court within that time.

To his request there was some demur, and some observations about precedents and impropriety; but the court at last acceded to the proposal.

Before the half hour had expired, the real robber and murderer was brought before the judges in the person of one of the before-mentioned thimble men! He had fled from the scene of his guilt to the remotest parts of the country; and, after being disappointed in several attempts to leave it, and hearing that he was pursued, with the cunning of the fox, he had *doubled;* and having disguised himself by dyeing his hair, and otherwise metamorphosed his dress and countenance, he again made for the vicinity of the place where he had done the deed.

But at the very time when he began to consider himself safe, and was indulging in a day's rest, he was seized by his indefatigable pursuer, who had followed him through all his windings, with a determination not to be baffled while the smallest hope of success remained.

After divesting his victim of the money and other articles, the murderer had sewed the large bank notes into the lining of his trousers; imagining, no doubt, that he would be able to issue them with safety after the murder was forgotten. On after thoughts, he had again torn them out and burned them, but still continued to keep the watch, which, by means of a false crown, he had contrived to secrete in his hat. The watch, and one of the notes, which had slipped through a hole from among the rest, and escaped the burning, were found on his person. These were incontestable proofs against him; and, terror-struck by the unexpectedness of his capture, and smitten by the pangs of a guilty conscience, he had already confessed the whole.

When this circumstance was announced, an involuntary shout of triumph burst from the crowd who now thronged the court-house, and stood around the doors, anxious to learn the issue of these strange events. A complete revulsion of feeling had supervened; and they now rejoiced in the innocence of that individual, of whose guilt, but a few hours before, they had not entertained a doubt.

Hugh M'Arthur bore this unexpected brightening up of his prospects as he had borne his former reverses, without any extravagant expression of emotion. His manner was composed, with a slight degree of—it might be assumed—indifference, as if he still wished to make it appear that the change was to him a matter of no very great importance; but the events of the day had been working a silent change in his heart, and he felt a sentiment growing within him which he had never before experienced. He was still retained a prisoner; but his confinement was a mere matter of form: no one now entertained the slightest doubt of his innocence, or of his being ultimately set at liberty.

On the day after his trial, he was visited in the jail by a female, having the appearance of a lady: and in her though much altered, he instantly recognised his former *protegé*, Lilias, now Mrs. Stevenson. Such a meeting under any circumstances would have been interesting; but recent events, combined with the time which had elapsed, the changes which had taken place in the fortunes of either since they parted, and the place in which they met—all tended to make it doubly affecting. From her it was that he first learned the extent of their mutual obligation. It was her son—the very child she had nursed while he supported her, who had so ably pleaded his cause, and whose efforts in his behalf had been at last crowned with success in the detection of the real murderer. That these should still continue his firm friends was only what he would have expected, but how they came to be in circumstances to befriend him so effectually required some explanation.

The reader may now be told, that the name of Lilias's seducer was Mr. Stevenson. His addresses were rejected by the lady, for a union with whom, as already noticed, his friends so anxiously wished; and this disappointment, connected as it was with previous events, operated so powerfully upon his mind, that he did not afterwards seek any other alliance. After Hugh M'Arthur left the country, he fell into ill-health, and became melancholy. A lingering disease, and the prospect of its probable termination, entirely altered his ideas of the world, and of his past life. He never approved of some parts of his conduct; but he now reflected, with feelings of the deepest remorse, on those promises which, prompted by early passion, he had made and never performed—the broken vows and solemn obligations he had come under to his once innocent and unsuspecting servant girl—the sacrifice of that innocence which she had made to him, and the degradation and misery into which it had subsequently plunged her,—all these were conjured up by the solitude of a sick-room; and his own conscience—that stern monitor within—now accused him loudly for his infidelity.

He now expressed a wish to make some reparation to the only individual whom he considered himself to have wronged. Lilias, he said, was the first and only object of his affection: to please his friends he had abandoned her after he had done her a deep wrong; and now, to quiet his own conscience and remove a stigma from the name of his son—for he acknowledged the child as his—he considered it his duty to give both a legal claim upon those comforts which he might leave behind him. And he declared that, unless he were permitted to do this, he could not leave the world in peace.

He was himself an only son, and his mother doated upon him with more than common fondness. Her former abuse of the unfortunate participator in his youthful passion had sprung from an overstrained anxiety for his respectability in the eyes of the world; but now when he spoke of leaving it, her maternal solicitude for his peace of mind overcame every other feeling: her cordial consent was easily obtained, and he and Lilias were married.

This timely gratification of his wishes brought back his banished comfort. The consciousness of having acted according to the dictates of virtue and justice produced the happiest effect upon his spirits: the change extended itself to his corporeal frame, and his health began slowly to return. After living happy for a number of years, he died, bequeathing his name and the whole of his fortune to his wife and son, with the exception of a small annuity which they were to pay to their early preserver, if ever he should be discovered. With every intention to discharge the debt with which they had been intrusted, they had not been able to find the means till the newspapers announced the commitment of their creditor for murder: then all was bustle and anxiety with both mother and son, and the full determination to do for him whatever his case would admit of.

The events narrated in the former part of this story, though for the most part of a gloomy texture, were the means of evolving the true character of the extraordinary individual who forms the subject of it. As the thunder-cloud carries in its bosom the electric flash which penetrates the gloomy recesses of the cavern, those dark suspicions in which he had been involved emitted a ray which penetrated that obscurity in which his best actions lay concealed. And, in the reflux of that tide which had lately threatened to bear him to destruction, his merit became the theme of every conversation; the fortitude which he had displayed received its full reward of praise; and people marvelled at and magnified those stern virtues which, under his dark exterior, they had never before been able to discover. These feelings manifested themselves in the most hearty congratulations on his deliverance, and the deepest sympathy for his unmerited sufferings. He saw and knew that these expressions were unfeigned. The anxiety of Mrs. Stevenson, the exertions of her son, and the bequest of her husband, all originating at a time when no sinister purpose could be placed against them—these were proofs of a generous and disinterested philanthropy, which came warm to his heart, and, under their genial influence, united with the circumstances already noticed, that ice which, in the frost of neglect and early scorn, had grown over his better feelings, melted away. He received and returned the looks and the words of kindness in the true spirit of social intercourse; and in the scene which was thus opened up, he found what to him, after so many years of seclusion and solitude, was an unexplored paradise. After his liberation, the annuity, which he continued regularly to receive, and the bounty of his friends, more than supplied his few wants: he was in independent circumstances, and, as long as he lived, it was his delight to contribute to the happiness of all around him.

If this story possess any moral, it is this : *That kindness is the best teacher of philanthropy, and the only nurse of the social virtues.* It may also remind us, that it is not always the fairest exterior that encloses the noblest spirit. We ought ever to keep present to our judgment the distinction thus laid down by Shakespeare :—

> In Nature there's no blemish but the mind,
> None can be call'd *deformed* but the unkind :
> Virtue is beauty; but the beauteous, evil—
> Are empty trunks o'erflourish'd by the devil!

## THE FATE OF THE FAIREST.

> Oh ! there are some
> Can trifle in cold vanity with all
> The warm soul's precious throbs—to whom it is
> A triumph that a fond devoted heart
> Is breaking for them—who can bear to call
> Young flowers into beauty, and then crush them.
> LANDON.

"THE NETHERTOWN," where the scene of the following story of the heart is laid, consists of a moderately extensive farming establishment, with about twenty low, ill-constructed, old-fashioned houses standing mostly to the northward of it, some "haflins seen, and haflins hid." Of the farm it is superfluous to speak: a neat house, barn, and stables, erected a few years ago, and covered with blue slate, have made it modern enough. But in the appearance of the other houses, all the rustic simplicity and rude architecture of an earlier age may still be traced. After all the innovations and improvements to which the first thirty years of the nineteenth century gave birth, there they stood with their low walls, built in some instances with clay instead of mortar—roofs composed of alternate layers of thatch and turf—chimney-tops with a rope of twisted straw around them to keep them together, and doors so low that their inhabitants were obliged to "loot low" before they could enter. Another feature of days departed was the little gardens, in which were cultivated small quantities of cabbages and potatoes surrounded by what, to a stranger's eye, or indeed to any eye, might seem a nettle bank instead of a wall. The houses were disposed in no regular order, but stood in groups of two or three together, generally in the lowest places of an undulating surface, while the intermediate and higher ground was occupied as gardens in the way already noticed. Narrow green lanes formed the only communication between them,—sometimes crooked, sometimes straight, as the fancy of our forefathers had been.

To the eastward of the Nethertown the country is open, and the prospect varied by patches of wood, hedges, farm-steadings, and little eminences. But, on the west, a continuation of high ground, which rises at no great distance, and terminates in a precipice of considerable height, shuts in the view in that direction. These hills are characterised by that abrupt scenery which marks the boundary of the Ochils. In one of the ridges there is a deep gorge, or opening, through which winds a hill road, where, at certain seasons of the year, the setting sun, striking down between the almost perpendicular banks on either side, floods with light a long stripe of corn field, stream, and lake, while the surrounding country is lost in shadows.

At the extremity of the gorge, where "a hamlet smiles," a rough bank slopes to the margin of a gurgling stream, which wends its way through an adjoining hollow called *The Den.* Here the ever-blossoming furze, the wild flowers which shoot forth in all the luxuriance of uncultivated nature, and the stream, with its struggling waters more than half-concealed by the matted grass which fringes its edges, formed a scene perfectly in unison with the rustic habitations above.

Farther down the Den, and a little to the northward of the houses, there is a level spot called *The Green,* where the waters of the stream were collected in a number of small dams called *demmens,* for the purpose of bleaching. And here, on a summer's evening, while the sun shoots his last red rays from the hollow pass, are often seen a band of laughing girls from the houses above, with naked feet of fawn-like lightness—arms bare nearly to the shoulders—neckerchiefs carelessly thrown aside, or disarrayed in such a manner as to show the whiteness of necks and bosoms, on which the noon-day sun was not permitted to look—eyes all bright with the beam of youth, and locks braided with the greatest care,—gathering in their linen which had been exposed, during the day, to bleach or dry.

"*Where the carcase is, thither shall the eagles be gathered,*" is a Scripture apothegm: *Where young women are, there will the youth of the other sex be found also,* is an aphorism scarcely less true. There also might have been seen a band of youngsters from the neighbouring farms, with faces newly washed from the sweat and dust of the day. There lurking affection shone out; and while mirth convulsed the features and shook the nerves of every one present, the eyes of youth and maiden met with a quick and bright intelligence that sent the heart's blood dancing to the cheek.

In its own appearance, and the appearance of its inhabitants, there was much in the Nethertown on which the eye of the philanthropist might have rested with pleasure. The groups of young and happy faces at the Green, the contented looks of the older part of the community, and the absence of everything like bustle and confusion, gave an air of quiet happiness to the whole. Amid this scene of rural simplicity and retirement, men had tenanted the houses where they first drew breath, till the snows of four-score years had whitened their heads and bent their bodies. Maids had there become mothers and grandmothers; and individuals over whose heads nearly a century had passed, had died in the very bed where their feeble cries were first heard. Indeed, had it not been for a smithy and wright's shop, it is highly probable that the Nethertown would not have received a single new inhabitant in many years. These, however, served occasionally to introduce a stranger to this little society, when an additional hand was wanted, or a vacancy occurred, at either of the establishments. The place seemed a sort of concealment which poverty had never been able to discover, and its inhabitants looked like happy fixtures. But to estimate the happiness of any society, it is necessary that we should be acquainted with the history and feelings of the individuals who compose it, and such an acquaintance would, to a certainty, have operated as a sad drawback upon those romantic visions which the contemplation of such a scene was calculated to inspire.

This imperfect, and, perhaps, unsatisfactory sketch, is the result of observations made, during a short period of his life, which the writer passed in the vicinity of the Nethertown. He was then an occasional idler at the Green, and sometimes, though seldom, a listener in the houses. In this way he became acquainted with most of its inhabitants; but as the heart is often arbitrary in its selections, there were only two who particularly interested him.

The one was the sewing-mistress, an individual well down the vale of years. She had married young, and her husband had been torn from her by death shortly after. In her the influence of years had mellowed the affections of a heart naturally warm, and that love which had once been centred in a single object, now took a wider range, and displayed itself in the tenderest sympathy for the sufferings of her fellow-creatures, and a kindly deportment to all who came within the circle of her acquaintance.

The other was a young woman in the last of her *teens*, who hitherto had attracted little notice. Her father, in the prime of life, had been a farm-servant, but from increasing years and infirmities, he had lately abandoned this employment for the more humble occupation of a labourer. Her mother was a tall and rather coarse-looking woman, with nothing to distinguish her from the class to which she belonged. In their family they had been particularly unfortunate: some had made early and imprudent marriages; some had wandered they knew not whither; others were confirmed drunkards; and of six children, Christina alone, who was the youngest, promised to be the stay and comfort of their old age. Recent times had made the art of weaving almost as common among women as it was formerly among men; she had been taught this art, and as her apprenticeship had expired, she now lived with her parents, ministering to their increasing wants with her scanty earnings.

It seemed as if Providence in bestowing her had meant to compensate for the profligacy of their other children. Her disposition was gentle and amiable. Filial affection, and a desire to obliterate from her parents' minds the recollection of their children's disobedience and misconduct, made her diligent at her work. In winter her lamp might be seen throwing its cheerful light from the window where she wrought, and the music of her shuttle heard every morning long before the other girls of the place had thought of quitting their beds. At fairs, and other places of resort, she was seldom seen; gossiping parties she never frequented; even at the Green, that common haunt of fair faces and happy hearts, she was a rare visitor; and except at church on Sabbath-day, she was almost never from home.

In person, she was rather under than above the middle size, but of the most exquisite proportions. Her features were of that pensive cast which is not incompatible with the play of innocent mirth; and in the calm of her deep blue and eloquent eyes there was a tender light which seemed never to have been clouded by angry or tempestuous passions,—affection, gentleness, and peace dwelt in them. It would be difficult to convey an accurate idea of her complexion; it could not properly be classed with either the pale, the brunette, or the florid, though it certainly approached the first more nearly than either of the other two. Her being employed mostly in the house had protected her from that *tan* which is the consequence of exposure to the sun; and while the wanderings of the "violet vein" might have been traced along the transparent whiteness of her brow or cheek, the blood seemed to mantle beneath a thin veil of snow, slightly tinging the pure covering with its warm stream. When she was excited by the recital of wrongs patiently borne, or touched with the tale of joy or sorrow, the inspired blood appeared to mount, a brighter spirit shone in her eye, the flash of soul beamed from her whole countenance; and having seen her thus, it were impossible to form an idea of anything more interesting or more unaffectedly beautiful. The only young woman in the Nethertown, or near it, who at all approached her in personal charms, was the shoemaker's daughter, Jeanie Muir. While some affirmed that she was nearly as fair, others maintained that she was far behind even in this respect—but all allowed that she was totally destitute of that inspired beauty which the heart alone can convey to the countenance.

No one had ever suspected Christina of being in love; and what was still more strange, no one had ever heard of her having a lover! She had never once thought of the subject herself. A shrinking sense of the ill-fame which had fallen on more than one of her brothers, and a wish to shield her parents from the scathing thought of their degradation, had hitherto occupied her mind to the almost total exclusion of anything else. But this could not last: the vivid expression which at times brightened over her countenance proved that she was made for the extreme of either happiness or misery. There was in her nature too many of those qualities which constitute the one or the other, for both spring from the same source, to admit of a cold mediocrity. The *fate of the fairest* was yet in the balance, and equally poised, but her hour was approaching.

Early in the spring of 1830, a young man called James Dixon came to the village seeking employment, and the wright engaged him. "His face was handsome, eyes fine, mouth gracious." That facility of purpose, and quickness of perception, which are so often found in youth—a warm heart, and a wish always to please, formed the basis of his character.

He had, moreover, a sort of natural gallantry and good humour, which, added to his other qualities, soon made him a great favourite with the young women of the place. He was violent in his likings, but inconstant. He spared no pains to gratify the slightest freak of fancy, but the whim of to-day lost its relish on the morrow.

When the bleaching season arrived, the young wright became a constant attendant at the Green; and his handsome face, his smile, his humour, and his wish to please, added a new source of attraction to the little evening parties which frequently assembled there. Passing along a green lane on his return home one evening, he chanced to meet Christina, and tried to detain her a few minutes by conversation; but she seemed to be in a hurry, and answered him without stopping —this was the first time he had seen her.

Some days after this event, her mother being fatigued, Christina, after her daily toils, went to the Green to "bring in the claes." Here she found herself in the company of six or eight young persons of both sexes, and among the rest *Jamie the wright*. Upon this occasion he seemed to take no notice of her, but his pleasantries, and the humorous tricks which he played upon the other girls, were unceasing. He put two pieces of paper on each side of his pocket-knife, and by a dexterous sleight,* made them believe that he wiped them off one by one, and then brought the whole back and replaced them with a whistle. He tried to pin bits of brown paper or

---

* The trick is performed thus: wet the blade of a knife, and place two pieces of paper at about an inch and a-half, or two inches, separate on each side; hold it in your left hand in a position nearly horizontal, resting the point upon your knee or on a table, and with the forefingers of your right hand wipe off the paper which is nearest the point on one side, saying at the same time "There is one there." Give the knife a sudden turn, but instead of turning the other side up, turn it quite round, so that the same side may be uppermost again, and before the deception can be discovered, pass your fingers quickly over the place from which you had formerly wiped the paper, saying, as before, "There is one there." Repeat the operation with the remaining paper, changing the words to "There is none there." You will thus have one side of the knife with two papers on it, and the other with none, while the onlookers will believe that the whole are off. Flourish it in the air, putting it over your shoulder, and whistling at the same time, then bring it down with that side uppermost on which the two papers are still sticking, and say, "There are two there." After this you may amuse onlookers as long as you please by showing the knife alternately with and without papers, only taking care to turn it rapidly. Some practice is necessary to enable a person to perform the trick with dexterity and success.

rags on their backs, and mimicked their affected wrath when he was discovered. He offered to assist them in gathering up their clothes, well knowing that his services would not be accepted, and when they came to drive him away, he fled; while the offended parties, taking the hint, chased him round the Green, throwing wet clothes at him as they ran. By these good-humoured oddities, he succeeded so well in drawing the attention of the spectators, that in a short time they seemed to have forgotten everything else in laughing at him. Christina was among those who looked and listened; and oftener than once she laughed till her eyes filled with tears. The merriment and fun was kept up till she was ready to depart, when, as if to play a trick on her, the young wright snatched up her basket and ran off with it. But instead of running round the Green with it, he carried it directly to her mother's door, and set it down with the greatest care, then turning round, held up both his hands, as if to deprecate the wrath of the panting maiden who followed. Breathless with running, she could scarcely speak; but instead of teasing her like the others, he had done her all the service in his power, and she thanked him with a smile. The young wright felt the power of that smile, and answering it with another, he ran back to the Green. But his tricks and oddities were over for that evening; the whole party appeared dull; and after standing for a few minutes, during which a yawn went round, broke up simultaneously.

"O love! what art thou in this world of ours?" How simple and almost imperceptible are thy beginnings, and yet what havoc of peace and happiness hast thou made in many a heart! For the next five or six days, Christina was not at the Green. But when her mother's bleaching day again came round, she again came to "bring hame the claes,"—again she met Jamie Dixon, and again he ran off with her basket. The unaffected wish to please rarely fails in its effect: again the artless maiden thanked him with a smile, but on this occasion it was accompanied with a few words expressive of her gratitude for his kindness. After this, she went oftener out "to take the air," in the evening or at mid-day, than was her wont, and as a matter of course, was oftener in the way of meeting the young wright. At first, a mutual smile of recognition, and the common observation about the state of the weather, constituted the whole of their intercourse. But ere another month had elapsed, they would stand together for a few minutes to tell or hear some piece of news, and then they would part, as they had met, with a smile—each turning to take a backward look at the other. Sometimes it happened that both looked about at the same time, and then they would smile again. By and by these little conversations became more frequent and prolonged; they would look around to see if they were observed, and pass abruptly if any one was near. After this, it was soon noticed that at the Green and elsewhere, Jamie the wright always appeared to be happiest and in the highest spirits when Christina was present, while the smile was oftener upon her cheek when he was near than at any other time. If he spoke in her praise, she would blush, turn away her head, pick up a blade of grass, and busy herself in folding it up, as if she had not heard him.

In small societies, every trifle becomes the subject of conversation. Suspicions were now entertained of their being in love; and those suspicions were confirmed, when, after having gone up the burn one evening to gather water-cresses, Christina was seen slowly returning with the supposed object of her affection by her side, and observed to part from him before they reached the houses, each taking a separate road. Her neighbours now threw out sly hints in her presence, which brought the crimson rushing to her cheeks, and put the state of her affections beyond a doubt.

Her smiles were now entirely suppressed in the presence of her lover, and if she met him at the Green, or in any of those little parties which sometimes assembled in the lanes during leisure hours, the few words she uttered were always addressed to some other. But if he left the party first, her eye followed him till he disappeared, and then she sighed deeply. If a footstep were heard approaching the window when she was at work, she would pause and listen attentively till the individual passed, and if it chanced to be him, she would sit for a time apparently absorbed in profound thought, with her eyes fixed on vacancy, and her hands idly folded across her bosom.

These little occurrences were carefully noted by the neighbours, and Christina was frequently compelled to hear an account of her own blushes and sighs, and to be taxed with that affection which she could so ill conceal. Too modest and timid to confess openly her feelings, and by far too honest and ingenuous to deny what she secretly felt to be true, she had no other resource but to bear all in silence, and labour in future to suppress her sighs, and curb her blushes.

Lovers are objects at whom every one deems himself entitled to level the shafts of raillery; and the young wright had also to endure his share; but to him it gave little annoyance. He could make jests at his own expense, and laugh with those who made them for him. Sometimes he would deny every thing with humorous effrontery, and at others he would plead guilty to every charge which was brought against him. Thus he puzzled and baffled those who wished to tease him; and when they found that their efforts were ineffectual, they in general soon gave it up.

Matters thus went on, till new events gave to the good people of the Nethertown new topics of conversation. Christina and Jamie Dixon were looked upon as affianced lovers; and though they were seen together, it was considered merely a thing of course, and scarcely spoken of. The ramble to the hill for blackberries—the walk up the burn to gather flowers —and the errand to the town, deferred till evening that they might go together, continued as before.

The growth of affection is often of such a nature, that it were difficult even for those who have experienced it in all its stages to describe it. A look when hundreds are between, and no word can be spoken—a touch of the hand—a cadence of the voice, even in common conversation—may make a deep impression on the memory, "and come, and come again," in moments of solitary musing, till the imagination has magnified it into an ideal world of tenderness and love. Love is like an indigenous plant; nature has provided for its growth, and no extraordinary care or cultivation is required to bring it to maturity.

Thus it was with Christina. Formed by nature for the most tender and lasting affection, love had opened up to her a new existence, and supplied her with a new train of thoughts. Her heart no longer wandered, like the bee, from flower to flower, among that little round of associations which had formerly occupied it. One image alone was imprinted upon it —the name of one object was written there; and these were all in all to her. To recollect every varying shade of his countenance—to ponder over every word he had spoken—and thence to draw indications of all those amiable qualities which add to domestic felicity;—to form excuses for his trifling faults, and in his virtues to find sure signs of that excellence which, when matured and known, would draw the esteem of all;—these occupied every hour of her waking time, and every day added something new, which "lent to loneliness delight!" Not that fears did not sometimes intrude—for fears and ardent affection are often married together; but when they were past, they only served to make the pleasing reflections which followed more pleasant, as pain, when it is removed, serves to heighten the enjoyment which we derive from health, while yet the contrast is fresh. Upon the whole, her life at this period resembled a happy dream, over which hope was the presiding power, while fears only came occasionally. And in that dream the summer passed away—the autumn faded into winter—the winter brightened into spring—and spring was again expanding into summer—without having produced any material change.

The buds and blossoms were bursting from the trees; the birds "made wild music rife" on every common and in every grove; the Green was again covered with its load of clean-washed linen, and again at eventide fair forms, happy faces, and hearts full of glee, flitted round it. At this gay season there is an annual fair at the little town of N——, and thither, on the appointed day, Christina's lover easily persuaded her to accompany him. On the road, and in the crowded market-place, he treated her with the most sedulous attention. He took her to see the shows of wild beasts, and the exhibitions of jugglers; then he led her down to the harbour to "see the shipping;" and while she hung on his arm, he pointed out every novelty which he supposed worthy of her notice. He was constantly by her side, protecting her from the pressure, and choosing for her those situations where the objects of interest might be best seen. When they had satisfied their curiosity with these, he led her up to the hill above the town, where they had an extensive view of the Frith. It was a spring-tide, and its bosom presented a scene to her so new and striking, that she seemed to forget all, save the youth by her side, in silent wonder. Far off, amid the dim haze of the waters, the distant ships might be seen emerging, as it were, from the clouds, and appearing no larger than so many white specks on the horizon. Somewhat nearer they lay still and motionless, with all their spread of canvas, like leviathans slumbering on the deep. Nearer still, or rather immediately below, some were drawing in to the little port, while others were moving majestically past, with their white wings spread to catch the breeze—breaking the blue waters into foam, and leaving a long rippling track behind them.

All this was new to Christina. Her heart was in unison with the picturesque and beautiful, and she thought she had never in her life seen any thing half so worthy of admiration. Those who have looked, for the first time, on a number of new and interesting objects, in the presence of the being whom they most love, and felt their interest increased by the consciousness that *that* being was participating the same pleasure, and sharing the same emotions, with themselves, may perhaps be able to form a better idea of what her feelings were upon this occasion, than any which words could convey.

The day had been remarkably fine, but toward evening the sky became cloudy,—a few peals of distant thunder were heard, and a rattling shower of rain forced the lovers to hasten to the town, and take refuge in a close called the *Wide Entry*. This was nothing more than a passage through below the houses; and, in a few minutes it was crowded with people seeking shelter from the shower. While standing here a rude fellow, who fancied himself pinched for room, began to thrust a young woman, who stood next him, out into the rain, by offering her such indignities, as made her prefer being drenched to the skin to returning and standing beside him. Christina, who knew the girl, requested Jamie, in a whisper, to interfere in her behalf. He did so; and, as several others appeared willing to take her part, the fellow was driven forth to seek shelter elsewhere, while she was again received under the protecting roof, and better accommodated than before.

The violence of the storm had abated, and dwindled into a drizzling rain; and twilight was begun when the lovers, under the canopy of a solitary umbrella, set out on their homeward journey. Neither the inclemency of the weather, nor bad roads, were any inconvenience to Christina, since they afforded her companion an opportunity of performing many little acts of kindness and attention, which enhanced her comfort and happiness. When they were within a mile of the Nethertown, a small party of acquaintances overtook them, and some miscellaneous conversation ensued; but the new comers soon passed on; and, when they were out of hearing, Christina's companion inquired at her, "who it was that walked on the left hand side of the road?" She informed him that she was the shoemaker's daughter, and the very woman on whose behalf he had interfered during the rain; that she had come from her service to spend the summer half-year with her father; and, moreover, that she was wont to be considered the bonniest lass about the Nethertown. She concluded, by artlessly asking again "if he didna ken her?" "I never saw her afore," was the inconsistent reply, for he *had* seen her only a few hours ago: "but I think she is a bonnie lassie."

The individual spoken of was indeed a dashing lass—tall,

dark-haired, and dark-eyed. Christina knew all this; but when she heard her lover speak of her beauty, she felt something like a cold damp at her heart—an involuntary feeling for which she could not account, and the smile of happiness, which hitherto had brightened her countenance, forsook it for a season. Perhaps her lover discovered the change, and what had caused it; for he endeavoured to obliterate both by increased care and kindness. Her heart was not made for suspicion, and before they reached her father's door, her confidence—if it had ever been shaken—was perfectly restored. To the threshold of that door he accompanied her; and, after shaking her by the hand, and holding it for a few seconds gently pressed in his own, he bade her *good night*, and left her to dream of him and happiness.

During the whole of the next day she did not see him. This naturally created some alarm, but her heart was fruitful in forming excuses for his absence. At last evening came, but with it came not her lover, as was his wont. What could she do? Propriety forbade that she should ask an explanation. After a restless night, morning dawned—it passed away, and still she saw him not, though she learned that he had been out late last night, and even heard herself censured as the cause. This information fell heavy on her heart; still hope was not extinct, and throughout the day she tried to comfort herself with the idea, that something unexpected had prevented him from seeing her. In the evening of the second day, after finishing her task, she walked out, not perhaps without the expectation of seeing him. She did see him, but what words can describe the hopeless and dreary feeling which settled over her at the sight! He, too, had walked out, though apparently not for the purpose of seeing her. With him walked the very woman about whom he had inquired on the road two evenings ago—whom Christina had characterised as "the bonniest lass about the Nethertown." They paid no attention to her—they did not even see her. Her situation, however, gave her an opportunity of marking them too accurately for her own peace. She saw his eye distinctly, and it seemed to beam with all that tenderness which it was wont to express when turned upon herself. She saw him smile, and his smile appeared the same as that which had long been the light of her eyes—she heard him speak, and in his voice she fancied she could trace those endearing accents which had so often lulled her into utter forgetfulness of everything else—she saw and heard all this, and she was miserable. The scene was too painful to be long endured. Her visions had vanished, and in hopeless dejection she hurried back to her home, and threw herself upon her bed, to hide in obscurity her heart's despair.

In justice to the other, we must now notice the circumstances which produced the scene narrated above, for as yet his error was owing to levity and thoughtlessness, rather than to infidelity. The day after the Fair, he was so busy at the shop that it was not till evening he could find leisure to see her who anxiously awaited his coming; and when he did walk out with this intention, before he had proceeded many steps, he met the dark-eyed dashing Jeanie Muir. She thanked him, with a host of smiles and blandishments, for the service he had rendered her on the preceding day, and he could not do less than listen. She was fair, and forward as she was fair. He had a sort of natural gallantry, which made him desirous to please; and they stood together till, thinking it too late to follow out his first purpose, he abandoned it for the night, without once thinking of the anxiety which his absence might occasion to one who so tenderly loved him. On the following evening, as he left the shop, he again met Jeanie. She felt proud of his acquaintance; and from a wish, no doubt to make the most of it, she had again thrown herself in his way. She was going she said to take a walk, and asked him, in a half laughing way, if he would not accompany her? He assented, and chance brought them where their looks and words were as daggers to the heart of one who was but ill-prepared for such a scene.

He saw Christina, however, as she was hurrying from a sight which she could no longer endure. Conscience rebuked him for his levity; and, as soon as he could conveniently get away from the other, he hastened to join her. Even then she did not refuse to see him; but, believing, as she did, that his affections were estranged, how could she receive his attentions? She tried to summon a smile to her countenance, but tears came instead; and, to conceal them, she turned away her face. She attempted to speak, but her voice was broken, and her words unconnected. In spite of all her efforts, he saw she was changed; and, conscience-stricken, he left her without a word.

From this night Christina was visibly altered, though she strove, with all a woman's wiles, to hide the change. When others were present, she still attempted to speak and laugh, and appear as cheerful as she had been before. But the veil was too thin to deceive even a superficial observer.

Ill may a sad heart forge a merry face,
Nor hath constrained laughter any grace.

Her words flowed not from her heart as they were wont, and her laugh was forced and unnatural. Instead of walking out when her work was done, she would sit lonely by the fire, twisting and untwisting a bit of straw; or she would take down her hair, and while it hung loosely about her face, with her scissors clip the pieces of paper which held it into strange and fantastic shapes, and then put them into the fire one by one, and watch them as they blazed. During these reveries, if she was spoken to by any one, her name had always to be repeated oftener than once before she could be restored to consciousness.

This alteration in her manner did not pass without remark. The gossips, however, only attributed it to one of those casual coolnesses which are so frequent among lovers, and from which even the fondest and most faithful are seldom wholly exempt. But in a short time her mother became anxious for her health; and thinking that too close an application to her work might have brought on lowness of spirits, she earnestly urged her to take a jaunt and see her friends. With her mother's wishes she readily complied, and was absent for two days, but returned without any sign of having brought along with her a lighter heart. It was rather late in the evening before she reached home; and the next morning, as she was returning from the well with water, some young people from the houses which she passed stopped her to inquire the news of her journey. One of them noticed the late hour of her arrival, and asked if she came without company. She averred that she did; but he pretended to disbelieve her, and said, that "Jamie Dixon had not been seen last night till *after* her return." When the name of her former lover was mentioned, she tried to smile, but the paleness of ashes was on her lip—it quivered —the blood forsook her cheek, and she fell apparently lifeless at their feet! Was she gone? No: a faint breathing told she was not dead. They raised her up, and sprinkled water over her deathlike forehead, and into the palms of her hands, and gradually restored her to consciousness. But the shock she had received was too violent to be immediately got over; and it was not till after she had been confined to bed some time, that she was able to resume her usual occupations.

Here we must once more advert to her now faithless lover. Petted by what he was pleased to think her coldness, and pained by his own reflections, but still disposed to shift the blame from himself, he hastened back to the very individual who had been the cause of all. While with her, his manner was uneasy; he appeared, as he deserved to be, unhappy; and by either real or well affected concern for his uneasiness, she succeeded in drawing from him an account of what had happened. She felt proud of the confidence he had thus reposed in her; and she professed so much friendship for him, and seemed to sympathise with him in such a way as to induce him again to seek consolation, or at least court forgetfulness, in her company. Had he been left to himself, affection would have soon returned to assert its sway, for his heart was neither callous nor corrupt. But the time was critical, and in the freshness of his pique she acquired an influence over him which she was perfectly willing to exercise for her own advantage. Facility on the one hand, and rashness on the other, were his principal errors. He received a letter from an old shop-mate in Edinburgh, informing him of an opening for him there, with the prospect of high wages. This information was immediately communicated to his newly-acquired friend. Art and intrigue are practised in cottages as well as courts, and there is a rivalry among women when their affections are engaged, which, though less obvious, is as earnestly pursued as the more open contentions of men. She urged him to embrace the offer, and, as an inducement, stated that she had determined to go there herself in quest of service. To wean him from any hankerings which he might have for the place, or any of its inhabitants, she also repeated some tattle which she had heard about a lad who was said to "be after his auld sweetheart," and who was supposed to be gone with her to see her friends. The scheme succeeded; and, on the night on which Christina returned from her jaunt, the two were together concerting measures for taking their departure on the following day. Both of them, accordingly, left the place early next morning, and as they had kept their intention secret till they were ready to set off, their departure was not generally known in the Nethertown till after Christina had swooned.

After this, James Dixon never returned to the Nethertown. Had he stayed there a week longer, his feelings, probably, would have flowed back to their old channel; but rash and reckless of consequences, he had exchanged the rural quiet of a country life for the confusion of a crowded city, and the Nethertown and all it contained, if not forgotten, might be for a time so confounded with other images as to leave but a faint impression on his mind. It is, moreover, questionable if he knew the extent of the misery he had occasioned till it was too late to remedy it; for if subsequent accounts were true, in six months going to Edinburgh, he married Jeanie Muir. But this, ... believed, was never told to the victim of his former attachment.

It is painful to trace the progress of disappointment from the first shade of paleness which exhibits itself on the countenance, through all its future stages,—languor, weariness, and disease,—till it ends in the darkness of death. But *the Fate of the Fairest* must be told; and if it should be instrumental in teaching the virtue of *constancy* to one inconstant lover, or in saving one gentle heart among the softer sex from the pang which its opposite might occasion, the writer will account himself amply rewarded.

When but partially recovered, Christina resumed her work, and was as diligent as she had been before; but she never regained her former cheerfulness. By degrees, she began to absent herself almost entirely from company, always indicating a wish to be alone. Her colour, too, it was remarked, had never been what it was previous to her sudden illness, but no one appeared to entertain any apprehensions for her perfect recovery, and the matrons merely observed, that "Christina was surely growin' guid noo, for they never saw her at the Green."

Time stays not his flight for the happy or the unhappy, though to the latter he may seem to linger; while the former may fancy him too swift. The fields had exchanged their rich green for "the hues of coming ripeness," when Christina began to complain of weariness after her day's work; but still she spoke not of pain, or any fixed disorder. Harvest came, and she went forth with the reapers, in the expectation that the fresh air and exercise would be beneficial to her. But the canker-worm was at her heart, and neither air nor exercise could scare it away. It was truly touching to see her sit, during the intervals of rest, with her features composed into the deepest melancholy, while peals of laughter were ringing around her; and it was still more touching to see her sometimes attempt to laugh at—she knew not what. Her strength was unequal to the task, and, after a trial of two or three days, another took her place, and she returned to her former employment.

The harvest season passed over; the corn was secured from coming winter; the sombre hues of autumn were on the naked fields, and the trees had begun to shed their sere leaves at the summons of the blast.

A little after daybreak, the east appeared overspread with clouds—
> Which, streak'd with dusky red, portend
> The day shall have a stormy end.

They vanished before sunrise, and for two hours after the morning continued calm and beautiful. It was the Sabbath, and Christina was preparing herself for church; her friends would have dissuaded her from going out in her infirm state of health, but she wished to go, and they consented. Before the service was concluded, sleet and rain fell, and the wind blew keenly from the south-east. In returning, she got slightly wet, and almost immediately on reaching home complained of unusual weariness, headache, and oppression of the breast. Pain in her side was the next alarming symptom. Medical assistance was called in, and succeeded in affording a temporary relief, but there was no permanent improvement: her strength had departed, and no power of art could bring it back. Her medical adviser now recommended walking in the open air when the weather was mild, and cheerful company when it was not. With these directions she endeavoured to comply; but her weakness had increased so much, that her walks in general terminated at the house of the sewing-mistress, in whose words let what remains of her story be told.

"When she came to see me," said this kind-hearted individual, "her conversation was always of a solemn and impressive nature—death, and the things of another world, were the subjects upon which it most frequently turned; but not a word did she speak of her faithless lover, nor did she ever make the slightest allusion to her own particular case. I frequently attempted to draw her attention to passing events, and to amuse her by telling cheerful stories; but all was in vain. Though she appeared willing to listen, her mind soon wandered from the subject; and when I asked her opinion, I often found that she had forgotten, or rather never heard, what I had been saying. At last it occurred to me, that if she could be brought to disclose the story of her ill-requited affection, it might relieve her sinking spirits, and even yet give her a chance of recovering. With this idea in my head, I watched for an opportunity to lead her on to unbosom herself, without importuning her with questions.

"One day, after we had been speaking of the felicity of a future state, I remarked that love—overflowing love—would be one of the principal sources of happiness in heaven: love to God, and love to each other—a love which could neither be interrupted by accidents, nor unreturned. At these words, a faint red once more tinged her pale cheek, she sighed deeply, and I almost trembled to proceed; yet the time seemed favourable for my purpose, and I went on to say, that the little unalloyed happiness we could enjoy here would be still less, were it not for those sympathies and affections which Heaven, in mercy, had vouchsafed us—the love of friends, sisters, brothers, parents, children, and the yet more tender ties by which young hearts are linked together. I remarked farther, that those affections from which we derived our purest enjoyments were, from unavoidable circumstances—the unworthiness of their objects, and the imperfections of our fallen nature—sometimes turned into bitterness, and made the means of poisoning the fountain which they were intended to purify; but where this was the case, it was our duty to forget the past as speedily as possible, and in future be more careful to fix them only on such objects as might be worthy of our regard.

"As I spoke, I purposely avoided looking at her, lest she should suspect my intention; but as I concluded, I looked her full in the face, and I shall never forget the appearance which she at that moment presented. A bright hectic burned on her cheek; her eye—dry, feverish, and 'full of fearful meaning,'— was fixed on my countenance, and her hands were clasped across her bosom. She did not attempt to speak for some minutes, and fear made me silent also; for I recollected the scene which had followed the rash mention of her lover's name when she was much stronger than now, and apprehensive for the same consequences, I would have given worlds to recall my words. She rose from her seat, and made an attempt at utterance, but her emotion was still too strong, and her voice died away in a broken murmur. After heaving a deep sigh, she was able to articulate,—'Oh,' said she, 'I would tell you a secret, which you already know—but I know not how it is, I cannot speak.' I begged her to compose herself, and sit down, and when she was better, I would be happy to listen to whatever she had to impart. She sat down accordingly, and tried to calm her feelings and collect herself for the task, but soon expressed a wish to go home, saying that she was too much agitated to tell her story distinctly. To this I did not object, and when she rose to depart, after looking earnestly at me for a short time, as if to ascertain the extent of what I felt on her account, she pressed my hand in her own—thin and shadowy —and said she would return to-morrow.

"When she returned, the melancholy serenity of her countenance was restored. She was pale—paler than I had ever seen her before—but there was no agitation in her manner, and her eye, though it did not sparkle with health, beamed with a pure seraphic brightness, as if it looked far beyond the mists of time. She was herself the first to allude to the subject. With the most perfect composure, she told her whole story from first to last—from the time she met her faithless lover at the Green, to their last parting. She said she had often tried to discover what it was that made him so dear to her, and had as often fancied that it was merely his kindness and his good humour which she admired, but that she never knew her own heart till she was shocked with the idea of being forsaken.

"When she concluded, I said she should try to think no more of him, or if that were impossible, that it were better to despise, or even hate him, than thus to wear out her existence in useless regret and unavailing sorrow.

"'Oh, no!' she replied. 'I do not think of him now as a lover—that is past—but I can neither despise nor hate him; I could not do that even in the bitterest moments of disappointment—I love him still! And oh!' she continued, in an excited tone, 'oh if I could but meet him in heaven, this—*this* would more than reward me for all I have suffered on his account!'

"I was so struck with this instance of pure and forgiving affection filling the warm heart of the apparently dying girl, that it was some time before I could answer her. I applauded her constancy, and that gentleness of heart which sought no revenge—what else could I do?—and tried to flatter her once more with hopes of recovery, telling her of others who had been weaker than she was yet, and who, nevertheless, had lived to a healthy old age; but her only answer was a mournful smile.

"From this time forward, though the process of decay went on, her spirits seemed to be relieved of a burden. Gradually and gently she faded day by day; but death made his approaches in loveliness, not in terror. As she drew nearer her end, her countenance assumed an expression of tranquil and almost unearthly beauty; and her eye, which retained its lustre to the last, seemed to glow with heavenly light. Sallowness and gloom were not among the symptoms of dissolution: and on the evening before she died, one would have thought that she might melt into the essence of a spirit without suffering a single pang. On the following morning, which was the market day, while her former companions were preparing themselves to visit those scenes which she had seen along with them but one short year before, she closed her eyes in a gentle slumber, and so tranquil were her last moments, and so calm and bright was her countenance even after the spirit had fled, that it was with some difficulty those who watched could tell she was dead."

At the Nethertown, and on the Green, she was soon forgotten by all save a few; and her grave has already sunk nearly to a level with the grassy heaps which surround it. I have stood over that grave; and while memory wandered back into the past, and pondered on the brief career of her whose affections " blighted her life's bloom," the words of a great delineator of the human heart involuntarily occurred to my recollection,—" A broken heart is a distemper which kills many more than is generally imagined, and would have a fair title to a place in the bill of mortality, did it not differ in one instance from all other diseases, namely, that no physician can cure it."

Such was the fate of artless maid,
Sweet flow'ret of the rural shade!


## THE DECLINE AND FALL OF THE GHOST.

What may this mean,
That thou, dead corse, . . . .
Revisit'st thus the glimpses of the moon,
Making night hideous; and we fools of nature
So horridly to shake our disposition
With thoughts beyond the reaches of our souls?
SHAKESPEARE.

JOHNNIE HUME was an Aberdonian of birth and rank—that is to say, a ploughman, and the son of a ploughman. I cannot swear that he was quite so intelligent as his clansman, the historian of England; but there is one thing certain: Johnnie was sprung from one of the most ancient and noble families upon earth, and his blood had never been contaminated by any deteriorating admixture with the blood of a meaner race. Johnnie could trace his descent from an ancestor whose dominions were more extensive than those of Pompey the Great, Peter the Great, Cæsar the Great, or even *Sandy* the Great. The founder of Johnnie's family was Noah, who reigned over the whole earth; and, though he had neither wars nor taxes, prime minister nor privy counsellor, governed his subjects without rebellion, and died in the full possession of his regal authority.* Such being the ancestry of Johnnie Hume, it cannot be denied that he was both anciently and honourably descended.

Johnnie was a little man, of plethoric body, with a short face, full, round, and rubicund—exceedingly expressive of self-complacency. His eyes were small, and almost entirely concealed beneath his shaggy eye-brows, which gave them the peculiar advantage of seeing without being seen. His mouth was large, and the under lip turned down with a graceful curl, resting confidingly on the soft, glittering, cushion-like redundancy of his short, broad, and sagacious chin. This lip was particularly serviceable to Johnnie when he and his social neighbours happened to meet over their evening dram; and it was curious to observe the gradual unfolding of that pouch-like appendage to his mouth, which, so soon as his fingers touched the glass, turned slowly upward, and formed itself into a regular and capacious receiver for the dearly loved liquid.

In his worldly circumstances Johnnie was "geyly provided for," as he himself expressed it, being in possession of a small farm, at that period when low rents and high prices raised so many of his fellow-landloupers to the quality of lairds. But though Johnnie possessed all the avarice of a man of the world, he was not possessed of the capacity of rising to a higher place in society. Though he was habitually cautious in parting with money, and habitually careful in collecting the last farthing of the smallest debt that was due to him, he had still to sustain the character of a liberal, good-hearted man among his ale-house companions; and this bottle generosity sometimes proved too hard for his domestic economy. Johnnie was no "scrub," as he himself asserted; but if, in settling accounts, there happened to be an odd halfpenny, which the payer claimed in discount, for want of change, or some other reasonable consideration, he never failed to show his sense of the value of it, by repeating the money table which he had learned at school—"Twa bawbees mak' ae penny, an' twall pennies mak' ae shillin', an' twenty shillin's mak' ae pound; sae ye see," said Johnnie, "though this be a little sum, it mak's a pairt o' a muckle ane,

---

* It is recorded of this potentate, in the writings of Robert Burns, that
<blockquote>Graceless Ham leuch at his dad,<br>
Which made Canaan a Nigger.</blockquote>

This seems to have been a sort of rebellion, though not to such an extent as to derogate from the sovereign dignity of Johnnie's ancestor.

an' I canna want the bawbee!" But though Johnnie's nature and education neither desired nor required the delicacies or refinements of life, his familiarity with the gill-stoup, and that sottish inactivity in the general management of his affairs, which a habitual addiction to the use of ardent spirits never fails to produce, served to prevent his fortune from exceeding his capacity to enjoy it. Yet, after all, Johnnie was a substantial man, who could at any time change a pound to a neighbour who required it; and this command of money made him respectable among the rich as a subject of sport, and honourable among the poor as an object of convenience.

Johnnie's family consisted of four children, of the same sturdy constitution, and stubborn disposition as himself. It was the subject of his proudest boast, that he had "gien them a' a gueed edification; for there wasna ane o' them but was sax winters at the sceul." Yet, after all this long course of instruction, when he wished to avail himself of their learning, to relieve him from some arithmetical perplexity, he found their boasted education insufficient to tell him what was the cost of a boll of meal at one shilling and fourpence the peck.

Johnnie's family grew up around him, in the light of his own example, and soon became the faithful representatives of their father in mind and in body. His eldest son, the inheritor of his patronymic, at the age of twenty-four was deemed fully qualified for the management of a farm of his own; and was, accordingly, provided with the portion necessary for commencing business on his own account. A small farm, adjacent to Dubbyside, became vacant; and old Johnnie, with great adroitness, negotiated a bargain with the proprietor, in behalf of his hopeful son. This farm was beautifully situated on the banks of the Tay; but the sweetness of the surrounding scenery added nothing to its value in the eyes of its intended cultivator. Johnnie was luckily ignorant of every production of nature, with the exception of wheat, barley, oats, turnips, and rye. Nevertheless, he succeeded in his calling, and soon ceased to be considered as a dependent member of the family. But while Little Johnnie (as he continued to be called for distinction's sake, though the largest man of the two) increased in wealth, his venerable father declined in health. Though he was originally possessed of a stronger constitution than any other animal, carnivorous or herbaceous, on the farm of Dubbyside, he had poured more whisky over his throat than would have killed all the horses in his stable, and all the cows in his byre; and it so happened, that Johnnie became so seriously indisposed, that he was no longer able to travel the short distance which lay between his own house at Dubbyside, and the little inn at Drumdreggle, where, for the last twenty years of his life, he had been accustomed to repair for nightly consolation. But, alas for Johnnie! those halcyon days and merry nights were gone; and he was the most miserable of men! His mind was completely destitute of all internal sources of enjoyment; and therefore completely unprepared for the society of solitude.

His memory and imagination had never been developed by exercise; and he had, therefore, nothing to recall, and nothing to anticipate. The past presented no comfortable recollections, and the future exhibited no cheering hopes. He only possessed the present, and to him it was present misery. His good-nature, which was the best quality in his composition, at length gave way under the painful circumstances of his situation; and he became peevish, fretful, and discontented with himself, and every thing around him. He was now a prisoner to nature for his previous contumacious disregard of her laws; and the only liberty which he possessed, was the privilege of swinging backwards and forwards in his old arm chair, with the pleasure of grumbling at every one who came within reach of his voice. But as he had lost all respect in his family, his admonitory addresses, and paternal reproofs, were generally answered by a scornful laugh, or a contemptuous repetition of his words.

Johnnie's disease, encouraged by the harsh treatment he received from his friends, and strengthened by his own discontent, soon reduced his bluff, good-humoured countenance to the most meagre dimensions; and being no longer able to keep his seat by the fire, he was gladly consigned, by his careful family, to the closer and more dreary incarceration of an old box bed, where even his last remaining consolation—the pleasure of grumbling—was fairly cut off; for, as the *lids* were kept shut, the household operations were concealed from his view; and he had no motive for the exercise of his only available faculty. Yet he was sometimes so overcome with a desperate desire for utterance, that, raising himself up on his arm, and knocking against the wooden walls of his prison, he not unfrequently addressed his dear goodwife in such language as the following:

"Ho ye, Janet! D'ye hear me na—eh? Gae doun to Willie M'Bickers, an' be hanged to ye! an' tell him if he does na send me twa bottles o' his best maut whisky, he'll never see my face again at Drumdreggle; for I'm deein' for want o' a cure. Open thae lids, ye doure auld dromedary!" he would continue in a louder tone, "d'ye think that I'm to be keepit mowtherin', mowtherin' here like a mole in a peat stack, without ever seein' a blink o' licht for the lee-lang day but what comes in at the key-hole?"

To this violent remonstrance the tender-hearted goodwife only replied, by observing to her equally delicate daughter: "Let him craw there like a cock i' the crib—he may weel fleg the chickens, but he canna brack the eggs noo!"

After a hearty laugh at her mother's wit, Tibby also had her humorous remark on her father's misery. Johnnie was too much accustomed to the want of affection in his family, to feel very acutely this utter contempt of his commands, and shameless disregard of his comfort. Yet the pain of his disease, aided by such ungentle treatment, sometimes operated so forcibly on his exhausted temper as to render him completely furious; and upon these occasions he tumbled about in his wooden dormitory liked a chafed tiger in his cage, imprecating curses on himself and all who were within hearing of his still stentorian voice. These fits of rage soon exhausted his little remaining strength; and they were generally succeeded by intervals of peace and repentance. During one of these melancholy qualms, the sad and solemn idea that he was a dying man at length fairly forced itself upon his stubborn brain; and as it was seemly for a man in his circumstances to settle his earthly affairs, Johnnie wisely bethought him of making his will. He had enjoyed no *will* of his own for some time past; but in this instance, some of the members of his family seconded his motion with great readiness; others who thought it would be more for their benefit that he should die intestate, opposed his inclination with great bitterness. And thus a debate arose in Johnnie's household, which was as noisy, as selfish, and, I had almost said, as sensible as any which has occurred in the British Parliament since the days of Pitt and Fox. Nevertheless, when the house divided, Johnnie's party prevailed; and, strange to tell, he experienced great kindness and attention from both sides ever afterwards; for the contending parties seemed to vie with each other in obeying his commands and supplying his wants; and between this period and the final settlement of Johnnie's last will and testament, his friend Willie M'Bickers of Drumdreggle had been several times called upon in his behalf, and divers bottles of his best medicinal water kindly procured, and tenderly presented to the old invalid by his loving relatives and—expectant legatees.

Johnnie had no knowledge of legal forms; and he was only possessed of as much skill in the art of writing as to enable him to sign his own name. He was therefore incapable of preparing himself the necessary instrument for securing to his heirs the property which he intended to bequeath; and to call in the assistance of a professional gentleman was quite contrary to Johnnie's ideas of economy; for, as he wisely remarked, "a lawur wud tak' as muckle to tell fowk what they were to get, as a' he had to gi'e them." But he discovered a cheaper method of managing the affair, and one which answered the purpose as well with his simple family as the most nicely adjusted testament could have done; for they were not acquainted with the method of breaking obligations by the assistance of law.

After receiving from the hands of his dutiful wife a glass of double strong *destructive*, which had the happy effect of strengthening him to make his will, and of hurrying him out of the way, for the benefit of those whom it concerned, he raised himself up on his arm, with all the sottish good humour of his better days beaming in his countenance, and thus addressed his faithful spouse—

"Ho ye, luckie! D'ye hear me na, eh? I fin' mysel' a gueed deal revived by that spcen'ul [spoonful] o' drink, woman; and if a *little* dee [do] muckle gueed [good], *muckle* 'll dee mair; sae hand me anither glass o't. D'ye understand me na—eh? Wha kens but I may live to bless ye mony a lang day yet; but it's best to be prepared for the warst, as worthy Mr. Humelrigs was wont to say; sae ye'll send aff immediately for my friends, Will M'Bickers and Sandy Hapabout, that they may come and bear testification to the guids I intend to contribute amang ye. D'ye understand me na, eh? An' hear ye me, luckie—may the gear that I gi'e ye blaw aff frae yer hand like birk seed frae the bensil, if ye forget the injunctions I leave ye, or mak' ony tirrivee about my testimony after I'm gane!"

This was no time to dispute the desires, or disobey the commands of Johnnie. The liquor which he requested was therefore granted him; and a special messenger despatched with all speed for the two individuals whom he had appointed as his executors, who both made their appearance in good time to drink his foy, and listen to the instructions which he had to give concerning the division of his property. Suffice it to say, that the whole affair was settled to Johnnie's satisfaction; and though there was a little natural grumbling among his family about the shares he had allotted to each, the peace was wonderfully preserved—no heads being broken, and no blood spilt upon the occasion. But Johnnie's eldest son, who, by the law of primogeniture, should have inherited the whole, was excluded from all participation in the distribution of his father's effects —the old testator evidently showing, by his judicious conduct in this respect, that he possessed more sense in his own brainless head than the collective wisdom of all our infallible ancestors is worth. For his son had previously received a sufficient portion in the stocking of the farm which he then occupied; and his own words upon the subject manifest more propriety of thought than the world was inclined to give him credit for. Addressing himself to one of his advisers, he inquired—

"An' fat think ye o' Johnnie, man? He has a gueed farm, a gueed house, a weel filled stable, an' a weel filled byre; an' I dinna ken fat mair he would be at, man."

After the affair was fully settled, by way of confirmation of the solemn engagements which had been entered into, the venerable testator and his two executors got gloriously drunk together, and fairly forgot before they parted all the obligations they had contracted since they met. Johnnie first became humorously drunk, uttered some popular oaths, told several facetious fictions, and laughed heartily at his own good-natured jokes. Anon, he became seriously drunk, and diverted his rude associates with several pathetic lamentations over the errors of his past life. Then he became confoundedly drunk, cried with one side of his mouth, and laughed with the other, while prayers and blasphemies tumbled over each other, as they galloped forth with fearful rapidity from his garrulous jaws; and, lastly, he became speechlessly drunk, and never again moved lip nor limb in the capacity of a mortal man!

Shortly after this event, a wag of the neighbourhood composed the following

### EPITAPH.

Here lies the dust o' Johnnie Hume,
  Beneath the mountain daisy;
His spirit fled for want o' room,
  An' left his body crazy.
But Johnnie, when his wame was toom,
  Was unco ill to please aye,
Sae to avoid his glumsh and gloom,
  An' keep his temper easy,
They ga'e him drink, till in a fume,
  He vapour'd aff to Lizzy! *

The news of Johnnie's death spread fast and far over the

---

* His first wife.

surrounding country, and at length reached the ears of his distant son, who, influenced by an earnest solicitude about the disposition of his father's better part, soon put on a decent coat and a decent face, and hurried away to the house of mourning, with a suitable lamentation on his lips.

After a few brief inquiries as to the manner of his father's exit, Johnnie the younger fully explained the object of his visit, by requesting to know "fat had been left as his *legatee* o' the gear that he had helpit sae weel to gather?"

He was faithfully presented with a silver-hinged snuff horn, which his father had bequeathed him, on account of the identity of his name with that which was engraved on the Scotch thistle that ornamented the lid of it. Though his brothers were prone enough to covet, they were too fearful to keep, anything which their father had assigned to another; for, as long as his body remained above ground, they apprehended that he would start up from his silent slumbers, and upbraid them for their infidelity, should they violate his will in the slightest degree. And thus, his lifeless remains commanded greater respect in his family, than he had ever possessed while alive. Johnnie, however, seemed to be less influenced by his awful veneration for the dead, for he rejected his father's bequest with the bitterest contempt, asserting, at the same time, that he had no use for horses without hoofs. "But ye'll hae preef o' the injustice o' yer dealins afore lang," continued he, "for cheatry aye kythes upon the livin' an' the dead; an' I'm muckle mista'en if my father get rest in his beerial place, or I get the guid o' my ain?"

Thus saying, the disinherited son strode haughtily out of the house. But he had said enough to awaken the fears of his superstitious kinsfolk, and they now felt greater pain from the apprehension of Johnnie's return in the character of a ghost, than they had done at his departure in that of a father. Every case with which they were acquainted, in which apparitions had manifested themselves to men, was conjured up to recollection; and the various circumstances connected with their appearance compared with those under which Johnnie had departed from this world; and, after long and anxious consultation, it was finally agreed that there was a probability of his return. But though they frequently cast their expectant eyes towards the bed where the lifeless body was laid, as if they thought he would rise up and rectify all past errors, by remodelling his will, no voice was heard, and no muscle stirred on the rigid convexity of his countenance. Day, however, soon passed away, and their apprehensions grew more terrible as the gloom of night approached, and an awful night it was; for the storm which had been long gathering in dark and dismal masses in the sky, at length burst forth with appalling violence, and soughed and howled among the hoary trees that surrounded the little farm-house of Dubbyside; and the fitful pauses and melancholy moanings of its inconstant voice might well have astounded stouter hearts than those which beat in the superstitious breasts of the Humes. In their ears every gust of the tempest rang like a voice from the dead. They believed that all the inhabitants of the unseen world had been convoked by the spirit of their father, to revel and roar around their desolate dwelling; and the various contortions which their countenances exhibited would have excited the risibility of the gravest observer, "if any laughter at such time could be."

Sleep was banished from every eye; and to add to their trepidation, the midnight hour was approaching, when the spirits of darkness are allowed the unlimited exercise of their own wicked wills. Short sharp shrieks, resembling those uttered in the first moments of mortal agony, began to swell, mingled with more distant wailings, like the dreary lamentations of madness, and followed by long, low, dismal groans. The solemn pauses which occurred in these terrible sounds were occasionally broken by the watch-dog at the door, whose yelling and growling seemed to bespeak a consciousness of "unholy spirits near." The door and windows creaked and rattled to every gust of wind, which, entering by their crevices, shook the old curtains of the bed of death, and waved the flame of the ghastly candles that were placed around it, now flaring with pale brilliance, and then sinking into a feeble spark, which imparted a dim, fantastic appearance to the antique furniture that filled the apartment, and increased the gloomy horrors of the scene.

Amidst these fearful alternations of glare and gloom, and surrounded by sights and sounds of woe, sat the simple family of Johnnie Hume in an agony of speechless apprehension, but not in silence; for there was a clattering among their jaw bones, which made them one of the noisiest little companies that ever was convened around a cottage hearth.

The old clock had no sooner began to rattle out the midnight hour in her accustomed way, than the snow-white linen cloth, that was so neatly folded over the round oak table, which stood in the centre of the room, flew away of its own accord, and disappeared through the cat-hole; and the bottles, glasses, and crockery which it supported rolled on the floor with a crash like the meeting of many waters. Unearthly sounds, too, began to arise in the garret, rattling and rumbling as if a shower of cannon-balls were descending upon the devoted dwelling, while long dismal shrieks, mingled with groans and lamentations, continued to swell in the distance, with appalling distinctness.

Terrified by this unaccountable storm of voices, the whole family fled from the chamber of death, and took refuge in the kitchen, where they concealed themselves under such articles of furniture as might afford the best protection from the grisly spectres which they every moment expected to burst upon their sight; and in an inconceivably short time every one of them was so judiciously stowed away that no mortal observer could have supposed the house inhabited. In this state of dreary durance, they lay quietly till the cheerful beams of the morning sun began to visit them in their separate cells. When at last the cock's shrill larum "roused them from their lowly beds," and restored them again to the blessings of light and liberty, they all assembled in the kitchen to consult about the best means of preventing the recurrence of such a disturbance.

"Gie Johnnie his share o' the gear," said one.

"Get my father beeried," said another.

Thus the family of Johnnie was again divided, and a stout debate ensued; but the amendment prevailed over the original motion, for it had avarice on its side, and they had every reason to believe that the unearthly noises which they had heard were occasioned by a general muster of the spirits of darkness, who had assembled to receive the ghost of the deceased into their society, and instruct him in the mysteries of their commonwealth. Prompt measures were accordingly taken to have Johnnie conveyed to his long home; and though they scarcely deemed the coffin's lid would hold him fast, they had some hopes that he would never again find his way back to disturb them in their quiet possession of Dubbyside. But, alas, how frail are human hopes!

On the second night after Johnnie's interment, when the family were all in bed, they were again alarmed by several sharp raps upon the window, which recalled all the former scene of uproar and terror to their drowsy recollections; but none of them could find courage to demand who was there, nor even to turn their heads in the direction from which the sounds proceeded. This undoubtedly was the Ghost; but on this occasion he was either more lazy or in better humour; for he did not prosecute his "cantrips slight" so long or so zealously as he had done before.

Next night, however, he returned at the accustomed hour, and began his nocturnal exercises with greater vigour. The whole family again took refuge from their fears beneath the massy folds of their heavy home-spun blankets, which were alike impervious to sight and sound; and nothing but the application of fire could have induced them to come forth from their comfortable concealment. There was one of the family, however, who began to entertain the serious intention of speaking to the Ghost; and this courageous individual—(who could have believed it?)—was one of the fair sex—in short, no other than Tibby Hume—Johnnie's beloved daughter; and

> Who could appease like her a father's Ghost?

Full of her romantic project, the fair one arose from her warm bed, and arraying herself hurriedly in a petticoat and short-gown, that she might appear decently before the ghost of her father, proceeded cautiously towards the door,—

> And turn'd the key wi' cannie thraw,
> An' owre the threshold ventured;
> But first on Sawnie ga'e a ca',
> Syne bauldly out she enter'd.

The full moon was shining with unclouded splendour while the trembling girl cast her eyes fearfully around in hopes to find the object of her search; but she discovered, to her horror, that she was alone!

> Had he sunk in the earth, or melted in air?
> She saw not—she knew not—but nothing was there!

She leaned against the wall, and listened with breathless attention; but there came no sound upon her ear, save the beating of her own heart. At length she mustered courage to articulate faintly the name of him whom she sought, but not the endearing name of father. At that moment a solitary figure in white made his appearance from behind one of the stacks. It was not, however, the form of Sandy Hapabout, whom she in reality wished to meet, but it was indeed the ghost of her father, whose presence, above all things, she desired to avoid. She tried to run, but in her confusion fairly mistook her course, and instead of doubling the jaw-hole, which lay right ahead, she ran directly over its slippery verge, and fell with a fearful splash into its polluted waters, which were not a little troubled on her account. There she lay, with her eyes steadfastly fixed upon the apparition, which did not seem to possess the smallest grain of gallantry in its vapid composition; for instead of coming directly to the assistance of the bemired maiden, it turned aside and hobbled away with all its speed, as if it had been a mere mortal, and susceptible of suffering suffocation by the noisome effluvia which arose from the dangerous pool, where the disconcerted beauty was *plowtering* for freedom! Nor did he once look over his shoulder to see whether his daughter was drowning, but repeating his accustomed song in his usual slow, melancholy tone, "Johnnie's a' wrang! Johnnie's a' wrang!" finally disappeared at the stable door, which seemed to open of its own accord for his reception.

As soon as the terrified girl could muster strength to move, she crawled into the house, and gave a solemn recital of all she had beheld; and her account was amply corroborated by the evidence of her bedraggled garments. The Ghost did not leave his grave for nothing. The traces which he left behind him proved to the satisfaction of all that it was no pleasure jaunt or idle freak that brought him so far abroad in the moonlight. In the morning, three of the best cows were found to have escaped from the byre, and busily employed regaling themselves upon one of the best pea-stacks in the barn-yard. The whole of the pigs had also been turned adrift, and were assiduously engaged in breakfasting on the contents of a potato pit which they had just disembowelled. A pair of the best horses, too, wondering at their unwonted liberty, were running races around the steading; and the hens were cackling, and cocks crowing, in joyful chorus, on the tops of the highest stacks. There was a general jubilee at Dubbyside, where all seemed to rejoice but its human inhabitants. The Ghost was certainly liberal in his notions, since he so generously conferred on all that were bound the freedom which he himself enjoyed. But there was evidently something beyond a mere love of liberty intended to be understood by this transaction. The number of domestic animals let loose seemed to indicate the share of his live stock which Johnnie the Ghost should have bequeathed to his son, Johnnie the Mortal, as we must henceforward distinguish him. The Humes were not altogether without a sense of their ghostly father's intention; but, like all other reasonable beings, they were slow to acknowledge, even to themselves, an understanding of any mystery, the clearing up of which was likely to operate to their own prejudice; so that it became a question among them, whether the presence of the Ghost or absence of the cattle and poultry, would be the greatest evil. Avarice, however, prevailed over fear, and they still retained the property of which the living and the dead seemed striving to deprive them. The indefatigable Ghost still continued to haunt the place of his former residence, reminding his family of the injustice of which they were guilty, and awakening them to a sense of the restless life which he was living upon their account.

Though it was known all over the neighbourhood that "Johnnie was gaun again," as the country people expressed it, and though the most of his former friends carefully avoided his supposed haunts after nightfall, there was one individual who was not to be daunted in the performance of what he believed to be a benevolent duty. He therefore braved every danger, and attended regularly at Dubbyside in the capacity of comforter to the distressed household. But Sandy Hapabout was in love, and to be in love is almost as good as to be in armour; for all lovers, since the days of Cervantes, have been successful in their "misventures." Though Sandy's mistress was once deceived by meeting a ghost instead of a gallant, she was not always so unfortunate in her assignations; but, despite all interruption from mortal and immortal apparitions, spent many a delightful hour with her faithful swain.

On one very stormy night, Sandy Hapabout knocked gently at the door of Dubbyside, and was promptly answered by his ever watchful mistress.

> The wind blew as 'twad blawn its last;
> The rattling showers rose on the blast;
> The speedy gleams the darkness swallow'd;
> Loud, deep, and long the thunder bellow'd:
> That night, a child might understand
> The deil had business on his hand.

Sandy confessed that it was an "awfu' thing to be out in sic a nicht"; but he turned it to good account, by making it a proof of the ardent passion which he felt for his fair Tibby. Tibby believed his assertions, of course, and smiled graciously upon the devoted attachment of her faithful swain. The night was too stormy for them to enjoy each other's company, sweet as it was, in the open air. Sandy accordingly advised, and Tibby agreed, that they should seek shelter in the barn.

> And who can tell the rapturous caress
> That followed wildly in that dark recess!

Suffice it to say, that the moments flew as expeditiously as if old Time, instead of dribbling them out grain by grain from his weary hour-glass, had been crushing down whole hours at once with a steam engine of sixty horse power.

> But pleasures are like poppies spread,
> You seize the flower, the bloom is shed.

While the young hearts of this happy pair were fluttering with the most exuberant delight, the awful ghost made his accustomed call at the door; and his long, melancholy cry, "Johnnie's a' wrang! Johnnie's a' wrang!" rung like a death knell in their ears, and thrilled their nerves like an electric shock—chasing away every pleasurable sensation, and leaving them in a wonderfully romantic situation for two modern lovers. The lady clung to her gallant, while he gallantly butted with his head among the straw; and after a little walloping with their legs, both succeeded in obtaining a tolerably comfortable burrow. But, alas? what covering could conceal, or what stronghold protect them from the approach of an enemy who found no impediment to his march in the strongest doors and the firmest locks? and such an enemy was close at hand. He again uttered his dolorous cry, "Johnnie's a' wrang! Johnnie's a' wrang!" and the door flew open at the sound, as if touched by a magician's wand, or charmed by the presto of a conjurer.

Sandy gasped with apprehension as the Ghost advanced towards the place of their concealment; and every tramp of his feet on the floor seemed to communicate a convulsive energy to the fingers of his gentle mistress; for she clasped him so closely about the throat, that he could only groan out, in stifled accents, "Dinna worry me, Tibby—dinna worry me," when the unmannerly ghost actually planted his heavy iron-shod shoe upon the extended leg of the enamoured rustic. But, as if inspired by some heroic impulse of the heart, Sandy soon convinced the solemn intruder that he was not to be trodden on with impunity; for springing forward with the celerity of a mountain-cat, he seized the weighty apparition by the ankle with such a determined grip, that the ghost soon became more alarmed than the mortal; and totally forgetful of the dignity of his character, called out, in a voice tremulous with consternation,

"Wha the de—de—devil are ye?"

"Aha, lad!" said he of the straw, "I ken ye noo;" and in confirmation of the popular adage that "knowledge is power," Sandy tugged so strenuously at the brawny limb of the spectral aggressor, that he soon laid him as prostrate as himself!

Thus fell in an unfortunate hour the ghost of Johnnie Hume, who had "kept the country side in fear" for many a month, and afforded stout arguments in favour of the ghost system in many a lengthy debate. "Misfortunes love a train, and tread each other's heel;" and Johnnie's did not end here. He had yet to suffer "a deeper wreck—a greater fall;" for Sandy still held him fast by the ankle, and in the ineffectual struggle which he made to escape, he unluckily projected his anterior parts over a hole in the floor, which happened to be directly above the chaff-house; and as the ponderous ghost descended head foremost through the aperture, his depending weight proved too much for Sandy's extended nerves, who accordingly slipped his hold, and down went Johnnie to that dusty den, like Satan when "hurled headlong flaming from the ethereal sky."

Sandy stalked about for a few minutes in silent admiration of his own prowess. He had performed an achievement worthy of the greatest hero; for what was the sack of Rome to the overthrow of a ghost, or the valour of Brutus to the bravery of Sandy Hapabout? The Roman trembled before the eye of his evil genius, but the ploughman overcame his spiritual enemy. Nor can Scotland, the land of heroes, produce a single name worthy to stand beside Sandy's in the annals of Fame. Even the immortal Wallace fled before the ghost of his faithless follower; and the hero of Flodden field trembled at the appearance, though he disregarded the warning, of an old spectre who met him at Linlithgow. But Sandy grappled with and overthrew a ghost—not a meagre, white-headed, decrepit starveling, like that which terrified the ill-fated James IV., but a full-grown vigorous ghost, scarcely less formidable for weight and bulk than that which, issuing from the brain of Horace Walpole, made such a fearful commotion in the Castle of Otranto.

Sandy stood still for a moment, and shook himself like Samson; but what was Samson to Sandy, or the pulling down of the pillars of Gaza to the overthrow of a ghost? He could contain himself no longer, but called out in a rapture to the betrothed of his heart, who still lay crouched among the straw,

"Ho ye, Tibby! Get up, woman; there's na need for terriation noo, for the ghost's coupit heels ower head i' the chaff-house, an' he may plowter about long enough there or he get the gait oot again. He's been aye cry cryin' that he was a' wrang; but he'll no be sae far wrang in crying that he's a' wrang noo."

Tibby did get up; and after bestowing due praise upon her eliverer, and arranging matters for their next meeting, they tore themselves asunder. Sandy went home to boast of his own prowess in discomfiting the ghost of Dubbyside; but Tibby spoke not a word of what had happened.

Next morning at daybreak, when her brothers went into the barn, they were alarmed by an unaccountable noise in the chaff-house; for the impatient ghost, after resting from the labours of the night, had risen "like a giant refreshed," with the firm intention of breaking through every obstruction. It was now dim day-light, and the Humes had no fear for the ghost. They accordingly armed themselves with pitch-forks, and other warlike instruments, as if to contend with a physical foe; and placed themselves in such array as that they might be able to act on the offensive or defensive, as occasion might require. Every brow was knit, and every arm raised to strike, when one of the heroes advanced briskly and opened the door; but alas! what was their consternation when the ghost—the grim grisly ghost—shook his winding sheet, and gnashed his teeth in their faces!

> They would have crossed themselves all mute,
> They would have pray'd to burst the spell;
> But at the stamping of his foot,
> Each hand down powerless fell!

Their lethal weapons dropped harmlessly to the ground; but though their arms were paralysed, their legs acquired a double degree of swiftness; and off they scampered one and all, without waiting a moment for the benison of their ghostly father. But the more haste the less speed, as the old proverb has it; for two of them reached the door exactly at the same time, and squeezed themselves so firmly into the narrow passage that they could neither get backwards nor forwards. The ghost beheld this new disaster with despair, for he was anxious to escape; but his retreat was now cut off by the bodies of those who had fled from his frown. He cursed his unlucky fate, and scratched his shaggy head in perplexity; but as ghosts are destitute of brains, it was in vain to dig there for wisdom. Fortune, however, favoured, where foresight failed. The two living fixtures, believing in their terror that it was the hand of the ghost that detained them, called out, each for himself, at the same time—" O let me gang, an' Johnnie sall get a' that belangs to him!"

This supplication contained a hint which brightened up the invention of the ghost, and aroused all the activity of his nature; and, again assuming the solemn dignity of his spiritual character, he addressed the trembling suppliants, with a hollow voice, in the following words:

"Gin ye honour the words o' yer faither, and do justiceness to the claims o' yer brother; gin ye promise, upon yer lives an' yer oaths to gie Johnnie his ain guid share o' the kye, an' the ca'ves, an' the ploughs, an' the carts, an' o' a' the ither gear upon my farm o' Dubbyside; an' his ain share o' the notes i' th' aumry, an' the siller that I left i' the leather pouch aboon the bed;—gin ye'll promise to dee a' this, without cheatry or lounry, ye'll ha'e lowsance frae yer bondage, an' there sall be nae mair bickerment about the matter. But gin ye break yer oblifications, or look ower yer shouthers afore ye be past the knocken stane, I'll torment ye as lang as ye live, an' gie ye to the devil for a greeshoch when ye dee. D'ye understand me na—eh?"

The poor trembling mortals gave solemn promise of obedience, and the wily ghost stepped briskly forward, and seized one of them by the skirts of the coat, to pull him out of his wedge-like position, that both might go free, when at this important moment, the indefatigable Sandy Hapabout again made his appearance, and greeted his friends in the doorway with a hearty salute. But the only answer he received to his civil "Guid mornin'," was a convulsive gape of the jaws, and an involuntary oscillation of the tongue. This unmannerly silence was too much for the patience of Sandy to endure; and, imitating the ludicrous contortions of countenance which they exhibited with the skill of a practised ape, he exclaimed,—

"Guid sake, bodies! what are ye puffin' an' blawin', an' gapin' an' gautin' there for, wi' faces like a nor'-wast meen, girnin' an' grainin' as if ye were tethered to a stake, an' twenty bleed-hounds howling at yer heels?"

Still no answer was returned; and, advancing a little closer to discover the cause of their speechless trepidation, the hero of the chaff-house caught his eye; and, peering over the shoulders of the two immoveable doorkeepers, with a grin of humorous recognition—for which Sandy was famous—he called out in a merry tone to the retiring spectre—

"Aha, lad! are ye aye there yet? I thought ye wad 'a been wearied o' the barn, an' hame ower to yer ain fireside lang syne; but a guid caff bed's no that encomfortable for a mornin' sleep, an' ye was gey an' late up last nicht, as ye ken yersel', forby ithers that baith saw an' heard ye."

Alas for the unfortunate ghost! His glory was now departed—his fall was complete! The terrors of his voice and the mystery of his character were dissipated by the salute of Sandy Hapabout. Even the poor trembling doormen caught courage from his familiarity, and fearlessly broke the promises which they had so solemnly sworn but a minute before. Sandy, to make a passage for himself, drove them out of the door, and all three turned in to talk with the harmless apparition, who, instead of disappearing in darkness, or vanishing in light, as any reasonable ghost would have done, stood bolt upright before them, in all the substantial materiality of a mortal man.

It were useless to tell what excuses he made, or what falsehoods he uttered, to palliate the enormity of his conduct; but the identity of Johnnie the Ghost with Johnnie the Mortal being fairly ascertained, all his previous pranks, which had occasioned so much alarm at Dubbyside, were easily accounted for. When he came in the evening to examine into the state of affairs at Dubbyside, he found his mother and brothers in the kitchen, and availed himself of their absence to slip into the chamber of death, where he dexterously attached a small cord to a corner of the table-cloth, and, passing it through the cat-hole, again retired to the outside of the house, where he busied himself with other preparations for his nocturnal project. When the clock struck twelve, which was the hour determined upon for the commencement of his operations, Johnnie pulled the cord, and away went the table-cloth like a "thing of life," while its precious furniture fell to the floor, and was shivered into a thousand pieces. The first trick was successful, which encouraged Johnnie to proceed with the rest. Hurrying around to the back of the house, he ascended a ladder, previously prepared, and displacing a portion of the thatch of the roof, through which he inserted a large round stone, with a strong cord attached to it, he rolled it along the wooden floor of the garret, lifting it up and letting it fall at pleasure; and with this simple apparatus he produced those unearthly sounds which sent his friends to seek sanctuary among the barrels and tubs in the kitchen. He was civilly dismissed to seek redress for his grievances in some other quarter, and never again lodged a night in the chaff-house, nor sung the burden of his wrongs to the tune of his departed father. But as long as he lived he was known by the appellation of Johnnie the Ghost; and now that he has become that immortal essence whose character he ventured to assume, he is still remembered as the Ghost of Dubbyside, and his fame is likely to be permanent.

But I must now do justice to Sandy Hapabout, and make an end of my tale. Sandy received the reward of his valour in the lass of his love, who was united to him shortly after the Fall of the Ghost; but what was the result of his marriage, or the glory of his future exploits, I am not privileged to unfold. It is said, however, that he frequently boasted—as well he might—of the victory which he obtained over the Ghost at Dubbyside; and we may be allowed to believe, that more good accrued from that bloodless struggle, which shook the reign of superstition in the place where it happened, than mankind ever derived from the sack of cities and the dismemberment of empires.

## THREE HANSELMONDAYS.

O happy, happy holyday!
  Though angry winter frown,
When friends, residing far away,
  In country or in town,
Once more may meet around the hearth
Where all their early joys had birth.

AMONG the country people of Scotland the custom of visiting their friends on Hanselmonday, like many other usages of the olden time, is fast wearing out; yet it is still a day towards which anticipation is turned, and I doubt not but to many the very mention of its name will bring back pleasing recollections of happy hours spent in the humble abodes of hardy industry, and friendly greetings, and glances of affection which left a long-living impression behind them. Tales, too, and reminiscences of joy or woe are inseparably connected with that day in the memories of many a humble individual. The beginning of a deep-rooted and lasting affection—the long sought and eagerly expected confession of a mutual passion—the first sight of a future husband or wife—the meeting of relations who had never met before—the solemn interview after death had made its inroad among early acquaintances—the first visit to a paternal home after man's last enemy had thinned it of its blessings,—these, and many other incidents, of common occurrence at this season of the year, have stamped Hanselmonday in deep and enduring characters on many a heart. "I did not see him after my father's death till Hanselmonday;"—"It was on Hanselmonday that I first met Peggy;"—"Mary and

me went to her father's, for the first time, on a Hanselmonday;"
—"It was three weeks before Hanselmonday when Johnnie was born;"—these, and many more of the same kind, are familiar words among the sons and daughters of "rustic toil;" and what a host of pleasing or painful recollections do they carry along with them!

Many years ago my father's family came to reside within a moderate distance of a small village, where lived an uncle whom I had never seen. Having resolved to pay him a visit on Hanselmonday, I set off early on Saturday morning, and, by dint of hard travelling, reached my destination a little after mid-day.

My uncle's family consisted of his wife, an only daughter, and an unmarried sister, familiarly known by the appellation of "Aunty Eppie." They all greeted me with a warmth which I had scarcely expected; but if one welcomed me more cordially than another it was my cousin Rose, an interesting girl about my own age, which then did not exceed eighteen. Having never known any relation save her parents and her aunt, she seemed to look upon me as an accession to the number of her friends and her stock of happiness. As I was to stay a week the elder females insisted that I should "rest myself" for the remainder of the day, but Rose would by no means agree to this. In the afternoon she led me out to see her little garden, —a small patch of ground overstocked with flowers of every description.

I was never an enthusiastic admirer of flowers. From a very early period my attention had been too exclusively engaged by other concerns to admit of its being thus divided. To look upon them in those repositories of art where they have been congregated by man, or to see them in wild luxuriance "bloom along the vale," or by the stream, or on the hill, without knowing any thing of their properties, or even their names,—was always enough for me. But my pretty cousin was a lover of flowers, and a cultivator of them in her own way, and had, moreover, a smattering of botany. She spent many of her leisure hours in cultivating her little parterre, and on this occasion apparently took great delight in exhibiting her floral treasures. In return, I tried to learn the names of her favourites—extolled the beauties of some which I had neither seen nor before heard of—admired the neat and orderly appearance of her garden—racked my memory for all the professional slang I had ever heard used by gardeners and amateurs; and, in short, praised the whole with an enthusiasm which must have been very extravagant. To this senseless rhodomontade she listened with apparent satisfaction, occasionally giving me the history of several of her "mute friends," and regretting that the season did not permit me to see them in all their loveliness.

Among them were some pinks and polyanthuses, which had been the gifts of two female friends, Mary Auburn and Peggy Simpson. But the plant upon which she seemed to set the greatest value, and bestow most care, was a tuft of carnations which had been given her by a journeyman gardener called George Robertson, at that time residing at Corolla Castle, a gentleman's seat in the immediate neighbourhood. Of this individual, Rose gave me to understand that he was "reckoned very clever by the people about—he knew a great deal about flowers, and was better acquainted with his trade than the master gardener—so the folk said." But she "knew very little of him—scarcely any thing at all; for though he sometimes came owre on an e'enin' to see her father, she had seldom spoken to him." This homily on friends and flowers was concluded by pulling away some weeds about the size of pins from the carnations, and carefully drawing the earth up to their roots,—all which appeared to me superfluous labour.

On the following day, which was the Sabbath, we went to church. She took my arm as we set out, and for half the distance appeared perfectly delighted with my company; and, if truth must be told, I was as well pleased with her as she seemed to be with me. But unfortunately for our conversation, three young fellows overtook and passed us on the road. Rose looked after them wistfully till they were at some distance, sighed two or three times, and then became unusually silent. For the remainder of the road, and during the service, she appeared distracted and thoughtful; but as we were coming out of the church, a person, whom I recognised as one of those who had passed us, spoke to her. I did not hear his words; but, in answering him, I heard her say, "He is my cousin." A few more words passed between them in a sort of half whispering tone, after which she again took my arm. On the road home, her liveliness returned, and our mutual happiness was restored. Had I been possessed at the time of only a tolerable knowledge of the workings and wanderings of the young heart, it is probable these little incidents might have given me feelings very different from those with which I was then occupied; but my knowledge was, like the knowledge of eighteen, neither extensive nor deep, and they gave me no uneasiness.

With the morrow came Hanselmonday. My uncle, or rather his wife, kept a small shop for supplying the neighbourhood with grocery and other wares of a promiscuous description. In the course of the afternoon, I sauntered into it, and being a holiday, I found him attending it in person. When I entered, he was in the act of almost forcing a quantity of cheese and a small sum of money upon a rather elderly and poor, but decent-looking woman.

"Na, na," said she, in answer to his pressing, "I hae nae right to appear like ither folk at ither folk's expense; a throughbearin is a' I maun look for; an' if that be granted, I hae great reason to be thankfu'."

"Hout! havering body!" was the good-natured reply, "ye'll get a throughbearin; but od, woman, ye're aye wurkin to our guidwife, an' it's only pride that winna let ye tak payment!" With these words he thrust a home-made cheese, and a small sum of money, into her lap.

"Deed, sir, I dinna ken what to think o' ye noo!" ejaculated the good woman; "at this rate, I'll no win out o' your debt as lang as I live."

"The woman's gaen clean crazed, I declare!" said the other, "to stand there an' ca' *me* 'sir!' as if I were either a knave or a knight; an' crack about *debt*, as if I were ane o' her creditors. If we're a' spared health we'll see ye gin supper-time, an' if there's onything owre after that, we can settle about thae accounts the morn. But, Marion, I maun e'en flyte wi' ye for that ill-faur'd custom ye hae o' mockin' little folk wi' great names—ca'in them 'sirs,' an' 'masters,' an' a' that. The sorrow confound ye if ever ye ca' me ought but 'David' after this."

"Ah, David!" I could hear her say, as she was going away, "we hae but few men like you. Though ye were to gie awa the half o' yer substance, ye wad aye mak it appear that ye was giein naething. I can mak ye nae return for a' your kindness to me; but may the blessing o' the widow rest on your head, an' the head o' your bairn, an' your bairn's bairns, to the latest generation."

When she was gone, "That's Marion Simpson," said my uncle: "I was just giein her something, when ye cam in, to help her to appear like her neighbours when we a' gae to see her the nicht. At her husband's death, she was left wi' twa sma bairns; an' though she has had a sair struggle wi' the warld, she's aye been honest, an' provided for hersel' an' them wi' her ain industry. They'll baith be a comfort to her yet, I hope: the lassie is sae already; but her son—God bless him—

wha was as weel behaved a callant as ever breathed, had the misfortune to engage wi' the laird o' Rummlegairy; and as his life was made perfectly miserable, in a fit of despair he ran aff to the sea. But I scarcely think he can like the wild life o' a sailor; and I hope he'll come hame after a', and be a blessing to his mother in her auld age."

In this hope, I, as a matter of course, participated, and made some half boyish observation about the pleasure it must give him thus to deserve and receive the blessing of the widow.

"I've wrought hard," said he, "for the little that I hae; and, as auld folk maun aye be giein advice to young anes, ye maun listen to me a wee. Tak gude care o' ony siller ye may get; an' if ye hae a shilling to spare, never try to imitate the rich, nor even the poor, in their dinners an' their dresses, their drinkings an' their vanities;—lay it by: it may be of mair use to you than a' your kin. And when you can fairly manage your ain ends, if ye can help an honest man or woman in their straits and struggles wi' poverty, never tie your purse-strings, nor turn a deaf ear to the complaints of those that are in distress: try to relieve them if ye can; and if your heart is what I wad hae it to be, ye'll derive mair pleasure from this than from counting over useless thousands."

The evening of Hanselmonday was one of general festivity. At first, the neighbours, with their families, to the number of a dozen, assembled in my uncle's house. Here they were plentifully served with bread and cheese, and good ale was handed round to "*synd it doun,*" as they themselves phrased it. After this, a glass was offered to each, and the lasses were requested to sing; to which, after the usual show of reluctance, they consented. In reflecting on the subject since, I have often thought that, from the songs they selected, which were generally those they could sing best, a shrewd guess might have been made at the feelings of the respective singers.

There was one blue-eyed, mild, and rather melancholy looking girl, who was prevailed upon, with some difficulty, to contribute her share. This was Mary Auburn. She sang a mournful ballad, which told of disappointed affection, and desponding constancy. I had no skill in music, and never in my life knew one tune from another; but the low mellow voice of that girl thrilled my very heart. Hers was that sort of singing which a deep sympathy with the words of the poet, drawn from experience, and assisted by a voice naturally musical, alone can produce. The following are some verses of the song which I still remember:—

"With a face falsely smiling, while sad is my heart,
   Among the gay circle I sit;
When the laugh rings around me, I suddenly start,
   And laugh, though I cannot forget!

"Ah! think not that frowns were the cause of my anguish:
   By smiles my fond heart was undone;
I trusted to kindness, and now I must languish,
   Since far, far away he has gone!

"He knew not the thoughts that around him were twining,
   As lonely I stray'd by the burn;
Nor knew that, when morning was blythsomely shining,
   I wish'd for the e'enin's return.

"The gloaming aft brought him again to my sight,
   The past fleeting hour to beguile;
And Love stole my heart, in his kindly "good night,"
   As he parted from me with a smile.

"Though he breathed not the accents of love in my ear—
   Yet now, when I fondly recall
His tones and his glances, the gathering tear
   In my eye glistens, ready to fall.

"Those tones aye fu' tender—that look aye fu' kind—
   Lang, lang in my bosom shall lie;
Though he left me nae promise nor token behind,
   *First love* with life only can die!"

As the fair singer breathed forth her soul in these simple verses, her voice faltered, and something very like a tear *did* glisten in her eye. I was struck by the girl's agitation. Could it be, that some deep-rooted attachment, formed and felt, but never confessed, such as often steals unperceived over the morning of life—some tender tie, which, in the flush and fulness of early feeling, had bound her to one by whom she was forgotten—some recollection of the past, cherished in silence, and changed into gloom by the hopeless aspect of the future,—was at the time withering her heart, and drying up the fountain of her enjoyment?

Widely different was the strain sung by Peggy Simpson,—a fair-haired, light-hearted, laughing damsel of fourteen, and as widely different was her manner of singing it. Joy seemed to dance in every tone of her voice, and it was with difficulty she could suppress a laugh at the close of every line, as she sung—

   Let the silly an' love-sick in silence draw nigh;
     Nae laddie hae I, an' the less do I care,
   Sin' I aftener laugh, and seldomer sigh,
     Than lasses wi' plenty o' lads, an' to spare.

Thus she went on with a light-hearted and humorous strain, which seemed in a great measure to obliterate from the minds of her hearers the effects produced by the former singer. In her, it was evident that the ruling passion of youth was scarcely, if at all developed. To the notice and admiration of the other sex she might have, and no doubt had, a liking; but she had not yet arrived at that period when love becomes the engrossing subject of every thought—when the little pleasures, childish passions, and personal considerations of the girl, are exchanged for another and a dearer self—for that absorbing and disinterested feeling which characterises a woman's first affection. Of love she had heard, and of love perhaps she thought; but it was only as another name for happiness: of its solitary musings—its tormenting jealousies, and needless alarms,—she knew nothing; and she could laugh and sing of it with a face full of glee, and a heart which did not belie her look.

This scene of harmony and mirth was interrupted by one of the seniors of the company addressing my uncle.

"Noo, Mr. Pennyworth," said he, "when we hae a' partaken o' your guid cheer, ye maun just honour us by gaun to see what my Luckie has provided for the haddin' o' Hanselmonday."

"Hout! awa, man, wi' your high names!" was the reply: "keep your mock-masterships for anither day. I've aye been plain David! sae am I yet. But, nae doubt, we maun gae an' tak vengeance on your guidwife's kebbuck an' her bottle; an' sae I think, if the company's agreeable, we had better commence the attack."

The business of the night was perfectly understood, and this proposal was responded to in the same strain of good humour in which it had been made. We went through the whole of the houses—eating and drinking, singing songs and telling stories in each. On reaching the abode of the widow who had benefited by my uncle's bounty, it was gratifying to see the look of satisfaction with which she placed her little store before her guests.

"Dear me, Marion, but matters are mendin wi' you," said one of them: "there's a hale kebbuck, I declare, an' no a bit heel, as I've seen ye hae."

"Ay, ay, lad, I'm able to get a hale kebbuck noo," was Marion's answer: "thanks be to Him wha sends us a' guid gifts, and His blessin' on some folk no far bye." As she spoke, she cast an arch look at her benefactor, and seemed on the point of disclosing the scene which had occurred at the little shop. But he shook his clenched fist, and she was silent.

From the manner in which this crusade of eating and drinking was conducted, it was evident that my uncle was regarded with a sort of respectful deference. He had, by dint of industry, acquired a little money, and in this lay the secret of his superiority. Nor was he altogether ignorant of the power with which his wealth had invested him, though he did not choose to display it. His constant endeavour was to conceal his power, and for this very reason, perhaps, he possessed it in greater perfection.

"The daft days" were not yet done. As Monday night had been given to what might be called public, so Tuesday night was to be devoted to domestic festivity. But upon this occasion the guests were more select; only Mary Auburn and her brother, and George Robertson were invited.

Up to this period I had enjoyed a principal share of Rose's attention, but now I was destined to meet a sad reverse. No sooner did the gardener arrive, than she entirely forgot me. It has been observed that "lover's eyes are sharp to see:" perhaps I had got enough of the disease to give me something of that quick perception which is meant by this phrase; for I soon became a more acute observer than I had ever been before, and more prompt at drawing inferences. I began to perceive that George Robertson was a stronger magnet to Rose's thoughts than I had ever been. She directed the whole of her discourse to him, and her eye was restless and uneasy when gazing on any other object. He possessed considerable liveliness of conversation, which her presence tended greatly to increase; and she was always the first to laugh at his sallies, though I, with less candour than ill-nature thought them very stupid. To the compliments which he occasionally bestowed on her she made no verbal reply; but I observed with mortification that they seldom failed to heighten the natural glow of her countenance, to impart a more fascinating lustre to her eye, and call into play a thousand nameless blandishments, which too plainly indicated the impression they had made on her mind.

A circumstance, however, occurred, which might have served to give me some satisfaction, though I do not recollect that it did so. Mary Auburn at last came in for a share of the gardener's attention. My uncle had been jesting her about giving him an invitation to her marriage, and she, to evade his good-humoured importunity, observed with a smile—the first I had seen on her face—"that she was going to the garret; for she wad never be married." The gardener overheard her words, and gallantly took up the subject.

8

"The garret!" said he, with well-affected astonishment; "na, na—nae garrets! I'll be caution for ye in ony sum no exceeding a Scots bawbee, that thae bonny een, that snawy neck, an' fair face o' yours, whilk ye spoil by haddin' down your head, hae gotten ye already mair than half-a-dozen wooers, and among them, if ye wale weel, ye may get a guid husband ony day in a' the year."

Her only answer to this raillery was a sigh.

"But may I gang on crutches a' the neist owk," he continued, looking at her earnestly, "if I wad hae you for a wife, though I could get you wi' a word; for I'm certain I could neither work nor sleep if ye were mine, but look at ye a' day, an' caress ye a' night!"

At this sally we all laughed except Rose—an unwonted thoughtfulness overspread her countenance, and for the next half-hour she spoke but little, and did not laugh at all.

The horticulturist appeared perfectly aware of this sudden change in her manner, for he again exerted himself, with even more than his former assiduity, and again all his best sayings were exclusively addressed to her. For a time she answered him in a quiet tone, very unlike the clear and joyous accents of her natural voice, and without looking at him when she spoke. But her resolution, whatever it was, could not hold out against his good-humoured attention. At first her countenance was lighted up with a faint and half-reluctant smile—then she looked at him, then she laughed, and then her eye again grew bright in the reflection of his, a glow of satisfaction suffused her cheek, and she appeared supremely happy.

"But those that are true lovers run into strange capers." The company began to speak of breaking up, and here one of those difficulties occurred which, though in themselves nothing, often perplex mortals sadly. Mary's brother had been unable to come; and as the night was dark, and she had nearly half a mile to go, it was indispensable that some one should escort her home. She was an interesting girl, in every respect as well deserving of attention as Rose, and I felt somewhat inclined to offer my services. But I was then little accustomed to the society of young women, rather bashful, and withal, at the time, rather discontented; so I said not a word. My uncle was the first to start up and offer to be her conductor himself. But he had caught a slight cold, and my aunts would by no means hear of his going out. Rose, who was now all glee and gladness, was the next to take up the matter. "She would run," she said, "for Andrew Outerlands;" and she did run—

but Andrew had gone to see his brother, and was not expected home till to-morrow. As she told this, she looked at me in evident expectation that I would volunteer. But by this time I had some sort of a presentiment of where matters would end, and with unmannerly obstinacy I still forbore. Through the whole of this dilemma Mary had been protesting that she could go home herself, and begging them not to trouble themselves; but this she would not be permitted to do. After a considerable pause, my aunt put in her word.

"What are ye a' makin' sic a wark about?" said she, "canna Geordie there, when he's sic a favourite wi' a' the lasses, gang an' see her safe hame?"

At these words Rose changed colour almost as suddenly as the pigeon's neck changes its hue when the rays of light strike it in a new direction. This was the arrangement she had been labouring to avert, but the consummation of her fears had at last come upon her. Still, however, she affected to be cheerful, and tried to laugh—nor were her resources yet at an end.

"It's sae far out o' his road," she said, "and sae far for him to come back when he has to work hard next day; Tam Brown, I'm sure, will be glad o' an opportunity to see Mary; I'll run and tell him, if he's no in his bed." She made her promise good, but to her disappointment Tam was absent, and supposed to be with his sweetheart. This was her last resource. The man of carnations and cabbage, after a struggle between what appeared to be his inclination and his duty as a gallant, was forced to obey the latter; and after the usual "good nights," and being "wished weel hame" by all and sundry, away he set with his protegé. It should have been noticed, that during the latter part of the discussion he had become in a great measure passive, and spoke but little, so that had it not been for that "index to the heart," his countenance, I should have supposed he did not dislike the part assigned him. But Rose was latterly too much taken up with her own thoughts to pay any attention to this.

On the following day, Rose was somewhat changed. On coming in from the yard with some vegetables for the dinner, she spoke of "delving up" the violets she had got from Mary Auburn; and the carnations, she "didna think they would flower," and wished she knew where to get something better to put in their place. Her buoyant spirits were gone: she went about the affairs of the house, and scarcely noticed any one—even I had some difficulty in getting a word from her. But what surprised me most was, that no one except myself seemed to notice the alteration.

That I was somewhat chagrined by the discovery I had made the previous night, will be easily believed, and at first I had almost determined to show that I cared nothing about her. But this determination did not hold long. Since I could not shine in her favour as the cynosure, I thought it might be best to come in for a secondary share, by endeavouring to be of some service to her. Here I had some difficulties and delicacies to encounter; but after reflecting on the matter, I resolved to commence by communicating my suspicions to her aunt, and taking her advice as to what it would be best to do, in order to bring the whole to a happy conclusion.

I, accordingly, with an impudence for which I cannot account, and to which I could never either before or since summon any thing similar, told her the whole story, heightened by all the observations and imaginations with which I then thought proper to crowd into it.

It is impossible to describe my surprise when she laughed heartily at my "delusions," as she called them.

"Na, na, laddie," said she, "ye ken little o' young women yet. D'ye think a lass maun aye be in love wi' ilka ane she laughs at, an' ilka ane she allows to speak nonsense to her? Gude saufe us! if that were the case, what a warld it would be! The lasses wad need a hantle mae hearts than ane to haud their love in; for there's no a lass in a' the country-side but may laugh at fifty fules, an' let fifty fallows she cares naething about crack havers to her in the course o' her lifetime. Hech, sirs! Na, na! I'll warrant the lassie is as deep in love wi' you as wi' Geordie, an' no ower the ankles wi' ony o' ye!" Here she took another hearty laugh, in which, maugre my disappointment and mortification, I was forced to join. "An' as to the lassie's being dull an' thoughtfu'," she continued, "a body canna aye be giggling an' laughing. I'm sure she cracked an' leugh as muckle yestre'en as might weel ser' for a hale owk."

With this assurance I was forced to be satisfied.

Throughout this and the following day, Rose's thoughtful disposition continued, though she made some efforts to conquer it. At dinner she was desired to bring some milk; she obeyed without speaking, and bringing an empty vessel, placed it on the table with great care.

"The lassie's gaen gyte," said her mother, "it was milk your father bade ye bring, an' no a toom dish!"

"I'll wager my lug," said her aunt, "if her mind wasna chasin' mice, it was rinnin' after a new mutch, or a braw frock, or something o' that sort, that ye'll hae to gie her siller to get some day soon."

"Deed was't," said Rose, with a smile, which seemed to shine through a mortifying sense of the blunder she had committed.

After it was dark, a gentle tap was heard at the door; Rose answered it, and a short conversation in whispers ensued. Rose speedily returned, and addressing her mother said— "Peggy Simpson has been here, asking my assistance to shape a new gown. May I rin ower for half an' hour?"

"Far be't fae me, lassie, ever to say no," was the reply. "The widow an' the fatherless should aye be treated kindly. It might hae been your ain turn to want your father instead o' hers; sae e'en gang if ye like. But what for did the lassie no come in?" Without taking time to answer this interrogatory, Rose was off in an instant, and with a lighter step, and in better spirits, than she had exhibited for several days.

I was in bed, but not sleeping, when she returned, and I could hear her mother attempting to chide her for her protracted stay. But on her naming over several little acts which she had done, she was easily forgiven.

"Weel, weel, lassie," said her mother, "I'll never be angry at ye for takin' the lesson ye've often heard me repeat—aye to be kind an helpfu' to the poor, an' them that hae few helpers. But mind, Rose, ye are my only bairn: your father likes you aye to be i' the house at e'en; an' ye maun never stay out sae late again if ye can help it."

From this night Rose's sprightliness and loquacity returned in even a greater degree than formerly. I found myself again fully reinstated in her good graces; and her endeavours to amuse me were unceasing. In the exuberance of her glee she even charged me with dulness, and asked if I could not laugh and speak nonsense like her. The overflowing of a happy heart was evident in almost everything she said or did. The change was so remarkable that to account for it perfectly puzzled me, till toward night, when I accidentally overheard that Rose was not the only visitor at Mrs. Simpson's on the preceding evening. This confirmed me in my own opinion; and somewhat piqued at the jeering repulse which I had formerly met, I resolved again to mention the matter to her aunt. But when an opportunity occurred she did not permit me to break the subject, and saluted me with "Ye were thinkin' Rose was in love," said she, "because she was dull yesterday. If that was the case she's soon win ower her ill turn, as ye wad say. What think ye noo o' your nonsense about love? I'm sure she can laugh the day as weel as ever she did."

I would have said what I thought, but wanted resolution. The opportunity and the night passed over, and on the morrow at an early hour, after shaking of hands, and with hearty wishes for each other's welfare, as John Bunyan saith, "I went on my way, and saw them no more" for a twelvemonth.

If the reader will be pleased to direct his mind's eye over the period of his past years, he will find the images which his memory may retain so evanescent and unsatisfactory that I flatter myself he will easily be induced to pardon me for passing over one of the earth's entire revolutions without a single word.

The Hanselmonday returned, I renewed my visit, and Rose, who was still uppermost in my thoughts, was the first object to attract my attention. From the moment on which I saw her I lacked not a subject on which to think. She was indeed sadly altered. Pale and listless, the speaking lustre was gone from her eye, and her voice had lost its clear and thrilling melody. No object of sight, or topics of conversation, however uncommon or lively they might be, could attract her notice. Or if she did listen with a momentary interest, or try to speak, the effort appeared too painful to be sustained, and her mind soon wandered back to its melancholy haunts. Her little garden, and her flowers, seemed to be almost the only things on earth for which she cared : there she would sometimes work though it was winter, and stand and gaze upon its quiet occupants as if the world contained nought beside. And while thus employed in "idle reverie," the blood would occasionally rush to her cheek tempestuously, then slowly subside, leaving it paler than before. Anon a faint glow would succeed, followed by a deeper desertion. And when her spirits were exhausted and worn out in this apparently mental struggle the whole would end in a lasting fit of abstraction and melancholy silence.

Her parents complained of the lowness of her spirits, and spoke of her being in ill health. Like other parents, whose affections are centred in a single object, they alternately gave way to apprehensions and hopes of her recovery ; but they never once seemed to suspect that her heart could be in the least accessory to the melancholy change. With me it was otherwise, and I found Aunty Eppie had adopted my opinion, though she had never ventured to mention it to any one else.

I observed that she used some stratagems to get me by myself, and when she had accomplished her purpose, " Laddie," said she, " I'm fear'd ye guess'd ower true the last time ye were here; for, if I'm no far cheated, that gardener chield has ta'en awa Rose's heart wi' him, an' left the rest o' her here, poor thing! to wither like a geranium set out-bye in winter. She's never been like hersel' since Whitsunday, when he left the place. And yet, I ken na how it is, but I could never muster courage to speak o't either to her father or her mither: it wad vex them sae to think that their only bairn wad tak' up wi' a fallow like him—here the tae day, and wha kens whar the next."

Many plans were thought of, and much was repeated which had been thought of before to no purpose, and we ended where we began, without eliciting anything which could be of the least service; only we both agreed, that as her parents could do nothing, it was best to keep the secret from them still.

On this occasion there was no Hanselmonday festivities at my uncle's; fear and anxiety prevailed where mirth and good cheer were wont to preside. But the widow and her daughter were still fresh in my memory; the scene in the little shop, a twelvemonth before, had prepossessed me in their favour, and I could not leave the place without seeing them. I accordingly paid them a visit, and the conversation, naturally enough, turned upon Rose, her indisposition, and the probable cause of it. With this I found them much better acquainted than I had been prepared to expect; and from them I learned that George Robertson had left Corolla Castle for the Edinburgh nurseries, a practice not uncommon among young gardeners. After being there for a few days, he was offered an advantageous situation in Wales, which he at once accepted for a year. These circumstances, after his arrival in Wales, he narrated in a letter to James Wilson, another of the gardeners at the Castle, with whom he had been on very intimate terms, and who was also a great favourite with Marion. The letter, after inquiring for Rose, stated that he had anxiously wished an interview with her, on the night previous to his leaving the Castle, as he had something of importance to communicate; and that he had gone over to buy some articles which he did not need, in the hope of being able to see her for a few minutes by herself. But there was such a flow of mirth in her manners, and contrary to his expectation, she misunderstood his hints so often, seemed to avoid being alone with him with so much care, and had so many jests about his "going to Edinburgh to get a wife," and "the worthlessness of the country lasses," that his resolution entirely failed him, and he went home, with feelings of the most painful disappointment, to spend his last night in her neighbourhood in a state of sleepless agitation. All this, Jamie Wilson had been enjoined to keep a perfect secret; and the letter concluded by desiring him to give the writer's "compliments" to Rose; and, if she showed any signs of concern, or seemed to take this mark of attention kindly, to say that he intended, as soon as circumstances would permit, to come back and see her.

The *compliments* were accordingly given as directed, and poor Rose on receiving them—if one can be said to receive that which is nothing—almost fainted. But when she was told the sequel, she soon recovered so far as to be able to laugh, and to say, that "she doubted, if he had nae ither errand, it wad be lang afore he came back."

The evident agitation which the mere mention of the subject had occasioned her, made the people afraid to speak of it to her afterwards. A letter, however, was, by the advice of the kind-hearted widow, despatched with all possible speed to her distant admirer, informing him how matters stood, and requesting him to write to Rose direct, and state what were his intentions, or otherwise the consequences might be fatal.

Months passed on; no notice was taken of the letter, no accounts of her lover arrived, and Rose's melancholy and indisposition evidently increased, but still she spoke not. At last a stranger came to visit the place, and with him came the clearing up of the mystery.

Samuel Simpson, the widow's son, had sailed for some time in a vessel trading to the West Indies, and while his ship was undergoing repair, he had taken a trip down to see his mother. Several months before, he had met George Robertson, at one of the sea-ports on the west coast of England, and heard him state, that he had, by the unexpected death of an uncle, fallen heir to a valuable property in Jamaica, of which he was going to take possession, having been advised to do so by an eminent lawyer. This intelligence reached Rose before Marion could take any means to prevent its spreading, and from that time her melancholy abstraction became more painfully evident.

Such is the substance of the information I received; and I was solicited to try my utmost for the relief of my dejected cousin, but not to mention the news to her parents, which, I was assured, would only aggravate her distress. The propriety of this I could easily see; but alas! what could I do? The first part of the story promised fair—the letter seemed to indicate a mutual affection; but what followed came like a death-blow to hope. The heir of a rich uncle—embarked on a long voyage, and gone to take possession of a valuable property!—the probability was, that he would think no more of Rose, or if he did think of her at all, it would be as a dream of the night, which is thought of only to be forgotten. I felt that it was a hopeless case, and I could not help saying so.

On returning to my uncle's, I found Mary Auburn there before me. She was endeavouring to cheer and comfort Rose, in such a manner as led me to suspect that she also was in the secret. "Your melancholy thoughts make ye ill," said she, as I entered, "but you should aye try to be cheerfu', an' hope the best. If ye only kent what mony a ane has suffered, an' how lang they've lived, an' how happy they hae been made after a', ye wad never despair." To this Rose listened with little attention. But it appeared to me that the two had done something more than exchanged hearts since I last saw them together. "Sing 'The Desponding Maiden' to me," said she, "I like to hear you sing, Mary."

Mary obeyed; but her singing was no longer the same. The music might be as accurate; but to me it seemed to want that tone and feeling which on a former occasion had sent every word warm and thrilling to the heart. Her anxiety for her suffering friend was moreover evident; but it was the anxiety which is felt for another—her own melancholy was gone. Though her sympathy was sincere and unaffected, there was peace and quiet beneath, and her eyes no longer drooped, but beamed with a placid lustre on all they met, and had occasionally an expression of archness which appeared quite new, and almost foreign to her former nature. To have known her before, and seen her now, one would have thought that she had forgotten the cause of her own sadness in sympathising with the secret sorrows of her friend. Poor girl! she had need of sympathy. But, alas! in such matters what can sympathy avail? Her peace of mind was evidently gone, her beauty withering, and her frame hastening to premature decay. I felt that such was the case; and, with a heavy heart, I took my departure.

Distance, and I know not what, prevented me from hearing a single word of her for the year following. Nay, let the truth be told,—

Of such materials wretched men are made!

—though for nearly two months she was seldom absent from my thoughts for two hours together. As spring advanced, and the busy season of summer came on, I entirely forgot her; and it was only the approach of winter which brought back the image of the pale and interesting girl who had once attracted so much of my attention. Though the days were shortening, to me they seemed to lengthen; and as their number diminished, my anxiety on her account increased. At last the third Hanselmonday arrived, and I set out on my annual pilgrimage. During the tedious journey, many and varied were the thoughts which passed through my mind; but, I recollect well, that which affected me most was the possibility—nay, probability—that my cousin, with all the buoyant spirits and gay fancies which characterised her at our first meeting, and that melancholy abstraction which pervaded her manner when I saw her last—that she—the young, the beautiful—might have sunk into an early grave, the victim of unrequited love! And then the grief of her parents for their only child—the joy of their hearts, and the light of their eyes—snatched away in the very opening bloom of her existence, presented itself to my imagination. I saw the look of deep sorrow with which they would meet me, and felt the pang which my presence would impart. Such were my feelings, as I stood before the door, which that day twelvemonth I had been so eager to enter, and some minutes elapsed ere I could muster resolution to knock.

It is the lot of man to hope for things which can never be realised, and to fear that which may never come upon him; and of these hopes and fears, more than "life's realities," his existence is made up. The door was answered by Rose herself; and I was welcomed with a smile as congenial as any I had ever seen play upon her countenance. In a moment she had me by the hand, and, without giving me time to make those inquiries which were rising to my tongue's end, she led me into the house, where, I need not say, my reception was most cordial.

The comfort and cheerfulness of the family were perfectly restored; and the smiles and blushes of Rose alternated in such a manner, that had my feelings been what they once were, it is probable I should have looked upon them as a happy omen. She seemed as happy and as free from care, as cheerful and as assiduous to please, as ever she had been; yet somehow she was not the same. There was an air of mystery about her, for which I could not account; and I did not fail to remark that certain significant looks and winks passed between her and her aunt. In about a quarter of an hour after my arrival, Mary

Auburn came in, and again the same telegraphic communications were made, and the same air of mystery prevailed; but it was only for a minute; for, as if anticipating an inquiry which they wished to escape, they kept chattering and asking me questions with such volubility, that I was completely cheated out of the explanation which I had intended to ask.

In the meantime the task of diverting me was an easy one; for, while my ears drank the music made by cheerful voices, my eyes lacked not subjects for pleasing contemplation. Rose, I have already said, was restored to perfect health and cheerfulness. The change in Mary was no less remarkable. From being a modest melancholy girl, with eyes oftener fixed on the earth than on any other object, and a complexion rather pale, she had brightened into exquisite loveliness. A lasting smile played around her mouth; her laugh seemed to rise direct from the heart, like waters from a fountain; and there was an archness in her look, that bespoke the possession of a secret which she had no immediate desire to communicate.

"Ye've complimented baith Rose an' me," said she, "on being bonnier than when ye saw us last. When ye have na gotten a wife, an' we want husbands, whatfor dinna ye fa' in love wi' either her or me?"

"Because," I replied, "I'm fear'd neither her nor you would fa' in love wi' me."

"But ye ken," said she, "the men maun aye fa' in love first, an' tell their love too, an' bide our scorn awhile to the bargain; for though the lasses, puir things, should fa' ower the lugs in love, they daurna speak a word o't; an' then they may a' dee o' broken hearts, an' ne'er ane ken—no even their nearest freends."

"What might hinder them to let their love be kenn'd as weel as the men do?" quoth I, willing to hear what she would say.

"Maybe they wad mak an odd warld if they were aye able to tell o' their likings," was her reply; "but nature has ta'en care to keep that power for ither kind o' cattle. An' if ye only kenn'd the struggle a woman has afore she can tell the man she likes best some wee hints aboot her affections, after he has deaved her for years wi' his, ye wad never speer that question. A woman's heart is like a mouse-trap—love may get in, but it can never get out again, unless the minister len' a hand to open it."

"Hoot, lassie!" said Rose, loth to be silent while others had the privilege of speaking—"hoot, lassie! what gars ye tell him about women, an' their hearts or their heads either—let him learn for himsel'."

This tattle was interrupted by a tap at the door. Rose, who had been looking out at the window, did not answer the summons, but hastened into the other apartment, or "ran ben the house," as her aunt would have said. Her mother opened the door, and George Robertson was ushered into the house, or rather ushered in himself; for, in his impatience, he passed the hostess in the doorway. After casting his eyes around the apartment with a hurried glance, "Where is my wife?" he exclaimed. A titter from behind the room door, while it announced the person he sought, invited him to join her. We could still partially observe them through the half open door; and after a hearty embrace, and a kiss, to procure which seemed to be the object of "the base cutty's manœuvre," as Aunty Eppie observed, they both returned to the kitchen.

This was surprise enough. The West India proprietor returned from his rich possessions—from his sugar plantations, his slaves, his rum, and his tobacco—and married to a country girl—the husband of my cousin! This was certainly "true love," as the popular ballad-makers say. The good people on all sides saw my wonder, and hastened to give an explanation, the substance of which is as follows:—

At my last visit, though I had despaired of being able to afford Rose any relief, the widow, with stronger faith, had deemed it her duty to make an effort. Accordingly, she charged her son, ere he set off for his vessel, with such a letter as she could write to the supposed West India proprietor. In this she set before him, in strong but simple language, the pains he had taken to gain Rose's affection, the stolen meetings which she herself, trusting to his steadiness, had assisted him to procure, and all those little flatteries which sink so deep into the heart of a female. She next depicted, in her own way, the unhappy effect which these had produced, and were likely to produce, on the poor girl. And, that nothing might be wanting which she could supply, she concluded by threatening him with the "widow's curse," if he should sacrifice, on the altar of his better fortune, the heart he had so earnestly sought, and forget, in the day of his prosperity, those who had loved him when he was poor and a stranger.

On entrusting this letter to her son, she instructed him, as he valued his mother's blessing, either to deliver it himself or see it put into such hands as would convey it to its destination. Fortunately his vessel was freighted for the same port; and, shortly after landing, he had an opportunity of delivering the letter into the hands of George Robertson himself, corroborating its contents, of course, by stating what he had seen.

By this time the brilliant prospects of the individual to whom it was addressed had totally vanished. Owing to a train of tricks and circumstances, which would be fruitless to detail, his uncle's property had proved little better than a delusion. He had, however, been offered a situation of trust and emolument on a neighbouring plantation; and that love of money which is natural to man in his civilised state, together with the uncertainty in which he had left his affair with Rose, had almost induced him to accept of it. "It might be," he argued, "that her supposed partiality for him was merely the creation of his own ardent wishes; and, as she was naturally kind to all, that he had been favoured with only a common share of her smiles." From these considerations he imagined that it would be better never to know the truth than to be shocked by a disappointment, and he was either determined, or determining, to stay where he was; but when he received Marion's letter, it needed not the fear of her curse to frighten him home. He left the scene of his delusive hopes without a sigh, and hastened to seek happiness in peaceful industry and domestic affection.

From the time of his arrival, Rose's health and spirits began to return. The state of her feelings at last dawned upon her parents; and, so far from forbidding, they facilitated the marriage. The bad conduct of a former master made an opening for the young gardener in his own calling; and everything appeared to promise happiness and prosperity.

Scarcely had these particulars been communicated, when in came "Sam Simpson, the sailor lad."

"What!" said Mrs. Robertson, as we must now call her, seeing she was no less a personage than the wife of the master gardener at Corolla Castle, and only come to spend Hanselmonday with her parents,—"whatfor dinna ye salute Mary's husband, an' wish them baith joy? Ye're but an unmannerly kind o' a cousin to stand and stare that gait at a new married couple."

Mary laughed: so did her husband; while I stood bewildered with accounts of weddings. The occasion of her downcast looks and dowie sangs was discovered at last. Samuel and her had been great cronies from the time they were children up to his running off to sea. During his short visit to his mother, they had renewed their former acquaintance; and he had then and there fairly asked her to be his wife, promising, at the same time, if she would accept him, to quit his present occupation, and settle himself at home as soon as possible.

"Yonder comes Jamie Wilson an' his sweetheart," said Mary, wishing to turn the conversation from herself.

In a few minutes, the said Jamie Wilson and Peggy Simpson arrived. He was a fine looking young man, and his companion, too, was improved. Her cheerfulness remained the same; but that thoughtless gaiety which, two years ago, gave lightness and music to her singing, was exchanged for a demeanour more sedate and womanly; and there was an expression in her bright eyes which bespoke deeper and maturer feeling.

"I like to see ye come that gait," said my uncle, as he welcomed them. "I hope I can prophesy whar this will end, an' God send my prophecy may be happily fulfilled! See that ye dinna tempt an' torment ane anither wi' dortin' an' drawin' back, like young fools as ye are. Be kind, an' carefu' no to gie offence; but tak my advice, an' see that ye are able to provide a comfortable hame for yersel's afore ye gang thegither."

Peggy blushed as they both took their seats. In a few minutes more, her mother arrived also. She had stayed behind on purpose to let the young folk get their crack; and as she looked upon her children — the one already married to an amiable and deserving woman, who had long loved him, and the other in the full prospect of being soon united to the man of her affections—as she looked upon them, and contemplated the happiness of those whom she had been instrumental in bringing together, a glow of happiness suffused her countenance, which seemed to take many years from the past, and bring back to her care-worn features "the light of other days." Her satisfaction was, perhaps, augmented by a sense that where she had experienced kindness and received assistance she had also conferred some benefit.

## MARGARET CLINTON.

*She weeps not, yet often and deeply she sighs—*
*She never complains, but her silence implies*
*The composure of settled distress.*
SOUTHEY.

THOSE who confine their reading exclusively to works of fiction, and form their estimate of mankind from the information they thence derive, will, on bringing matters to the test, infallibly find themselves deceived; and those who go forth into the great world to make love, or war, or anything else, after the fashion of these works, may lay their account with disappointment. But neither of these evils can accrue from a narrative like the following, in which it has been the writer's intention only to lay before the reader a few simple facts, with the recital of which he was himself deeply affected.

Margaret Clinton was born—the exact *when* and *where*, the narrator of her story was never told, and he never had the curiosity to inquire. Her mother died when she was very young, and the care of rearing and educating her devolved upon a married aunt, who, in conjunction with her grandmother, kindly undertook to provide for their infant relative. In about three years after the death of his wife, Margaret's father again thought proper to enter into the married state; and from that period little intercourse subsisted between him and the maternal relations of his infant daughter. But though this was the case, she could scarcely be said to feel the want of a paternal home; for her grandfather and grandmother looked upon her as all they had left of a beloved daughter who had gone before them to a better world; while her aunt, who had never enjoyed robust health since her marriage, and in whom a sort of melancholy tenderness had been fostered by the death of two children, regarded her with an affection which could not have been surpassed had she been her own.

With these relations she passed the helpless years of infancy without suffering much from the deprivation of a mother's care. As she grew in strength and in beauty, age, with its concomitants, began to steal upon the venerable pair, so that her society and little services became to them indispensable. From the quiet and orderly seclusion in which she thus lived, a natural bashfulness of disposition, and a tinge of melancholy, which she partly inherited from her mother, had been nursed into a painfully acute sensibility. An inquisitive look would embarrass her; she could scarcely speak in the presence of strangers, and she always seemed to prefer being alone to any society save that of her dearest friends.

When she was about seventeen, her grandfather died. This was nothing extraordinary: fathers and grandfathers must die, and there are many who can forget them fast enough. But to Margaret Clinton, "in life's morning march," when the feelings are most intense, and with a temperament which gave a melancholy permanency to every emotion, the death of this aged individual, who had been to her all she could ever know of a father, was the source of deep and lasting sorrow. Still, however, her home was the same. By the last will of the old man, his youngest son, who was unmarried, was to succeed to his little farm and other effects, with the proviso that his mother should remain in the house as its mistress for the remainder of her life. He took possession accordingly. In a little while, matters went quietly on in their usual way, and the venerable patriarch, who slept with his fathers, seemed to be forgotten by all save his aged partner and Margaret, who might still be seen, on a Sabbath day, shedding a tear over his grave.

The lease of their little farm, which consisted of only a few acres, expired in less than two years after the old man's death; and as the laird did not choose to renew it, those who remained were forced to remove from a spot in which they and their fathers had been rooted for more than a century. This, too, was nothing extraordinary: people must often remove at the end of every year, and those who have hearts which "recognise no being and no spot" are certainly the happiest in such circumstances. But to Margaret Clinton, who had never before known what it was to *flit*, and whose affections—balked of their natural range by her timidity—had twined themselves around every feature and every object connected with the place, it was distressing to leave it. Her spirits drooped as the time drew near; during the preparations for removing, her colour often changed from the flush of feeling to the "paleness of fear," as the recollection of her former haunts, or the certainty that they were to be hers no longer, passed over her mind; and when she did leave this home of her happiest days, her tears flowed plentifully.

She was not, however, allowed to sit down in idle sorrow. The fatigue of travelling, added to the infirmities of age, proved too much for her grandmother, who, after arriving at this new dwelling, was for a long period confined to bed, so that the task of nursing her, and attending to the concerns of the house, devolved wholly upon Margaret; and the constant claims on her attention thence arising, tended materially to relieve her mind from those morbid impressions which it was but too ready to receive, and permanently retain.

About this time, the uncle, who had succeeded to his grandfather's effects, formed a sort of secret attachment to a young woman in the neighbourhood of their former residence. He proposed, was accepted, and now began to make preparations for his marriage. To this, his aged parent, as she was in no state to offer objections, gave her consent, with the understanding that she was still to remain in the house, and that it was also to afford an asylum to her otherwise homeless grand-daughter.

The marriage was accordingly consummated; and this, too, was only a thing in the common course of events. Nevertheless there are some with hearts so sensitive that common occurrences, and matters which to others would be unimportant, are to them subjects of deep and distressing thought; and of these Margaret Clinton was one. To see another take her place by the fire, and to be spoken to as a lodger and a stranger in the house where she had once been as mistress, was not to be borne without some feeling of pain. The solitude in which she had been reared, and which hitherto had guarded her from the effects of the passion of love, only served to deepen every impression after it was made; and her affections were now destined to be poured forth in a stream, the stronger and the purer, perhaps, for their having been so long locked up in her own bosom.

A young man of the neighbourhood happened to see her one day as she was returning home with her weekly store of articles for household use. Where combustibles are lodged a single spark will often suffice to set the whole on flame. The sight was enough: and he tried in future to throw himself in her way as often as possible, never failing to behave toward her with the most marked attention. At first she seemed inclined to shun his company, and appeared rather annoyed by his advances; but the heart of woman is not constituted to resist continued kindness. In due time he found an opportunity to confess his passion, and offer her his hand. Though timid and bashful, all the gratitude and tenderness which characterise the best of her sex were in her nature; the discomfort of her present home added another powerful argument in his favour, and her consent was won. They plighted their faith; and in the prospect of being united as soon as was consistent with the circumstances of both, they were supremely happy—but it was "happiness too exquisite to last."

Shortly after this era in her life her aunt, whose health had long been delicate, became so ill as to be wholly confined to bed; and Margaret was once more called on to come and live with her, less as a protegé than a sick-nurse. She went, and the enchanted dream in which she had been living was for the time dissolved by seeing one of her nearest and dearest friends withering away in the merciless gripe of consumption, and to all appearance near her journey's end.

She had scarcely been a fortnight with her aunt when her lover was taken ill with small-pox. The disease at first, though virulent, was not deemed dangerous; and no one thought of sending word to her. But in a short time alarming symptoms began to appear; and while people were consulting about the propriety of giving her notice, the rumour of his illness was handed from mouth to mouth till it at last reached her. With a heart weighed down by apprehensions for the fate of her aunt, and a frame worn out with watching night and day by her bedside, she set out on the following morning to see the object of her first and deepest affection.

After a hurried and fatiguing journey, in a hot day in June, she arrived in the vicinity of the sick man's dwelling. But as the mother of her intended bridegroom had always been inimical to the proposed connection, and as it was her house in which he lay, she did not go directly there, but bent her steps first to the habitation of a female acquaintance, who had been intrusted with the secret of the approaching marriage. This individual knew the sight which awaited her, but she wanted courage to prepare her for it; and instead of attempting to do so, she offered to accompany her to the scene of suffering. Her offer was accepted, and they went together. On entering the house, his mother quitted the apartment without bidding them welcome, and left them to introduce themselves.

When Margaret entered the apartment, her lover was lying quiet, but his terribly altered appearance might have served to appal a stouter heart than hers. Her limbs could scarcely carry her to his bedside, and when she did reach it, she stood over him, silent and motionless, while her soft hazel eyes, instead of melting, seemed to burn. For a while her very breathing seemed to have forsaken her; every sense appeared suspended, and she stood rigid, pale, and statue-like, in the astonishment of grief. At last she raised her hand to her forehead, as if to shade her burning eye-balls, and something between a shriek and a stifled groan escaped her as her consciousness returned. The sound attracted the notice of her lover: he knew her voice; and, with a desperate effort, wrenching open his eyes, turned them on her for a moment with a look of surprise and kindness. As soon as he had satisfied himself of her presence, he closed them again, and held out his hand. She took it; and heedless alike of the contagion which it might communicate, and the notice of those who were observing her, she pressed it to her lips, "and pressed and pressed again," as if her life lay there. This mark of tenderness, so unlike everything he had been accustomed to receive from her, appeared powerfully to affect the individual on whom it was bestowed. The rising blood once more reddened over his disfigured face, and he made several ineffectual attempts to speak: at last he was able to say in a low voice, "Peggy, I am dying! and I could wish you to think of me sometimes when I am gone. Yet"——— He muttered something more, but the words were inarticulate. The strong emotion had increased his fever; his throat seemed to close, and he sunk reluctantly back upon the bed.

Little as he had said, his words were too many for her to whom they were addressed. As he concluded, her powerless hand dropped his. The faint red faded on her cheek and lip; she staggered backward, and would have fallen had not her friend supported her from the house.

After this short and painful interview, her shaken nerves were in no state to support her back to the dwelling of her dying aunt; and by the advice of her female friend, who again accompanied her part of the road, she went to her grandmother's, where she passed a sleepless night; and early on the morrow she returned to the house of her friend.

Whatever the state of her mind may have been, she was now doomed to experience one of those treacherous gleams of hope, which occasionally brighten a dark prospect, as a ray of sunshine may sometimes be seen shedding its lustre over the evening of a dark and stormy day, ere the world is wrapped up in a darker and more stormy night. Her stricken lover had passed the hours of darkness better than had been expected; he had, moreover, been able to swallow a few teaspoonfuls of wine in the morning, and some faint hopes were entertained that the disease might have reached its crisis. This her humble friend made the most of. She had seen her agitation during their previous short interview; and she was afraid that her reason might be touched, or that she might sink altogether under the pressure of her own feelings, were she to see him again in his sunken state. She, therefore, endeavoured to cheer her with hopes of his recovery; and after representing in strong terms the evil which might accrue from those emotions which her presence would produce, she succeeded in persuading her to return to her aunt, without attempting to see him again.

Though her journey, with all its consequent delays, had detained her only a night, and part of two days, the malady of her aunt had, in this short period, made fatal strides toward its termination. She just arrived in time to be recognised by the expiring woman, who took her hand, pressed it with a feeble grasp, raised her dim eyes once more to look her in the face, and died.

Real sorrow is seldom capable of playing extravagant tricks, or acting fashionable vagaries—though there is a fashion in sorrow as well as in everything else. A carelessness of praise or blame from the world, and tears shed in solitude, are its legitimate expression. Such was the grief of Margaret.

She might have now been free to go whither her heart directed; but the confusion consequent on death, and the many ceremonies to be performed—ceremonies which custom has made it sacrilege to neglect, preparatory to depositing the dust in its last dwelling—these, together with the urgent request of the widower, "not to leave him," detained her till the funeral was over: so that it was the morning of the third day before she could set out on her return to him, on whose life her own for the time seemed to depend.

As she pursued her journey with an emaciated frame and weary feet, there was in her heart a sad contention between hopes and fears—hopes which with *ignis fatuus* gleam flitted quickly past; and fears which, like the cloud of night, hung heavily and dark, and weighed her spirits down with damp and gloomy foreboding. She was within a mile of the habitation which contained him; no tidings had reached her since her visit, and though she might have obtained information of him at several houses which she had passed, her lips ever refused to frame the question; and with a strange fatuity she shrank from knowing the truth, and clung with a desperate hold to the small remains of hope that existed.

The mile was diminished to less than half that distance, when she saw a young woman who belonged to the place coming directly to meet her. The truth, whatever it might be, was now about to be forced upon her, and her heart palpitated with terror lest it should be as she feared, yet wished not to believe. They met and stopped, as if by tacit consent. The unhappy girl had made an attempt to compose her looks, and collect her bewildered thoughts; and she took her part of a trifling conversation, which lasted two or three minutes, in a calm tone of voice. Still no question could she ask regarding the cause of her journey, till the other said, in an abrupt and half-careless manner, "Ye'll hae heard o' George's death, nae doubt? an' ye'll be come to see the corpse afore the buryin'?" On hearing these words, an ashy paleness overspread her countenance, yet, strange as it may seem, she neither trembled nor wept, nor manifested any other sign of sorrow; but after standing for a minute's space, as if she had been stunned by a violent blow, she resumed her journey without answering the young woman's interrogatory, or seeming to remember that an answer was required.

The sun gained the meridian, and was calmly sinking in the bosom of evening, ere she arrived at the house of the female friend, who accompanied her on her first visit to the deceased. Here she spoke with apparent composure of his death; and after listening to a detailed account of his last moments, expressed a wish to see his remains before they were consigned to mother earth. Her wish was readily complied with. The lid of the coffin was lifted up, and her friend, at her request, removed the cloth which covered the face of the deceased. When this was done, she stepped round to the head of the coffin, and for some minutes leaned over it with fixed eyes. Her countenance, which was pale before, exhibited little change, and, save a momentary shudder, she showed no other sign of emotion. She then stood erect and said, in a calm tone of voice, "Ay, it's a' ower noo!" The words were uttered without being addressed to any one; and, without offering to condole with friends, or waiting for their condolence, she left the house with as much apparent composure as she had entered it.

At her grandmother's, whither she instantly returned, she appeared equally composed. This aged relative was glad to see her so little cast down, as she thought, under a trial which she had feared might prove too much for her fortitude; and thinking it might be of use still further to divert her mind, she set her to perform some little services about the house. To these services she manifested the utmost readiness; and as her uncle and his wife were absent, she went on with them for a time, as she had been wont to do when she had the sole management there. But she had already taxed her powers of concealment to the utmost; and that fortitude which hitherto had resisted the pressing claims of so many creditors, at last became bankrupt. She threw down the things which were in her hand, turned her face to the wall, and after standing thus for a few seconds, walked hurriedly to the door. The aged dame felt some misgivings as to her peace of mind, and followed her out as fast as her feeble limbs could carry her, but Margaret was nowhere to be seen. The neighbours were made acquainted with the circumstance, and a young woman, who had formerly been in her confidence, was sent out to seek her. There is a plantation immediately adjoining the site of the houses here alluded to, and to it had she fled, like a wounded fawn, to conceal her anguish from the eye of day. Here, after a short search, she was accordingly found, seated on the earth, her form more than half hidden by the depending branches of a tree, and her face buried in her hands, while tears flowed fast from under them.

It was long before she seemed to recognise the presence, or to hear the kind expostulations of her former friend. When the violence of her emotion had somewhat subsided, she seemed to observe that she was not alone, and, uncovering her face, she attempted to dry her tearful eyes with her apron; but no sooner had she raised them to meet those of her friend, than, as if recollecting the circumstances under which that face and form had last met her eye, a convulsive shudder shook every part of her frame—she bent her head suddenly down between her knees, covered her face again with both her hands, and yielded to an agony of grief. When this burst of feeling had again exhausted itself, and after being earnestly urged to "come into the house," she removed her hands slowly from her face; and while her head drooped on one side, as if its weight were too much for her to support, and the tears gushed fast from her eyes, she said, in a tone of melancholy earnestness,— "Oh! I dinna care whar I gang now!"

It could serve but little purpose to dwell on this scene of sorrow. That which gave life its charm, and, like the summer sun, made all things bright around her—that was gone for ever. Her hopes of happiness were fled—her heart was desolate.

Excessive grief, like everything else which is excessive, must soon come to an end, by either destroying itself, or all that is destructible of those on whom it preys. But it may be, and sometimes is, followed by a sedate and settled melancholy, which, though little noticed by careless eyes, may last for years, or for life. Soon after these events her tears ceased to flow in the presence of others; she made no further allusion to the subject, and in a short time her countenance had assumed a part of its wonted composure.

On the ensuing Sabbath, when her uncle, with his wife and the other friends of Margaret's deceased aunt, went to church, dressed in the garb of woe, but with only a common share of sorrow in their countenances, she walked a space behind, clad in deeper mourning than any of them, with eyes which were never raised from the earth, and a look in which her feelings were more forcibly portrayed than in the sables which she wore.

It has been said by one,* whose gloomy observations on the lot of man often approximate too nearly to truth, that "misfortunes love a train," and "tread each other's heel." The quiver of Fate was not yet exhausted. Margaret Clinton was requested by her friends to sort the habiliments which had belonged to her deceased aunt; and, weak as she was from the violent shock which her nerves had sustained, she complied. But scarcely had she commenced her task, when she was overtaken with pains in the head, weariness, and loss of strength. This forced her to abandon the idea of proceeding; and "What was she to do now?" was a question which for a time she could not answer. Here she had no one to attend to her, or even to give her a draught of cold water should she be seized with severe or protracted distress, which she foreboded was awaiting her. She had but one alternative: once more her weary limbs dragged her fainting form back to the residence of her grandmother; and there, after being confined to bed for two days by severe headache and sickness, she caught the infection of that fatal disease which had cut off her lover, and her life was considered in danger. Death was spoken of in her presence, and she spoke again of the King of Terrors without shrinking. She could even introduce the subject herself with calmness, and without manifesting any of that reluctance to die which is often observable in the young, and in those who are snatched away ere they have experienced those disappointments with which maturer years are familiar, or had an opportunity of trying those pleasures which imagination holds up so temptingly to view, and proving that they are not what they seem. Throughout she endured patiently, and was seldom heard to complain. Did she die? No: death comes oftener in imagination to the assistance of the playwright and the writer of tragic fiction, than in reality to those who have little or nothing left for which they would wish to live. After the disease had spent its force in the usual way, she began to recover.

The writer of these pages had an opportunity of seeing her shortly after she got better. The church where he attends sermon is situated at a short distance from the parish burying-place. Thither he occasionally went, to muse away the interval of public worship among the mansions of the dead. On the day alluded to, he wandered in that direction, as was his wont; and on entering at the gate, which stood open, he was sur-

---

* Dr. Young. See "Night Thoughts."

prised to find that a female figure had taken possession of the solitary spot before him. It was Margaret Clinton, sitting by the grave—of whom, the reader need not be told. He would have spoken, and tried to condole with her on the severe shock she had sustained; but there is something so sacred in the solitude of deep sorrow, that he felt it might be intrusive in him to "intermeddle therewith," and, stealing silently and hurriedly away, he left her—the only living thing in this "city of the dead."

Two years have now elapsed since her bereavement, and some may suppose it forgotten. Yet decide not on her memory till you have made a simple trial. Are you an old acquaintance?—speak to her and she will answer you with a smile. But mark that smile!—it grows slowly, like an exotic plant in an uncongenial clime: its decay is like its growth, gradual and slow, as if the effort which called it forth were required to keep it alive throughout; and when it has faded from a face which it had scarcely brightened, her features relax into an expression of deeper melancholy than they had previously worn; and it is only by speaking to her again that she is brought to recollect your presence.

Such was Margaret Clinton when the writer of these pages saw her last. Her affecting, but ill-narrated story, may be concluded by the following verses, which were composed, shortly after her lover's death, by one "alike to fortune and to fame unknown."

### The Unmarried Widow.

O Grave! what woe is wrought by thee!
What clouded years of misery!
What loving hearts hast thou bereft!
What joyless, hopeless mourners left!
MARY HOWITT.

She was not by the bed of death
  To see his manly strength decay;
Or mark the last convulsive breath,
  That feebly heaved his suffering clay.
No! hands less kind, and hearts less true,
  Were gather'd round his dying bed,
To watch death's shadows, as they grew
  Slowly o'er his devoted head!

Yet once I saw her, with those eyes,
  As bending o'er his couch she stood,—
With hopes, that vainly strove to rise,
  With fears that curdled cold her blood.

Of these I saw the shadows pass
   Across her eye, along her brow,
Like things seen in a magic glass—
   Alas! methinks I see them now!

Yet once again I saw her near,
   Ere the black coffin lid was closed;
Even then, her dark eye shed no tear
   O'er his cold limbs in death composed.
And yet—oh! what a spectre host
   That sight must wake within her brain!
Of every parted look, the ghost!
   Of every perish'd smile, the pain!

*There*, visions of that happy time
   When hearts, whose faith had long been tried,
And made but one responsive chime,
   In wedlock's bands of love are tied;
*There*, the concentred wish of years—
   The long, long cherish'd dream of love—
The source of countless hopes and fears,
   Lay with the winding-sheet above!

The house—the home—the happy hearth—
   A husband's smile, the children's glee—
Their harmless sport, and noisy mirth,
   And the embrace, caressingly,
Of him she loved, when eventide,
   Which homeward brings the laden bee,
Should bring that loved one to her side,
   Her heart from every care to free.

His hand to press—his eye to meet—
   His frugal meal to dress with care;
To hear him talk in accents sweet—
   In all his joys and woes to share:
These were her fancy's golden mine—
   These were her riches—these her store;
Her heart a consecrated shrine,
   With all its treasures brimming o'er!

These to her soul's enchanted cell,
   At morn, or noon, or evening time,
Had come—like spirits bright that dwell
   In worlds beyond the reach of crime—
To steal her from herself away,
   A new and happy world revealing
Where Love ruled every smiling day,
   In the unbounded flow of feeling.

That light was quench'd, that music hush'd,
   In silence and in hopeless gloom;
Her visions in that hour had rush'd
   All downward to their silent tomb.

With his cold shrouded corse that lay,
　From whom they came, on whom they turn'd—
All perish'd—cold and pass'd away,
　Like dust which hath been long inurn'd.

But though her dark eye did not swerve,
　As there she gazed upon the dead,
Yet, in the trembling of each nerve,
　The anguish of her heart I read.
The shudder, that so quickly flies
　Electric o'er each arm and limb,
Speaks a far deeper grief than eyes
　Which many tears have render'd dim.

With wayward footsteps, moving slow,
　And eyes upon the cold earth fix'd,
As she from thence essay'd to go,
　All faint and pale, I saw her next:
Pale were her lips, so lately red;
　Her cheek had sadly changed its hue,—
The sparkle from her eye had fled,
　And on her brow deep shadows grew.

A love-lorn, hope-forsaken shade,
　She glided through the twilight's gloom,
As if full fain she would have made
　Her nearest resting-place the tomb,—
With him to moulder side by side
　In the cold chambers of the dead,
Who sought in her a living bride,
　And share in death his bridal bed.

Ay, she hath loved, ill-fated maid,
　As she can never love again.
Though her last hour be long delay'd,
　And from his prey Death long refrain:
Her heart hath pour'd forth all its ruth,
　And pour'd it forth, alas, in vain!
The faith of age, the love of youth,
　And ashes in their place remain.

## THE COVENANTER'S GRAVE.

> How vainly seek
> The selfish for that happiness denied
> To aught but virtue!
> Madly they frustrate still their own designs.
>       SHELLEY.

### CHAPTER I.

IN the parish of Abdie, and almost immediately under the churchyard wall, lies the little loch of Lindores, which, in the calm twilight of a summer's evening, appears like the eye of

Nature looking up to its Maker, in the spirit of meek and quiet devotion. This loch is studded with two small islands, both of which were, at a former period, covered with willows so thickly, that, seen from a distance, the dark foliage of the trees seemed a solid mass of green. Overlooking the loch, on the abrupt acclivity which forms its southern bank, stand the ruined walls of what was once a shepherd's cot, known by the name of "Sitmalane." On its eastern shore rises a hill of considerable height, the ridge of which is surmounted by a peak, called "The Black Cairn." On this peak, at some forgotten period of the country's history, a small tumulus had been formed, from which human bones have been dug, and over the stones of which the annual deposits of the moss and lichens of ages had formed a sort of soil, which at last produced vegetation of another description; so that the circular area of which it is composed, has long been covered with grass, while all is heath and barrenness around.

Descending from this bleak region—the haunt of unsocial birds, and the home of the mist—to the cultivated slope, and the dwellings of men, on the western shoulder of the mountain, and near to where it verges to its northern extremity, stand five or six trees of moderate size, with rough gnarled trunks and drooping branches. These mark the place where once stood a humble dwelling called "The North Cotton," which, at the time of our story, was tenanted by a shepherd of the name of William Turner. A little way to the southward of this tenement may still be seen three ashes bearing all the symptoms of sickly age: these once overshadowed a human habitation called Waaltower, and they still preserve its name. It was formerly a small pendicle, which, with its low thatched house, overshadowing trees, and crystal spring bubbling out from the veins of a decayed rock immediately above the premises, had long been the dwelling of contented and peaceful industry. There the family of the Stewarts had resided for several generations, without much either of improvement or deterioration in the manners and circumstances of the race. They were poor, hardy, hospitable, and industrious, as all poor people must be, who wish to be honest. About a quarter of a mile farther onward, in the same direction, a few hoary sycamores mark the site of Lookhame. The place was what, in the language of those days, was called a farm. It was little superior in appearance to the other two, only it had more land attached to it; and, at the time to which the reader's attention is about to be directed, it was managed by David Banster, assisted by his son

Richard; the latter of whom was more commonly known by the name of Black Ritchie, a cognomen which, it is supposed, he had acquired from the darkness of his hair, or some other personal quality. Such is a brief sketch of those dwellings of our forefathers. But the plough has passed over their foundations; the last fragment of their walls has long since disappeared; and the crops of many years have been reaped from the place where their hearthstones once were lying.

William Turner had a daughter, whose beauty made her the admiration of the neighbourhood. Jane was one of those beings of uncommon loveliness, who sometimes spring up in the least cultivated districts, and among the rudest people, to enliven with their sweetness "the desert air," and raise a feeling of wonder in the bosom of the traveller, why such flowers should bloom in the midst of what he deems a waste. Her affections had been sought, and her smiles courted, by many youths of her own rank. Nor among those whose expectations might have justified them in looking a little higher, were there wanting some who felt a secret satisfaction if they could only succeed in being near her, or in attracting her attention for a few minutes. This, however, was no easy matter; for beset as she was with lovers, and eagerly as her heart and hand had been sought, she appeared to be in no hurry to give either of them away. Though she might be partially impressed by the novelty of a first sight, or the respectful deference of a first conversation, it is probable, upon better acquaintance, that she discovered most of her admirers to be actuated by motives which did not accord with the pure and warm aspirations of her heart.

Be this as it may, she still continued the object of general admiration; but that admiration was now offered at a more respectful distance. Though every peasant still persisted in putting on his best dress, and his best looks, wherever she was expected to be present, there were only two who could be said to aspire to her hand. These were Alan Stewart, and Richard Banster, *alias* Black Ritchie. The last, it was supposed, owed his favourable reception at the North Cotton principally to his skill in rural economy, and the fluency with which he talked of rural affairs to the old shepherd. Sometimes he would exhibit his own knowledge with good effect; at others, he would listen with apparent deference to the maxims of his host; occasionally, he would dispute a point with considerable ability, then yield as if overcome by superior argument. By these, and similar means, he succeeded in making himself a welcome guest with the father, whatever he might be with the daughter.

His person, moreover, would have rendered him no despicable wooer in the eyes of many a maiden. He was about the middle size, well made, and had a set of features upon the whole rather pleasing than otherwise, which were set off by small black eyes, possessing that peculiar twinkle which is sometimes expressive of humour, but much oftener indicates that species of cunning by which the man of the world can turn almost every circumstance in the lot of others to his own advantage. His physiognomy exhibited traits of a passionate disposition; but so carefully subdued, and concealed under an insinuating address, as to be scarcely noticeable. Both he and his father bore what is generally styled a respectable character in the neighbourhood, though obscure hints were sometimes given of undue advantages having been taken, and bargains pushed to the very verge of honesty. In short, such was the policy of the Bansters, that *perseverance in the process of accumulation* might have been their motto; and the result was, that, considering their station in society, and the poverty of the country in which they lived, they were uncommonly wealthy.

Alan Stewart, on the other hand, it was whispered, was induced to continue his attentions by encouragements of a less equivocal nature with which he was sometimes favoured by the maiden herself. He was taller than his rival, and equally well formed, nor were his features less regular, though they wore a very different expression. Taken altogether, he might be said to belong to a quite different caste. The distinguishing characteristics of the Stewarts had long been a high-minded honesty, which scorned alike to take advantage of the rich, or to oppress the poor. It was the internal self-rewarding principle, not the assumed and hollow show, upon which they acted. Alan might have been taken as a good specimen of the family character. He avoided the tricks of the bargain-maker, not because they might be discovered and subject him to contempt, but because he reckoned them in themselves mean and unworthy of a man. He sought no cover for his actions, and he never stooped to seek by art or intrigue what he could not obtain by plain dealing. The consequence of these principles, and this line of conduct, was that the Stewarts had never attained to anything like worldly wealth. But though they were not rich, their labour made them independent; and the strict integrity of their character commanded the respect of all who knew them.

William Turner was aware of all this. He acknowledged the high minded honesty and upright intentions of Alan, and he admired them; but he would have admired them still more had they been recommended by a little of that wealth, and a few of those worldly possessions, which would fall to the share of Black Ritchie at his father's death. The union, however, of such a character with a prosperous fortune, he knew, was a thing but rarely attainable. Experience had taught him to believe, that though the rich may preserve, and even augment their wealth, without any dereliction from duty, the poor, unless placed in very favourable circumstances, must be content to remain in their poverty, and look for the reward of their integrity, not to those wonderful and unexpected overflowings of wealth, which the poetical justice of story tellers sometimes bestows upon humble merit—but in that secret satisfaction which a consciousness of rectitude never fails to confer.

On the other hand, he could not conceal from himself several things, which he did not consider altogether commendable, in the conduct of Black Ritchie, although his expectations prevented him from looking upon them with that abhorrence which otherwise he would have done. Like most fathers, he would have preferred one who did not want for the good things of this world as a husband for his daughter. But, unlike some fathers, he could both appreciate the virtues of the poor and estimate the errors of the rich; and in this dilemma he determined to leave his daughter to choose for herself. But in taking this step she did not appear to be in any haste.

Though the spirit of persecution had been raging in the west for a considerable time previous to that of which we speak, hitherto Fife had remained tolerably quiet; and though the Covenanters in this quarter were both numerous and influential, as the agents of government had their hands full elsewhere, they had hitherto received but little molestation. But the successful attempt made upon the life of Archbishop Sharp was now destined to give a new impulse both to the persecutors and the persecuted,—the former becoming more zealous in their endeavours to root out and destroy, and the latter more determined in their resistance. Hackston, Balfour, and several others who had been present at that tragic affair, fled westward; and, as these were the principal leaders of the Covenanters in Fife, they were followed by many of the best and bravest men of the county, who deemed that they might be of more service to the cause for which they contended, by joining the great body of their distressed brethren in the west, than they could possibly be by their most strenuous efforts for its advancement in their scattered state at home.

Among those who thus went forth to succour their oppressed fellow-worshippers, and peril their lives for their religion, was Alan Stewart. Besides those considerations of duty, which were sufficient to justify him in taking this step, he had other motives for so doing, the source of which must be sought in human weakness. Though he had good reasons for believing that Jane secretly preferred him to every other, yet she was far from returning his affection with that tenderness which he imagined it deserved. Her manner was often capricious, and at times, as he thought, even unaccountable. With his head full of these reflections, he chanced one day to come suddenly upon her in a rural spot. He accosted her with all his wonted tenderness, and inquired after her health in the kindest manner. These inquiries she answered rather carelessly, and without lifting her eyes. This might be the effect of mere thoughtlessness, or it might be that she wished to enjoy his efforts again to establish himself in her favour.

There are times, however, when the mind is more prone to take offence at a supposed affront than it would be at others to resent a real injury. For this apparently cold reception, Alan was not prepared; and instead of pausing to ask an explanation, or to continue the conversation, he unconsciously assumed a haughty stride, and passed on.

"Is it thus," thought he to himself, after passing her, "that my affection is to be rewarded? does she answer my inquiries without turning on me a single look, as if I were an object of disgust?" And with these thoughts he walked off to chafe himself into a temporary fever of resentment.

This was a result perfectly unexpected by the other party. She felt as if she had done something wrong; and when she saw he did not stop, she gazed after him more wistfully, perhaps, than she had ever done before. Had he looked about at that moment, gladly would she have welcomed him back, and rallied him on his hastiness. But he cast no retrospective glance, and was soon out of sight.

"He disregards me," thought she to herself, when he had disappeared; "ay, he disregards me! and this is my reward for having preferred him to every other man on earth! Well, if he cares so little for me, he may yet learn that I care as little for him."

After this rencontre, they did not see each other for several days; and when they again met, his salutation was measured and distant, and her reply, if possible, more cold than before. This tended to make matters worse. Both wished for a reconciliation, but pride fairly forbade either to make the attempt.

—— How wayward is this foolish love,
That, like a testy babe, will scratch the nurse,
And presently, all humbled, kiss the rod?

. . . . . .
How angerly they taught their brows to frown,
When inward joy enforced their hearts to smile!

In this state of mind, absence, which under any other circumstances would have been reckoned a severe misfortune, appeared the only alternative. Accordingly, after having obtained his father's full consent, Alan set off to join the Western Covenanters, in the anticipation that distance might soften the poignancy of his reflections; and not without the hope that a temporary separation might work a favourable change on the object of his affections.

Hitherto, Jane Turner had never directly discountenanced the attentions of Black Ritchie. She had given him, indeed, but little encouragement, though, from deference to her father, she always treated him civilly, and never showed any marked dislike to his presence. This served to keep his hopes alive; and, now that his rival was out of the way, he grasped eagerly at the opportunity which thus presented itself for pressing his own suit more closely. He became unceasing in his attendance upon Jane—vilified Alan upon all occasions—misrepresented his motives, and decried his actions—boasted of his own wealth and expectations, and finally urged her, in the most pressing terms, to marry him.

To this proposal Jane was far from listening with a favourable ear. She had now become better acquainted with the true state of her own feelings; and his addresses, which she had before endured, rather than encouraged, became almost intolerable. Still, with that sensibility which is peculiar to females, she shrank from the idea of giving him pain, till the upbraidings of her own conscience forced her to the disagreeable alternative.

"No," said she, "it cannot be. I cannot love you. Why, then, should you urge me into a union, which, without affection, must prove a snare and a curse, instead of a blessing, to us both? In moments of light-heartedness and vanity, I may have tampered with your affections—I may have given you reason to think that I had no aversion to you. The recollection of this is bitter to me. Pardon the frailty which permitted it, if it has caused you pain; and let us cut off all occasion for such weaknesses in future; for, to do otherwise, would only be to add perjury to folly, and from this may God preserve us both!"

These words she pronounced in such a tone, and in such a manner, as to leave no doubt of her sincerity; and she firmly persisted in never afterwards giving him an opportunity of speaking to her in private.

But, as often happens in such cases, rejection, instead of allaying, served rather to increase his passion. Richard had long been accustomed to have everything his own way; and he could not submit to the idea of being baffled here, where his heart, naturally strong, though perverted by selfishness, was chiefly concerned. Hopeless as his suit now was with the maiden herself, he still imagined that he might be able to work upon her father, and, by fair speeches, induce him to interpose in his behalf. Minds more delicately formed would have hesitated before entering upon such a task; but an excess of delicacy was not among his faults. After duly prefacing his discourse with all necessary civility, he took advantage of every circumstance with which fortune seemed to favour him—his rival's poverty, and his abandoning his own friends, in a time of danger and alarm, to fight for strangers, as he termed them. And after expatiating on his own prospects, the extent of his abilities, and the unchangeableness of his affection, "I hope," said he, "that you will intercede with your daughter to prevent her from throwing herself away on one so utterly undeserving, and use that authority which every parent should possess over his own children, in bestowing her where she may have better things to expect."

Here, however, he had overshot his mark. He forgot that the person whom he addressed had himself never been rich. His attack upon the character of Alan Stewart was also inconsiderately made; and the worthy shepherd did not fail to discountenance it.

"Poverty," said he, "unless it should proceed from idleness or evil habits, is no disgrace. The poor man, who preserves his integrity, may be more honourable in the eyes of his Maker than the rich man who has no temptation to dishonesty; and why should he be less respected by his fellow creatures? Riches in this world, unless used for the purposes of benevolence and charity, form no passport to the next. The people of God have often been poor and persecuted, as at this day; and for those who stand back, when the lives of their fellow worshippers are in danger, and when tyrannical power would fetter, not only the hands and the feet, but the very thoughts of free-born men, were they called upon to make any great exertion for their friends, it is to be feared that selfishness, which makes them renounce their public duties, would also induce them to abandon their private ones. I am now old and unfit for journeying far; but had I been, as in the years of my youth ——"

"Pardon me!" interrupted the other—and as he spoke his wonted coolness seemed to have forsaken him. He appeared fluttered, and his voice gave signs of perturbation—" pardon me, I should have taken up arms myself, but that I could not think of being separated from the object of my affection. And when you have considered the comforts she will enjoy with me —comforts which she can scarcely expect with any other—I hope you will, at least, use your influence in my behalf."

"I will not stop," said the old man firmly, and drawing himself up to his full height as he spoke,—"I will not stop to rebuke your inconsistency. But for my daughter, had she, indeed, been throwing herself away, as you would insinuate, I should have deemed it my duty, as a father, to interfere; but I will neither compel nor advise her to marry any one contrary to her own inclination!"

"But were any thing to occur to prevent Alan from returning, surely I should be preferred to every other?"

"My daughter should still be free," was the reply; "free to choose for herself; nor would I interfere with her choice, unless it were a bad one."

"But still," said the other, in a voice in which rage and disappointment were strongly blended with an effort to appear calm—" but still——" here he stopped, and after a short pause resumed, his passion getting the better of his assumed calmness —"I will argue no more with you! I must contrive other means of procuring happiness than reasoning with one who is alike deaf to remonstrance and pity."

After this interview, to the great astonishment of his relations, he wandered about for two days moody and silent, and sometimes muttering to himself. On the evening of the third, he had in a great measure resumed his former manner; but before morning he had gone no one could tell whither.

Revolutionary struggles, and periods of civil commotion, never fail to bring to light talents and abilities which otherwise would have slumbered in obscurity. This, to a certain extent, was the case with Alan Stewart. He had joined the Covenanters previous to the affair at Drumclog; and his conduct in that short but desperate conflict attracted the notice of those who acted as leaders of the party. He was introduced to his countryman, David Hackston, and, through the agency of that gentleman, promoted to the post of training and disciplining such of the Fife men as from time to time joined their body. This was an arduous task. The art, which he had to teach others, he had himself to learn. But his heart was in the cause. He had caught the enthusiasm of the period, and, by perseverance and industry, he overcame every difficulty. Though dissensions, and a blind trust in Providence, rendered the west country army less formidable than it might have been, there were soldiers and brave men among them. From these he took lessons in military tactics—familiarising his mind with the art of war; and while he taught this to others, he became himself skilful in the use of his weapons.

The intervening period between the battle of Drumclog and that of Bothwell Brig, may be briefly passed over, as it imports but little to the present story. The spirit of fanaticism—the schisms and discordant feelings which pervaded the camp of the Covenanters are well known; but in these Alan took no part. On the contrary, he strove, though in vain, along with the more disinterested spirits of the time, to remove the causes of discontent and animosity.

On the fatal day of Bothwell, while by far the greater portion of the army, misled by their own feelings and the fanaticism of their preachers, were listening to a ill-timed discourse, the Fife company were among those who, for a time, successfully disputed the passage of the bridge. Headed by David Hackston of Rathillet, under whom Alan acted as a subordinate, they kept the enemy in check till their means of farther resistance were nearly exhausted. And when, in answer to their demand for a supply of ammunition, their infatuated brethren on the height had sent a barrel of raisins instead of gunpowder—when the hopelessness of their situation was discovered, and each one looked in the face of his fellow in the blackness of despair,—Alan, and the Fife men who were under his command, determined still to do everything in their power to cover the retreat, and save the lives of those who were now about to pay dearly for their inactivity.

With this intention, while many fled for their lives in every direction, Alan's little band retired slowly, and in good order, to a place where some vantage ground afforded a prospect of enabling them to offer a more protracted, though now hopeless, resistance. In this position they remained while the enemy's advanced guard were employed in cutting down the loiterers, and despatching those whose wounds prevented them from following the main body. But having now brought their cannon across the bridge, the unbroken front of the Fife company soon attracted notice. They began to play upon them with grape-shot; and a portion of their ranks having been swept down by this terrible species of missile, a troop of horse, who, falcon-like, had watched the opportunity, dashed at them in full career. But ere they could reach the destined prey, the ranks of this gallant band were re-united; and desperate was the struggle which followed. The discharge of pistols—the clash of swords—the curvetting of wounded horses, and the shouts of the soldiers, mingled with the shrill notes of the bugle, and the groans of those who were every moment falling mortally wounded, formed a scene which no language can describe. The dragoons had incurred some disgrace in a former affair with the Covenanters, and were eager to wipe it off, while those with whom they were engaged, as they neither asked nor expected quarter, and could not fly from such enemies, fought with a ferocity unknown in regular warfare. In this short, but desperate melée, there was one horseman who acted a conspicuous part. He seemed to be inspired with something more than the soldier's wish for fame. His brow was knit, and his dark eyes appeared to be lighted up by some deep-rooted feeling of hatred. His countenance seemed expressive of the savage ferocity of the secret assassin rather than the generous daring of the gallant soldier. In that desperate conflict, oftener than once had he singled out Alan Stewart as his victim, and as often had he been balked in his purpose by interposing foes. At last they met in what might have been deemed mortal strife, and for a few seconds success was doubtful. But the trooper, in his fiery zeal to destroy, soon gave his cooler opponent an opportunity of making a cut at his bridle. It succeeded; and the horse, missing the rein on one side, wheeled round: a second stroke, and the hamstrung animal rolled on the ground with his rider. This, however, would have availed little; for the ranks of the Fife company were now waxing thin, and those who remained fought with fearful odds. But just as they were on the point of being borne down by superior numbers, the adverse party were charged in flank by Hackston (now on horseback) and Balfour, who, at the head of a small squadron of cavalry, were doing all that men could to save the lives of their infatuated countrymen. This charge took the enemy by surprise, and, unable to stand the attack of this little band of heroes, most of whom were the veterans of many fights, they wheeled round and fled, leaving behind them many whose last fight was over. But they left also one still living, and unwounded, who had been disarmed ere he could extricate himself from his fallen horse, and who now stood, in the midst of his enemies, in sullen expectation of his fate. The same expression of deadly hatred was upon his countenance, but the fire of his eye was quenched in the fear of death. Still, he showed no sign of remorse, nor did he seem to shrink from that which he could not avert.

"Renegade and apostate!" said Alan Stewart, addressing himself to the disarmed trooper, "I spare thee for the name which thou bearest, and the home where thou wast nursed. Back to thy blood-thirsty crew! but when thou seest the defenceless before thee, spare them as thou hast thyself been spared!"

This was the last attempt at resistance on the part of the Covenanters. The flight and carnage had now become general, and the shattered remains of the Fife company took advantage of the momentary respite which was thus afforded them to make their escape.

Alan Stewart was among the few who escaped from the fatal field of Bothwell; and, after skulking for a few days till the heat of the pursuit was over, he deemed it best to return home. This, after innumerable escapes and hardships, he accomplished, and had the satisfaction to find his native parish still in a state of comparative tranquillity. The Presbyterian form of worship had been kept alive and fostered by Mr. Adamson, a zealous native preacher, without interruption. Alan's reception, too, at the North Cotton, was all he could have wished it. The smile with which Jane welcomed his return—the tear which trembled in her eye, and all but flowed down her cheek—and the tremour of her voice, which she in vain strove to overcome, as she answered his first questions,—these spoke a language which her lover well knew how to interpret. Separation and absence had taught her "a deep lesson." Time passed on. They were as happy in each other's affections as the troublous times in which they lived admitted of, and there appeared no obstacle to their speedy union.

## Chapter II.

It was now the month of September, but agriculture was then in a very indifferent state in the country, and harvest was not yet begun. Jane had gone to Sitmalane, a distance of little more than a mile, to visit an uncle, who was then lying ill, and Alan had gone thither in the evening to escort her home. The two had tarried till it was dark, that they might have the satisfaction of each other's company, unobserved, on their return. The night was cloudy, and fitful gusts of wind came rushing from the hills; but this to them was nothing. Arm in arm they descended the steep bank to the margin of the lake; and as they tracked its winding shore, they conversed in the low and earnest tones of confidential affection. But even when they spoke not, their souls seemed to hold converse, and their pace became gradually slower and slower.

After a pause, in which Alan felt half ashamed of keeping silence so long,—" This night," said he, " with its fitful breezes and threatening clouds, reminds me of one which I passed among some bushes, under the shelter of a rock, after the battle of Bothwell."

" Bothwell!—Oh, that is a terrible word!" said she to whom he addressed himself; " I shudder whenever I think of it," and she did shudder as she spoke. " The heaps of slaughter!—the hopes of many a hearth lying cold on that field! Oh, had you fallen!"

" But tell me, Alan," continued she, after a lapse of some minutes, " how could you, averse from cruelty—gentle and unoffending, as you have always been—deal the death-stroke, and shed the blood of your fellow-creatures?"

" I can scarce tell you," was the reply. " I have often turned away, with a sensation of horror not to be described, from seeing the deadly stab inflicted, by the hand of the butcher, on an inferior animal. And at Drumclog, after an engagement had become inevitable, a strange feeling shook my frame, as I looked on those around me, full of life, and strong in health, and thought how soon they might be weltering in their gore, or lying cold and mangled corpses; and in this feeling I almost forgot that the same fate might be awaiting myself. This agitation of mind continued, in all its force, till the foe were almost on us; and, when the word was given, my hand trembled as I raised my firelock to take aim; but, to my surprise, in a few seconds I became cool and collected, and a thousand lives appeared as nothing, when sacrificed in such a cause."

" But to die!" said Jane, " Oh! it must be terrible to think of that. I cannot yet comprehend those feelings of which you speak. To leave friends and kindred—all who love you, and all whom you loved! And then such a death!" she continued, her imagination portraying the horrors which her lover had escaped, "no friendly hand near to help—no pitying eye to shed a tear above you—no affectionate voice to speak the last farewell—but all around heaps of slain, and the dying groans of mangled wretches writhing in their last agonies! What can support the spirit in the prospect of such a scene?"

"My love," said he, "death on the field of battle is not, I think, so terrible as you have painted it; but even if it were, to the Christian, whose belief is in accordance with his profession, there is one great source of courage and consolation. It is this which supports the poor persecuted wanderer, under all his sufferings; and it is this which enables the martyr to meet death triumphantly at the stake or on the scaffold."

"Yes, yes," interrupted Jane, "I understand it now—the approbation of One."

"There is, moreover," continued he, "a something in the consciousness of being engaged in a just cause, which exalts the spirit above the fear of mere bodily suffering. There is a secret satisfaction in believing that the sacrifice of property, liberty, and even life itself, is made for the general weal, and that posterity may reap a harvest of happiness from the blood that is shed on a battle field, which inspires fortitude, and makes endurance its own reward. There is a sympathy extending itself to the humblest being who bears the human shape, and to the remotest futurity, which merges every selfish consideration, and all feelings of fear, in its own abyss, as the ocean drinks up the rivers—it is this sympathy, acting upon a powerful mind, which makes the patriot of humanity contemn the favour of kings and mighty men, wealth, idleness, and ease, and brave danger and death in their most terrible forms; accounting the life which he sacrifices in the cause of truth as a thing of no value."

As he concluded, his voice rose to a pitch of enthusiasm, and his eyes sparkled with deep feeling. Jane looked on her animated lover in silent admiration. After a pause, she spoke. "I wish I could emulate such glorious examples also. But I am only a woman; and my feelings have been doomed, by the weakness of my nature, to act in a narrower sphere."

"Why do you say so?" broke in her companion. "The nature of woman is susceptible of the noblest feelings that ever animated the heart of man."

"I will tell you why," was the answer. "I have often fancied that I could meet hardships, and endure torture, with patience; but it would have been only to save some dear friend from pain. I have imagined that I could encounter death; but it would have been to save the life of one,"—here she hesitated a moment, as if she had been about to utter something wrong, and then, with a strong effort, she proceeded,—"Yes, to save the life of one dearer than life. I have thought all this; but, among these, my heroic musings, the idea of enduring ought for others never came. It was only the belief, that you would cherish my memory, and love me when I was no more, that could have enabled me to suffer and to die without shrinking! But perhaps," she added, sinking her voice, " were I called upon to suffer in a common cause, or to die for conscience sake, God might give me strength to endure that also."

"He would! he would!" said the other, glad in this exclamation to find a vent for those feelings with which her confession had almost overpowered him. " Fear not for your fortitude: 'as thy day is, so shall thy strength be;' as the sympathies of women are ever more active, and their selfishness less strongly marked, so their patience in suffering is often greater than that of men."

"I know not that," said she, with a deep sigh ; " but I have more to tell. In those musings of which I spoke, I have fancied, that when I was gone, were Alan to love and marry another—pardon my weakness—the thought would diminish my happiness even in another world!"

"Alan will never love or marry another," said he to whom she spoke, and clasped the speaker to his bosom; " we will live and die together!"

As he concluded, there was a deep and solemn pathos in his voice. He would have continued, but their farther conversation was here interrupted.

The foot-path was on the side of a deep trench, which separated the arable land from the marsh. The space between this and the clear water was occupied by a boggy surface, covered with high grass and sedges, which were cut every year by the peasantry for fodder to their cattle in winter. Here our travellers were alarmed by the violent barking of a little dog which accompanied them; and on looking, they thought they could perceive men on the path before them. "They are soldiers," said Jane, in a whisper, while she almost trembled with apprehension ; " I see the glitter of their weapons." At the same moment, a harsh voice commanded them to " stand, if they were his Majesty's loyal subjects." This left no doubt; and as Alan was unarmed, their only chance of safety seemed to be in flight. Close to where they stood, a plank had been thrown over the ditch by the cottars, for the purpose of carrying out grass from the bog; over this they instantly crossed, and made their way, as silently as possible, among the sedges on the other side; while their pursuers—for they were now pursued—missed the narrow bridge, and fell into the trench. The bog, from the season of the year, was tolerably firm, so that the lovers found little difficulty in passing over it; while the sedges, in this place higher than a man's head, and the darkness, left no trace by which they could be followed, except the noise of their feet.

They were now at the south-eastern angle of the lake, where the deposits of a burn had covered the marsh with a firm crust of gravel and sand, brought down from the hills by its wintry torrents. Upon this bank they emerged from their sedgy cover, and in the darkness stumbled upon the moorings of a little shallop, which had been drawn up there as a place of safety. The circumstance appeared providential; and embarking as quietly as possible, they pushed from the shore. At that moment, the shadow of a dark cloud rested upon the bosom of the lake, rendering all objects alike invisible; and a hollow breeze, whistling through the reeds, chafed its surface, and made the waves fret against the shore, so that it was impossible to distinguish the dip of oars from the other sounds which prevailed.

"They must have been ghosts," said one of the foiled pursuers, who, to the number of ten or twelve, had now reached the place where they had just departed; "or, if they were human beings, the devil hath carried them off bodily; for it was *here* that I heard the last sound of their tread, and now, *here* is nothing save darkness; these confounded winds and waters seem to be laughing at our disappointment."

"They were no ghosts," said another of the party, in a voice which Jane distinctly heard, and which seemed not altogether that of a stranger, though so altered that she could not recollect when or where she had met the speaker; "it was no ghost. I could swear to the voice of one of them at least. Curse on the day I first saw her!—and to escape me thus! But no matter, say I, for the present. Come, my lads, we have other game afoot, which will better pay us for the hunting down; you know what the Curate hath promised if we succeed."

These words contained a mystery which Jane could not unravel. She did not dare to speak for fear of a discovery; and Alan, who was now propelling their little vessel with a full stroke, heard them not. He made directly for the easternmost of the willow-covered islands, as a temporary resting-place, where they might consider what were best to be done. Having found it, and drawn in the boat, he proposed to leave it and Jane at the island, and swimming quietly ashore by himself, try to procure some of their friends to assist in escorting her home. "Anderson," said he, "or Galloway, or any of the Bothwell men at Lindores, will be ready at a word."

To this Jane strongly objected. Peril only served to strengthen the tie which bound her to Alan; and to quit his side when his freedom, or even his life, might be more in danger than her own, appeared worse than death. Yet she felt her spirit rise superior to fear; and though she spoke with emphasis there was neither tremor nor hesitation in her voice. "No," said she, "why should they seek me? I have been guilty of no crime, and you have been at Bothwell; this they may construe into a crime. But if there is danger before you I will share it, and if it be death let me die by your side; if we stay, let us stay together; and if you go I will accompany you."

This island is not far from the shore. The bank jutting into the lake diminishes the watery distance; and, while the lovers thus conversed, their notice was attracted by human voices almost opposite to where they were. "Alan was a fool," said one, "for sparing the life of an enemy who would not have spared him."

"Fool or wise man," said another, "with sixty such as Alan, to the hundred of our foes, they would have fled before us like sheep before the shepherd's dog."

In the voice of the speakers Alan immediately recognised Anderson and Galloway, the individuals of whom he had formerly spoken. "My love," said he, "these are our friends; we may both go with safety now." And in a minute more the white foam was flashing from the prow of the little boat as she cleft the waters for the shore.

Anderson and Galloway were accompanied by five others, all of whom had been at Bothwell. One of their number had seen soldiers arrive at the Grange in the forenoon, and, after alarming his companions, they had kept concealed till nightfall. Believing themselves to be the principal object of this mission, they had determined to seek some place of security farther off for a season, but not till they apprised Alan of their intentions, and invited him to join them. This was their present errand, and they travelled armed.

Alan narrated the escape which they had just made. And

on Jane's mentioning what she had heard about the "game" to be hunted,—"Well," said Anderson, "should we chance to meet them to-night, if they are not too many, we may give them hunting till they are tired of it. But when you speak of the Curate," he added, addressing Jane, "I guess *their* game must be Mr. Adamson."

"If such should be the case," said Alan, "God grant we may be able to defeat their purpose!"

Ruminating upon these circumstances, they began to track the shores of the loch in the direction of Waaltower, without any fixed purpose, but not without the hope that they might be of some service to their pastor, who, they had heard, was to attend a dying man at a cottar town upon their road.

For some time past the east had given signs of the approaching moon. She now rose above the horizon, and her light made distant objects visible. The northern sky was covered with a dense body of dark vapour, from which ever and anon large masses of cloud were detached, and, being driven upward, pursued their way to the zenith in sublime confusion. The wind, which before had only breathed occasionally with a sort of whistling cadence, now sounded, among the distant woods, like the fall of waters rising at uncertain intervals and then floating away upon the wings of silence. The whole seemed to indicate the approach of one of those nights in which terrible gales, accompanied by hail and rain, alternate with seasons of the deepest calm.

The party proceeded quietly along the margin of the lake till they came to where the path diverges from the level shore to climb the ascent to the houses on the hill. But, before quitting the water's edge, their attention was arrested by a confused noise of voices. They had scarcely concealed themselves among the bushes and brushwood when they heard the deep and sonorous voice of a man earnestly expostulating with some others who appeared to be dragging him away contrary to his inclination.

"Listen to me for a moment," said the pastor, for it was he. "Here are none to oppose you. Suffer me to return and speak a word of comfort to that dying man, from whose bed-side ye took me, and to offer up a prayer for the welfare of his immortal soul ere it depart and be no more!—then will I accompany you cheerfully and in peace."

"Accompany us cheerfully and in peace as it is, reverend father," said one of the party whom he addressed; "and try to move your feet a little faster, or we may find means to quicken your pace for you. Take his arm, Gilbert," he continued, addressing one of his companions, "and we will assist the good man on his journey heavenward."

While this discourse was going on Alan and his friends lay quiet in their place of concealment; and after listening for a time,—"Our conjectures were right," said Galloway, in a whisper. "It is our faithful pastor in the hands of his enemies!"

"It is too sure," said Anderson, in the same under tone. "But if they compass his captivity it shall be with a redder price than their victory at Bothwell cost them!"

"Let us on them, then," exclaimed the other; "the sooner the better."

"Nay, nay," rejoined Anderson, "that were a foolhardy step. Hear ye not the moaning of the winds behind us? It has been steady for the last five minutes. And see ye not the heavens how they darken? I am mistaken for once if the elements come not to assist us. Let us bide their time. Our feet are not tied: we may hunt the hunters a little. Nor will our courage, I trust, evaporate for our keeping it a few minutes. And mark me: this squall once come, the prey is in our hands, and they, at least, shall set the snare no more for the innocent, nor seek the slaughter of the unoffending!"

Alan, meantime, was endeavouring to calm what he conceived would be the fears of Jane; but of his efforts she stood less in need than he had imagined. The near approach of danger, the distant growl of the coming storm, and the fate which too surely awaited the prisoner—were he allowed to remain in the hands of his enemies,—in the excitement of the moment, tended to awaken a sentiment within her to which she had hitherto been a perfect stranger.

Alan, on the other hand, felt that he wanted that alacrity which animated him to rush into danger and defy death at Drumclog and Bothwell. He had now a new tie to bind him to the world; and, for the sake of protecting her, he felt as if he could have almost played the coward, and remained behind in the projected attack. She, however, seemed to read his thoughts in the embarrassment of his manner; for, laying her hand gently on his arm, with a voice in which a slight tremor bespoke her affection for him rather than fear for herself,—
"Go," said she; fear not for me: I will call on the God of battles, that he may give you success, and spare the effusion of blood. I would I were a man, that I might fight by your

side, and restrain your hand in the moment of triumph. But I forget——"

The wind blew louder every minute. The first drop of rain now began to rattle to the ground, and she was interrupted in what she would have said by Anderson inquiring if Alan was armed.

"No," was the reply.

"Here, then, is my gun," said he, as he put his heavy firelock into his hand. "I have a sword which will stand me in better stead. She carries exactly six inches and a half on the fire at a hundred yards distance; at thirty you may take dead aim—mark that, and her ball whistles true."

The blast came, as had been anticipated. The wind blew a perfect hurricane; and the rain mingled with hail, poured down in such torrents that the earth seemed to smoke beneath its violence like a smouldering furnace. The soldiers, with their prisoner, were now two hundred yards distant, and the whole party started at a brisk pace in the pursuit.

"Oh, take not life if ye can help it!" they could hear Jane say, as they departed.

The storm, which raged with terrible violence, beat directly on their backs; and the moon, breaking from an unclouded part of the southern sky, gave them a distinct view of their enemies. To overtake them was only the work of a few minutes; but such was the fall of rain, that, before they reached them, fire-arms were of no use. The soldiers had no idea of being pursued till they were commanded to "Let go" their prisoner. At this hasty summons they faced suddenly about, and made an effort to fire upon those who gave it. Not a gun, however, went off; and, before they could recover from their surprise, the others rushed upon them with their swords, while they, blinded by the storm, which beat furiously in their faces, could neither see the number nor appearance of those by whom they were attacked; and, after making a few random strokes, they turned, and fled before the elements, rather than from the power of their enemies. The whole was but the work of a moment; and Mr. Adamson was again free. But, in the first onset, there was one among the soldiers who appeared more loth to fly than his fellows. Anderson had rushed on him, and knocked him to the earth without wounding him, and he now stood over his fallen foe with his sword lifted high to sever his head from his body. A moment more, and the deed had been done; but Alan, who saw his purpose, took the blow upon the barrel of his gun.

"What do you mean?" asked Anderson, with some warmth.
"Don't you know him?" said the other.
"I do," was the reply; "but what of that?"
"We must not trample on the fallen," said Alan. "To do so were to degrade ourselves beneath our persecutors."

"As you will, then," rejoined the other; while the soldier, getting upon his feet, took the opportunity to follow his companions with what speed he might. "But, confound it!" he continued, "I believe you have made me hack the barrel of my own good gun in two, instead of cleaving that recreant's skull; for, in truth, I had given both heart and hand to the job—and to strike an old friend instead of an ass's head! My good Ferara, too!" he continued, examining the gun and his sword at the same time—"better steel was never hardened by fire and water. But I fear it has met with more misfortune here than a' the hard hacks of Mary's popish hallions ever brought it." The barrel of the gun was indeed deeply notched; but the edge of the trusty blade was uninjured.

This conversation was interrupted by Mr. Adamson, who, raising his voice with solemn emphasis amid the storm, said, "My friends, let us thank God, who hath given us a bloodless victory. It was in him I did put my trust, and lo! he hath sent you to my deliverance; and, that ye might speed in your errand, he hath summoned forth the storm to fight for us. To his name be the honour and the glory."

Jane's happiness at the accomplishment of their purpose without the shedding of blood, was felt rather than expressed; and as Alan again took her hand, her eye beamed in that uncertain light with those feelings for which she found no words.

Though the storm still continued to rage, and though they were still in danger from the rallying of their enemies, the next care of the watchful pastor was to return to the bedside from which he had been taken. But the sight of the soldiers, and the confusion and terror which they had occasioned, had quenched the last feeble flickerings of life in the bosom of the dying man, and the scene was changed from that painful suspense and suppressed sorrow which precede the last moments of human life, to wailing and lamentation for the dead. Here, therefore, they made no tarry, but pursued their journey in a body to the North Cotton, where they hoped to rest safe for the night, it being a place difficult of access, except in the day-time, and otherwise not likely to be suspected.

Here they arrived, drenched with the rain; and, having

satisfied the good old shepherd as to what had occasioned his daughter's stay, and dried their clothes before a blazing fire, with which his hospitality soon provided them, it became necessary that they should determine on what course they were to follow. On this subject the opinions were various, and the debate was warm. Some were for going into concealment, or fleeing to distant parts of the country; others were for quitting it altogether, and seeking in America that freedom which, they said, was denied them in their native land; while Anderson, with characteristic hardihood, proposed that they should embody themselves, and brave their enemies to the teeth while a man remained. "Who knows," said he, "but we may make the Sheels Brig retrieve the disgrace of Bothwell, and send our own Black Cairn down to posterity associated with the heights of Drumclog? What say ye to fighting for our rights, instead of fleeing for our lives?"

With this proposition Alan would have coincided. He felt strongly inclined to do so; but he knew the licentious brutality of the soldiery, and there was one, now deservedly dear to him, who, he feared, might be exposed to all its consequences by such a course. He therefore was silent. Not so their venerable pastor.

He said, he doubted not but that it was the intention of the Prelatical party to annoy the Presbyterians of the neighbourhood in general, and himself in particular, to the extent of their power; and that for this purpose the soldiers had been brought from the West. "But why should we fear?" he added: "let us not shrink from our duty, though it may be attended with danger; the reward is only promised to those who strive. Let us raise up our voices against our oppressors even in the day of their power, and assert, as God shall give us strength, that freedom which he hath conferred on all his rational creatures, though wicked rulers, for the present, have wrung it away. Self-preservation might prompt us to flee from this unhappy country; but let us remember, that to flee is not always to escape danger; and moreover, were no one to act from higher principles, tyranny and injustice might become co-existent with time. This cannot be! Justice shall yet flow down our streets as a stream, and judgment as the mighty waters! Yes, justice must ultimately triumph over oppression, and truth scatter error, as the coming of the morning scattereth the shadows of night. We know not what are the purposes of Providence concerning us—whether we may be honoured, as the small beginnings of a great and glorious consummation; or whether darkness must still rest upon us for a season. But let us obey the still small voice of conscience, which biddeth us be bold in the cause of freedom and of truth—for your own rights, and for those of your children; and though ye should fall by the sword, and your flesh become food for the ravens, and your bones whiten the fields like the snows of winter, yet it may be that Providence will raise up a seed from your ashes, who may put to flight the oppressors of conscience, and triumph over the enemies of religious liberty. My brethren, is it not so?"

This short address produced a decisive effect; for in those days the teachers and the taught were mingled: they were knit in the bonds of friendship, and their cause was a common one.

In accordance with these sentiments, a day was appointed for a general meeting in the fields to worship God. The place of meeting was to be the hollow on the hill, to the southward of the Cairn, where, from the nature of the ground, they could not be discovered at any great distance. It was agreed that they should assemble early; that as many as could procure arms should wear them for the defence of themselves and their fellow-worshippers; and that watches, or sentinels, should be placed on the most commanding points of their station, to prevent them from being surprised by any sudden attack. With this agreement, and the understanding that those present were to give notice of the meeting, as quietly and as extensively as possible, among their friends, they parted.

But let us now follow Black Ritchie. This individual, on his suit being rejected, sank into a sort of moody despondency, which soon terminated in the most implacable hatred, not only to his rival, but even to the object of his former affection, and a determination, if possible, to ruin both. To effect this the civil and religious discords of the time offered the readiest means. He never doubted that the Government party would prove the strongest, and, procuring secretly a recommendation from the Curate of the parish to Claverhouse, he set off to join them in the West, without acquainting any one with his purpose. But Claverhouse's troop being at the time full he found a place in another regiment, where his animal courage, and abhorrence of the Covenanters—qualities at that time held in high estimation—procured him speedy promotion. The licentious life of a soldier, and the rapine and cruelty in which he was daily engaged, soon extirpated the last remnants of humanity, and gave the worst passions a perfect predominance over him. The victory at Bothwell accelerated the time for gratifying his private revenge; and by his representations in private letters to the Curate of the ease with which a military force might be procured, and the solicitations of the Curate in the proper quarter, a party of a hundred horse were sent to propagate the tenets of those in power at the sword's point. Among these he held a commission, and, as he was a great favourite with the officers who commanded them, he had a principal share in directing their operations. On the day of their arrival he learned by accident the place where Mr. Adamson might be found; and, after night-fall, taking along with him a dozen of his followers, he determined to try the experiment of making him prisoner before it should be known that they were in the neighbourhood. In this expedition they encountered Alan and Jane. Though both of these escaped, as has been already narrated, he was near enough to hear that voice, the tones of which had once made his heart thrill. His ideas of love, which had never been of the purest kind, were now much changed for the worse. The sound of her voice, and the idea of being so near her, brought her charms forcibly before his polluted imagination; and, by obtaining possession of her person, an opportunity now seemed to present itself of gratifying his passion, and satisfying his revenge at the same time. That the accomplishment of these foul projects might be more complete, he wished, if possible, to effect her ruin with her own consent, which, he doubted not, some favourable opportunity would enable him to obtain. And if this should fail him, it mattered little, as the means of snatching success were now, he supposed, within his reach.

Chapter III.

On the appointed morning the family of William Turner were early astir. Alan Stewart was also with them; and, after their morning devotions had been duly performed, and an early breakfast hastily despatched, they armed themselves and prepared to depart. The place of meeting, though out of sight, was only at a short distance; and, for some hours previous, numbers of country people had been seen flocking to it, in the dusk of the morning, by the most unfrequented paths.

"Jane," said Alan, as they were on the point of setting off, "I am sorry you cannot accompany us."

She did not speak, but held out her hand to him. He

clasped it in his, and both seemed to labour under some strange feeling for which neither could account; but it was only momentary, and she bade him adieu with a smile.

Jane was left behind to notice her father's flock, and attend to the wants of her mother, who was then infirm and old. And when her father, lover, and brothers were gone she busied herself in the performance of these duties—now in the house attending the wants of her mother,—now gathering the sheep, with her father's dog, when they attempted to scatter; and, when neither of these required her attention, leaning over her Bible by one of those gnarled trees which stood beside the dwelling, and reading from its pages. But, in spite of her assiduity, a heaviness was at her heart—a lowness of spirits hung over her, and something like those forebodings of approaching calamity, for which no one can account, seemed to oppress her mind. The train of her thoughts became solemn, and she turned to the Lamentations of Jeremiah. The pathetic wailings of the prophet over the desolate temple, ruined cities, and fallen glory of his people, were in unison with the tone of her thoughts, and she became deeply interested in that strain of mourning and woe. While thus engaged she was startled by a step stealing towards her, and, on looking up, a man stood before her without the dress, but with the arms of a soldier. Her surprise was yet increased when in the features of the intruder she discovered those of her former lover, Black Ritchie.

"Jane," said he, with a voice in which an attempt at tenderness struggled with the insolent tones of authority, "can you forgive me for leaving you? If you only knew what I have sacrificed to see you again ——"

The sight of a disagreeable object recalled her wandering thoughts, and she interrupted him by boldly demanding, "What injury have you done me that you should ask forgiveness? I never wished your stay."

"I know you did not," said he; "but if you only knew the affection which I had for you, and have still, you would not treat me thus."

At this appeal she felt touched. She felt as if she could have pitied him; but she felt also that firmness was indispensable. "My heart is already given to another," said she, "and my hand is promised. If you loved me, as you say, you would cease to urge a suit to which I cannot listen."

"But are you aware," said he, "what you have to expect with him to whom you have rashly given your heart, and promised your hand? Do you know that he has carried arms against his king, and that his life is forfeited to the laws of his country?"

"I know that he was in arms," she replied; "and I only esteem him the more for perilling his life in the cause of those who could offer him no reward. *He* did not forsake the faith of his fathers."

The sarcasm, which these words implied, was not without its effect on him to whom they were addressed. He felt that to consideration of this sort he could lay no claim. He, too, had perilled his life, but for what? The comparison would have thrust itself upon him, but he was a man of the world.

"You may esteem him still," said he, "but take the advice of a friend, and leave him to his fate. He has been guilty of high treason, and he must soon pay the ransom with his life. Think what you could do then."

"I could die with him," was the brief but energetic reply. "Selfishness is the bane of this world's attachments; but where true affection exists, it is a stranger."

"Jane," said he, emphatically, "you do not know your own heart when you talk thus. His feet are already in the snare. His enemies have concerted their measures so as to render escape impossible. If you knew the certainty of his fate, you would not speak of dying with him; but try, by every means in your power, to cultivate the affections of those who may be able to afford some protection to you and your relations in times like the present."

"Were my heart again free, I would only cultivate the affections of those whom I deemed worthy of my esteem and love," replied Jane, warmly. "But who has set the snare of which you speak, and who is it has brought his enemies hither? Is this your doing?" Though these were questions which he might have expected, he felt his cunning at a loss to answer them. After a moment's pause, "Ritchie," she continued, "they say you are among those who have denied the faith which you once pretended to profess; and that you took an active share in the massacre at Bothwell. Is this true?"

At a loss what to say, "Has he told you that too?" he stammered out.

"No," was the reply. "But I have been told by those who saw you there."

"Well, Jane," said he, "I will not attempt to deny it; nor can I regret it deeply when I reflect on the protection which this circumstance may enable me to extend to you and yours, if you only accept my offer, and say that you will love me."

"Ritchie," said she, drawing herself up and speaking with emphasis, "I never could bring myself to despise you till now! You have become an apostate from the faith of your fathers; you have united yourself to the enemies of your country, and imbrued your hands in the blood of its best friends; and now you have brought these enemies here to hunt, like blood-hounds, for their prey; and for this you ask my love, and promise me protection on condition that I should basely abandon those who are deservedly dear to me, and sell myself to you for the sordid prospect of a wretched life with one so worthless!"

The energy with which she spoke went far to convince Black Ritchie that the first part of his game was already played, and without success; but he determined to make one other cast and see what luck awaited him. "No," said he, "it is not you alone whom I would protect: I may be able to save your friends also. Think of your father and brothers, and the treatment they have to expect from merciless soldiers! The place of their meeting on the hill is known to their enemies. A party of dragoons, strong enough to cut every man of them to pieces, are already on their way to attack them; and, unless I interpose, no power on earth can save them from their fate. Think of this, and tamper with me no longer."

"I will not tamper with you," said she, fixing on him a look which, abandoned as he was, he knew not well how to abide. "You have brought the wolves of your party on the sheep of another's fold. But their Shepherd, if He will, can protect them from the rage of their foes; nor think that He will long suffer the wicked to pass unpunished, or that you can long prosper with innocent blood on your hands, and the blackest perfidy in your heart. Yet, for yourself, save them if you can. It may wash a stain from your guilty conscience, and avert a pang from your dying bed! Do this, and you will have from me that regard which a generous action always deserves. For the lives of those who are dear to me I will respect and ——" love you, she would have said; but she shrank from uttering the word to which her sincerity was a stranger.

His hopes of success from the means to which he had hitherto trusted were now at an end. The hour when his presence would be required elsewhere was, moreover, approaching. "I see," said he, and as he spoke he looked at his watch, "it is in vain to argue longer with you; but I now bitterly repent me of my former conduct"—this he said in a whining tone—"and, to convince you that I am not so bad as you suppose, if you will only lead me the nearest way to the place where your friends are assembled on the hill I will warn them of their danger, and point out to them the only way which remains of escaping from certain destruction. But make haste; for I see there is no time to lose." As he concluded he put up his watch, which hitherto he had held in his hand as if to note the hour exactly, though, it may be supposed, he kept it only as something at which to look while palming what he knew to be a deception on the innocent girl who stood before him.

Gladly, and without a moment's hesitation, did Jane embrace this proposal, and with a hasty step she led the way to the hill. At another time the circumstances might have caused her to hesitate and suspect; but the words "certain destruction," and "no time to lose," left neither room for suspicion, nor time for delay.

The sun was now high in heaven, and the sky without a cloud. The landscape around presented a scene of calm and tranquil beauty. The fields of grain, almost ready for the sickle, nodded in the vales below, and adorned the slopes of the receding mountains with a rich yellow. Farther off, the Tay, now bright in the sunshine, and the dark masses of Clatcher-craig, frowning over it, gave relief to the eye. Immediately beneath them, the lake lay expanded in sleeping beauty, reflecting all the gorgeous hues on its banks, and the varied scenery of hill and corn-field on its unruffled bosom, while the Grampians, in the extreme distance, already crested with snow, shut in the prospect. But neither of them paused to look upon the scenery. Jane was too anxious for the safety of those who were dear to her, to think of aught save the means of facilitating their escape; and the mind of Black Ritchie was too much occupied with that infamous scheme, to the completion of which he now looked forward, to enjoy the charms of inanimate nature.

In a few minutes they reached those regions where the process of cultivation had never come, and threaded their way among the long broom, and furze bushes, pruned into conical shapes by the sheep that browsed their tender shoots in winter, —Jane, to whom the way was familiar, always going before. Oftener than once had he come close up to her with the intention of speaking; but upon these occasions she always quickened her pace, and he drew back as if he either wanted words to express his purpose, or was awed into silence by her extreme beauty, and the firmness which she had already displayed. A struggle between his lawless passion, and the remains of shame, or some other feeling which he had not been able entirely to banish, was evidently taking place in his bosom; but his brute propensities having of late been accustomed to unbridled scope, he soon appeared to master this sentiment, whatever it was, and only waited for a fitting opportunity.

The path on which they were—formed partly by sheep, and partly by foot-passengers—led over the very summit of the Cairn. They had reached a small hollow, or rather open space, immediately below it on the north side; and here, pushing suddenly past her, he turned round, and looking her full in the face, "Jane," said he, "you must stop till I speak to you. The violence of my passion has made me deceive you: I cannot save either yourself or your friends, unless you yield to my wishes even here—you understand me!"

There was a fire in his eye, and an indescribable something in his manner, as he uttered these words, which seemed to suspend alike the powers of speech and motion in the maid whom he addressed; and she stood, for a moment, petrified as it were before him, as his guilty purpose, of which she had not even dreamed, flashed upon her. Her situation was indeed terrible. A dreary silence reigned around them, and no living creature was in view to whom she could apply for help.

"You have nothing to hope from resistance," he continued, after a pause. "Your friends are too far away to hear your cries, or render you any assistance. I know the very spot where they are assembled, and every thing connected with their proceedings. I even knew that I would find you alone to-day."

Hopeless as was her situation, she had yet one resource— that trust in a Supreme Being which conscious rectitude of purpose, and previous freedom from great offences, in connection with religious habits, alone can bestow—a trust which, though it does not, and cannot always ward off evil, never fails to exercise a sublime influence on the mind, and to support it under adversity, when mere worldly motives might prove too weak. It was this which prevented her from sinking into despair, and giving up all for lost. The short interval which elapsed while he was speaking, had enabled her to collect fortitude for the occasion; and when she spoke, it was with a firmness which could hardly have been expected.

"There is a God above!" said she, "whose eye is now upon us. In his hands I trust my innocence. He can preserve it."

"Ay," said the other, in whose face his own tumultuous and guilty passion now flushed with a fevered redness, " but without a miracle that God, of which you speak, cannot rescue you out of my hands; and do you think he will work one for such as you? But I have no more time to waste."

With these words he advanced a few steps towards her, while she retreated so as to preserve the distance between them still undiminished; but some unseen power arrested him in his purpose for a moment, and both again stood still. The extremity of her fate now seemed to be approaching. She breathed a silent prayer; and as her eye turned upward, in the act of devotion, she caught a glimpse of a well-known figure on the height above them.

"Yonder," said she, "is a man on the Cairn."

"Where?" said the savage, in a tone of surprise and disappointment, as he turned to look for the object of which she had spoken; but observing nothing, he again turned toward her with increased insolence, like one who expects to drive a better bargain from having discovered a deception in the article he was about to purchase—"where is this deliverer of yours? Has he hid himself, like an owl who is ashamed to show its face in daylight, or melted into air, like a ghost at the crowing of the cock?"

"He disappeared but just now behind the bushes," was the reply.

"Come, come," said he, "this is a mere scheme to gain time, but it is found out, and can avail you nothing." As he spoke, he advanced close up to her, and as she did not now retreat, he stretched out his right hand to lay hold of hers, still holding his carbine in the other; but before he could touch her, he was grasped by a powerful arm from behind. In a moment the carbine was wrenched from his grasp, and thrown to a distance, and Alan Stewart stood before him.

As one of the watchmen, Alan had been stationed on the Cairn. He had marked the approach of Black Ritchie; and guessing that his intentions could not be good, but loth to alarm the meeting for a single individual, he determined, if possible, to make him his prisoner for the time, and succeeded in surprising him at the very moment when he fancied he was about to achieve his guilty purpose.

This was no meeting for explanation. The eyes of Black Ritchie shot forth "living fire!" Once he had been foiled in fight by Alan—self-love made him attribute it to accident—and twice had he owed his life to him. To be under such obligations to the man he hated served but to stimulate his hatred. With frantic haste he unsheathed his sword, and, uttering an awful imprecation, dashed at the individual who but a moment before might have shot him dead, or stabbed him to the heart, with far less trouble than it cost to take his carbine.

Alan had only time to unsheathe his own weapon when he was attacked; and for a few seconds the combat was kept up by the one party with a fury which resembled that of inspired madness, while the other satisfied himself with parrying the thrusts, and warding the blows which were aimed at him, till the rage of his opponent should exhaust itself. This task a consciousness of superior strength and skill enabled him to perform without any great exertion. With admirable dexterity did he defend himself from the most reckless thrusts and desperate blows, foiling every attempt made at his life by his opponent. The contest was by no means equal. Ritchie soon began to suffer from the violent efforts which he had been making. In a short time he was almost wholly at the mercy of his antagonist, who, with a sweeping stroke, carried his sword out of his hand, leaving him apparently defenceless. The habitual benevolence of Alan would have probably prevailed once more, but he was not allowed time for its exercise; for no sooner was Ritchie deprived of his sword than he drew a pistol, which he had concealed about his dress, and holding it close to the other's head, fired. Alan succeeded in turning up the muzzle of the weapon so far as to save his life, and the flash only scorched his face.

Jane's feelings during the conflict it would be difficult to describe. The sight of two men engaged in desperate strife was what she could ill endure to behold; yet the interest which she took in one of them riveted her to the spot. The glancing of the weapons in the sun—the ringing sound which they emitted, as they repeatedly clashed against each other, and the uncertainty that death might be in every blow which descended—kept her in an agony of feeling; and while the combat lasted, she trembled in every nerve for the safety of one who was but too dear to her. But when she saw the sword fly from the hand of his enemy, the *woman* in her heart prevailed, and for a moment she shared the triumph of her lover. The sight of the pistol again struck her with deadly horror; and when she saw it fired, it seemed as if all the lightnings of heaven had scorched her heart. She closed her eyes on what she conceived the death scene of her lover; and, as the lids were drawn downward by an unnatural action of the nerves, she only found power to open them again when she heard Alan, with a stern voice, address his enemy in these words: "Call on God to forgive your sins, and prepare to die!"

To this Black Ritchie made no answer. His only regret was that he had not succeeded according to his intention; and to have asked pardon from Heaven would have been to acknowledge guilt, and give the conqueror cause to triumph. He was silent, and his days had then been numbered. But Jane no sooner saw Alan look at his sword's point, and read his stern purpose in his eye—that eye in which she had so often looked with the stealthy fondness of a first affection—than pity took possession of her heart, and, forgetting the doom which he had decreed her, and the agony of terror from which she had so lately suffered, she rushed forward to intercede for the life of the vanquished.

Women are ever ready to overlook misdeeds in misfortune. Sympathy is the source of their " weakness and their strength." "Alan," said Jane, "spare him, I beseech you, that he may have time to repent of his crimes. To me he would have proved—" She checked herself, conscious that the disclosure would operate the wrong way, and concluded with—" If you could see his heart you would let him go!"

"If his guilt has been great," said Alan, "he has the less reason to expect mercy."

"I neither ask nor expect it," said Ritchie, sullenly.

"Eternity is an awful word!" said Jane, without noticing him, "and he is not prepared for it. But haste," she added, the recollection of what he had told her at that instant recurring,—" Leave him in the hands of his maker, and let us hasten to the meeting. He told me, before we left the house, that a party of dragoons were on their way to cut these unoffending worshippers to pieces. Haste, haste, and let us give them warning!"

This was indeed no reason for allowing him to live—rather the contrary. But, with Alan, that gentle voice had never pleaded in vain. He could, it is true, take the life of an enemy in a battlefield, and in the heat of an engagement, without much remorse; but coolly and deliberately to inflict a mortal wound on one who lay weaponless before him—his heart revolted at the idea. He abandoned his purpose; and casting on his vanquished enemy a look of mingled pity and contempt, "Come," said he to Jane, as he took her hand, "let us go;" and with these words they hurried off on their monitory errand, leaving Ritchie to his own meditations.

Black Ritchie followed them with his eyes as they ascended the Cairn, and while thus employed the very demon of madness seemed to revel in his heart. After a world of cunning and sophistry to find that his diabolical scheme was cut short at the very moment when success seemed certain, and to see the object of his selfish solicitude led off in triumph by his rival— himself, too, mastered in fight before her eyes, and then left as one whose life was not worth taking. These thoughts stung him like a thousand furies, and he walked to and fro, almost bursting with rage, till his eye fell on the spot where his own loaded carbine was lying.

Jane and Alan were soon over the height. They shot down the declivity on its farther side, and crossed the narrow hollow where the broom and brushwood, on either hand, rose higher than their heads. But as they were pressing up the short ascent, which now lay before them, to reach the table-land above, the report of a gun awoke the mountain echoes—a ball whizzed through the air—a quick shiver of the hand he held in his alarmed Alan—a lightning thought of the cause shot through his heart, and he turned his head with eager haste. But, while in the act, the maiden at his side bent forward, staggered, and, despite of his efforts to support her, fell to the earth. To his inquiries she made no answer, and he could not repeat them; nor was it necessary—all was already explained. Her eyes were still raised to his; but there was a deep languor in their expression, and in her bosom he saw blood. He gazed on her for a moment as she lay there, and that moment was in itself an eternity. It was one of those moments which stamp impressions on the hearts of men which future years have no power to wear away—a moment never to be forgotten.

The shot had not been intended for her, but the half frantic miscreant had either mistaken his aim or the ball had not proved true to the direction he gave it.

She was not dead: and after breathing for the space of a minute she found strength to speak. "Alan," said she, in a voice scarcely audible, but which was heard distinctly by her lover, who bent over her in that indescribable state of feeling when the ear is stretched to catch even the faintest breathing, "Alan—dearest—I cannot tell you now how dear to me—you have been—The day of our earthly love, I feel,—is nearly done—The happiness—the endearing tenderness, in the prospect of which—my spirit lived, these were not reserved for me, —I—had made you my idol!—But—the—dragoons ——." Here her voice failed her.

Alan could only press her hand in reply. But, mastering the weakness of his sorrow, and gathering strength for the terrible emergency in which he was placed, with the utmost tenderness he raised her in his arms, and with a speed resembling that of the hunted deer—a speed which no common motive could have supplied—he bore her lightly over heathery knoll and furze-covered bank to the meeting of the Covenanters. The alarm had been already given. Their other sentinels had apprized them of the approach of cavalry; and the service was hastily concluding as he laid down his lovely, but more than half-lifeless burden.

The sympathy of those present for the beautiful sufferer was sincerely felt, though little was said. Even her father and brothers suppressed their grief, not knowing but that ere an hour was ended, they might be with her in another world. Escape was considered impracticable, as their enemies were mounted, and the country around was open. It was, therefore, determined to retire to the sheep-fold as a place where they might better defend themselves against an attack, and for this rude fortification they instantly departed. In the short but hasty march which followed, there were numbers who would have lent their assistance in removing the wounded maiden, but Alan would accept of none: as he brought her there, he bore her thence.

The sheep-fold was no other than a narrow space, enclosed with a turf wall. And in one place, where the wall had been carried a little higher for the purpose of supporting a roof, the other materials had been strengthened by alternate layers of stones, in the same way as the houses of the Scottish peasantry were built about half a century ago. The walls, though no more than breast high, promised them considerable protection against a distant fire—the circumstance which, of all others, they most dreaded; they also offered a manifest advantage in case they should be forced to dispute it hand to hand. Here, having taken up their position, and hastily barricaded the gap which served as an entrance, they determined to make a desperate resistance.

The attack, however, with which they were threatened, was delayed a short time in consequence of the nature of the ground. It was found that cavalry could not act, with any prospect of success, in such a situation; but dismounting, the troopers advanced in small parties with open spaces between them, their object being not to present anything like a close front to the fire which they expected from the fold, till they should get as near to it as possible, and then, concentrating their force, beat down a portion of the wall and rush in.

On the part of the country people there was a backwardness

to take away life, which might have proved ruinous to their cause, had it not been for some veteran spirits among them. As soon as the enemy were within proper distance, Anderson and his fellows of Bothwell-field fired with good effect. This acted as a stimulus to the others, and as many of them as had fire-arms followed their example, and gave their foes a warm reception. But, nothing daunted, they pressed forward, while the shouts with which they cheered each other, the volleys they discharged in their advance, and the irregular fire from the fold, made altogether a scene of noise and confusion, such as that peaceful solitude had never before witnessed. The birds of prey, startled by the unwonted intrusion, rose from their places of concealment, and circling high in air mingled their shrill screams with the discordant sounds below. The volumed smoke, part of which slowly climbed the sides of the narrow gorge, while part stagnated in the hollow, obscured the combatants; and from its dense masses, piercing groans were heard to issue when the other sounds intermitted.

But Alan neither saw nor heard what was passing around him, so intently were his eyes fixed on that form of perishing beauty which he still continued to support. What his feelings were, words may not express. He staunched the bleeding wound that disfigured her fair bosom, and watched the changes which came over her face as the stream of life ebbed to its last feeble tricklings. When the shades of death began to gather thicker, strange to say, he felt his spirit more composed. At last her head dropped yet more heavily on his arm—he raised it tenderly. She turned her eyes, which still beamed with a faint lustre, upon him once more; then, as if oppressed by sleep, they gently closed, and all was still. He felt her arm, and pressed his hand against her bosom, but there was no pulse in her veins, and the flutter of her heart had ceased for ever—she was dead!

With as much care as if she had been his living bride, and only in a gentle sleep, from which he feared to wake her, did he deposit her lifeless remains upon the matted grass which grew within the fold; and, after covering her face with his handkerchief, he arose from the turf, still wet with the warm blood, with as much apparent calmness as if it had been from a repast. "Thou, who art the God of armies!" said he, in a voice of prayer, low but audible, "Thou, who permittest thy people to be thus tried, grant me strength, I pray thee, and make me instrumental in saving the lives of those who are yet to serve thee."

By this time the firing on both sides had ceased, and the work of death was carried on foot to foot and hand to hand. The assailants had succeeded in demolishing a part of the enclosure, and they now pressed hard upon those who defended it. A number of the more active, and among the rest several of the Bothwell men, were already dead, or lying mortally wounded; and the country people, though they fought with enthusiasm at the commencement, like all undisciplined troops, soon evinced by their conduct that they were unfit for protracted strife. Appalled by the carnage which now swelled around them, and the piercing groans which ever and anon rose above the din of battle, many of them stood almost wholly inactive. Nor were there wanting some who would have actually fled from the horrid spectacle, had it not been that they were hemmed in on every side. Only Anderson, and a few of the more determined spirits, animated by the voice and pressence of their reverend guide, still continued to defend the place with desperate bravery. But of those the numbers were diminishing every minute, and it was evident they could not hold out much longer against the superior force with which they had to cope. Already they appeared to be giving way, and terror was fast seizing on the undisciplined mass. But, at this critical juncture, Alan threw himself into the breach with a desperation which nothing could withstand. In an instant the foremost of the foe had sunk beneath the blows, which appeared to be dealt with more than mortal strength; and the bravest, seeing the fate of their companions, recoiled before him. He pressed into the thickest of their numbers, which formed a sort of avenue to receive him, while those on either side, instead of rushing into the fold, turned after him, as though it were his destruction alone which they had determined to compass. This gave a momentary respite to the defenders of the place.

"Out, and let us attack them in the plain field!" cried Anderson; and, gathering fresh strength from the favourable change which a single arm had wrought, he rushed forth with his hardy followers at his back.

There was a simultaneous movement within the fold: a new spirit seemed to reanimate them; and the whole body, indifferently armed as many of them were, fell on at once, with such ardour, that in a few minutes those who remained of the dragoons were compelled to fly to their horses, and abandon the field at full gallop.

It was high noon when the last sounds of strife ceased, and

the trample of the last horse's hoofs died away on that solitude; and glad were those of the combatants who remained at these indications of victory. But of those who had accompanied them thither only an hour before, there were many who had ceased to share their feelings—many whose ears could never again be greeted by these nor any other sounds till the archangel's trump shall summon them to doom. There they lay, heaped where they had fallen, with ghastly wounds gaping to the sun, while the crimson tide, the last drops of which had already flowed, dyed with a still deeper red the purple bloom of the isolated tufts of heath which grew around.

Among those who were mortally wounded, but not yet dead, was Alan Stewart; and near him, in the same state, lay Black Ritchie, whose fate at last had found him. Both were carried to the nearest house—a house which, like the others, has long since disappeared, leaving, to mark its site, only one tall ash, and two or three others of more stunted growth, known by the name of "Gulie's Tree."

In this lonely cottage, the last moments of Black Ritchie were such as to terrify all who were near. That retrospection of the past which a near prospect of death seldom fails to bring along with it, to him afforded no foundation on which to rest a single satisfying thought. The events of his past life, which had been one continued scene of selfishness, now crowded upon his imagination, and filled him with fearful fantasies. A vivid remembrance of all his evil deeds seemed to have disordered his brain; and, after a fit of moody silence, during which he repeatedly wiped the cold sweat from his brow, his words broke forth in raving.

Those whom he had over-reached by his cunning, and those whose blood he had causelessly shed, all stood before him, he said—him, the accursed of God, and the hated of man!—ready to tear him limb from limb while living, and to torment his soul eternally when dead. "Jane! Jane!" he would cry, "what do you there among that cursed crew? and that ghastly wound!—who gave it? I swear it was not me! I would have sent a ball through the villain's brains, had I known him." Then, turning his starting eyes on some one by his bed-side, he would continue: "Take away that female spectre—her beauty is loathsome, and her charms are an abomination in my sight; yet it was that beauty, and those charms, which urged me to the deed! Yes, it was these which made my eyes dazzle as I pointed the carbine, and my hand tremble as it pressed the lock. And now her black eyes are staring at me as if I were her murderer! O the curse!—the curse!—they are worse than burning coals!" Thus he continued to rave and writhe in the agonies of mortal pain, augmented by the madness of his despair.

These fits of frenzy soon exhausted his remaining strength; but still life seemed loth to loose its hold. His voice became weaker; and, when the films of death began to obscure his sight, he cried out that the fiends of hell, in the form of spiders, were weaving fiery webs in his eyes, and called on those around him to tear them away! They tried to convince him that it was a mere delusion; but his frenzy was not of the kind which admits of conviction. He imprecated the most terrible curses on their heads, crying out, that they too were his enemies; and, in his frantic efforts to rid himself of these imaginary tormentors, he would have torn his own eyes from their sockets had he not been restrained. To prevent him from destroying himself, it now became necessary to hold his hands. The struggle which this occasioned increased his agony. He gnashed his teeth and foamed; while the breath issuing from his nostrils resembled smoke more than the respiration of a human being. In this state he continued till death terminated his earthly sufferings.

Alan Stewart was laid on a bed in another apartment of the same cottage; and, at his request, the body of Jane was brought and placed beside him. When this was done, and her cold hand clasped in his, he seemed to have no farther care, nor any earthly wish unsatisfied. With the assistance of those who watched him, he gently parted the raven locks on her forehead, now cold and pure as marble; and, while he pressed his lips, already growing pale from the loss of blood he had sustained, to its snowy whiteness, he expressed an unfeigned acquiescence to the decree which awarded them the same fate, and acknowledged its mercy. He was not made for the weakness of sorrow, and the near prospect of his own dissolution calmed his spirit; yet the tears tracked each other down his cheeks, and his voice was partially broken, as he said: "Yes, in mercy was it sent—that fate which will soon reunite us. To thee my spirit turned amid the din of battle; and during the solitary march by night, when I knew not but I might encounter foes at every step, and when no friend was near, it was the thought of thee which made me superior to suffering, and enabled me to travel in darkness, and cold, and hunger, without weariness; and now, had I been left behind thee, the world could have been but a dreary void—a wilderness, in which I should have sought in vain for repose."

His life had been one of high-minded honesty, softened by the purest benevolence, and an unceasing wish to promote the happiness of all. But though a stanch supporter of what he conceived to be the cause of truth, mercy was ever uppermost in his heart, and his end was such as might have been expected.

As death approached, he fancied he saw Jane, clad in flowing robes, and looking inexpressibly more beautiful than she had ever done before. He spoke of the seraph-purity of her eyes, and the brightness of her form; and said that she beckoned him to come away. A smile of ineffable happiness overspread his countenance, and in that smile his spirit passed from its earthly tabernacle, while death fixed the expression, in unchangeable serenity, on his lifeless features. These fancies, doubtless occasioned by the weakness of his last moments, and a gentle delirium which came on before death, were, at that period, attributed to a supernatural opening of his eyes— a vision vouchsafed to him of the things which pertain to another world. The days of miraculous intervention are long since past, and philosophy accords not its sanction to the idea; but even philosophy might well be loth to rend away those sublime emotions which such an illusion has a tendency to raise in the minds of surviving relatives.

Influenced by this circumstance, the friends of the unfortunate lovers looked upon their remains as hallowed dust; and as the common burial-place of the parish was in the hands of their enemies, they did not inter their bodies there, but bore them to the brow of a hill, on the estate of a laird who was friendly to the Presbyterian form of worship, and, having dug a grave sufficiently large, at the still hour of midnight they placed them side by side—heaped up the mould—replaced the turf—and left them to that union and repose in death, which they had been denied in life.

As long as their story was remembered, the veneration of the peasantry around protected the place from violation; and when Time and Death had done their work upon those in whose memories it was chronicled, the mystery which brooded over the whole affair, and the strange circumstance of bodies being interred in a place so lonely, encircled with a sort of superstitious awe the grassy mound which still continued to be called *The Covenanter's Grave*. Thus it remained, with little alteration, till the beginning of the present century; and in the memory of many still living, it stood high, and distinctly marked. But the improvements of later times have levelled it with the surrounding field. The last mark of its having been once used as a place of sepulture is obliterated; and unless this frail record should, for a time, rescue it from oblivion, its very name may soon pass away.

Little more remains to be said. Mr. Adamson, though threatened with the punishment which was awarded to many of his brethren, continued to preach and teach till after the Revolution, when he died in peace, and was buried in the churchyard of his native parish. But the fears of those among the country people whose friends had been engaged in this affray were awakened; and being anxious to see them out of danger, it was resolved that as many of them as possibly could should quit the country privately. To assist them in this plan, a Mr. Turner, who was related to the North Cotton family, and who had then the command of a trading vessel, after leaving his ship's cargo at Dundee, sailed up the river Tay, under pretence of taking in some articles for another voyage, at the village of Newburgh. They had reached a place midway between Balmerino and the Castle of Balenbriech about sunset. Here they came to an anchor; and after it was dark, on an appointed signal being made, their boats, which were already manned, put off for the shore, and in less than half-an-hour the *articles* came on board in the shape of between forty and fifty men. They fell down the river with the night tide, and ere morning they had crossed the bar at the entrance of the Frith, and were in the German Ocean, on their way round the eastern coast of the island to America. In their adopted country they became prosperous and happy; and it was remarked, that from among their offspring arose some of the most zealous contenders for the freedom of the United States.

## THE STRANGER.

O Woman! in our hours of ease
Uncertain, coy, and ill to please,
And variable as the shade
By the light quivering aspen made,
When pain and sickness wring the brow,
A ministering angel thou!
Sir Walter Scott.

In the southern part of an obscure country parish, in one of the midland counties of Scotland, there is a deep ravine called

"The Rasp-berry Den." At the head of it a spring of limpid water bubbles up, producing a stream which traverses its bottom for the whole length—here fretting and brawling, with angry din, among the rough pebbles—and there

in pools as clear as glass,<br>Kissing, with easy whirls, the bordering grass.

After escaping from this narrow gorge, it traverses corn fields and way-sides, for nearly half a mile, and then loses itself in a lake.

On one side the den has been ploughed to the very margin of the stream. But the other, which is as steep as an earthen bank can well be, offering but little temptation to the agriculturist, has been allowed to remain in a state of nature. The primrose peeps forth in the early spring time; and the raspberry bushes, from which it derives its name, mingle with the darker green, and gayer blossoms, of the tall broom which luxuriates along the bank—offering to holiday ramblers a delightful shade from the rays of the summer sun. There, as it chanced, on the afternoon of a beautiful summer's Sabbath day, sat together an individual of either sex whom the ripe raspberries had lured to the spot.

In a certain sense of the word, both might be said to be young, yet not alike in youth. The maid could scarcely be more than eighteen, and the other was at least twenty-six. What were they? does the reader ask. Nothing very extraordinary—neither heroes nor heroines—princes, nor people of illustrious lineage; but common folk, and come of common parents. The one was the daughter of a laborious widower, whose mother had died when she was yet an infant, and she now kept her father's house. The other was a farm-servant on the next estate, and a native of a different county.

The two beings whom we have just introduced had frequently met before; a manly figure, a ready wit, and an honesty of purpose easily discovered, in the one; and an unobtrusive feminine beauty, gentleness of manner, and sensibility of heart, the prevailing attributes of the other, had given birth to a mutual esteem.

Their conversation turned upon the things of another world —the sermon, and other familiar topics—then changed, as conversations must, till at last they talked of the affections and passions of the human heart—its deceit, disappointments, and sorrows. This was a dangerous subject for those at the age of at least one of the parties, perhaps for both. A strange feeling, which showed itself in her countenance, almost overpowered the half girlish heart of Emily; and the other, as he looked on her, felt embarrassed, he knew not how. He thought of love —of domestic comfort—of the affections of woman, and the happiness of those who are fortunate enough to possess them— and so absorbing were his thoughts, that he had nearly forgotten to speak. The emotions of both appeared to grow too strong for utterance; and their observations became shorter, less connected, and less frequent.

In this lapse of conversation, Emily remarked that she had often felt as if she could confide in those around her: and yet she had seen others so often deceived, and been so often deceived herself, that she never could speak her thoughts with freedom; and thus she had been under the necessity of keeping them, whether pleasing or painful, for the most part to herself.

"They do not deserve to be trusted," said her companion, taking her hand as he spoke; while the tone of his voice, and a sudden flush in his countenance, bespoke the depth of his emotion. "Yet there is at least one honest heart," he continued, "which you might trust if ever you should need a friend; and believe me when I say that I would be proud to be thus trusted. Hark!" he added after a short pause, and pressing her hand close to his bosom as he spoke—"hark! it beats high at the thought."

She made no effort at resistance—she was a stranger to art— her heart was full—and her hand was passive. They sat for some time in silence. He pressed her hand yet more close; then, as if impelled by a feeling which he could not control, he raised it to his lips, and kissed it with tremulous tenderness. But ere his emotion could have subsided, he suddenly dropped her hand, rose hurriedly, and said he must leave her. He had only proceeded a few steps, however, when he turned to look again. Emily sat motionless as a statue, and her eyes were fixed on him with a look which went to his heart. Their glance sank to the ground with the quickness of lightning the moment they met his; but they had already told too much. His step faltered, and he stopped. He was in love — he acknowledged it to himself; and he began slowly and hesitatingly to retrace the few onward steps which he had made, with the intention of declaring it, and conjuring her, by all that was sacred, to promise that she would yet be his wife. Already he had drawn in his breath to speak; but emotion choked his utterance, and he stood speechless. Previous to this period, his head had been filled with schemes of ambition which were incompatible with marriage. There was a struggle between the passions in his bosom, and, ashamed of standing still and saying nothing, he once more moved slowly away.

Both went home that evening with hearts full, and neither slept; so that, after a night of restlessness, when morning came, the recollection, or rather the feeling, of "those deep and burning moments" were alike fresh in either heart. But ere evening came again there was a difference between them. Emily had learned to conceal her emotion, to subdue all outward signs of inward grief, and to laugh and talk as usual. Her companion had nearly supplanted his by day-dreams of the wealth and the name he would make in the world. Love and ambition seldom exist long together—and ere a week had elapsed a dim reminiscence was all that remained with him of those once warm feelings. He carefully avoided her company; for he had learned his own weakness, and determined not to trust his cherished dreams of future eminence with such temptation. With Emily it was otherwise. To have known that her affection was returned—that she was beloved by him, and to have heard him say as much, would have consummated her utmost wishes. As the stream wears its channel the deeper for being confined by its banks, her affection had only concentrated itself for being narrowed by the bounds of concealment. Hopes and fears fed it alternately, and uncertainty fanned the secret flame. Wherefore is it that the warmest and best affections so seldom meet a suitable return?

The year wore by, and Emily removed with her father to a distance of many miles, leaving behind her that magnet to which her soul still turned with the quivering fervour of first love. After another year she saw him again in a public market; but then he regarded her with the look of a stranger.

Thus it is with the different sexes. With man love is a feeling which overflows his heart only at intervals; and, though its sway may be despotic for the time, the thousand pursuits of his life; the every-day projects to which his attention is called; the cares and the bustle to which he is continually engaged,—to these, soon or late, it must yield, and he is left again a free agent. But with woman, love is a component part of her existence—one of the elements of her being. She was sent into the world to love, and to be beloved; and constancy, which even reason cannot change, is too often a feature in her character.

Years rolled on and Emily was forgotten; though *she* could not so readily forget. She heard nothing of the man to whom she had unconsciously given her heart—who had been her happiness and her heaven for a few brief moments; and of whom, despite herself, she still continued to think. Notwithstanding, she also knew the ridicule which is so often and undeservedly heaped upon old maids, and the helpless condition to which single women among the lower orders are often reduced in the decline of life—their dependence upon the charity of friends, and frequently on the still colder charity of the parish, for a wretched home and a scanty subsistence. She knew all this; and to avoid such scenes of misery and wretchedness she had reconciled herself to the idea of becoming the wife of another—any one, in short, who could offer her the prospect of a comfortable home. But even in this she seemed destined to be unfortunate; for, though she was not without lovers, they one by one gradually dropped off without assigning any reason. That she was beautiful they all confessed; that her deportment was modest and becoming they could not deny. But somehow there was a something awanting to fix their affections; and what that something was they could not tell—it was her heart, which was already another's. This being the case, the only effect produced by her beauty was somewhat similar to that of a frozen lake when the smooth ice is, as it were, kindled into flame by reflecting the light of the sun. Every one can admire the brilliancy and splendour of such a scene, though no one would care for breaking the ice and plunging in, conscious as he must be that cold water awaited him beneath. Emily could speak of love as she had heard others speak—she could reflect the language, so to speak, as ice reflects light; but for all save one the cold water was beneath. The bright spirit of affection failed to sparkle in her eye—the heart sent no fresh colour to her cheek—the mighty charm was awanting.

There are some who suppose it quite possible for a woman, by the mere fascination of her face and person, to keep love alive in one of the other sex for any length of time. Instances of this kind may have occurred, but they are rare. Man is a calculating being, and even where he is most disinterested he always expects something in return. His benevolence is the hire of gratitude, paid in advance; his generosity is bestowed to buy fame; his friendship is conferred that he may have friends; and his heart, when he gives it, is only given in exchange for another. His love may live long upon little, and Hope may feed it for a time with fantasies of its own forming; but deprive it of that little, and those fantasies, and the sentiment will soon cease to exist, though the dregs which it often leaves behind it,—regret, shame, indignation, despair—either or all of these may, in effect, resemble it so closely as to be mistaken for it by the individual himself.

\* \* \* \* \* \*

Emily, after various *flittings,* now lived in a house on the outskirts of a small village, or rather group of houses, called the Grange, in the immediate neighbourhood of the extensive Limeworks of P——. Most of the young women here were weavers; and Emily, from necessity or some other reason, had also "learned the loom." From the proximity of the Limeworks, many of these female artisans had sweethearts among those who were employed in blasting and burning the rock; and this being the case, it was to be expected that they should take a sort of interest in the gossip and whatever else was going on in the quarries. But Emily, though among them, was not of their number. She had reached her twenty-fourth year with her heart still faithful to its first impression; and at this age, early as it was, she had wholly abandoned the thought of marriage.

While matters stood thus, a sort of sensation was given to the place, and a fresh subject for conversation afforded, by the arrival of a new workman at the quarries. He had been brought from a distance by the master quarryman, and received high wages for the purpose of introducing an improved method of blasting the rock. He was a stout, well-built man, muscular and handsome; and though computed to be nearly thirty years of age, his looks, which were not the worse for wear, were such as to procure him very general admiration among the female part of this little community. Those who had conversed with him said he was quick-witted, affable, and obliging. But what served to give a double interest to his arrival, and make him ten times more spoken of than otherwise he would have been, was the circumstance of his being silent as to his friends and connections, and his former place of residence; he had not even told his name, and no one as yet had ventured to inquire it of him. This mystery, it was surmised by the more discerning part of the community, he kept up merely for the purpose of making a wonder. And if such were his intention, he perfectly succeeded; for *the Stranger,* as he was called, with all his sayings and doings, became the subject of more frequent conversation and conjecture than King Solomon would have been, though he had come back with a cart-load of wisdom in

his train. He had told that he was not married; and more
than one of the young women, while they manifested no small
anxiety and wonderment about his parentage and the place of
his nativity, had already formed designs upon his heart, and
wished secretly for opportunities of becoming acquainted with
the Stranger. If any two of them met, ten to one but the
Stranger was, if not the first, at least the second or third word
which was spoken; in short, the Stranger seemed to have
possessed them with a sort of mania.

Emily saw and heard all this without any anxiety or wonder
about the matter; and of the young women of the Grange she
alone had not seen him. What was the Stranger to her?

On the forenoon of the fourth day from his arrival, as he
was employed in driving a charge, the powder ignited, and it
went off, throwing him, along with several large fragments of
rock, into the air. After the smoke and dust had cleared
away, he was found lying, apparently lifeless, on a heap of
sharp splinters and loose stones at some distance. He
soon began to breathe; but his head, face, and other parts of
his body, were so fearfully scorched, and the blood flowed with
such rapidity from a number of deep wounds, that there was
scarcely any hopes of his surviving beyond an hour at most.
His fellow-workmen, however, made what haste they could to
remove him from the cairn on which he had been thrown; and
that he might not "die in the fields like a beast," as they
expressed it, one of the stoutest of them, after wrapping a mat
around him to prevent the blood from smearing his clothes,
took the corpse-like figure on his back, and they proceeded in
a body to the Grange. The house in which Emily lived happened to be the nearest, and to it they brought him. So
convinced were they of the hopelessness of his case, that they
had deemed it unnecessary to send for medical assistance. But
as fortune would have it, just as they brought the bloody,
mangled, and scarcely breathing form of the Stranger up to
the door, a surgeon chanced to pass, who kindly offered to
examine and dress his wounds, which done, he retired, promising to return on the morrow to see what would be the issue.

From the moment the Stranger was brought in, Emily had
taken a deep interest in his fate. Dismay, surprise, and sympathy, were portrayed in the countenances of all who were
present; and in these feelings she was only a participator with
the others. But her heart beat violently with some unwonted
and strong emotion, as he was laid on the bed; and after the
surgeon, and most of his fellow-labourers had left him—when

his moanings intermitted, and he sunk into a state of comparative quiet — she watched his troubled rest and heavy breathing with an anxiety as intense as if he had been her brother. And ever and anon, as the sigh of pain convulsed his bosom, or the shade of increased suffering passed over his swollen and distorted countenance, her silent but earnest prayer would ascend to the throne on high, to plead with Him who sitteth thereon, for the recovery of the Stranger.

After a few hours of that stupor which had been occasioned by the complete exhaustion of nature, he awoke in a state of mind similar to what may be supposed of one awaking from a trance, or—if such a thing could be—from the dead. All was confusion and chaos. The deprivation of sense had been so sudden, and his brain so much stunned by the concussion, that he could recall nothing distinctly. A sense of pain, and a confused recollection of a stupifying shock, blended with a dim idea of his having been far from home, and among strangers, was all he possessed. He had been, moreover, totally blind from the moment at which the explosion happened, and, consequently, could obtain no information from sight of what was passing. In this strange state, he at last found strength to inquire "what had befallen him, and where he was?" But how was the interest which Emily had taken in him increased, and the wild beat of her heart renewed, when in these accents, now tremulous and weak, she recognised the same voice which had once told her, in tones of emotion never to be forgotten, "that there was at least one honest heart which she might trust." Alas the change! She had been but too rash and ready to trust; and now the man who could forego the faith and the affection of a heart worth more than all he had to give in exchange, was thrown upon her care in such a state that a single rude breath would have sufficed to extinguish the feeble flickerings of life's taper in his bosom, and leave him a prey for the worms to fatten on.

If he had been regarded with feelings of sisterly affection when he was a stranger, now that he was known, he was watched and nursed with all the tenderness and care with which a mother watches and nurses her sick infant. His case was an extraordinary one, and as such excited general sympathy. Cordials, to prevent nature from sinking under the pain he endured, and clothes to keep him warm in his exhausted and almost bloodless condition, were contributed in abundance by the people around; and the Stranger was cared for as if he had been the patriarch of the place.

In a few days the surgeon, who had visited him regularly from the time of his misfortune, pronounced him free from fever, and in a fair way of recovery. The swelling, too, of his head and face, began to abate a little, and he could partially open his eyelids. On the following day, the surgeon, after examining them, gave it as his opinion, that though they might continue weak for a time, they would ultimately recover from the injury they had sustained. When he heard this, his spirits seemed to be relieved from the burden which hitherto had pressed on them—the fear that though he might live, he would be an object for life; and a bright expression grew upon his countenance, as he raised his dim eyes, for the first time, to that face and form, which was again bending over him, as if to be satisfied of the truth of what the surgeon had said.

Though he was now considered out of danger, he still continued to suffer acute pain; and as lying in one position often became irksome, Emily would sometimes sit behind him for hours supporting him in bed, with his head resting on her bosom, and her hands thrown across his breast, to keep the clothes close about him. One day as she sat there, after heaving a deep sigh, he once more took her hand, but he took it with feelings widely different from those with which he had grasped it on a former occasion. Then he was an object of general admiration among women. The symmetry of his form, and the healthy hue of his manly countenance, secured to him their favour wherever he came, and he felt confident of success wherever he might choose to apply as a suitor. But his heart was the theatre of ambitious schemes; and though neither dead to feeling, nor deaf to the voice of nature, he was too busy to appreciate the worth of woman's love, or to relish the soft endearments of domestic affection. Such was he, and such were his hopes and prospects then. But now, his ambitious schemes had vanished—death had been before his eyes, and the grim phantom had hunted them out of sight. He was feeble as a child—his face ploughed with scars—his vanity subdued—with much in his appearance to excite pity, and nothing to draw the admiring gaze, or fascinate the heart of a female. And in this state, he felt that the care and tenderness of Emily were worth more than worlds to him; and he would have given worlds, had he been possessed of them, in exchange for the prospect of living and dying beside her. He knew that she had once loved him: her look had told it—a look which his weakness had summoned from the oblivion in which it had long lain, and again placed before him with accusing accuracy. But how could she endure the idea of such a wreck as he now was for her future husband? The question staggered him. Though he had fancied himself more than equal to the task, for a time he could find no words to tell her that his only hope of happiness lay with her. And at last, when he could speak—in broken and unconnected sentences, such as have ever formed the language of the deepest and most heartfelt affection, and in faltering tones, such as have often been found more eloquent in woman's ear, than all the tropes and figures of speech put together—when *he* could speak, *she* was silent. But though she did not answer him in words, he felt the wild beat of her heart at his back, and did not drop her hand, but continued to hold and press it, and entreat her to pity, if she could not love him, till the maid, with deep blushes, and in tones as tremulous as his own, had promised to be the wife of the Stranger.

His recovery, though slow, was perfect. His looks, though considerably injured, are still the index of his heart; and when his face, brightened with the beam of affection, is turned on the woman who is now his wife, to her it seems to possess all the beauty she could wish, and even more than its former fascination. They live together blessed in the reciprocity of love, which has stood the test of *years and intimate acquaintance*—that test of all others the most trying; rich in reflected smiles and mutual confidence; and *strangers* only to the curse which prevents many people from being happy, because they cannot be miserable in a fashionable way.

## DISINTERESTEDNESS.

—— My desires
Run not before mine honour.
*Winter's Tale.*

"WELL, then, to-morrow night," said George: "Fortune favours true lovers, they say. I shall have everything in readiness, and on love's wings we shall fly away together."

"What must be, must be," replied Miss Caroline, in a low tone of voice. She was about to say more, but her father, Mr. Hanson, at that moment entered the room.

She was somewhat disconcerted, but her father noticed it not. "Caroline," said he, "you had better retire: I have some important communications to make to Mr. George here, and it may be as well that we are alone." Caroline bowed, and blushingly withdrew.

She was scarcely gone, when Mr. Hanson abruptly began,— "I am sorry, my dear sir, that the intelligence I am about to communicate to you, and which it is my duty to do, is of rather a startling nature. I have just received a letter from a friend of mine, stating that the house in Madeira, with which you are connected, has failed."

"Failed!" ejaculated the individual spoken to, apparently stunned by that single word; "*failed*, and my whole fortune gone!" then, after a short pause, in which he partially recovered himself, "Well, it can't be helped;" and with this last remark, upon which he laid a particular emphasis, he affected to set the matter at rest.

"But that is not all," rejoined Mr. Hanson. "My friend states that there are strong suspicions of fraudulent dealings— that the partners are in danger of being imprisoned—and that he writes thus early in the hope that he may be instrumental in enabling you to avoid a jail."

"A jail!—They have my all already; they may have me for the keeping sooner or later. Man was made to rot; and if it must be in a jail, there is no great use in raising objections." Here again he assumed an air of indifference.

"No, my friend," said the other, "you shall not go to prison if I can keep you from it. We may succeed in convincing the creditors of the firm that you at least are honest; and when we have satisfied any reasonable demands which they could have upon you, I will endeavour to establish you in business for yourself, if you will allow me to number myself among your friends. You are a young man, and you may realise a fortune ere the finger of age has set its seal upon your brow."

George's brow was knit. He listened to the proposal with marked impatience. Conflicting passions were at work in his bosom, and he seemed struggling against the impulse of his heart and his better self. But at last his countenance brightened. He accepted Mr. Hanson's offer, strove to express his gratitude, and declared that his life should be spent in endeavouring to prove that he was not altogether unworthy of such a friend.

On the afternoon of the same day, he received a letter from the managing partner of the firm. It was as follows:—"My dear sir,—In consequence of Mr. S. having failed, and the circumstance being known that he lately stood engaged with our house to a considerable extent, a report has got into circulation that the firm is also bankrupt. This report is utterly false, and I write thus early to set your mind at ease, lest it should have reached you," etc.

This letter completely changed the aspect of affairs. But notwithstanding the happy information which it conveyed, Mr. George continued thoughtful during the remainder of the day, rather avoiding than seeking company. He was late in going to bed, and rose early on the following morning. His first business, after dressing himself, was to obtain a short interview with Miss Caroline, the concluding words of which were— "Though I could have been unjust, I cannot be ungenerous. I shall never love another, but I dare not wait your reply—it would unman me. Farewell, dearest Caroline. Look sometimes at the picture, and do not altogether forget its original—farewell." After this abrupt interview, he took a formal leave of Mr. Hanson, and again thanking him for his intended generosity, set off for town—business, he said, calling him thither.

Mr. Hanson was the representative of an ancient but decayed family. He was a man of generous and philanthropic disposition, but strongly imbued with aristocratic feeling. Caroline was the eldest of two daughters, and every way his favourite. She was a girl of elegant form and fascinating appearance; her education had been in a great measure received at home. To perception naturally quick, she had added varied and extensive reading, and possessed a fund of knowledge and a discrimination of character rarely to be found in one of her years. Mr. George was sprung from what, in the estimation of Mr. Hanson, was a degenerate branch of the same family,—a branch which had supported itself for the last two generations by trade and commercial speculations, and between it and the original stem little intercourse had subsisted. Upon a heart actuated by the best intentions, and feelings which shrank from the meanness of double dealing, he had ingrafted some strange notions of his own about happiness. He considered it as a creation of the mind, rather than the creature of any particular station in society, and fancied that, with so much of Fortune's favours as would raise him above the fear of want, and place the necessaries and comforts of life within his reach, and a *friend* (he meant a wife) with whom to share these, and some other extras, such as his thoughts and affections, he could be perfectly happy. These ruminations naturally gave a sort of romantic turn to his thoughts, (perhaps there are few who have not, at one period or other of their lives, experienced something of a similar kind;) and this is the only excuse which can be offered for some of his actions. What appeared his greatest difficulty was the choosing of his friend. His limited fortune prevented him from looking very high, and he was deterred from descending very low from a knowledge of that want of general intelligence which was known to prevail there. He, however, determined to proceed cautiously, and when he had found one to his liking, to spare no effort to make her his own. He had been admitted as a visitor at Mr. Hanson's; and, availing himself of this privilege, had contrived to be oftener there during the last two years than either he or any of his family had been for at least half a century before.

On the day after his departure, Mr. Hanson chanced to pass a secluded spot in a woody hollow, where a little rivulet played over a ledge of rock, forming a miniature cascade, above which, in a recess of the rock, an arbour had been erected. This had been the favourite haunt of Caroline for some time past, and here, on the evening just alluded to, he was surprised to find her seated on the bench, and gazing intently on a miniature which she held in one hand, while she supported her head with the other; and as she sat thus, tears, which she could not suppress, at intervals flowed down her cheeks. She did not notice his approach, so that she was rather taken by surprise. The unwonted signs of sorrow visible in her countenance, naturally led her father to inquire what had caused her inquietude, and whose picture it was upon which she was gazing so intently. After recovering herself a little, "Sit down here, my dear father," said she, "and I will tell you all. I have nothing now to conceal. I may well be ashamed of some parts of my conduct, but it is perhaps as well that you should know it."

Here she proceeded to narrate to him that conversation, the end of which forms the beginning of this story; but as she only gave the leading particulars, it may be as well to introduce the reader to it as it really occurred.

It was after a walk to the very arbour in which the father and daughter now sat, during which mutual confessions and explanations had been made, that George and she were seated in a room by themselves. After a pause of some duration, "Well, you have confessed you love me," said George to his fair listener, "and that you would be happier with me than with any one else."

"Yes, I have confessed all that," was the reply of the playful girl, and in her tones, assumed levity, natural candour, and unwonted seriousness, seemed strangely blended.

"But your father—can we ever gain his consent?"

"Now that I think of it, I am afraid we never can," was Caroline's reply, and here all her former gaiety forsook her; "and were we to do anything without his knowledge, I fear he would disown me. Oh, this is the only thing I cannot bear to think of; and besides, were I to come to you with nothing, I would not be worth the taking."

"It is yourself, my love, not your fortune, that I wish to call my own. But do you recollect the account of my limited circumstances, and humble prospects, which I formerly gave you?"

"O yes, I recollect all that, and your candour, in this respect, only served to increase my esteem for you."

"And do you think you could submit to the economical way of living which it would be necessary to adopt? We should neither be able to keep nor to see much company, but you should have every moment of a lover's and a husband's time, which he could spare from his daily avocations. Could you bring yourself to conform to such a way of life?"

"O yes," was again the reply to these questions. "Let not that woman say she loves a man who cannot make her tastes —mode of living—all she is or can be—conform to his circumstances. Love is not selfish in its demands, though men may sometimes think it so. And were it not that you would deem me forward, I would tell you that, for the last twelvemonth, I have been careful to learn, not only what pertains to the management of a house, but the doing of everything which is required to make it comfortable. And I am proud to say, that there is now nothing that a servant could be required to do, which I could not perform in her stead, if fortune should demand it of me."

"What could be your reasons for learning all this?" again inquired her enamoured listener.

"I believe I never made any strict search for my reasons. In truth, I rather wished to conceal them from myself. But I now suppose, some indistinct idea, that you would one day do as you have done, and that I might be called upon to perform a part in life quite different from that at present assigned me, must have been at the bottom of the whole."

"My angel!" exclaimed the enraptured lover, as he seized the hand of the fair speaker, and pressed it to his lips.

Love is a mysterious power: it often oversets the resolutions of the wisest heads as if in sport. But it is as capricious as it is powerful, and is itself liable to be overset by the merest trifle.

Here the impropriety of the step she was about to take, and the grief which it would occasion her father, had been so forcibly presented to Caroline, that, for a time, she had almost determined to abandon those prospects of happiness which love so temptingly held out to her, and to follow what her heart told her was the path of duty. But the solicitations of her lover, the recollection that her sister was on the eve of returning home—her education being completed—to supply her place, and the hope that, after all, her father might not take it so much to heart; these, backed by the strong current of her own affections, at length prevailed, and she consented to an elopement on the following evening.

Mr. Hanson listened patiently to his daughter's recital, and when she had concluded, he angrily put the question, "And why did you not run away with the fellow?"

"Have patience, dear father, and I will tell you all. I did not run away, because he would not take me with him. The last time I saw him, which was only for a few minutes, he told me of the kindness which you had lately shown him, and said that though he could have acted the part of a villain formerly, now that you had proved yourself a friend in what appeared the extremity of his fortune, he could not, for a moment, think of robbing you of what he was pleased to call your greatest treasure; and that, rather than be the cause of giving you the smallest uneasiness, he would forever forego his own prospects of happiness."

"And what did you say to all this?" again inquired the father, his passion gradually subsiding.

"Indeed, I was so struck with the nobleness of his sentiments, and the passionate earnestness with which he uttered them, that I could not say a word. And, besides, he did not give me time, for he hurried off, and left me to mourn his absence as I do now."

"What! is it possible that you really love him?" exclaimed Mr. Hanson, in a half bantering, half angry tone. But now it was evident that his passion was working itself into a calm.

"O father!" said Caroline, "need I answer you that question after what I have already told you?"

The next morning Caroline was summoned to her father's apartment, when he inquired, in the most affectionate manner, "if she thought George Hanson really loved her, or if it were not rather her fortune to which he was partial, notwithstanding all his professions to the contrary."

"As to that, my dear father," said she, "I can have little

doubt; for, setting aside the circumstance of my fortune being in your disposal, while he was here, a letter from the young and beautiful widow of the late Mr. Mowbray, whose fortune would more than double mine, even if I were to marry with your approbation, fell into my hands. It was addressed to him. Some irresistible impulse prompted me to read it, and from the tenor of that letter, it was evident he needed only to make a proposal to be accepted."

Mr. Hanson, after a short pause, resumed, "I have been thinking a good deal about the matter, and I believe I must write him an invitation to come and spend a few days more with us as soon as he can find it convenient." George Hanson was not long in returning, and the result was—what the reader has perhaps already anticipated,—a marriage.

All men's characters are mixed: there is something to be borne with, and something bad in the best, and there is often some brighter traits even in the worst, if we could only discover them. Accident, or a word elicited by some strong emotion, may sometimes bring the latent principles to light. Thus Mr. George has often been heard to aver that he had never formed a proper estimate of his wife's character till he heard her say that for him she had been learning to be a servant; and upon these occasions she always remarked that she never believed there could be candour in a lover till he told her that he was not rich. Mr. Hanson, too, had his observation. He said, that had it not been for the circumstance of George's going away without his daughter after she was willing to run off with him, he should have set him down for a scoundrel to the latest day of his life. To these remarks may be added another of a more general character: "Money should never be despised in matrimonial alliances; but those who marry exclusively for a fortune need not be disappointed if afterwards they should miss a friend."

## THE DRUNKARD.

"Oh, that men should put an enemy in their mouths, to steal away their brains."—
SHAKESPEARE.

### CHAPTER I.

WHILE a few words in the way of advice from a metropolitan physician, who adds M.D. to his name, and rides in his carriage, are sometimes considered worth almost as many guineas, there is another class of medical practitioners who, with humbler aims and more circumscribed prospects, must often perform much real drudgery for a few shillings. The individuals who compose this class derive their origin, for the most part, from the middle and lower ranks of society; and after having obtained, with considerable difficulty, a medical education, and qualified themselves to practise as surgeons, they establish themselves in our provincial towns, villages, and obscure country districts, often spending laborious lives in visiting the sick-beds, and endeavouring to alleviate the sufferings of a poor and scattered population, who, from the very limited nature of their incomes, can seldom afford to give them more than the most scanty remuneration. What they lose in profit, however, they may, perhaps, gain in honour and professional importance; for whatever degree their respective colleges may have conferred on them, in the estimation of their patients and the public, they are all *doctors*, without distinction; and of many of them, at least, it may still be said,—

> Their virtues walk their narrow round,
> Nor make a pause nor leave a void;
> And sure the Eternal Master finds
> The single talent well employ'd.

But though much of their care, and by far the greater part of their time, must be unavoidably devoted to the poor, the patronage of the rich must always be an object of ambition, and, in some instances, an auxiliary without which they could scarcely subsist; for it may be easily supposed, that where a great quantity of labour must be performed below the average rate of rewards, unless the labourer should contrive to get occasionally into the service of those who may be able to pay him better, he could scarcely find it possible to keep himself and his implements in repair. But as the merchants, manufacturers, farmers, &c., who, when not eclipsed by greater lights, may be regarded as the aristocracy of such places, are always conscious of their own importance, and, in many instances, jealous of conferring their favours, this patronage can only be obtained by very delicate management. Should there chance to be a rival of the same profession in the place, then matters are rendered still worse: all the difficulties are doubled, and it requires more than an ordinary degree of tact and perseverance to overcome them. For these reasons, an introduction to the family of a wealthy citizen, or even of an ordinary farmer, is frequently regarded as a very important obligation by the party introduced; and in a state of society where men who act upon the principles of disinterested benevolence, are not over and above rife, it may be expected that cases will occur in which calculating individuals may not be altogether averse from taking advantage of the feelings of those they have obliged. This is, no doubt, telling truths which are as obvious as can well be imagined, and with which the world might have been familiar long ago; but then, as they are truths respecting a particular class, of which the world, when in health, seldom takes time to think, for that very reason their repetition may be pardonable.

Roland Bridges had been early smit with a love of the medical profession: from a boy it was the object of his ambition to be a surgeon, or a *doctor*, as he phrased it; his parents, who were only small farmers, or rather *pauchlers*, did not thwart his inclination; and after having gone through that preparatory course of instruction which was to fit him for his intended station, he settled in the town of Auldenburgh. Here he engaged for "bed and board," with the wife of a respectable shopkeeper, and took a small room fronting the street, over the door of which he got the word LABORATORY painted in blazing characters; and then in the window of the said room, he exhibited, to all and sundry, his "well crammed magazines of health," in the form of a goodly array of bottles —square, globular, and round—containing liquids of various colours, from the transparent, the pale blue, and the light crimson, to the deep purple, and the almost inky black.

About three months previous to the time at which Roland Bridges began his Esculapian labours, another individual, whose name was Arthur M'Quiddit, had come to reside in Auldenburgh. In stature he was about the middle size, square made, and well proportioned; his forehead was erect, but rather low; his hair dark, thick, and curled; his eyes were of the same colour, not remarkably large, but penetrating, and deep set in his head. His complexion had in it, perhaps, a little of that dusky hue which, for want of a better name, has been called *iron coloured;* but this was either never noticed or immediately forgotten in contemplating the general expression of his countenance, which was strongly marked, and had in it a something between good-nature and sarcasm—a sort of mixture which, according to the mood of the beholder, with a little assistance from imagination, might have been easily resolved into either of these qualities. In addition to this hasty sketch of his personal appearance it must be stated that, after having served the usual time in a writer's office, and passed some eight or ten years with various masters in a number of different places, following the same profession, he had now commenced business on his own account. For such an undertaking he might have been considered perfectly qualified, both by education and experience, his age being somewhere between twenty-eight and thirty: and with a prepossessing address, pleasing manners, and a sort of satirical humour, which he knew well when to curb, and when to let loose; backed by some pretensions to fortune, which he was supposed to possess, he had found his way into a number of respectable families, where he was received upon all occasions as an agreeable guest. With the better sort of people in general he maintained a favourable footing: business, too, seemed to be increasing, and thus his prospects were every way encouraging.

Roland Bridges, on the other hand, who was six or eight years younger, was but indifferently qualified for elbowing his way into the better circles. Neither his conversational powers nor his wit were greatly inferior to those of Mr. M'Quiddit, but he wanted that art, so to speak, which is often necessary to procure a field for the display of these talents. He possessed a stock of varied and useful information, and could speak with propriety on most subjects when in a company with which he was perfectly acquainted, and at his ease; but among strangers he was bashful, diffident, and sometimes even awkward in his attempts at conversation; and instead of thrusting himself into an opening wherever it appeared, and attracting and dazzling the attention of his listeners, in most instances he would have required a guide to lead him forward. On numberless occasions he fancied that he could say fine things, and really had these things at his tongue's end, but somehow, when an opportunity for saying them occurred, he could rarely utter a word; and as conversation can seldom be long kept to one subject, it had in general changed before he could settle on the manner in which he should introduce himself. When he came to Auldenburgh he had, moreover, an established rival in the person of Dr. Drugster, who had long been in quiet possession of the practice of the place, and was backed by a numerous circle of friends and acquaintances. With these disadvantages his assistance was seldom sought except by the poorest of the inhabitants; the fees which he could take from them were always of the most moderate description; and in some cases, so far from receiving anything, he was obliged to part with a shilling or a half crown, which he could ill spare, to save his patients from death by starvation. His prospects were thus the very reverse of *flattering*, and after having passed something more than two months without any perceptible improvement, as he was returning from visiting a patient in the country he met Mr. M'Quiddit, who had sauntered out to take a walk, and who, it seemed, knew him, though neither of them had been formally introduced to the other.

"Happy to see you, Dr. Bridges," said he, advancing to shake hands with him; "and as we have both come to this place with pursuits and prospects almost the same I think we should be better acquainted."

There was such an appearance of frank hilarity in the manner in which these few words were spoken that Dr. Bridges felt at once inclined to return the salutation in the same spirit in which it had been made. "I am happy," he said, "at any occurrence which promises to make me acquainted with you. But," he added, with a faint smile, "I suspect no one except an experienced lawyer would attempt to establish the similarity, not to mention the *sameness*, of our pursuits."

"As to that," rejoined the other, "it does not require so much experience as you would imagine. For instance, *you* came here to live upon the diseases of men's bodies, and *I* to make my bread by preying upon the crotchets and caprices of their minds; *you* are to give personal attendance and advice wherever there is real distress, *I* am to be attended in all cases of bad humour or imaginary wrong; *you* are to use your utmost endeavours to promote head-breaking, if you are your own friend, and then spread plasters for the heads which have been broken, and sell physic and cordials wherever you can find a market—no offence, for I will make my own calling as black as yours presently; and *I* am to foment mischief to the extent of my ability, setting people by the ears upon all occasions, that they may break each other's characters without mercy; and then I am to sell threatening letters, warrants, and other legal papers to whosoever will buy them. And now, I think, my friend will acknowledge that our pursuits, though not exactly the same, are pretty nearly allied."

Dr. Bridges could not help laughing heartily at the ludicrous comparison which had been thus placed before him. "I must confess," he said, "that you have succeeded much better than I had anticipated; and I wish to Heaven you could now establish as good a parallel between our *prospects* as you have done between our pursuits—yours, they say, are flattering; but what with the want of employment, and what with employment without reward, I verily believe the people of this place intend to transform me into a skeleton for the benefit of science; and for any reasonable argument which I could oppose to such a proceeding they may even complete the work as soon as they please, and then hang me up in their old steeple or elsewhere for the edification of the public."

"We must try and baulk them of their intentions though," said the other: "and I will tell you how we shall do it—it shall be in this wise. Wherever I can find an individual dying of a broken head, or a broken heart, not forgetting broken legs and arms, and all manner of diseases, I will either send him to you, or direct him to send for you; and swear, at the same time, that you could *cure* him, though he were dead, which would be no great falsehood after all—seeing that herrings, as well as other kinds of living creatures, are mostly cured after that event has taken place. And that you may not be at all burdened with gratitude, for which some people are sad anglers, wherever you find a patient who wishes to have his will made, or an individual who has got the vapours, and is dissatisfied with his friend or his enemy, or his master or his servant, or his brother or his sister, or the whole world together, then send him to me, and declare, that if the devil himself had wronged him, I would find means to do him, the devil, and the world, the most perfect justice."

This second sally produced another laugh, in which Mr. M'Quiddit was not slow to join; more conversation followed, and when the two parted, it seemed as if they had been friends for more years than they had really been acquainted hours.

Shortly after this conversation, as Dr. Bridges was one evening busily engaged in his little LABORATORY, or rather pretending to be busy, compounding and preparing medicines, for which he had no immediate demand, Mr. M'Quiddit came in rather abruptly—"What!" he said, as he entered, "still busy with extracts, and essences, and tinctures, and other preparations, which healthy people seldom think of purchasing."

"In good sooth, I am busy with the things of which you speak, because I have nothing else to do," said the pharmacopolist.

"Well; and if a friend should procure you some other work, what in the name of wonder *could* you do?" again inquired the lawyer.

"Why, as to that, I cannot exactly say," rejoined the other, catching at the same time the tone of good-natured banter in which he had been addressed; "but something I certainly could do. For instance, I could poison people as fast as the most dignified M.D. of the whole profession; I could keep accounts, too, and make demands upon their purses like a very lawyer; I could let blood, from a thimbleful to the last drop which could be with safety extracted; I could plaster a wound, after the most approved fashion, or if the said wound were sufficiently large, I could play the tailor, and stitch it up at once; and if you, or any friend, would be so kind as to employ yourself a little in the way of bone breaking, I hereby promise to mend the whole in the most scientific manner—that is to say, one half of my patients shall be lameters for life, and the other half shall have their legs as strong and as crooked as any lover could wish the legs of a rival to be; and lastly——"

"Nay, hold there; what you have already said is enough for me," said the lawyer. "And now, when I can get in a word, I may tell you for your consolation, that my landlady's youngest son has been pleased to consider your case so far, as to allow a cart-wheel to pass over his arm, by which the bone has been broken between the wrist and the elbow, so that you may now have an opportunity of mending it, and making it as crooked as you please. Dr. Drugster would have been called, but I peppered them with some phrases about *recent discoveries, improved methods*, and so forth. And now, Master Hippocrates, will you be pleased to select such of your tools as may be needful, and make haste, for I have run all the road to tell you."

Dr. Bridges, as may be easily supposed, lost no time in making the necessary preparation, and hastening to the boy's relief. The fracture was a simple one, the bone was soon set, bandages, etc., applied, and the first part of the business finished: he, however, continued to give his attendance till the cure which he had begun was completed, and then the mother was pleased to say, that she could not tell which of her boy's arms had been broken.

It was Christmas, the annual round of festivities had begun, and when Mrs. M'Intosh's turn came, out of gratitude, she could do no less than invite the doctor, who had been so successful in rescuing her boy from deformity, to be a partaker in the hospitality of the season.

Mrs. M'Intosh was the widow of a respectable cloth merchant, with two sons and two daughters, one of each grown up; the son had continued to keep the shop after his father's death, and though not remarkably rich, they were well connected, and well received in the best circles of the place. Dr. Bridges was, therefore, fain to attend on the appointed evening, in the expectation that his doing so might be the means of introducing him to better and more extensive practice than he had hitherto enjoyed. When he arrived, among a number of other guests, he found Mr. Forester and his daughter; the former a rich widower, who had retired from business to live upon his money, and the latter a delicate but interesting girl, in her twentieth, or one-and-twentieth year. From the circumstance of Miss Forester having been born and bred among them, and living rather retired, she had not hitherto attracted much notice. She was spoken of rather as an affectionate and dutiful daughter than as a beauty; and while all admitted that her conduct in every respect was most exemplary, very few talked of her charms. But notwithstanding this silence, there was a peculiar charm in her quiet unassuming manners—a charm which, in some eyes, might have compensated for many personal defects, of which, however, she had none. She did not appear to consider herself as deserving of attention, she gave herself no airs to procure it, and she never seemed to think herself in the shade when it was withheld. Though her face and figure were not of that sort which draw immediate admiration, yet when once observed, she lost little by being compared with others; her charms, such as they were, had rather a tendency to grow upon the heart of the beholder; and as she was the last of her father's family, and likely to inherit whatever he might leave behind him, this consideration was by far too important to be wholly overlooked. The lining of a purse has often more attractions than the colouring of a cheek, or the brilliancy of an eye, and thus she had become the subject of *interested*, if not interesting, speculation, with those fathers and mothers who were anxious to see their sons well married; but of these sons themselves, no one as yet had proposed for her hand, or even paid her any marked attentions.

Few persons who will give themselves the trouble of casting a retrospective glance over their own experience can be ignorant of a certain tendency in the youthful mind to give a sort of arbitrary preference to some particular individual, even in the largest company. That individual may be a perfect stranger, and the preference may be founded upon the most trifling circumstance—the colour of the hair, the eye, or the complexion—the form of the mouth, the forehead, or any other feature which chances to strike the fancy of the observer; or it may owe its origin to a well-worn ornament, or a fanciful piece of dress, or, in short, to anything; but when once it has taken possession of the heart, there it remains, till something more interesting is seen, or till some reason appears for withdrawing it: and thus it was with Roland Bridges. After he had surveyed the company at leisure, measuring their most interesting points with his eye, and scanning their various tempers and characters in his own mind, he at last settled upon Miss Forester, as one who deserved a decided preference. The only other individual present who, in his estimation, would at all bear to be compared with her, was Miss M'Intosh, who appeared to be some years older, and who, by most judges, would have perhaps been considered the better looking of the two. There was, he readily acknowledged, an energetic expression about her countenance, which contrasted finely with her delicate complexion. He was also forced to confess, that she had exquisitely formed lips, dark commanding eyes, and a fine expanse of forehead, on which, when the light fell upon it from a certain direction, two or three lines were just perceptible. These, as may be readily supposed, were not the work of time: they rather seemed to indicate strong thinking faculties, in connection with strong passions; the last of which, however, she never exhibited in such a way as to detract from her fame. With these attributes she was, at least, a fair specimen of female beauty. But though Roland Bridges would have acknowledged frankly that she was so, he still persisted in giving the preference to Miss Forester, who—while the elder females were busy in discussing scandal, and other serious subjects, and the younger ones were dealing around their smiles and small talk, and setting all the sail they could to catch the gale of admiration—was for the most part silent, and seldom raised her eyes from the table. He soon began to entertain a very high opinion of her modesty and delicacy of feeling; and after looking round the company to try if he could discover any counterpart to these, when his eye returned to its former object, he was not displeased to find that she had been stealing a glance at himself.

When the repast to which they had been invited was over, and conversation had walked its round, Mr. M'Quiddit, reckoning, no doubt, on being supported by the younger part of the company, proposed that they should have a dance. This proposal was not at all in accordance with the etiquette of the higher circles, and for this reason, perhaps, Mrs. M'Intosh rather seemed to demur as to the propriety of adopting it; but she had herself been bred in the country where unfashionable revels of this kind are quite common; and as she recollected having been as happy in her younger days dancing to a *blind fiddler* in her father's kitchen, as ever she had been at a regularly got up ball, she offered no serious opposition. The motion, moreover, was warmly seconded by Miss M'Intosh, while her eldest brother, who was an amateur violin player, offered his services upon the occasion, and in the end the table was removed, chairs were lifted back, and a space cleared for a *reel*. Dr. Bridges offered his hand to Miss Forester, Miss M'Intosh accepted that of Mr. M'Quiddit, and when all were accommodated, to it they went with at least a whole world of good-will.

Miss Forester did not dance with any very extraordinary degree of spirit—that was not her forte. The animating exercise, however, seemed to bring the simple elegance of her form more prominently into view, while it certainly added a fresher colour to her cheek. The excitement of the music, too, to which she was far from being insensible, gave a brighter sparkle to her eye; and when she sat down, Dr. Bridges felt inclined to be better pleased with her than ever. He even congratulated himself on that penetration which had enabled him to discover and to appreciate, almost at first sight, the charms of one who was so little anxious to exhibit them, and who was, at the sametime, so deserving of notice. In the course of the evening, he had an opportunity of dancing with her several times: indeed, he danced with no other; and the attention which he thus bestowed exclusively upon her, seemed to have the effect of bringing her all at once into general notice. Of six or eight young men who were present, each and all appeared to have become rivals for her favour; every one seemed anxious to have her for a partner, and among them she was scarcely allowed to rest for a single minute. In this manner an hour or two passed rapidly away; and when the time came at which her father thought proper to go home, numerous were the gallants, and not the most backward was Dr. Bridges, who offered to escort her; but after assuring them with a *naïveté* which was peculiarly her own, that she apprehended nothing, she took the arm of her parent, and left them all alike disappointed.

On his way home, Dr. Bridges recollected the case of an unfortunate young man, who had been sadly addicted to the bottle, and who was, at the time, suffering severely from having stumbled over the perpendicular front of a rock while in a state of intoxication. As he had seldom been able to keep a shilling in his pocket if the means of spending it were within his reach, he was one of those from whom a fee could not be expected; but in every case where an individual recovers from what is deemed a dangerous condition, a certain degree of honour always attaches to the medical attendant; and this consideration, together with a sort of pleasure which he had often derived from a consciousness of having mitigated pain, made Dr. Bridges, at the time, more ready to listen to the calls of humanity, than the voice of selfishness. It was only ten o'clock: the poor fellow, he thought, might feel easier for having his wounds dressed, and he accordingly hastened to his bedside. But though his patient upon the whole did not appear to be worse, he was rather surprised to find his pulse considerably increased, with some other symptoms of nervous excitement, which he had not before noticed. On inquiring the cause of this change, he was told, that a few hours ago he had received a letter, stating the death of an uncle in the West Indies, who had left money and property to the value of £500, which would fall to him if he could only succeed in establishing his relationship. "But," continued the poor fellow, "I am so ill that I can do nothing, and there will be so much to prove—so many parish registers to examine—the dates of so many births, baptisms, and burials to arrange, and so many letters to write, that I have been thinking of sending for the town-clerk, and letting him manage the business any way he pleases."

Dr. Bridges saw at once that this was an affair which could only be managed properly by a man of business; and considering, at the same time, that it was one from which some emolument might be derived, gratitude made him recommend Mr. M'Quiddit, instead of the town-clerk, and as a very slight recommendation in such cases will often suffice to turn the balance, the former was employed.

Next morning, Miss Forester, as the consequence of having been exposed to the night air, after being heated with dancing, complained of hoarseness and sore throat. The affection did not appear to be at all serious; few would have thought it worth noticing, and she even thought so herself; but her only brother had died of consumption, which was brought on by a neglected cold, and her father, anxious for the health of his remaining child, immediately proposed sending for Dr. Bridges.

To this proposal Miss Forester did not readily agree. She declared that she would soon recover; and if a doctor were to be called at all, hinted that she would prefer Dr. Drugster.

"Why, what can make you prefer Dr. Drugster to Dr. Bridges?" said her father. "People are beginning to say that the latter has more knowledge of the healing art, and has been more successful than the former; and as it is hardly possible that he can have given you any real offence, I would almost be tempted to inquire what cause you can have for disliking him?"

"Indeed, indeed," said Miss Forester, rather disconcerted by the question; "indeed, I can have no cause for disliking him at all—only he is so forward, and it was him who made me dance so much. But I do not want a doctor at all, really I do not; or if you call one, call Dr. Drugster."

"Foolish girl!" said Mr. Forester, in a half angry tone; to make a long story short, I tell you Dr. Drugster has gone on a visit to his friends in the country, and we may all be dead before he comes back. But from your unaccountable apprehensions, one would almost be led to suppose that you believed this same Dr. Bridges was some great leviathan, who swallowed his patients, one and all, without distinction of age or sex, and that you were afraid of being devoured along with the rest. If you really dislike him, however," he added, lowering his voice to a tone of affection, "you have only to tell him the symptoms of your disorder, and then go to your own room."

Miss Forester was not perhaps greatly offended with her father's pertinacity, in this respect, after all. She felt, however—she scarce knew what—a sort of flutter and apprehension at the idea of her professional visitor, which, though not exactly so distressing as if he had been a leviathan coming to swallow her up, was nevertheless enough to disconcert her. How should she receive him, was with her a question of considerable importance, and one which she had decided half-a-dozen different ways in half as many minutes; but as she could not at the moment determine which was the best, the object of her anxiety and apprehension arrived before she could finally fix upon any particular plan, and she received him with a cold, distant, and somewhat embarrassed civility, which she either mistook for politeness, or adopted because she could not at the time substitute any thing better in its stead. While he was questioning her as to the symptoms of her supposed disorder, she answered in tones so low as to be scarcely audible, and hardly ventured to lift her eyes from the carpet. The professional part of his visit, however, was soon over, and when it had been despatched, as he still felt a wish to linger, with the intention of leading her into conversation, he expressed his regret at her having suffered from the effect of the last evening's revel, and then inquired if she "were fond of dancing."

"Not remarkably fond," was the somewhat laconic reply. But the desired effect followed. Some other commonplace remarks served as the prelude to a conversation which, to the parties themselves, at least, became interesting as it advanced; that reserve and diffidence which, in spite of every effort, occasionally clings to youthful individuals of different sexes, when they find themselves for the first time left to each other's company, seemed to wear off, and they began to feel almost as easy as if they had been old acquaintances, or rather friends.

"Though beauty, I believe, is a quality which is in general highly prized by young ladies," said Dr. Bridges, in answer to some previous observation, "yet I can easily suppose that it is not without its inconveniences; for had your own personal charms been less, you would have had fewer admirers last evening, and consequently fewer solicitations to dance, by which means you might have escaped your present cold."

This compliment was wholly unexpected: it was, moreover, bestowed on one who had been but little accustomed to such things; and thus the individual to whom it was addressed felt rather at a loss for a suitable reply.

"My present cold is a mere trifle," said she, "scarcely worth mentioning. But I hope Dr. Bridges has not conceived so poor an opinion of me, as to suppose that I am vain of what he has been pleased to call my personal charms."

There may be such a thing as a *possibility* of schooling people of both sexes into a method of managing conversations, and perhaps everything else, by rules previously laid down; but when such a course of instruction has never been attempted, blunders and mistakes, which may be either amusing or distressing, according to the nature of the case, must frequently occur. Of the truth of this, the experience of almost everyone will furnish him with at least some examples. While Miss Forester pretended to disclaim all vanity, the blush which rose to her cheek told that she was not altogether deaf to the voice of praise. This, however, the inexperience of the other led him to mistake for an expression of displeasure. He was not by nature very well qualified either for disguising his own feelings, or discovering the real sentiments of others. Highly susceptible of impressions, and but little practised in the arts of the world, as soon as this idea had got into his head, he felt like one who all at once discovers that he has done something to forfeit the very esteem which he was labouring to conciliate.

"By no means, ma'am," he stammered out; "I, I"—he would have made some apology, but he found himself getting more and more embarrassed, and he could only articulate the words, "I but spoke the truth;" after which he bowed and made his exit. Thus terminated an interview from which he had promised himself much pleasure, and from which, if he had deserved any, it was counter-balanced by at least as much vexation.

In an affair of honour, or in an ordinary case, the manner in which he had endeavoured to exculpate himself must have been regarded by the offended party as a high aggravation of the original offence; but in the present instance it were difficult to say if it was not the very best apology which he could have offered; for he was no sooner gone than Miss Forester, who had observed his embarrassment, and partly guessed the cause of it, began to accuse herself for having treated him uncivilly, and to wish that he had only stayed till she could offer some explanation. "It was kind in him," she argued, "to pay even an unmeaning compliment to one with whom he was so little acquainted: and then he did not look like a practised flatterer." The natural conclusion was that she had done wrong, from which it was only a natural transition to wish for an opportunity of remedying her mistake.

Her wish was not long in being gratified; for though Dr. Bridges did not call, as she had almost expected he would, next day, on the day following that his professional concerns led him to the same quarter of the town in which she lived. He had previously determined on going straight home, and thinking as little as possible, either of Miss Forester or his former visit, upon both of which it was somehow painful to reflect; but when he came in sight of the house he began to consider if it were not alike inconsistent with the established rules of his profession, and the safety of his patient, thus to discontinue his visits without any assurance of her health being fully re-established. He called to mind several cases in which a trifling indisposition, from being neglected, had produced the most serious consequences; and before he reached the door he had fully satisfied himself of the propriety of making another visit.

On this occasion he was received with the greatest cordiality by both father and daughter, the latter of whom was completely recovered. Mr. Forester, in particular, who, with some eccentricities, was warm hearted in the extreme, where he considered himself obliged, appeared to feel grateful for his daughter's speedy restoration, beyond what the case really merited.

"Welcome, doctor!" he exclaimed, shaking him by the hand at the same time with old-fashioned frankness; "and as I much doubt whether Eliza will have the grace to thank you for the services you have rendered her, you must permit me to offer you the thanks of her father, which, after all, may not be much worse than those of a foolish girl."

After some farther conversation upon common subjects, " I daresay you will find it rather difficult to establish yourself among us," said he; " for we are a bigoted sort of people. With us everything which is old is good, and everything which is new is worthless, at least for a time; but if you can only afford to wait till you get us on *the go* I have no doubts of your carrying all before you."

"I am aware," said the other, "that it is always an affair of some difficulty to get into practice; and where a professional rival is already established I know, too, that this can only be done either by servility or superior talents. The first alternative I cannot think of adopting; and as I have used my best endeavours to make myself master of my profession, if my abilities, such as they are, do not recommend me to notice, I must even try to live without it."

"I honour you for your sentiments," said Mr. Forester, with an approving smile. " But is it not hard," he continued, "in these days, when the whole of us must be gentlemen at once, for a young fellow to subject himself to all those hardships and inconveniences which he must unavoidably encounter before his talents can be discovered and appreciated by a world which grows old, and seldom wears spectacles, when looking for those who are willing to make their fortunes by an honourable application to an honest calling?"

" It may be hard, as you observe," rejoined the other; " but methinks those who never encountered hardships can hardly be said to conquer, even when they obtain a victory; and besides, I have not been such a stranger to those hardships and inconveniences of which you speak as to feel very uncomfortable in their company."

Though not exactly qualified to shine in a fashionable circle, or to attract general attention by brilliant conversational powers, there was about Roland Bridges a degree of firmness and manly sentiment, which formed at least a good basis for future eminence. This Mr. Forester, who was a man of considerable penetration, soon discovered; and after a long and interesting conversation, when he was about to depart, in addition to the father's assurance, that "he would always be glad to see him when he had a moment to spare," he had the farther satisfaction of seeing Miss Forester, who said, "she hoped, as often as his professional duties permitted, he would honour them with a call, without being sent for, as was the case the last time they had the pleasure of his company."

To the young surgeon these invitations were highly gratifying; but every one has heard of there being "a tide in the affairs of men"—that tide was now beginning to flow, and in putting him in the way of receiving such invitations, dame Fortune was playing exactly the same game which she has played to thousands. A few weeks ago, when his time was almost wholly at his own disposal, no one seemed to think his society worth the asking; but from the period here referred to, his prospects improved so rapidly, that in a few weeks more he had scarcely a moment to spare; and then he was pressed with invitations to dinners and tea parties on all hands. Most of these, as a matter of course, he was forced to decline; but whether invited or not, he seldom wanted some excuse for seeing Miss Forester, at short intervals; nor upon these occasions was a friendly welcome from her father awanting.

One evening, as he was on his way to make one of these casual visits, he met his friend Mr. M'Quiddit, who appeared to have been looking for him.

"Whither away in such a hurry?" said the lawyer, in his usual tone of light raillery.

"Only to Mr. Forester's, to whom you were so good as to afford me an introduction," was the reply.

"By the Apostle John, and John Bull," said the other, "and the bones of all the popes and cardinals who lived, died, and were buried before the flood, I could not possibly introduce you to a family to which I was never introduced myself, and with which, from the little company they keep, I have never been able to make an acquaintance."

"That is not exactly what I mean," said the surgeon; "but by introducing me at Mrs. M'Intosh's, you were indirectly the means of getting me introduced both here and elsewhere."

"Well, well," rejoined the lawyer, "I am glad to hear you say so; and as I have been the indirect means of introducing you, if you have no objection, you shall be the direct means of introducing me. This same rich citizen must have a *will* to make, and sundry things of that sort to do, which lie in my way; and there is no great harm in looking out for a job—sailors must keep their eyes on the wind, you know, though it is probable they see just as little of it as we do."

This request was at once complied with; and whether it were that Mr. Forester really entertained a previous respect for Mr. M'Quiddit, or that he only extended to him that respect which is due to a friend's friend, it matters little, but both were received with the usual welcome. The man of business and the surgeon repeated their visits oftener than once in company, and they always found the father the same, though by no means rash in extending either his friendship, or the circle of his acquaintances, it even seemed as if he had begun to entertain a very favourable opinion of the young lawyer; but somehow the daughter, after the first time, could rarely be prevailed upon to honour them with her company. She always found some excuse for leaving the room at the earliest opportunity; and Mr. M'Quiddit, either satisfied with the progress which he had already made, or having business of importance which demanded his presence elsewhere, began to relax his attention. In this respect, however, Dr. Bridges did not follow his example. The intimacy between him and the family of the retired merchant seemed rather to increase, while he at the same time seemed to be sensible, that it was to this friendship he owed at least a considerable portion of his success.

"Before Miss Forester caught cold," he said, on one occasion, "nobody thought of calling me; but since I had the honour of attending her, people seem anxious to become sick, that I may have an opportunity of either killing or curing them, and at the same time the inexpressible satisfaction of putting my hand as deep as I please into their pockets."

"And since this is the case," said Miss Forester, "out of gratitude for so eminent a service, you can do no less than regard me as your patron saint ever after; and if such a thing should happen to be in your power, I hope you will not neglect to have my name duly inserted in the calendar."

In answer to this piece of raillery, Dr. Bridges whispered something in her ear about "giving her a new name, and getting that name inserted in the parish register instead of the calendar of saints," which made her push him from her with a half playful motion of her hand; while it brought the blood to her cheek in a spring-tide flush, which made her glad to leave the room upon some pretended errand, from which she did not return till he was gone.

People are seldom long without some cause of anxiety. While everything else was prospering with Dr. Bridges, he had of late seen little of Mr. M'Quiddit, and he almost began to suspect that he had unwittingly given him some cause of offence. Though he could not discover what this cause might be, he felt extremely uneasy at the idea of such a thing being in existence. But one day as he was passing along the street, revolving the matter in his own mind, he saw Miss Forester approaching, in an opposite direction, and just as he was about to salute her, he was agreeably surprised by the friend of whom he had been thinking slapping him on the shoulder, and exclaiming, " What, doctor! so busy now dealing out medicines, writing out accounts like a lawyer, letting blood, and making crooked legs to other people, that I suppose you don't know your oldest and your best friends in passing."

The surgeon laughed, and shook him heartily by the hand, while Miss Forester passed on without speaking.

" By mine honour," said the other, in a tone loud enough to be heard at some distance ; " by mine honour, a noble looking girl that, and I only wish I knew where to find an individual of the other sex who might deserve such a treasure. But," he continued, lowering his voice to a confidential whisper, " they tell me you are the happy man yourself Ro' ; and now that we have met after so long an absence, pray be pleased to step into the tavern here, and permit me to drink her health, not forgetting your own."

Dr. Bridges said something about " not having been accustomed to frequent taverns," and was proceeding to decline the invitation, but his friend interrupted him before he could arrange his ideas.

" Well, I declare," he said, " one would almost be tempted to think you were going to turn puritan, and hold forth on the streets to a crowd of gaping ignoramuses upon the wickedness of the world, and the unpardonable sin of eating and drinking —concluding your sermons, as in duty bound, with a full assurance that fasting is preferable to prayer; and, in order to reach heaven, that men must take care to starve themselves while on earth. Well if you persist in these laudable intentions, you will be reckoned a saint: there can be little doubt of that. But in this degenerate age, saintship, I fear, will not sell at a great premium among your patients. The calendar, moreover, is already full ; and the publicans say that your tailor has forgot to furnish your unmentionables with pockets ; for they never see your money. These people really have influence ; and if they should raise the hue and cry, who knows what might be the consequence? Come, come, man! it is for your good I counsel you, and unless you are determined on becoming a *ranter*, you will not doubt me now."

Overcome by this species of oratory, which has in general more power over young people than most of them would be willing to acknowledge, Dr. Bridges suffered himself to be conducted into the tavern, where his friend immediately called for a quantity of liquor, of which, as soon as it was brought, he poured out a glass, drank it off to the health of Miss Forester; and then filling up another, handed it across the table to the surgeon.

When the liquor was finished—"Now," said Mr. M'Quiddit, "as I brought you here, I will deal honourably with you; your tailor's mistake shall not be brought to light if I can help it; for I will pay what I have called, and then, as you have so many patients to attend, and so much physic to mix, I will not press for your longer stay." With these words he was reaching his hand to the bell; but the other stopped him by saying, that "he hoped he did not consider him either unable or unwilling to take a glass with a friend, and to pay his share of the reckoning like an honest man."

"Well," said the lawyer, "if you will only promise to be a man, and drink half, I have no objection to sitting another quarter of an hour or so." Upon these conditions the liquor was called for, and the drinking of it commenced. Mr. M'Quiddit was of that particular temperament upon which ardent spirits produce comparatively little effect; though partially intoxicated, he could say things to make others laugh, without allowing a single muscle of his own face to be disturbed; even when so drunk that he could scarcely walk, he could still maintain all the gravity of a judge; and upon these qualities he could safely presume. With the other it was widely different: there was in his disposition a natural sensitiveness and excitability, which seemed to be the cause of much of his awkwardness and diffidence among strangers, but which, when acted upon by any stimulant, at once rose into noisy mirth. Some allusions to Miss Forester, which were made in the most flattering manner, had tended to elevate his spirits above the ordinary level; and thus before the second supply of liquor was concluded, he was exactly in that state of ebriety in which men are inclined to be pleased with the whole world, and to call for more of that which has made them so. Accordingly, when Mr. M'Quiddit again spoke of going home, he was warmly opposed by the surgeon, who now said, that "they might surely each spare a single afternoon from the drudgery of their professions, in which to enjoy themselves a little." It did not require any extraordinary degree of persuasion to induce the other to sit down—once seated, he again enlivened the conversation with quaint observations and humorous sallies, which never failed to draw peals of laughter from his companion; and when the afternoon was nearly spent, Dr. Bridges seemed determined to pass the evening in the same manner. Mr. M'Quiddit, however, represented to him in strong terms the impropriety of doing so, and, at a little after sunset, he succeeded in getting him to the door. The poor surgeon, as drunken people usually do, had all along supposed himself quite sober; but when he got into the street, he found that he could not walk; and his friend, if such he may be called, had to bribe the waiter to assist him home.

In the meantime, the servant of a wealthy individual, whose wife was on the eve of being confined, had called at his lodgings to tell him that her mistress was taken ill, and to request his immediate attendance; but as he was absent, his landlady had sent her to Mr. Forester's, where he had sometimes been found on former occasions. There, however, he was not; but the circumstance alarmed Miss Forester, and taking her mantle, she followed the messenger in the direction of the tavern, where she had last seen him, with the expectation that she might learn by accident the cause of his absence. She had not gone far when she saw him in charge of the waiter: as usually happens in such cases, he had grown much worse after coming out to the open air; the ribald jest, the silly question, the sentence broken off in the middle by a hickup, and the heavy *lurch*, told too plainly what he had been about; and Miss Forester, who, unobserved by him, had come near enough to see and hear these things, almost sickened at the sight.

Unfortunately, drunkenness is too common to excite much surprise in any rank of society; but still, to a virtuous woman, who has given her heart, with all its warm affections, to one whom her imagination has been busy clothing in the best attributes of humanity, nothing can be more distressing than to see that favoured object reduced with his own consent, and by his own act, to a state of drivelling imbecility, worse than the worst idiocy which Nature ever produced. Affection may try to plead excuses, and pass slightly over the darker evidence against him, but still, to a reflecting mind, the question must occur—What prospect of honour or fame for the man who can wilfully throw away his reason?

When Dr. Bridges arrived at his lodgings, his landlady told him that Mr. Potter's maid had been there to request his immediate attendance on her mistress's account. He had been previously engaged to give his attendance on that particular occasion, and the information which he now received tended materially to dissipate the fumes of the liquor. There was in

Mrs. Potter's case some peculiarities which rendered it a pressing, and if not properly treated, a dangerous one; it was upon Miss Forester's recommendation that he had been engaged; and as soon as he could walk without assistance, he proceeded to the house. But the girl, on getting home, had told her master in what state she saw him, and as time was too precious to be lost, Dr. Drugster had been already called. The consequence of all this was, that the servant, instead of admitting him to the patient, showed him into a separate room, and said, "she would tell her master." He immediately began to suspect that something was wrong. Had he been in the full possession of his reasoning powers, candour would have drawn from him a ready confession of his misconduct; but those who have made only a slight deviation from the paths of rectitude, can seldom stop till something more serious occurs; and when Mr. Potter confronted him, he began to stammer out some excuse about "being called away to attend a dying patient." As he spoke, his breath smelled strongly of the liquor he had been drinking, there was a haggard expression about his countenance, which told too plainly of his late debauch; and Mr. Potter, who, besides being naturally of a passionate disposition, already knew the real cause of his absence, and who was, moreover, quick-sighted enough to detect those evidences of intemperance which he still carried about his person, cut him short by observing, dryly—
"A pretty fellow, indeed; first to get drunk, and then follow the example of other drunkards, by adding falsehood to drunkenness!"

By this time, Dr. Bridges was in that state of morbid nervous sensibility, which often follows a fit of intoxication; the word *falsehood* stuck in his throat. For a few seconds he seemed at a loss what to say or do, and then trembling with passion, he exclaimed, "He is a villain who will say that I——I ever was guilty of falsehood!"

"I think, young man, you carry your head too high," said Mr. Potter, regarding him the while with a look which was meant to be one of calm contempt; "but I can forgive you, and time will prove who is the greatest villain. Recollect," he added, as he was leaving the room, "that Dr. Drugster served the people of this place, in the capacity of medical attendant, before they saw your face, and the good man can do so still, though some folks, who do not seem to consider punctuality a virtue, should choose to forget their own interest, and endanger the lives of their patients, by their bacchanalian exploits."

Thus left to his own meditations, the surgeon stole back to his lodgings, where he spent a sleepless night, in a state of mind not easy to be described. Next morning he received a very polite and very formal note, from Mr. Potter, requesting him to send in his account, and hinting that neither his presence nor his services would be required in future. Had his nerves retained their wonted firmness, and its mind its usually vigorous tone, such an occurrence would have probably made little impression upon either; but while both were out of tune, he felt that the excesses of which he had been guilty were, to say the least of them, in one of his profession, highly unbecoming; he felt farther, the risk which he ran of incurring the disapprobation of his friends and the public; under the pressure of these feelings, he had no heart to make the necessary calls upon his patients, and after pushing aside an almost untasted breakfast, he directed his steps to Mr. Forester's, in the hope that he might have an opportunity of explaining the whole affair to that gentleman and his daughter, before any exaggerated report could reach them.

The moment he saw Miss Forester, however, his resolution failed him: she appeared anxious to treat him with civility; but there was a something both sad and constrained in her manner. Those indications of feeling which are so minute that they might escape the observation of the innocent, after being seen for the hundredth time, frequently attract the attention of the guilty at the very first glance. Though she strove to appear kind, her eye did not meet his with that intelligence, warm from the heart, which was its wont; on the contrary, it either drooped, or seemed to wander in search of other objects. He immediately concluded, that some one had brought her intelligence of that which, in reality, she had herself seen; and while he wished to make the fullest confession of his fault, and to promise that it should never be repeated, he could not find words with which to introduce the subject. Miss Forester, on the other hand, was almost equally embarrassed. No one could have been more ready to forgive than she was, but then it became not her to interrogate; and thus their first efforts at conversation were of that kind which is sometimes resorted to as a substitute for silence.

"A most delightful morning this," said the surgeon; "the fresh air is so cool, and everything is so agreeable, I suppose it has tempted your father to take a walk."

"I rather think it was some business which led him out," said Miss Forester, affecting a careless case which she did not feel.

"I should have been glad to see him had he been at home," rejoined the surgeon; "but I suppose we must bear these little disappointments with patience—there is no other remedy for the evils of life."

"We should try to overcome them when it is in our power," said the other, attempting to smile; but the sudden recollection that the words contained an implied rebuke, quenched that smile in an instant, and she added, rather confusedly, "My father will soon be back—he promised to return by ten, and he is always punctual."

The word *punctual*, though spoken by a voice which was at all times gentle, grated harshly on Dr. Bridges' ear: it seemed to glance at the manner in which he had neglected his interest and his engagement in Mrs. Potter's case; the confusion with which it was uttered, he mistook for an indication of rising displeasure; and, again unmanned by his own recollections and fancies, he looked at his watch, pretended to remember the case of some patient, whom he should have visited, and took his leave abruptly. Whatever might be his former disquietude, it was now increased ten-fold; but he was not long permitted to muse on the consequences of his own misconduct; for the next individual whom he met was Mr. M'Quiddit.

"Glad to see you, doctor," he said, giving way to a suppressed chuckle—"glad to see you able to stir at all after your last night's glorification. But in the name of how many saints and martyrs shall I adjure you to tell me what ails you? for you look as melancholy and woe-begone this morning as if that great barrel, which men call the world, had been unhooped, and fallen to staves about your ears."

"If I look woe-begone, it is not without a reason," retorted the other, rather sharply. He then proceeded to give him a brief account of what had happened last night, and the note which he had received that morning, to which he was about to add some bitter reflections on what he considered the cause of his misfortune when his friend interrupted him.

"Pooh, pooh!" said he, "only one of those tricks of which the blind jilt Fortune plays a thousand every day. I can assure you she has played me twenty such in my time; but you are only a recruit, and too *raw* to be able to look upon these trifles with indifference. Nevertheless, you must give the good dame the *go by* in her own way, and when she sees she has a man to deal with she will be less ready to jilt you in future. But there is another thing for which I am really sorry—your ballast was rather out of *trim* last night, and ——"

"And whose fault was that?" interrupted the surgeon, in a tone of bitter reproach.

"Nay, hold there," said the other; "you would accuse me —I know it. But hark ye, and in your haste, do not forget to take reason along with you. I did but take you into the tavern to drink a friendly glass, and straightway you would have more. And had it not been for myself—little as you may think of the service—you might have been sitting there to this precious moment, or you might have sat till the day of doom, for anything I know to the contrary, leaving your patients to pack up their awls for the other world, and your physic as a heritage to the moths."

"I fear they would find some of it rather indigestible," said the man of medicine, laughing in spite of himself.

"That may be," continued the other, echoing the laugh of his friend; "and so much the better, seeing it would make the heritage last the longer. But as I have got you off this sand bank, and safe to sea again, I must now tow you into port; for you are in the *horrors* I see, or in the *dumps*, if that name please you better; and now listen to what I am about to say. I have been drunk fifty times—ay, a hundred, I daresay —and when I got sober again I was as sad and dejected, and all that sort of thing, as you can possibly be; nay, there were times, I believe, when I really thought the world was going to fall to pieces; but I always found that a single glass of the right spirit next morning sent the *blue devils* about their business, and restored me to my senses again. Now, your patients must be visited, and at present you have not the heart to go through with it; so come away and I will put you to rights in two minutes."

There was a something in this rodomontade, meaningless as it may seem, which, when aided by the voice and manner of a naturally good speaker, went directly to lessen the disgrace of drunkenness, and it really lightened Dr. Bridges' heart of nearly half its load. They accordingly went into the nearest public-house, where Mr. M'Quiddit called for a small quantity of their "best spirits," and when each had drunk their share the remains of his gloomy thoughts appeared to be dissipated as if by magic. So immediate was the relief which he experienced that he could not help thanking his friend as they left the house; who, in return, bade him "never droop, though he should happen to get a little top-heavy, but take comfort where he could find it."

He now proceeded to visit his patients as if nothing had

happened. Most of these patients, however, were already aware of what Mr. M'Quiddit had called his "last night's glorification;" the odour of his breath, upon the present occasion, did not discountenance the stories which they had heard; and in more than one family he was looked upon with suspicion. A drunken surgeon, or a drunken physician, is an anomaly from which every sane man must turn with feelings of dislike. In numerous instances the life of a patient may depend upon the nicest discrimination: a trifling delay, the circumstance of not detecting some obscure symptom, the prescribing of an improper medicine, or a mistake as to the quantity of a proper one, may, in some cases, prove fatal; and there is a general feeling that those who cannot at all times command their own reason should not be trusted where there are such dreadful risks.

From that day forward Dr. Bridges' practice began sensibly to diminish, and in a short time it was again almost wholly confined to the poor. Reports, the most prejudicial, as to both his moral character and professional abilities, got into circulation, no one could tell how; the public, as most people well know who have had to deal with it, is ever ready to run into extremes; these reports were believed without much examination as to their truth; and now when much of his time was again at his own disposal very few thought of enabling him to pass that time more pleasantly by inviting him to their tables. Mr. M'Quiddit, however, still continued to assure him that it was only a freak of Fortune, and that the blind dame, when she was tired of persecuting, would again smile upon him. He was also fortunate enough still to retain the friendship of Mr. Forester and his daughter, the former of whom did everything in his power to recall public opinion to its proper channel, while the latter, who was as willing to forgive as she was ready to sympathise, felt for what she considered his misfortunes, as acutely as if they had been her own, and frequently strove to support and cheer him under them. Had he been satisfied with the solace which she could afford, time and her father's friendship might have restored his lost reputation; but unfortunately, in spite of her endeavours to cheer him, and his own efforts to be cheerful, he felt occasionally that lowness of spirits from which, when their prospects are clouded, though it may be but for a season, few are wholly exempted; and then, recollecting the relief which he had experienced on a former occasion, he had again recourse to the bottle, and again he felt relieved. But the relief, not being a natural one, only predisposed him for an earlier and a deeper relapse into the same melancholy mood; and every time the experiment was repeated, it required a larger quantity of liquor to produce the desired effect. In the public-houses, too, and taverns, of which he became a daily frequenter, he soon began to forget himself. At first, this only happened when he chanced to meet his friend Mr. M'Quiddit, who was in most respects too many for him; but then matters were so managed, that the *carouse* was of his own proposing, and the man of business always took care to get him home before it was dark, for which he took no small credit to himself. By and by he began to court the company of still more despicable characters; for when once on the downward road of intemperance, people can rarely stop till they reach the bottom. In a short time he became a prey to hangers-on and common topers, who declaimed against Dr. Drugster, and the ignorant prejudices of the people, and flattered, and pretended to sympathise with him, for the liquor which, at his own expense, he allowed them to drink. As the legitimate result of such proceedings, he was on several occasions, in broad day, carried through the open street to his lodgings, with a crowd of boys laughing and hallooing behind him; even the poorest inhabitant of the place became afraid to trust his health in such hands; his means of supporting himself honestly were thus destroyed, his expenses incalculably increased, and debts accumulated; and last and worst, even Miss Forester was forced to acknowledge to herself, not without a shudder, that when she saw him he was frequently under the influence of liquor.

To her he had never spoken of his excesses; and now he was so much altered by that degrading vice, that he no longer seemed to think any apology necessary. She, on the other hand, saw with the bitterest regret the termination to which he was hastening, but still, with characteristic delicacy, she shrunk from the disagreeable task of admonishing and reproving. She knew that if her father should come to a full knowledge of his excesses, the connection would be at once broken off; with a woman's affection for a favoured object, she imputed these excesses to the misleading influence of his principal associate; and to break this influence she at last bethought her of an expedient.

"Jenny," said she to the servant girl, "do you know Andrew Baxter?" The girl blushed deeply, and acknowledged that she did know him. "Do you know, then," continued her mistress, "if he has received the five hundred pounds which were left by his uncle who died in the West Indies?"

"Why do you ask that question at me?" inquired the girl, still blushing.

"Because I think you know something of his secrets," said the other; "and because I believe your happiness is intimately connected with that circumstance. That you are under a promise of marriage to Andrew, I know; for I heard that promise made, though you never supposed any one was near—that it was by accident, you may believe—nay, do not run away, for your secret is safe in my keeping. And I know, too, that were he able to furnish a house, you would be married immediately; but as he has been thoughtless, and spent his money in the ale-houses, you must wait till the five hundred pounds, or at least a part of it, arrives."

"Ay," interrupted the girl; "and there are some folk, not far distant, who spend more money in the ale-houses than ever poor Andrew had to spend; but what is the meaning of all this?"

"I will tell you that presently," said Miss Forester, blushing in her turn. "Has Andrew ever spoken to you of the new house which Mr. M'Quiddit is building?"

"Ay has he," said the other; "and Andrew says that he is building it with his money, and if he was only able to *creish the clerk's loof* with twa notes or sae, he would be at the bottom of the matter in some way or other. But the clerk was angry at not getting the job, and he cannot face him without money; and he has been so thoughtless ever since he had the prospect of the five hundred pounds, that he never has a penny to spare; and as Mr. M'Quiddit says there is no security for a *farden* of his uncle's property ever reaching this country, nobody will lend him siller; and so he maun e'en wait till I get my half year's wages. I aye wished to tell you, but I never likeit to speak about it. For mony a time," she added, beginning to sob, "mony a time I think that Geordie Banks would be a better bargain without a bawbee, than Andrew wi' his five hundred pounds; but I likeit him first, and whatever he bids me do, I can never say no."

"You are a good and a warm-hearted lass, Jenny," said Miss Forester, endeavouring to comfort her; "and it is that partly which makes me interest myself in your affairs. I will not, however, attempt to deny that I have an object of my own in view; but of that I can tell you afterwards. In the meantime, you know that my father never allows me to have more than twenty shillings in my possession at a time; nor do I blame him for his care, for it has often been the means of preventing me from spending money foolishly; but here is a necklace and a ring, which are worth at least three pounds—dispose of them as you will; take the money to Andrew Baxter, and do not leave him till you have seen him on his way to the town-clerk. Tell him, farther, to do everything in his power to bring this affair to light; and despatch, for my father will be back by twelve."

While Miss Forester and her maid were thus arranging matters of their own, her ill-fated lover, and his never-failing friend, were regaling themselves in a neighbouring tavern, with what they were pleased to call their *morning*. For the benefit of the uninitiated reader, it may be here stated that *morning* in the language of a certain class, does not mean the natural return of light, but a glass of some strong stimulant taken before breakfast, for the purpose of winding up the animal machine after a debauch, to enable them to perform the duties of the day, and also to serve as a *whet* for that meal. Dr. Bridges had been late in rising: it was nearly ten o'clock when they sat down to prepare themselves for future usefulness; and, as Mr. M'Quiddit said all his fine things over in his best style, and rallied his friend on his want of spirits in the most amusing manner, the latter ventured upon two or three *mornings* instead of one, and ultimately forgot that anything more than *mornings* was necessary till dinner time. Upon this occasion, however, Mr. M'Quiddit was decidedly opposed to drinking deep, and so they whiled away their time in sipping small quantities at intervals, singing songs which they thought very merry, and saying things which they fancied others would deem fine, if they were only favoured with an opportunity of hearing them. In this manner two hours passed away: it was noon, and then the man of the law proposed that they should each take off a glass, and quit the premises like men who had determined not to forget their business for their pleasures.

By this time Dr. Bridges was exactly in that state which may be termed "gloriously drunk." He fancied himself as rich as a Jew, as strong as Samson, and as happy as the happiest man that ever lived; and when the other proposed that they should take a walk previous to commencing the labours of the day, he assented with a hiccup, and a declaration that "he would go with him to the world's end."

When they had proceeded some way along the street, " Glory be to the Giver of all good things!" exclaimed Mr. M'Quiddit, " but where are we now? As I am a good Christian man, and neither a Mahometan, nor a Jew, I declare we are before the door of your intended father-in-law, and in no other part of the world. But then he is such a disciplinarian, and such a saint, that you dare not venture into his presence, after you have been tasting."

"But I dare though," was the brief and energetic reply; and therewith the whisky-inspired speaker wheeled off like a whirlwind to prove the truth of his assertion. But his companion caught him by the coat-tail, and detained him, whispering at the same time, "Hold, hold—nay, come along this way a little, and I promise you I will tell you something which shall be for your advantage." Though sometimes inclined to be boisterous and self-willed in his *cups*, he was easily led away by a show of friendship; and thus counselled, he followed the man of business in silence, till they reached the outskirts of the town; but here, as the other still continued silent,—probably from a wish to enhance his information by delaying it for a time—he lost patience.

"Come come, Quiddit," he said, "do tell me what you brought me here for, and don't keep me wondering out my very soul about what is perhaps only a mere trifle after all."

"Not such a trifle either," rejoined the other.

"Well, well, tell me—tell me," said the surgeon, "I am all out of *impatience*, as you know,—ha, ha, ha."

"Well," said the lawyer, yielding at last to his importunity. "I brought you here as a friend, to tell you, that I fear your affairs are getting rather embarrassed. There is that bill which becomes due by the end of next week, you know. Now I much doubt if you have the ready."

"Why, where is the hundred pounds you promised to borrow for me?" inquired the other, growing serious for a moment.

"To say truth," replied the lawyer, "money has become so scarce in these latter days, that I have not been able to borrow a farthing, though I have done all that a friend could do; and after having failed myself, I even went so far as to give your note to an intimate acquaintance to try what he could raise on your account, but I am almost certain he will not succeed."

"That accursed bill," muttered the surgeon in a low tone of bitter reflection,—"cannot borrow a *farthing*, and I have not one to meet the demand. Well, there is not much friendship, after all, in bringing a man so far to remind him of his poverty. But the thought has made me sad, so come away back, for I must have another glass, or, if you won't, by Heaven! I go alone."

"Why, man, do not twist your mouth so terribly on one side, and look so cavalierly at me," said Mr. M'Quiddit, "I have no mind to fight, I assure you, and if I had, I should never think of beginning with my friends. I should have never thought of mentioning either the bill or your poverty, were it not that I have a plan in my head, which, if properly followed out, will enable you to pay the one, and remedy the other."

"Well, I am a fool—a hasty fool," said the other laughing; "I acknowledge that. But you are a good-hearted fellow, my dear Quiddit—I know you are. But you must tell me this same plan immediately; for, as I said before, I am all out of *impatience.*" Here he again laughed heartily at what he supposed his own jest.

"Since you desire me to proceed," said the lawyer: "there is Mr. Forester, who, with a few exceptions, is the richest man in the town. With all his riches, he must, as a matter of course, give his daughter a handsome portion when she is married; and besides, as he has no other child, she must ultimately be his heir. Now, I believe the girl loves you to distraction—upon my soul I do. And what hinders you, I would ask, from going to this Jew, this Crœsus, this same hopeful father-in-law, and demanding pretty Miss Eliza in marriage at once? Why, man, she would be better to you than all the physic you ever sold, or are likely to sell—By Heaven! she would be the making of your fortune in a single day."

"You are right—you are right!" rejoined the surgeon, slapping the former speaker on the shoulder as he spoke. "A glorious fellow, Quiddit! but, by Jove, you are right—she does love me; for now that I recollect, when I once gave her a hint about getting her name inserted in the parish register, she blushed as deep as a midsummer rose. And now I *will* have her—yes: by all the asses whose pates I ever plastered, when they complained of fever, and all the boobies whose blood I ever let, when they supposed themselves dying of plethora, I swear I *will* have her!"

"If you can get her," said Mr. M'Quiddit in a sneering tone, but so low as not to be heard by his enthusiastic companion, and then raising his voice, he added, "But do you think you have really fortitude sufficient, to go through with this affair which is to be the making of your fortune? Young fellows like you, are sometimes faint-hearted when they must come to the scratch in matrimonial matters."

"I must confess," said the other, still rubbing his hands in great glee, "I must confess that I have thought of the thing before, and wanted heart to go through with it; but if I had another glass, I am in the trim to go through with anything just now; and so, good morning, Arthur—my fortune shall be made before I see you again—good morning."

"Nay," said the cautious man of business; "if you are for another glass, I must go with you, to see that you do not take too much; for of late you have been rather given to forgetting yourself."

"Thank you, thank you," said the poor drunkard, "you were ever my friend, and you must be so to the end."

Instead of one glass each of them drank three, of what, in cant phrase, is called *double-strong*, which, poured into an empty stomach, produced a powerful effect upon the nervous system of the poor surgeon, who would have still called for more, had not his friend urged him to go and despatch his business immediately.

"But perhaps Ma—aster *Frosteter* is not at home," said the former, when they were once more in the street.

"Oh yes," rejoined the latter, "the old hunks was to be home precisely at twelve o'clock, I know that—nay, no offence, I respect him as much as you or any man living. And now, despatch, my dear fellow—strike the iron when it is hot, and God go with you, as the minister would say—The devil, I mean," he muttered between his teeth, as he turned away. "Why I should have given myself so much trouble in this affair, I know not; and yet, as I shall hardly be able to stave off that drunken blockhead Baxter for ever, unless I can send you a poking, and get my hand into the old miser's purse, by means of his daughter, I may soon be as poor as you are."

## Chapter II.

At the end of last chapter we left Dr. Bridges on his way to seek a wife, and here we must again take up his story. After various circumvolutions, upon which history cannot pause to dilate, he reached the house of his intended father-in-law in safety, though not without having been oftener than once in danger of breaking his nose against lamp-posts and other impediments. Here he was immediately ushered into a room, at the farther end of which sat Mr. Forester and his daughter —the last of whom appeared to have been in tears, but she rose and withdrew the moment he entered. Without seeming to notice her he staggered to the middle of the apartment, first overturning one chair, then nearly overturning himself upon another; and when, in spite of these obstacles, he had taken up his position, "Mr. *Fo—oster*," said he, "I wish you a ve—ery good morning."

"*Your* mornings seem to be pretty long ones—almost as long as they are in London," said Mr. Forester, eyeing him with a look of mingled pity and contempt. "But pray, what else have you got to wish, or say, or do here at present?"

"O—o—only this," hiccupped the poor surgeon, who was getting worse every minute, "O—only this—I came to demand your daughter—my pretty Miss E—E—liza—Miss *Frothester*, I mean, in marriage."

"Why did you not call her Miss *Froth* at once," said Mr. Forester, his features, in spite of himself, relaxing for a moment into a smile—then resuming his former calm, stern tone, "A strange mixture of bashfulness and impudence," he added—"A man here little more than an hour ago to borrow a hundred pounds for you, and now you are here yourself to make proposals for all I possess. But I pity you, poor thing!—I pity you!—You have been both a simpleton and a sinner, but more of the former than the latter, I believe, and though I cannot stand to speak to you now, I may perhaps see you to-morrow morning, if you should chance to be in your senses then."

Of this address the luckless surgeon had scarcely heard a single word; for the last few minutes he had been growing sicker and fainter, with almost every breath he drew, and before it was concluded he had sunk down upon the carpet, where those who have seen drunkenness in its most degrading form, will be at no loss to guess what followed. In order to prevent his being exposed to open shame, Mr. Forester had him conveyed as privately as possible to his lodgings, where he was immediately put to bed.

After nature, by her own efforts, had expelled from his system a portion of that poison with which he had been drenching it, he began to recover his senses, but it was only to make him wish they had been lost for ever. His potations had never been able to banish the idea of Miss Forester from his mind: to her, in his sober moments, his heart always turned as the star of his future destiny; and though his recollections were confused, he remembered enough to convince him that he had exposed himself in a manner which could hardly fail to make her despise him. He had also some indistinct ideas of her father's displeasure; and, in the midst of his other reflections, the *bill* came to sting him like an adder! He could no longer endure his own thoughts, and rising from his bed, he again hurried to the tavern, where he soon found oblivion of his care, in that madness which had been the fruitful source of all his misfortunes. From this place he was carried to his lodgings, with less ceremony than on the former occasion; and when he awoke next morning, with his throat parched, and his tongue almost as dry as if it had been baked in an oven, his landlady told him that a gentleman was waiting to speak with him. On hearing this intelligence he rose, huddled on his clothes, swallowed the water which had been brought for him to wash in, and scarcely knowing what he did, hastened to the apartment where he had been told he would find his visitor. There he found Mr. Forester, who rose and bowed to him very politely as he entered, but that bow seemed to strike him motionless, like a flash of lightning.

"Young man," said he, in a calm concentrated tone, and without taking any notice of the confusion of his auditor, who, between apprehension, and the effects of his late debauch, now began to tremble violently—"young man, I came not here to insult you: fallen as you are, and wretched as you have made yourself, I can still pity you. But from the headlong career which you seemed determined to pursue, it were madness to attempt to save you; and as I will not be insulted in my own house with such scenes as that which occurred yesterday, you will oblige me by never appearing there again."

"My dear Mr. Forester," interrupted the trembling doctor, in a faltering, and at the same time a pleading tone.

"Only a few words more," continued the other, "and I have done with you now and forever. I need hardly add, that Miss Forester sends you her forgiveness, and wishes you to carry your attentions elsewhere. With respect to myself, I could have wished to serve you; but those who cannot serve themselves, will never be benefited by the services of another. Your inability to meet the demand which the bank has upon you is already publicly known: no one will either lend you money, or be security for you; and as you have nothing to pay, and your presence here cannot possibly be of any use, your only chance of escaping a prison is in flight: and now my errand is said, and I wish you a good morning."

Lightning, thunder, or an earthquake, or all three together, could have scarcely produced such a stunning effect upon the

self-condemned doctor, as these words. Almost sinking under
a load of nervousness, embarrassment, and shame, he followed
Mr. Forester to the door, and gazed after him with a lack-
lustre stare, as long as he was in view. While he stood thus,
he was touched from behind by Mr. M'Quiddit, who drew him
a little aside, and then whispering in his ear: "I have been
looking for you this some time," said he; "do not start—you
were unfortunate in your last night's speculation: I know it;
but I have been myself threatened this morning—no matter
with what—I must have a dram to enable me to get through,
and I cannot go alone. Nay, not a word, I beseech you." So
saying, he led the way, and the other followed like a sheep to
the slaughter.

Upon this occasion, Mr. M'Quiddit drank recklessly and
deep, and the other followed his example; but as liquor always
operates most powerfully upon an empty stomach, and he had
not tasted victuals for more than twenty-four hours, in a short
time he fell from his chair, and in drawing his hand from his
pocket to support himself in falling, scattered several letters
and other articles around him. Mr. M'Quiddit then called the
reckoning, paid it hurriedly, and left the house.

Dr. Bridges was now carried to his lodgings by the people
of the tavern; but his landlady, with whom he was already
considerably in arrears, and who saw no prospect of getting
payment, absolutely refused to take him in; others were unwilling to run the risk of lodging him for nothing, and in the
end he was carried to an empty house, which served as a sort
of barn, and left upon a quantity of straw in a corner. Here
he lay till the afternoon was far advanced, and then a widow,
called Nelly Davidson, from the other end of the town, came
and requested that he might be brought to her house. What
motive she could have for making such a request, was not distinctly understood, but with her he found food, kind treatment,
and a bed for the present. He passed a restless night, however,
and when he arose next morning, an unaccountable change
seemed to have come over him. His air was dejected, and
his countenance strongly marked with a sort of unnatural
anxiety. Throughout the day he sat by the fire, without once
attempting to leave the house, and sighed frequently and
heavily; but when asked "what was the matter with him?"
he obstinately maintained that he was quite well. In the
course of the following night, he started wildly during those
short intervals of slumber which he was permitted to enjoy,
and on more than one occasion he had nearly flung himself

from the bed. When he arose in the morning, his countenance was, if possible, still more wild, anxious, and confused, than it had been the day before; his breakfast he scarcely tasted; and soon after he made several attempts to vomit. When a little recovered, he was most sedulous in his endeavours to please all who came near him, and it was with some difficulty he could be prevented from sweeping the house, and taking out the ashes for his landlady. In this state he continued for some time, without paying any attention to his professional duties; indeed, he scarcely mentioned them—then he became all at once immersed in business, and talked incessantly. He spoke of going to bleed one patient in the great toe for a pain in the loins, and to blister another on the thumb and little finger of his right hand for the toothache. He intended, he said, to take a third individual to a horse-pond in the neighbourhood, and duck him head and ears three times, for a scabbed nose; and he even spoke of having an old woman, who had long complained of rheumatic pains, hung up in the chimney, and smoke-drying her for three weeks. While thus suspended, the patient was scarcely to be allowed any solid food, but supported principally upon a hitherto unknown elixir, which he was to distil from a mixture of horse hair and ram's wool. All this, he assured his landlady, must be gone about with the greatest secrecy; for if it was not, his medicines and applications would lose their effect. These, and a hundred other whimsical notions, alarmed the good dame, who, when she could listen no longer, went out and begged a neighbour to "go in, and sit beside him, till she could run an errand of her own." When she returned, she begged the same neighbour to make what haste she could, and call Dr. Drugster; "for," added she, "the poor gentleman is certainly going out of his reason."

When the senior doctor arrived, his brother practitioner greeted him with a very profound bow, and a—"Pray who are you, sir? if I may presume so far."

"I am Dr. Drugster," said the Esculapian, taking a large pinch of snuff, and drawing himself up in a very dignified manner.

"Very well, doctor," said the other, it was very kind in you thus to come to assist me with my patients. But I assure you I understand their cases perfectly, and can treat them with the greatest confidence. I understand the *diagnostic* and *pathognomonic* symptoms of all their diseases; and the *nosology*—by the by, doctor—I beg pardon—but your own nose does not seem to be in a healthy state. There is a discoloration of the skin under the left orifice—the nostril, I mean—which must proceed either from some organic change in the cartilaginous structure above, exuding acrid matter, and thereby excoriating the cuticle over which it passes, or from some cutaneous disorder, which has its seat in the capillary system, immediately under the epidermis, or in the muscular fibres lying contiguous to the skin, but which, if not properly treated, may terminate in schirrous cancer. Now, sir, if you would allow me to prescribe for your case—and I assure you I have treated a thousand such—1 would recommend a quantity of blistering plaster spread upon a strip of blue flannel, about an inch broad, and placed so as to go quite round your nose: this would keep the place warm, and extract a quantity of the *serum* from the blood at the same time. It might also be useful to have a strip of the same breadth placed across your forehead, above the eyebrows, so as to extract the humours before they could descend. But what would be of more importance in your case than either of these applications, would be a *leech* of the *sanguisuga* genus, or a *gray German leech*, placed exactly here, sir, upon the extremity, just under this pimple; which would take a quantity of blood from the vessels, in the immediate locality of the disease; and if this did not restore your upper lip to its proper colour, it might be followed by *cupping* upon the chin."

How long this disciple of Hippocrates might have continued to lecture upon a discoloration of the upper lip, occasioned by a quantity of snuff adhering thereto, it were difficult to say; but Dr. Drugster cut him short by leaving the house. Soon after, he returned with two stout men and a strait jacket. The assistants were instructed to lay hold of him, and imprison him in this habiliment, which being done, the senior doctor then proceeded to feel his pulse and examine the other symptoms of his case; but after the most minute investigation, he could not determine with any certainty on the nature of the disease. Of all the maladies with which he was acquainted, it most resembled inflammation of the brain, or some of its membranes, and for this disorder he resolved to treat it, but at the same time to proceed with great caution, lest he should be mistaken. He accordingly confined his prescription to some palliatives for the present, and left him with the intention of returning as soon as possible to see what further confirmation of his opinion he could obtain.

When he returned in the afternoon, another scene, which would have been highly amusing had it not indicated a total derangement of the reasoning faculties, ensued.

On being asked how he felt himself. "Me," said the patient, in a tone of evident surprise, "I assure you I am quite well—as well as ever I have been since a thousand years before the creation of the world. Spirits, you know, sir, are not, and cannot be, affected with fevers and influenzas, and inflammations, and phthisis, and cachexy; neither are they subject to affections of the cerebrum and cerebellum, like mortals. But come away, sir, you are growing old, and you will soon die unless I renew you. I am the angel Gabriel, you know, and I can do these things. I will take you down presently, and then we shall get John Laventrough, the baker, to *poach* the clay, and the boy, Littlebaps, his apprentice, can carry water; and when we have got you pounded into a proper consistency, I will fashion you again in a twinkling. And then we can bake you a little in his oven, you know—not too much though —that would spoil the colour of your skin, which, if you were overdone, might be as brown and almost as old as it is at present: so we must take you out as soon as you are hard enough to bear handling. I promise you, however, that I will look after all this myself, and see that they do not put too much fire to the oven either. But you must come to me, sir; for were I to stretch out my wings to come to you, I might fly away altogether, and then you might die, and they might bury you while I was flying round the top of the steeple, and unable to alight—so come along, and I will begin with your nose and your upper lip, where I see evident symptoms of decay."

Though Dr. Drugster was a man of temper, he could not help being rather offended at the pertinacious liberties which his patient seemed determined to take with his nose, and other parts of his person; but this feeling was soon forgotten in the intricacy, or rather obscurity, of the case. As to the real nature of the disease, he was still as much in the dark as ever; and whether to treat it in a vigorous manner, or to do absolutely nothing, he could not determine. "Had it been inflammation of the brain," he argued, "the disease must have made more rapid progress, and to treat it as such might eventually endanger the fellow's life." On the other hand, to prescribe nothing after having been called, was equal to a confession of his own ignorance, which, with professional men in general, is the last alternative to which they can be driven. He therefore resolved, as on the former occasion, to adopt a middle course; but at the same time to make up as much as possible for the inefficiency of his prescriptions, by their number, and the magnitude of their names.

Shortly after Dr. Drugster left him, a new and, if possible, a still more ludicrous idea took possession of his mind. He told the widow that he was constantly tormented with evil spirits, who were every moment endeavouring to get in at his mouth, and possess him bodily; and after a few minutes, when she did not seem to notice him, he called out to her, in tones of the deepest terror, either to come with her besom and sweep them off, or loose his hands, and allow him to do it himself; for if she did not, he assured her that they would soon transform him into the *great dragon* mentioned in the Revelation, and then he would tear the rag which confined him to tatters, knock down the house, and set fire to the town! Terrified by his vehemence, she complied with the last request; and then he sat quiet for several hours, with his tongue extended over his chin, while he continued to strike it dexterously, first with the forefinger of the one hand, then with that of the other, dislodging, as he supposed, a demon with every effort, and thus making his hands take an equal share in the labour of self-defence. At times the strokes were so often repeated, that the quick rotary movement of his hands seemed to resemble a piece of revolving machinery; and then, as the imaginary attack of his spiritual foes was less ably sustained, about half a minute might elapse between his efforts to drive them off. When he had become a little accustomed to this sort of warfare, and had acquired a consciousness of his own superiority, he began to mutter to himself at intervals. "That's Beelzebub," he would say, "with a beard like a goat, and a face as black as a Highland sheep. That's Mammon, with an old stocking for a purse between his teeth. That's Lucifer, flying about like a lamplighter; and yonder is Apollyon: I know him by his long tail." Then, after a considerable pause, and an unwonted effort with both hands—"That's old Satan himself, with his coach drawn by four asses, and a grey cat for a coach-driver! but I have sent them heels-over-head, and there they lie sprawling! help them up, like a good woman—help them up, poor things! Now, now, they're off through the keyhole of the cupboard yonder like lightning—I don't think they'll care for coming back."

It were an endless task to attempt even to enumerate his whimsical notions. All the symptoms of his malady, whatever it was, kept steadily increasing; but still there was no indication of local pain, and when questioned as to the state of his health, he declared himself quite well. Dr. Drugster was now at his wit's end, and knew not what to think of it, unless it were, indeed, a case of insanity. His strength, however, was rapidly sinking—sleep had entirely forsaken him—his hands and feet were cold and clammy, while the former were tremulous in the extreme—his pulse was small, frequent, and indistinct; and had it not been for the arrival of a friend, with whom he had become acquainted at college, and who, in travelling northward, happened to think of paying him a visit, it is probable the record of his actions would soon have closed. Dr. G——, however, almost immediately detected the pathognomic symptoms of *delirium tremens*—a disease which, unfortunately, is at present but too well known, as having its origin in drunkenness, but which then was, and perhaps in some places still is, rather new to medical men. The treatment of Dr. Drugster, though not vigorous, had been the very reverse of what was proper; and as his constitution and complaint had already been too long tampered with, his friend resolved to stay for a few days, and render him all the assistance he could.

In these benevolent intentions, however, he was thwarted, by a most unlooked for occurrence. A branch of the —— Bank in Auldenburgh, had been robbed of money and notes to a very considerable amount, on the night previous to his arrival. When the robbery was discovered, a penknife, with a particular handle, which was at once recognised as having belonged to Dr. Bridges, and a letter bearing his address, were found lying near the *safe*, as if they had been lost by the robber in his hurry to escape. These were considered sufficient evidence; and early in the morning, the sheriff's-officers proceeded to take him into custody. Suffering as he was from severe indisposition, he was dragged to the jail, and shortly after brought up for examination. When asked by the sheriff-substitute, "What he knew of the bank being broken up?"—"Mr. Bank's leg broken," said he, after a considerable pause: "it matters little whether it has been *broken up* or *broken down;* the medical attendant must ascertain whether it is a simple fracture or a compound fracture, or a comminuted fracture, or a fracture complicated with dislocation. But if you would bring him here, I would settle the matter at once, and tell you what sort of splints to provide."

Dr. Drugster, who was next examined as a witness, stated the inexplicable nature of the disease for which he had visited him; and this, in connection with his own ravings, seemed to make the magistrate willing to believe that the whole of his illness, and the incoherency of his speech, had been feigned to elude suspicion. Nelly Davidson was then brought forward, and she declared upon oath, that so far as she knew, he had not left her house that night; but instead of being able to clear the prisoner, from her own evidence, she came to be regarded as an accomplice; and had nothing more transpired, it is probable an order for her commitment would have been issued before she had been allowed to leave the court. Even the exculpatory evidence of Dr. G——, who had never left him during the night, seemed to go for nothing, till an officer brought in two notes of the bank—one for £10, and the other for £20, which had been found near the door of the house in which Dr. Bridges formerly lodged. Had he continued to lodge there, this link would have made the chain of evidence complete, and had he lived so long it is highly probable that he would have been called upon to answer for his supposed crime on a scaffold. As matters stood, however, it gave a new aspect to the whole, and rendered the previous evidence unavailable. For had he been the robber, it was impossible upon any rational principle to account for the notes being found where they were; and when his previous habits came to be disclosed, the presiding authorities seemed to feel satisfied that the letter and penknife had been lost while he was in a state of intoxication—picked up by the robber, and then left where they were found, for the purpose of misleading the public functionaries, and criminating an innocent person. To this conclusion, the notes having been dropped near the door of his former lodging, seemed evidently to point; and upon these concurring circumstances—supported as they were by the unbiased testimony of Dr. G——, he was set at liberty. Thus—while a villain, by making, as he supposed, "assurance doubly sure," defeated his own scheme—the unkindness of his former landlady, and the opportune arrival of his friend, were the means of saving the poor surgeon from an ignominious death.

But though thus rescued from a prison, the last or fatal stage of the disorder seemed to be approaching; and though Dr. G—— had immediate recourse to spirits and opium, which are said to be almost the only remedies in such cases, it was a considerable time before sleep could be produced, without which there is no hope of recovery. At last, however, he did sink to rest, and when he awoke, his reason had returned. But owing to the mistreatment which he had received, and the extent to which the disease had been allowed to proceed, he was so weak that his friend did not deem it safe to leave him for several days. During this interval he became acquainted with the real circumstances; and when he was about to depart, he generously offered him the use of a considerable sum of money to assist in again establishing him in the world; but this was at once declined.

"No," said he, emphatically, " by my own folly I have lost my little stock-in-trade, as a merchant would say; I have lost my reputation, I have lost my health, and what is still worse, I fear I have lost the esteem of one who was dearer to me than all these put together; but now, when my reason is restored, I will not borrow money which I may never be able to repay."

"What do you mean?" inquired his friend, " without money you can do nothing—you cannot even *begin* to redeem your fortune! Pray, what have you to trust to?"

"I beg your pardon," said the other; " but I have thought of all this already, and I *have* my hands. When I was a boy they were accustomed to labour, and I will teach them that lesson again. What I earn in this way, as it will be hardly come by, so it will be likely to be more valued; and as I could not taste that curse of society, and keep in moderation, I now swear—but I will make no oaths—it is only the resolutions of children and changelings, which require to be so confirmed, and I am neither. Henceforth, and forever, my lips shall not touch it."

His friend tried to convince him of the folly of forming such resolutions, but he soon saw that it was in vain; and he left him, not without a suspicion, that these strange ideas might be only one of those obscure symptoms, by which lurking insanity may be sometimes detected. But in this he was mistaken; for as soon as he was gone, Roland Bridges began to question his landlady, in the most rational manner, as to what he owed her, and the amount of debts which had been contracted on his account since he became her lodger. He was, however, greatly surprised to hear her declare, that she " was paid up to last Saturday;" for his farther consolation, she showed him Dr. Drugster's account, which was discharged also; and told him that nothing was owing but his provisions for the present week.

"Did Dr. G—— pay all this?" inquired her lodger.

"Dr. G—— did not pay a ha'penny o 't," said Nelly, in a tone which was meant to be repulsive, but which, nevertheless, had something in it calculated to excite, rather than repress curiosity.

It did excite the curiosity of the surgeon, and he insisted on being made acquainted with the name of his benefactor; but upon this subject she was pleased to appear extremely unwilling to speak, and it was not till after a great deal of pressing, that she could be prevailed upon to satisfy him.

"As the lassie is alike beyont the reach of my kennin', and your thanks, I may e'en tell ye," she at last said. "And she made me promise faithfully neither to tell man nor woman, and I tak' Heaven to witness that had it not been for fear it might destroy the little health ye ha'e, ye had never heard a word o't. And wha should it be, after a', but Miss Forester. Had it not been for her, ye might been lying, at this precious moment, on the strae in the corner of Andrew Smibbert's barn, if ye hadna been lying whaur I'll no name; for folk were sae terrified at ye, that there was scarce anither in the toun would ha'e cared for your company. But she paid me handsomely to bring you here; and when you turned ill, she bade me send for Dr. Drugster, and she gave me siller to pay him too. But this is no a'; her faither has an ill-faured trick of keeping her aye short o' siller; and to assist you, the poor lassie selled her claes, and every thing of her ain that would sell, till she had little left but what was on her back. And if I maun speak the truth, she did it for ane that had done but little to deserve sic kindness at her hands."

"Good heavens!" said the astonished listener; "and do I owe my life and my all to her—well, this is more than I ever expected of woman! But she shall learn," he continued with growing emotion, "though I have been a madman and a fool, and could throw away my reputation, my health, and my reason, by my own folly, she shall learn that I am still a man, and that I know how to repair all."

"She'll learn naething about it, I'll warrant her," said Nelly, dryly. "And as to yer bein' a man; ilka drucken carle in the country side is a man, and a great man too, when he is fou; and then ye can a' repent, and promise reformation like very saunts, when your heads are filled wi' the horrors, your *gebbies* wi' wind, and your pouches wi' naething. But God be praised, the lassie kens the world ower weel ever to trust her happiness to a drucken man. I think some folk I had ance the misfortune to be ower nearly connected wi' learned her that lesson. But he was my husband," she continued, lowering her voice, and wiping away a tear with the corner of her apron; "he was my husband, and I ance liket him weel for a' that, and I should haud my tongue, now when he's at his rest. But mony a day I might have made my breakfast on the wind, and my dinner and my supper on the same thing, had it not been for her—may God reward her! and, if ever it is her fortune to be married, send her a kind husband!"

Roland Bridges felt bitterly these reproaches, which, though couched in general terms, were evidently pointed at his own conduct; but he was too deeply affected by what he had heard of Miss Forester, to give vent to any feeling, save that of admiration; and he now begged Nelly Davidson to try if she could procure paper and a pen. "For," continued he, "though I dare not look her in the face, I must thank her, and tell her that I am an altered man."

"Maybe your alteration may rub aff when it is dry, like a weaver's kiss," said Nelly, who seemed to be perfectly conscious of the superiority which her guest's ignorance of what had passed conferred on her, and who was, perhaps, willing to lose none of the importance which she might derive from such a circumstance. "But you may save yourself the expense of pens and paper," she continued, in the same dry tone, "and the trouble of writing, too, till you ken whaur to address your letter."

"That is what you can tell me, I suppose," said the other.

"That is what I can not, as I telled you already," was the brief reply.

"What am I to understand by all this?" inquired the surgeon, growing at last impatient of the tart manner in which she doled out her information. "Do you mean to say, that Miss Forester has left the place, and that you do not know where she has gone?"

"That is exactly what I mean to say," retorted the other; "and I say farther, that I believe you, and that daidlin' claikin' creature of a lawyer, Mr. M'Squintnib, have been the principal cause of her leaving it, and it will be lang before either of you bring her like into it again. But if she left the place to be out of his way and yours, he has been obliged to leave it too, to be out of the way of that punishment which he deserved for leeing and cheating."

Upon any other occasion, Roland Bridges would have scarcely borne the great freedom of speech, and the evident superiority of tone and manner which Nelly had thought proper to assume; but so many strange events had happened during his illness, and so much in which he felt interested was yet to be explained, that at present he took no notice of it. "What can Mr. M'Quiddit have done to deserve punishment?" he inquired, "and where has he gone?"

"As to where he has gone, I believe that is a secret he has

kept to himself," rejoined the widow. "But his deservings are by this time public enough, and anent them I think I can satisfy you, if you will have patience. First and foremost, he keepit thrang wi' Jenny M'Intosh, his landlady's daughter— and if we keep my ain Miss Forester out of the count, there wasna a bonnier lassie in the town than her—till she, poor thing, could scarce see daylight for him. But, amang a' the things that you men like, siller seems to bae an unco place in your heart; and sae, because Jenny's portion was like to be but sma', he thought proper to keep her between him and want, while he was a' the time laying close siege to Miss Forester; and, let me tell you, mair than ane or two wondered how neither you nor Jenny seemed to suspect sic a thing."

"He is a villain," ejaculated the surgeon, "and I should have known it."

"Then there was Andrew Baxter," continued Nelly, who had now got into the full tide of gossip—" by the bye, they say it was yourself that advised him to employ the rascal Squintnib about his uncle's property. Well, the poor lad—and a poor lad he is, for he never could keep a saxpence if a publichouse were within a mile of him—and Jenny Johnston, God help her, poor thing! they say they're to be married, but how she can ever think of being able to keep a house ower the head of sic a daidlin' creature, is mair than I ken. But as I was gaun to tell ye, the poor lad was staved off from time to time, wi' ae excuse after anither, till he grew impatient, and consulted honest Mr. Copyhold, the town-clerk. A weel, twa folk of the same trade in the same town are seldom great friends: so Mr. Copyhold demanded a sight of a' the letters and papers connected with the affair, and telled Mr. Squintnib, that if they were not forthcoming immediately, he would have him landed in jail for 'bezzling the man's property. Sae ye see, Mr. Squintnib promised faithfully to show him the whole of the papers next day; but before the next day cam, baith him and the papers were gane. And now Andrew maun want his siller, and Jenny maun e'en seek anither joe, for without the siller she says she'll never marry him. Sae there's the tap, tail, and mane o' the matter; mak o't what ye like."

"Strange, indeed," said Roland Bridges; " but what of Miss Forester? where is she? pray be so kind as to tell me that?"

"I've telled you twice ower already," said the dame, "that I kenned as little about whaur she is as I kenned about John o' Groat. A' that I can tell of the matter is, that after his wife's death, the folk here kenned unco little of Mr. Forester's affairs; and so, after you and Mr. Squintnib had baith tried to get Eliza—sorrow confound *him* at least for his impudence—he saw this was nae place for her and him to live in, and selled off his things by public roup. But before they left the town, Miss Forester sent for me to gie me what I verily believe was her last half-crown, and she bade me be as kind to you as I could at the same time; but I wish she had bidden me do something else, for I'm aye ill-natured when I think that you had some hand in driving my best, and, I may say, my only friend, from the house in which she was born and bred. But though she said she was convinced it was for her good to bide nae langer here, the tears ran ower her cheeks as she bade me fareweel, and then she turned back to bid me tell your friend Dr. what-d'-ye'-ca'-him, not to leave you till you was better, and said she hoped he would give you something to support you till you was perfectly recovered. Then she said, 'O Nelly, I'm vext to leave ye', and the tears ran ower her cheeks again like beads; and then she bade me gie ye a' the good advice I could; and when I said that drucken folk never listened to good advice, she shook as if she had been in an ague, and tried to smile as she bade me do the best I could. But, poor lassie, if she had only seen her ain pale cheek, drenched in tears, and sic a smile! I never saw its like before, and would never wish to see it again. But though she wished me to believe that her vexation was on my account, I could easily see that there was something else at her heart. Ah, little, little does a young scatter-wit like you ken what sorrow he may occasion to a woman, or how she may struggle sair, sair to keep it out o' sight, and assign twenty reasons for it beside the right ane, while he thinks a' the time he's only making sport."

This long speech of Nelly's, though certainly far from being an eloquent one, had made such an impression on the heart of her auditor, that when she concluded, he sat in deep meditation, without appearing to have anything wherewithal to answer; and then, after a short pause, she was left to take up the discourse again in her own way.

"Dinna tine heart, Mr. Briggs," she said, in a tone of real sympathy; "dinna tine heart. I'm a hasty body, and I've said ower muckle, but I'm sorry for ye now, and if ye would only tak' a thought and mend, wha kens what might happen—the thing is not impossible. I have kenned Eliza since she was a bairn, and though some women can change their joes, with as little trouble as they change their dresses, and nearly as fast as the moon changes her faces, I am far deceived if she ever marry anither; and if I could only see you fairly reformed, glad wad I be to hear that ye were man and wife."

What effect these harangues produced on the mind of the ex-surgeon, cannot be told, for he spoke not of the subject. But his next care was to see Andrew Baxter, to whose misfortune he considered himself as having contributed, and after a short conference, during which he represented to him, in strong terms, the folly of which they had both been guilty, they arranged matters for leaving the place together. In the evening, Andrew went to inform Jenny Johnston of his intended removal, and early next morning they started on their journey. After travelling one whole day, and a part of the second, they began to seek employment, which they soon found, and then Roland Bridges sold his watch, which was the only available property he possessed, bought a spade with part of the money, and some articles of dress, suited to his reduced circumstances, with what remained; and on the following morning, they both began the world anew as common day-labourers. Andrew, who did not want natural abilities, though hitherto he had abused them, was at first by far the best workman; and blistered hands and feet were rather severe trials for the other: but he had determined to persevere, and what cannot perseverance overcome? The toil to which he now subjected himself, soon hardened the skin upon such parts of his body as were exposed, braced his sinews, and called into vigorous action those resisting powers of Nature which enable the laborious classes to sustain, without serious injury, hardships under which those who are unaccustomed to them would certainly sink. As soon as he supposed himself sufficiently master of his new calling, he and his fellow-labourer began to work upon their own account. With indefatigable care and perseverance, matters prospered in their hands; in a short time they were enabled to become masters in a small way, by employing two or three men, which considerably increased their clear profits; and at the end of six months their prospects were better than either of them had ventured to anticipate.

About this time Jenny Johnston—led as it appeared by a liking for Andrew, which his *wierdless* habits had not been able to extinguish—came to reside in the same neighbourhood; and so delighted was she with the change which had been produced upon his manners and appearance, that, if his reforming partner in business had thought proper to become a rival, it were hard to say, if she would not have given him her hand out of gratitude. This however was no part of his design. They continued in company for a year and some months, endeavouring to make the most of everything; and then, after making a fair division of their profits, property in tools, &c. which left about *fifteen pounds*, for their respective shares, and seeing Andrew married to Jenny Johnston, as the best means he could think of for preventing him from falling into his former dissipated habits, Roland Bridges took his departure, like the patriarch Jacob of old, *with his staff in his hand.*

Thus provided, and thus equipped, he wended his way to a distance of some sixty miles from the scene of his disgrace; and with feelings and sentiments widely different from those with which he had begun the world, he again commenced his medical career, in an increasing village called Glenlaigh. The place, though small, possessed several advantages, being situated in the midst of a populous country district, which hitherto had only been visited, in cases of great severity, by a medical practitioner from a distance. Experience and misfortune had now taught him to restrain his former levity; disappointment had imparted a shade of thoughtfulness, if not melancholy, to his countenance, which, while it made him more interesting in the eyes of his new patients, and their friends, was at once imputed to habits of severe study; and though his practice for a time lay principally among the poorer sort, his success, and the zeal and attention which he displayed, soon placed him high in the esteem of all ranks.

Shortly after his arrival, he was called to visit the wife of an opulent farmer, who had been lame for more than a year. She had, as was supposed, sprained her ankle by a fall; little attention was bestowed upon it at first, but after it began to assume a serious appearance, the nearest medical gentleman was called, who continued to treat it, till it broke out into what he declared was an incurable sore, and then he advised immediate amputation. This, however, was not agreed to, and for several months the patient had been in extreme pain. But Dr. Bridges soon succeeded in giving her relief, and ultimately in healing the sore. Things of this sort frequently make a noise in a country district; the cure was considered as little less than a miracle, and his fame spread with the rapidity of lightning. The other medical gentleman had by this time saved a moderate competence, and considering himself insulted, when he was no longer praised, he left the place in a pet. Dr. Bridges was immediately called on to supply his place, and in little more than a year, he found himself in full employment, with handsome pay, from a number of genteel families. His retired, and almost abstemious mode of living, occasioned him next to no expense; and at the end of another year, he was comparatively rich, with the farther prospect of rapidly accumulating a fortune; but as his struggles with the world diminished, the gloom on his spirits seemed to increase. He had never been able to learn anything of Miss Forester, and, strange as it may seem, after such an interval, the idea of her, and of his former excesses, now began to haunt him like an injured ghost. During his struggles with adversity, other cares pressed upon him, and prevented him from thinking so much upon these subjects, as otherwise he might have done; hope, too, was there, to soften down whatever was disagreeable; but after three years had elapsed, when his other causes of anxiety were removed, and everything concerning her remained as dark as on the day of her departure, he felt "that hope deferred maketh the heart sick" indeed! It was no doubt a weakness—but from weakness of some sort or other what man is wholly free? and against it he could not strive. A slight review of his own thoughts, served to convince him that it was a lurking idea, of yet meriting her esteem, and perhaps obtaining her hand, which, like an unseen spirit, had enabled him to form his best resolutions, and supported him through all his difficulties; but now when he had acquired riches, and earned an honest fame, where was his promised reward? She might be still living in the belief that he was the same degraded, and dissipated thing, which he had once been—She might despise him, and detest his very name—She might be married, or she might even be dead! Every word of what Nelly Davidson had told him concerning her, he recollected with painful accuracy; he viewed the whole through the magnifying medium of his own imagination; and, if disappointment could produce an effect so saddening upon his own rougher nature—had she really loved him as he supposed she did—what might it not produce upon her, all gentle, and shrinking as she was?

From constantly pondering over such subjects, a deeper melancholy sunk over him, the routine of his professional duties became a weariness; and with the view of freeing himself, for at least a few days from that drudgery, and perhaps not without a distant hope, though a distant one it must have been, that something concerning Miss Forester might transpire during the journey, he resolved on paying a short visit to his friend, Dr. G——, who had just settled in Glasgow. He accordingly mounted the stage-coach on its way thither, and passed with it over many a mile, without feeling any alleviation of his care. On the road, however, he imagined that he could unbosom himself to his friend, and that he might reap at least the relief of his sympathy and condolence; but when he arrived he found that even this was denied him. The mind, like the body, from being overburdened, becomes weak, and ceases to perform its healthy functions. Upon this subject he had been so long silent, that he now found that he could not speak of it at all, without a most distressingly powerful effort; like the victim of disease, who calls for meat, and loathes it when it is set before him, as soon as he found himself in the presence of his friend, he shrunk from the idea of making the disclosure, and felt as anxious to return home as ever he had been to travel.

As his visit proved unsatisfactory, he determined to make his stay short. After spending a day and a night in Glasgow, he took leave of his friend next morning, and was proceeding along a narrow and dirty street, on his way, as he supposed, to the place from which the coach usually started, when a meanly dressed and pale-looking female attracted his attention. There was something in her dark eye and the profile of her countenance which he thought he had seen before, though he could neither recollect when nor where; but after reflecting for a moment upon the improbability of such an occurrence, he felt inclined to impute the whole to some distant resemblance, or to the effects of imagination, and without taking a second look he passed on. At the turning of the next corner, however, she met him full in the face, and seemed to solicit his attention, by a timid and supplicating look. The fine expanse of forehead, upon which the lines were more deeply marked than when he had seen it last, the dark eye, still the same, though clouded with care and anxiety—in short, every lineament of that countenance flashed at once upon his recollection, and there was now no mistaking the well-known features of Miss M'Intosh.

After salutations, and mutual inquiries had been exchanged and answered, she told Dr. Bridges that she knew him at first sight, and fancying that he had not recognised her, she had again ventured to throw herself in his way, to beg that assistance for another which she should have never thought of asking for herself; but though such a preamble seemed, in her estimation, to be absolutely necessary, it was not without a strong effort she could overcome her own feelings, so far as to tell him that the individual she alluded to was Arthur M'Quiddit.

"And how, if I may ask," inquired Dr. Bridges, in a kind and sympathising tone, "how is it that you come to be here at such a distance from your friends, and to take such an interest in him? Tell me, Miss M'Intosh, if I may still call you by that name, has he any claim upon you?"

"Upon me he has no claim," said the young woman, while a slight colour rose to her cheek, and a consciousness of the most disinterested intentions, and the most perfect innocence, overcame her former embarrassment. "Upon me he has no claim; and as to my being interested in him—alas! there was another, who with as little reason to be interested as I have, took almost as deep an interest in yourself; but I would not pain you, sir —God knows, I have enough of my own to think of."

"Do you know anything of her—of Miss—of Miss Forester?" inquired the other eagerly.

"Nothing," was the reply; but would to heaven I did, for here I have no friend—no one to whom I can speak. Poor Eliza, when I think of her I could almost weep, and yet I have nearly forgotten to shed tears on my own account, or that of any other, these two months have so changed and bewildered me! Before she left Auldenburgh, a sort of coldness had come between us; but it was my fault, not hers; and if she saw me now, and heard my story, I am certain she would forgive me."

There was something so touching in these allusions, and the manner in which they were made, that, had the speaker wept, Dr. Bridges had certainly done the same to keep her company. As it was, whatever dislike he might have for Mr. M'Quiddit, the feeling had never extended to her; he could only regard with sympathy and admiration those sorrows, and that disinterested affection, of the full extent of which he was as yet ignorant; and taking Miss M'Intosh by the hand, he pressed it warmly —as much as to say, we are fellow-sufferers, and then begged her to conduct him to some place where he might speak with freedom. By a short walk, she brought him to the outskirts of the town, and led him into a private road, which seemed to communicate with a neat looking little country house at a considerable distance. Here he felt that he was in the society of one to whom he could unbosom himself: a strange impulse urged him to tell his story, and he proceeded to give her a brief sketch of his fortunes, and the cause of his present unhappiness. He alluded, in feeling terms, to the first time he had met Miss Forester at her mother's, and spoke of

16

the impression which she had then made on his heart, and the hopes—vain ones as it now appeared—which he had long cherished of meeting her again, with so much sincerity, and truth to Nature, that it affected the other even more than her own sufferings. Nothing has a greater tendency to unlock the heart, and bring forth all its secrets, than a similarity of misfortunes and a ready confidence. When man or woman—but more particularly woman—has been intrusted with a tale of sorrow, akin to her own, and when this has been done without any appearance of reserve, it is hardly possible to resist the impulse to confide again, and thus make the obligation, if such it may be called, mutual. In the present instance, Miss M'Intosh felt what has been felt by others, and while a single tear stole down her cheek, she began to narrate some particulars of her own story.

She confessed, as plainly as female delicacy would permit, that she had been warmly attached to Mr. M'Quiddit, though up to that moment she had never acknowledged it to any one, and that she was the last to believe him guilty of meanness, or dishonest practices. For nearly three years from the time of his clandestine departure, she had heard nothing of him; and it was but little more than two months ago, that she received a letter, which did not bear his name, but which from the penmanship and a particular mark, she at once recognised as his. The letter stated that he had been unfortunate—that he was in extreme poverty—very ill, and that he had the prospect of dying amongst strangers, without being able to procure a nurse, or any attendance whatever. He spoke of her as being the only friend to whom in his extremity he could apply, and begged, if it were possible, that she would send him a small sum of money, to smooth his passage to the grave. A woman's hopes of being able to reform, and serve, and even save those she loves, are never at an end. When the caution, and it may be the stronger understanding, of the other sex would urge them to pronounce the case desperate, she is ever ready to step forward and exert herself to the last; nor are instances awanting in which she has succeeded, after men, with all their boasted powers, had yielded to despair. Miss M'Intosh did more than was requested of her: she fancied that in the midst of his misfortunes he might be ready to listen to the counsel of a friend, and with her care that he might still recover. She knew, however, that she could not accomplish the task she had assigned herself, with her mother's consent; and poor as he was, and blighted in fame and fortune as he had been, she left her home secretly to search him out, and administer such relief as she could. With much difficulty she discovered him, under an assumed name, but at first he pretended he was not the man she sought, and when at last he was compelled to acknowledge his identity, he seemed to be rather offended with the rash step she had taken, and entreated her to say nothing of having known him previously. Since then she had done her utmost to husband her little stock of money, living with a poor family, a few doors from him, and passing for a distant relation of his. But her means of supporting herself and assisting him were now completely exhausted: "And God only knows," she added, "what is to become of me! I cannot leave him to perish, and if I could, how am I to return home?"

At that moment Dr. Bridges saw his friend turn into the road which they occupied; from the time which had already elapsed, he felt certain that he must have lost the coach for that day; he felt, moreover, strongly interested in what he had heard, and resolving to postpone his departure till next morning, he gave her hastily some money; and after having learned the locality in which she lived, he promised to call in the evening, to see if he could be of any service to the sick man.

"If you are determined on doing so, some caution will be necessary," said the other; "for there is a mystery about him which I have never been able to penetrate. Had our meeting been less sudden and less unexpected I should have told you this at first, or perhaps I should not have mentioned him to you at all; but I had little time to think, and now I can only entreat you to recognise him as *Hubert Jackson*, to appear a perfect stranger, and not to speak of those scenes in which you knew him; for I have all along observed that any allusion to his real name, or to anything connected with Auldenburgh, drives him almost to madness."

"Leave that to me," said the other, and immediately joined his friend, Dr. G——, who was now close upon them. A short explanation of the causes which had detained him, followed as a matter of course, after which Dr. G—— expressed himself pleased with any circumstance which would give him the pleasure of his company for another day, and then requested his professional assistance, with respect to the patient whom he was then on his way to visit. "Her case," he said, "was a mysterious one, having completely baffled several medical gentlemen before he was called, and during his own short attendance he had not been able to render her any assistance." Dr. Bridges readily complied, and in a short time they reached the house to which they were going. The door was opened by a female servant, at whom Dr. G—— inquired, "how her mistress was?" but the girl only said, "she could scarcely tell," and then ushered them on tiptoe into her room. When they entered she was reclining on a sofa, and seemed to be in a gentle sleep. Dr. G—— paused for a moment, and would have turned back; but as she opened her eyes and sat up, before he could do so, he advanced to address her, and then turned round to introduce his friend. With the first glance, however, which he caught of that pale countenance, he had retreated like one in utter bewilderment, and before Dr. G—— could return to the room door, he was leaving the house. The last mentioned individual followed him out, and after he had somewhat recovered from the agitation into which he had been thrown, he endeavoured to account as succinctly as possible for his surprise, and sudden retreat. The features of the patient had been too deeply imprinted on his memory, to be easily effaced, and, altered in appearance as she was, by three years of disappointment and suffering, the moment he saw her reclining on the sofa, he recognised Miss Forester. But the meeting was so unexpected, she appeared to have endured so much, and the change which suffering had produced upon her countenance, was so evident, that his heart smote him as the cause of all; a simultaneous rush of recollections overpowered him, and he felt equally incapable of addressing her, or remaining in her presence. A short consultation followed, during which it was agreed, that to appear suddenly before her, in her present weak state, might produce disastrous, and even fatal consequences; but as Dr. G—— was now satisfied, that blighted affection had been the principal, if not the sole cause of her protracted illness, he was of opinion, that the sooner she could be made acquainted with his improved prospects, and the present state of his feelings, so much the better. For these reasons it was settled, that Dr. Bridges should return directly to his friend's house, while the other was to repair to his patient, and endeavour by such hints as he might think proper, to prepare her mind for seeing him.

When he returned to her apartment, Miss Forester inquired, with some eagerness, "what had become of the gentleman whom he was about to introduce as his friend?" whose name she had not yet heard.

"Why, as to that," replied the other, "I believe he had forgot some appointment, or something of that sort, and found it impossible to favour us with his company; but ever since I saw him, I have been determined to congratulate you on the hopes which I now entertain of your speedy recovery, and to banter you out of these melancholy thoughts which are at present preying upon your spirits. After him, I think I shall never again speak of any thing as impossible; for at no very distant period, he had wantonly thrown away his prospects, his reputation, and very nearly thrown away his life; indeed, there appeared to be but a hair's-breadth between him and his end; and now he is completely reformed, rich, respectable, and stands high in his profession; and I assure you———"

"And what is that profession? if I may be so bold as to inquire," interrupted Miss Forester.

"Nay, you must not fall in love with him so suddenly," resumed the other, "though I have been praising him, he may be both old and ill-looking, for any thing you know to the contrary, so you must wait till you have seen him, and then, as he is still unmarried, who knows what may happen?"

To the last part of this discourse she did not appear to listen, or, if she did, its import had escaped her. A bright crimson now flushed her formerly pale cheek, and her whole countenance bore such an expression of strong and deep interest, that Dr. G—— began to fear he had already approached too near the subject he was endeavouring to introduce, and almost trembled for the consequences. The blush, however, which alarmed him, was not one of passion, or of maiden shame, but occasioned by that mysterious impulse which hope and sudden excitement communicate to the heart; and while he stood confounded at the change in her look and manner, which his words had produced, "I conjure you, doctor," she said, rising from the sofa as she spoke, "I conjure you, unless you have strong reasons for withholding them, to tell me the profession and name of your friend."

"As to that—as to his profession," said the other, who was still wholly at a loss how to proceed; "as to his profession, I believe—I think I may tell you—that he is a surgeon; and for his name, really ma'am—I think—I suppose———"

"And his name is *Bridges*, you would perhaps say," added Miss Forester, completing the sentence with which he appeared to be so terribly puzzled.

"I believe your guess is not very distant from the truth," rejoined the other, while he could not suppress a smile at his own embarrassment.

"I thought I was right," said she, "from the slight glance I had of him when he was retiring."

As she uttered these words, she sank back upon the sofa, faint and exhausted by her own emotions. She did not swoon, however, as he had almost anticipated. Though he knew nothing of her previous history, except what had been hurriedly imparted by Dr. Bridges, she was perfectly aware of his having been at Auldenburgh while that individual was suffering from *delirium tremens:* this circumstance, and the evidence afforded by her own eyes, had partially prepared her for that information which he had communicated with so much embarrassment; and as he had been called by her own particular request, it is, at least, probable, that she might have been expecting some information of the kind.

"You will think me a strange creature," said she, after a short pause of exhaustion; "and for one so near her grave, as I have reason to suppose myself, I must confess I have acted unbecomingly."

"Not a word more of that," said the other, "but pardon me for speaking plainly. Short as was my interview with Dr. Bridges, I knew enough of your story to account for every particular of what I have seen; and as matters now stand, I think I may congratulate both him and you." Another deep blush was followed by a long and interesting conversation, in which Miss Forester took part with more strength and spirits than her medical adviser had supposed she possessed. Between them it was finally arranged, that if her father's consent could be obtained, Dr. Bridges should breakfast there next morning. Just as they had come to this conclusion, Mr. Forester returned from his forenoon walk, and, that nothing might be awanting, Dr. G—— waited on him in his own room. At first he seemed to hesitate, and would have, perhaps, declined the honour which was intended him; but on being reminded of the different position in which affairs now stood, and of his daughter's illness, with the probable cause of it, he at once gave his assent.

Deeply as Dr. Bridges had felt interested in Miss M'Intosh, the events which followed, and the important intelligence which his friend had to communicate, completely banished both her and Hubert Jackson from his mind; and it was not till next morning he recollected that he had promised to call upon them. As soon as he mentioned the circumstance to his friend, he offered to accompany him, and as he was by this time tolerably well acquainted with the town, they discovered the house in question without much difficulty. At the door they met Miss M'Intosh, who appeared to be suffering from recent agitation.

Believing that her former caution was vain, and that worse consequences might follow if she did otherwise, she had at last ventured to tell the sick man of his intended visitor; but as soon as she mentioned the circumstance, he fell into a most ungovernable passion, began to rave like a madman, and upbraided her with a wish to bring him to an ignominious death. These ravings were followed by a violent trembling, and a depression of spirits, as pitiable as the former had been appalling, and even after he had sunk to sleep, his dreams seemed to be haunted with images of horror. For these sudden and distressing changes, Miss M'Intosh could not assign a reason, and she now seemed to hesitate as to the propriety of admitting the two medical gentlemen; but as they expressed themselves ready to do everything in their power for his health and comfort, and she was still willing to believe that they might be of some service to him, she ushered them into his apartment.

When Dr. Bridges addressed him by his assumed name, and inquired how he did, he fixed his eyes on him with an appalling stare, but did not attempt to speak, and it was not till the other had repeated his words, that he broke silence.

"You need not mock me with that now," he said, at last, withdrawing his eyes at the same time, and fixing them resolutely on one of the bedposts: "I am Arthur M'Quiddit, as you perfectly know; and, what is more, I am dying; but what do *you* want with me?"

"To lend you all the assistance in my power," said Dr. Bridges, in a soothing tone.

"If that is all," retorted the sick man, "you may carry your assistance to those who can reward you for it, or, at least, to those who will thank you—for me I can do neither."

"I look for neither reward nor thanks," said Dr. Bridges; "but will you be so good as allow me to feel your pulse, and answer a few questions?"

To this he offered no opposition, but medical assistance came too late: to his visitors it appeared that his constitution had sunk under excesses of various kinds, to which he had been addicted; and though neither of them spoke, they both felt certain that his last moments were hastening on. As medicine could be of no use, they tried to draw his attention to the consolations of religion; but they had scarcely alluded to the subject, when he almost gnashed his teeth with rage.

"Demons and spirits of darkness!" he screamed in shrill and hissing tones, "if you *will* have me damned, let me die first at least! but wait till then; for I tell you, that I have despised and rejected the hypocritical cant and vile delusions which you would offer—my only hope is in annihilation, and why would you tear that away when I have most need of it?"

Convinced of the hopelessness of his prospects in both worlds, and unwilling to embitter by their presence the few hours he had to live, Dr. Bridges and his friend were about to retire, when they saw Miss M'Intosh, who, overcome by a feeling of horror, had shrunk back from the bedside, and now stood pale, trembling, and, to all appearance, ready to faint. They tried to soothe and comfort her, and while thus engaged, the scene seemed to affect the dying man deeply: a sigh heaved his bosom, he shaded his eyes with his hand for a moment, and then addressed Dr. Bridges in a tone of softened feeling.

"You have spoken of assisting me," he said—"I am beyond the reach of your assistance, but be kind to that woman—she has been kind to me, kinder than I deserved, and were I to live, I would be a better friend to her than ever I was to man or woman before. Be kind to her, and when I am dead, use your influence with her friends to take her back."

Dr. Bridges assured him that his request would be complied with, and offered him his hand, which he took, as a pledge. This done, they were again about to retire, when he interrupted them. "Stay," he said, "there is something yet which I would tell; but draw near, for I am unable to make myself heard at a distance." Dr. Bridges drew close to the bedside, and he proceeded to tell him of a tree which stood in a solitary corn field at a distance of several miles. After having described the place minutely—"Go to this tree," he continued, in a low husky voice; "measure exactly twenty feet from its root, in the direction in which the shadow falls at noon; dig there, and at the depth of about two feet, you will find a glass bottle, containing some papers, which may be of use to you or some one else." It was with considerable difficulty he could articulate the last words, and as he concluded, he pointed with his finger to the door as a sign that they might now depart.

It now behoved them to hasten to their appointment at Mr. Forester's, which they did with all possible speed, and there they found breakfast on the table, and Miss Forester waiting their arrival with some impatience. On this occasion, she had bestowed rather more care on her dress and person than was her wont. Her appearance was still emaciated; but there was a faint colour on her cheek, which, together with the sparkle of her excited eye, made her once more beautiful. The distressing scene which he had just witnessed could not prevent her lover from worrying himself with apprehensions on the road thither; but the moment he took the hand which she held out to welcome him, though she spoke not a word, the pressure of her slender fingers convinced him that he was forgiven, and that he still had an interest in her bosom. Sorry we are to say, however, that there was scarcely anything else in their meeting which deserves to be narrated. When the simple ceremony of shaking hands was over, Miss Forester retired to her own room for a few minutes, and when she returned, with the exception of an occasional flutter—the natural effect of pleased and excited feelings—she behaved as if nothing extraordinary had happened. With respect to the other, there was little in his manner worthy of remark, save that he seemed to have lost his appetite, and had he been left to himself, he would have certainly forgotten to take his breakfast. When reminded of what he had to do, he indeed set about the business in hand with much apparent satisfaction; but then after the first minute or so, he uniformly relapsed into inactivity, and the good things upon the table were suffered to remain untasted, till some innuendo, or commonplace remark, again called his attention to the strengthening of his inner man. It may well be supposed, that Miss Forester had no great reason to be pleased with this carelessness of a meal which, weak as she was, she had provided with much care; but such is the natural lenity of woman, that she showed no sign of having taken offence: on the contrary, she seemed to derive a sort of pleasure from the forgetfulness of her guest, and on more occasions than one, it was with some difficulty she could suppress a smile. When breakfast was ended, matters were so contrived, that they were left alone; and here those who have been in a similar situation must be left to guess what they said—the writer of this story not having been able to procure any information on the subject.

By the time this private interview ended, it was within an hour of noon, and as the sky was unclouded, and the sun throwing a distinct shadow from every object which intercepted his rays, the two friends set out to discover the tree which Arthur M'Quiddit had mentioned in the morning. By following his directions, they found the article in question, which contained the most important letters and papers connected with Andrew Baxter's West Indian property, along with a number of large notes belonging to the bank at Auldenburgh, which had unquestionably been abstracted when the robbery was committed. The notes were privately returned to the proper quarter as soon as possible; and as the robber had never been discovered, and no evidence now existed to warrant farther search, the whole affair was quietly hushed over. The other papers enabled them almost immediately to institute proceedings for securing to Andrew Baxter what remained of his uncle's property, which was still well worth attention.

Before Dr. Bridges and his friend could return to the town, Arthur M'Quiddit had escaped from disease and poverty, from the hands of that justice of which he appeared to be afraid, and from every earthly tribunal, and gone to give in his account before his Maker. Miss M'Intosh, however, remained to claim their care; she had been so terribly appalled by his last struggles, and the indistinct yet fearful allusions which he made to futurity before his spirit fled, that she was now seriously indisposed; and it required the most assiduous attention to prevent her from sinking under the effects of what she had witnessed.

Our story might now end, but as Sir Walter Scott had thought proper to introduce to the notice of authors, a numerous class of readers, from among whom he selected *Miss Buskybody*, as an example; and as it is unquestionably the duty of every scribbler to endeavour, as far as he consistently can, to please this and every other class who may honour his productions with a perusal, a few words more may perhaps be pardoned. Dr. Drugster was now dead, and by a subsequent arrangement, Dr. G—— took Dr. Bridges' situation, which was a very lucrative one, while he returned to the scene of his early labours. Mr. Forester also returned to Auldenburgh, and took possession of his former house. Andrew Baxter, who, as already hinted, had learned sobriety and industry from his connection with the surgeon, was again an inhabitant of his native town, living comfortably with his wife Jenny Johnston, and growing gradually rich upon the fruits of their joint labours. He was, however, soon raised many degrees in the estimation of his former acquaintances, by being put in possession of *three hundred and fifty pounds;* but though Jenny and his other friends declaimed loudly upon the villainy of Mr. M'Quiddit, in keeping him so long from his own, he only shook his head slightly, and thanked heaven in a whisper, that the villain had done what he did—intimating thereby his conviction, that had the money come into his hands shortly after his uncle's death, it might have found its way into the hands of others long ago. On the Sabbath after Andrew was made a gentleman, and just before the minister entered, the precentor rose up in the church of Auldenburgh, and proclaimed to the people there assembled, a certain laudable "purpose" at the time existing between Roland Bridges and Eliza Forester; and on the following week there was a marriage, to which Nelly Davidson was invited. In the course of the evening Dr. Bridges inquired at her if she were pleased with him now, and if she thought he had done his part, by bringing back one who, he hoped, would be as good a friend to her, and in other respects as valuable in the place, as ever Miss Forester had been? To these questions Nelly did not give a direct answer, but said, "she much doubted whether he would have ever been able to bring even a *beggar wife* to the town, had it not been for one who had more affection for him than he had for himself." With respect to Miss M'Intosh, it only remains to be stated, that she is still handsome, and has lost but little of her personal attractions. Her heart, however, does not seem to be of that yielding kind which, like warm wax, may be made to take a hundred impressions, one after the other; and having seen, and felt, and suffered, as she has done, there is little prospect of her changing her name.

---

## THE ILLEGITIMATE.

"Is it possible, on such a sudden, you should fall into so strong a liking with old Sir Rowland's younger son?"—*As You Like It.*

WHILE most of our large towns have been rapidly increasing, there are perhaps few old people who do not recollect several hamlets, or smaller villages, which have now almost entirely disappeared. Among these the Kirkton may be numbered: the improvements and alterations of the present century have nearly blotted its very name from the face of the earth; and such as it was, it can never be again. Standing at the base of a range of low hills, which screened it from the northern blast, it presented the very beau-ideal of irregularity. The houses, of which there might be between thirty and forty, stood in detached groups, with open spaces and garden ground between. Around most of the gardens, a row of trees had been planted, which, after having attained the growth of more than a century, gave the whole, when seen from a distance, the appearance of an open grove. The church, however, which, with its time-worn walls, painted windows, roof of grey slates, and antique belfry, stood upon a circular mound near the middle of the village, rose above the trees, and was seen from the surrounding country. Around the church lay the parish cemetery, separated from the rest of the houses by a low wall, within which the dust of many generations seemed to have augmented the original soil, till it was nearly as high as the top of the enclosure. The cemetery itself abounded almost to excess with that species of erect tombstone, which some one has somewhere designated "spectral." In some places they stood huddled together as if for company's sake, and in others solitary, as men are apt to do when disgusted with the world. Most of them were painted white, so that when seen in the far spent twilight of a summer evening, or by the waning moon on a winter night, a superstitious individual might have easily furnished himself from among them with a whole host of sheeted apparitions. These monuments, several of which evidently belonged to an early period, showed various degrees of perfection in the art. Some were smoothly wrought, and had all their lines and angles entire; others, of an older date, were so overgrown with moss, that they appeared to have neither lines nor angles; some were covered with quaint devices—some "with nameless sculpture decked"—while over a few of the oldest, the obliterating hand of time had passed, sweeping name, date, devices, and all before it, and leaving those whose memories they were intended to perpetuate, in as much obscurity as the "unhonoured dead." Around the churchyard on every side, and separated from it in some places only by a narrow footpath, the small smoky houses were congregated close, as if their original possessors had coveted these situations from their proximity to that "land of forgetfulness" to which they were at last to be removed. Below the church, on the north side, stood the mill from which the *mill burn*, making a circuit to the westward, swept nearly half round the village—now ready to overflow its banks, and anon diminished to the drippings of a scanty stream, as the dam above chanced to be open or shut.

To this place when a boy I was sent every morning, in defiance of my own inclination, that I might have the benefit of the instructions and the thrashings of Mr. Mathias Weatherspoon, who was the parish schoolmaster. Being somewhat of a dunce, I was far enough from being a favourite with the dominie; but to compensate for this, I had the good fortune to find a friend in his daughter, who, when her ireful father, for my misdeeds, had drawn me forth from that *sanhedrim* of numskulls with whom I was associated, sometimes took me into the house, and comforted me with smiles and kind words; or, if neither of these would do, her last resource was to tell me a story; and from her it was that I first learnt the following particulars of an individual, at the time living in the village.

On a summer morning, as the mill-master's servants were beginning the labours of the day, they nearly stumbled over a young woman, of rather interesting appearance, with a child in her arms, which appeared to be only a few weeks old, lying upon some straw in one of the sheds. When they discovered her, she was in such a state of exhaustion, that at first they supposed her dead. She was immediately carried into the house, where common humanity prompted Mrs. Henderson, the mill-master's wife to do everything in her power for the restoration of the stranger. When so far recovered as to be able to speak, there was a something in her manner—a bashfulness and a delicacy—so unlike the character of a common vagrant, that Mrs. Henderson began to take a sort of involuntary interest in her fate; and when it was farther ascertained that she had neither home nor friends to whom she could apply, Mr. Henderson offered her an empty house which he had in the village, at a very moderate rent, upon condition that she would work for him or his wife when they required her. These terms were readily accepted by the stranger, who seemed anxious to live for the sake of her infant, though it did not appear that she could bring herself to beg for that or any other consideration. The only difficulty now was, to furnish her with a few of those articles which were indispensable to housekeeping; but this also was got over. The wooden frame-work of an old bed, upon which the worms had feasted for nearly half a century, was brought down from the *couplebauks* of the barn; a remnant of an old carpet, with which the moths had long been familiar, and some worn out blankets, were supplied as bed-clothes; a chair without the back, and a four-footed stool, were brought from the kitchen to serve as seats; a wooden plate, a spoon, and an old pitcher, were added to the store by one of the farm-servants; and with these, and another culinary article, yclept a *parritch-kettle*, for which fourteenpence was subscribed, the stranger took up house.

The people of the Kirkton, however, were far from regarding these measures with a friendly eye. They had married, and intermarried, till nearly the whole inhabitants of the place were in some way or other connected; and to touch one, was to offend the whole. The former occupant of the house had been ejected by Mr. Henderson, in consequence of some quarrel; and when he left it, his friends consoled themselves with the idea, that it would never get another tenant. This was all they could do. Against the mill-master, who was also proprietor of his own farm, they had not the means of waging successful war; they were therefore compelled to brook, what they considered an unpardonable insult; but no sooner was the house again occupied, than they looked upon the unoffending occupant as an intruder, from whom, if they could not drive her hence, it was at least their duty to stand aloof: and, had it not been that some of the women were anxious to hear her story, they would have shown her immediately what she had to expect. That story, however, she did not appear willing to tell: some particulars she indeed gave, but they were neither full, nor satisfactory; and, when her neighbours discovered that she would communicate nothing more, it was at once decided that she had swerved from the paths of virtue—that her child was an *illegitimate*, and, as such, that they deserved to be treated with contempt. In this belief, they were confirmed by the circumstance of her boy's surname being the same as her own, which, they argued, could not have been the case, had she been married. But as time passed on, some individuals, who were less prejudiced against her, and treated her with more kindness, began to acquire her confidence; to them she at last unfolded the greater part of her story; and that story a little condensed, ran nearly as follows.

Her name, which she never attempted to conceal, was Katherine Elliot, and she was the daughter of a farmer, who lived near one of the shipping ports on the west coast of Scotland. When little more than a girl, she became attached to a young man, who was frequently employed about the harbour; he was equally fond of her, and as he had the advantage of a tolerably good education, they both hoped that in time he might get into some situation, which would enable him to ask her hand in an open and honourable manner. But, as matters then stood— he being poor, and her father comparatively rich—motives of prudence induced them, for nearly three years, to keep their attachment a profound secret. At last his prospects seemed to brighten: he was promised a place in the Excise, and already wearied with long waiting, to anticipate his good fortune, they were privately married. Almost every day he expected orders to present himself for examination, but several months elapsed without any thing of the kind having reached him. The war was then hotly carried on by sea, as well as land; the press-gang were busy in every port; and though he was not a sailor, as he had been frequently seen about the harbours by these officials, and was supposed to have some knowledge of nautical affairs, he was waylaid—hurried on board a tender—and thence draughted into a ship of war, which was on the point of sailing for the Mediterranean, without even having time to speak a word, or write a letter to his wife. On her part, she endeavoured to conceal her sorrow at this unexpected separation, as well as she could; but the time soon arrived at which the secret of their engagement could be no longer kept, and then her life became truly miserable. Day after day, she had to listen to the stern reproofs of her father, who spoke with bitterness of the shame and disgrace she had brought upon his family; and said, that he would have rather seen her buried, than dishonoured as she was. Morning, noon, and night, her mother abused without measure, or mercy, the man whom she loved, and to whom she considered herself bound by the holiest of human ties. The misery which she had to endure from these causes, was greatly aggravated by the conduct of an only brother, who would scarcely speak to her at all; he avoided her presence, as if it had been contamination to be near her; and, if at any time he did condescend to notice her, it was as "a fallen thing," and in that tone of mingled pity and contempt, which is a thousand times worse to bear than the bitterest reproaches. In vain did she declare that she was married, and that her husband would acknowledge her marriage when he should return—no one believed her, and driven almost to distraction, she at last formed the rash resolution, of quitting her paternal home for ever.

About this time, she heard that the ship in which her husband sailed, had sustained severe damage at sea, and had been ordered back to Plymouth, where she would lie till she could be repaired. The thought of reaching him, and getting their marriage publicly solemnised, struck her, and without speaking of her purpose to any one, she collected what money she could command, tied up a small bundle of clothes, and having previously ascertained that there was a vessel in the harbour, which would sail for the Ex with the night tide, she waited patiently till the family were asleep, then hastened to the shore, paid her passage, and went on board. After having performed more than half the voyage, the vessel was stranded in a gale during the night, on the west coast of England; and the crew, most of whom were drunk, thinking that she must soon go to pieces, took to the long-boat, leaving their passenger to the care of Providence. For their selfishness in this respect, however, they soon met what appeared to be a just reward. The moon, which hitherto had been clouded, now shone out, and from the deck she saw them struggling hard to clear the breakers, but a strong current and the heavy sea which was then running rendered their efforts unavailing; and in a few minutes a giant wave flung them headlong among those merciless executioners of the deep, where even their drowning cry was drowned by the louder crash of bursting waters. Almost immediately after this catastrophe, the wind began to abate; in half-an-hour more it was nearly a dead calm, and though the heavy swell from the ocean still continued to menace the vessel, she held together till the receding tide left her perfectly dry. Lighted partly by the waning moon, and partly by the rising morn, Katherine Elliot now proceeded to throw a rope over the ship's side, and by this means she succeeded in reaching "the smooth and hardened sand." The vessel had been thrown upon a solitary part of the coast, no one appeared to be stirring, and with a heart full of the events of the past night, and her own uncertain prospects she pushed on through field and brake, till she came to a road leading to the southward, and following it she proceeded sadly and silently on her journey, till fainting nature compelled her to seek rest and refreshment. She had many motives for despatch; even when she did stop, she felt inclined to be silent on the subject of the late wreck, lest any thing should transpire to detain her; and resuming her journey as soon as possible, she prosecuted it with indefatigable perseverance. Travelling on foot, however, is at best but a slow mode of proceeding; and after all her efforts she arrived at Plymouth just in time to see the ship in which her husband sailed, standing out to sea with a fair wind, and to learn that her destination was the East Indies.

This sight nearly overwhelmed her; it was several days before she could recover her spirits so far as to be able to leave the place; and while thus detained she met by accident a sailor, who was a distant relation of her husband's, and who had seen her father and brother at the quay, on the morning of her departure. When he saw them they had learned the name and destination of the vessel in which she sailed, and were speaking of the necessity of having her confined as soon as they could get her back. He had then only a few minutes to spare, and giving her hastily the small sum of ready money which he chanced to have about him, he requested her to meet him in the evening, when he would try to think of some means for her support. But that evening he was destined never to see, for in consequence of a rope giving way, he fell from the rigging of his own vessel, and was taken up a corpse.

Thus deprived of almost the only friend on earth to whom she could appeal, or who knew aught of her having escaped the wreck, and deprived at the same time of the only individual who had been a witness to her marriage, and could attest her innocence—hopeless, destitute, and unable to determine on anything, except that she would not return to her father's house to be a prisoner, she began to direct her steps to the north; but they were soon arrested by that event to which she had almost looked forward as the termination of her misfortunes. With no friend to cheer or support her spirits, in that most trying moment, she gave birth to a son, and in doing so she seemed resigned to the worst which could befall. But as soon as she found herself a mother, the wish to live revived in her bosom, her babe formed a new tie, which knit her once more to the world; and, contrary to her own expectation, she soon recovered. Without attempting to follow her through her subsequent wanderings and sufferings, it may be stated, that after her last shilling was gone, her spirits exhausted, and her body completely worn out with travelling, she arrived at the Kirkton, late on an evening in the month of June. The people were in bed; she had nothing to offer them in return for those provisions and that shelter which she required; her fainting limbs refused to support her farther, and sitting down, she gave suck to her infant with many a sigh, and then sunk back upon the straw, where she was afterwards found.

When the wandering mendicant has received his alms, and has prayed over his thousand times repeated prayer, for "a blessing on the house, and the head of the individual who doles it out," from him nothing more is expected; but it is different with those who have a fixed habitation. To sympathise with those who are in great distress of any kind, appears to be quite natural to humanity, in almost the whole of its stages of civilisation, and poor people in general are no doubt pitied, and relieved, and so forth; but then they must be so very humble, and so full of gratitude forever after, and so ready to comply with the wishes and opinions of their benefactors upon all occasions, that, to a proud and independent spirit, it may still be a question, whether the relief, or the destitution which it relieves, would be most easily borne? This piece of ethical philosophy, which is perhaps new to the schoolmen, though by no means new to their unscholastic brethren, Katherine Elliot either knew by intuition, or had been already taught by experience; and her knowledge in this respect, soon manifested itself in her conduct.

Notwithstanding their previous resolution, the dames of the Kirkton would have bestowed a sort of distant attention on their new neighbour; but she evinced no inclination to be their debtor, even for the merest trifle. This they attributed to *pride*, and as pride, in their estimation, was a more unpardonable crime, than any of which they had hitherto suspected her, they at once gave her up to her fate. The men indeed—married, as well as unmarried—were less hasty in their decision, and, when their *natural spirits* had been a little elevated by *artificial ones*, they showed their willingness, for a time, to befriend her, by giving her a clap on the shoulder, and calling her "a bonny lassie;" but she repelled these attempts at familiarity with indignation, and they too were forced to give her up—remarking as they did so, that "she was a *perjink* body, and carried her head owre heigh."

To this neglect she seemed to have reconciled herself, and she endured it without showing any symptoms of discontent. At the conclusion of the war, her husband came home, with his early prospects completely dissipated, and his constitution sadly shattered. But the air, and the occupations of the country, and perhaps more than all, the affectionate care of his wife, produced the most favourable effect upon his health and spirits:—both rallied, and for the six following years, he seemed to be as well as ever he had been in his life. During this period they had the satisfaction of seeing three children added to their family. The hardships of a seafaring life, however, often sap the vigour of the constitution, and induce premature decay. While he was yet in the prime of life, John Elliot began to suffer from declining health, and, after a lingering indisposition, which prevented him from engaging in profitable labour for more than two years, he was gathered —not to his *fathers*, for they slept in a distant part of the island, but—to his mother earth. During his protracted illness, his wife's anxiety to procure medical assistance, and every thing else which she thought might have a tendency to facilitate his recovery, or prolong his life, had induced her to mortgage their slender resources, to a very considerable extent; and when these items were added to the expenses of the funeral, she found herself deeply in debt—with the farther aggravation of three children, who, in common phrase, "could neither work nor want," to provide for.

Her circumstances at this crisis appeared to be desperate, and beggary, or parish relief, would have been her only alternatives, had it not been for her eldest boy, who bore his father's name, and who, though only fourteen years of age, now endeavoured to supply his place. By this time, *breaking stones* on the public roads, at so much per cubic yard, had become a common employment; to such laborious occupations, no apprenticeship was required; and to all the drudgery which they impose upon those who follow them, the boy willingly submitted, rather than see his remaining parent stoop to ask charity. The joint earnings of the mother and son, were once more found sufficient to support the family. It was, long, however, before they could even make an attempt to liquidate their debts, but those to whom they were owing, saw their determined honesty, pitied their poverty, and forbore to press for that which they had not to give.

Still they were not free from persecution. "The rich have many friends," saith Solomon; "but the poor is hated of his own brother." As an illustration of this aphorism, it may be observed, that there is a certain station in society which may be designated *honourable poverty*—that is, when an individual, without having any thing to spare, is still able to wear a tolerably good coat, and maintain a decent appearance in the circle in which he moves. Such an individual, if there is any thing of intellectual dignity or moral worth about him, may pass through the world very respectably, and be treated with much respect by his fellows. But there is another kind of poverty which is neither honourable nor respectable. When the soiled and tattered garb, the toil-worn countenance, and the anxious eye, tell, in language not to be mistaken, that the individual is fairly *under the world*, as it has been called, whatever may have been his talents or his virtues, from that world he need look for neither honour nor respect. Yet, under such poverty the noblest virtues, by a train of events, or by a single accident, may be buried; and there, but for some accident or favourable occurrence again to disencumber them, they may expire.

It was under the last mentioned species of poverty that the widow and her son were now labouring. They sought no assistance from any one, and, strange as it may seem, this very independence was imputed to "beggarly pride." Their general appearance spoke too plainly of their indigence; this opened the mouths of all who had a mind to speak; the unfounded suspicions of illegitimacy which attached to the boy's birth were again raked up, and he was christened in derision, *John the Illegitimate.* This phrase was rather a new one in their vocabulary—unthinking individuals seemed to imagine that it became their mouths, and it was rung in his ears till a sense of shame, if it may be so called, had nearly driven him from society. Nor was this all; the cup of their misfortunes was not yet full; conscious, as it would seem, that their poverty, and the circumstance of its being known that they were in debt, was the principal cause of that contempt with which he was constantly treated, the young man became careless of his own health. Whether it rained or was fair, early and late he pursued his laborious employment for the honourable purpose of being *even with the world.* This could not last; in a short time he was laid on a bed of sickness, his life came to be despaired of, and the mother, who had already watched the last moments of a beloved husband, now hung in awful suspense over what appeared to be the dying bed of her son—the prop and stay of herself and her fatherless children. A surgeon was called in haste, he was profusely bled, and from that hour Fate seemed to hesitate, if not to relent. For several days, however, no one except the surgeon would believe that he was better. His strength had been so terribly prostrated before the disease could be overcome, and he was so low, that for a long time his recovery was almost imperceptible. Many months passed over before he was able to resume his work, and when he did so, it was with scarcely a tithe of his former strength.

The reader must now be pleased to pass over a number of years, regarding which I can give him no information. In the early part of the summer of 1826, I was advised to try change of air for my health; like most others, I had some reasons for wishing to live, and I resolved to comply with the advice as far as possible, by spending a few days or weeks, as circumstances might warrant, with a distant relation, who lived near a place called Locharrow. In my way thither, I passed the scene of my schoolboy days, and as I paused to look upon it, I had almost exclaimed, in the words of the poet,

> A merry place it was in days of yore,
> But something ails it now—the place is cursed.

The Kirkton, as I had seen it, was no more. I was told that a public-house had been established in the village, and that the old-fashioned "little lairds," after *liquidating* the best part of their properties with the landlord, had one by one sold them, and gone to seek shelter elsewhere, or to conceal their poverty in their graves.  The old dominie was dead—his daughter married—the small smoky houses were razed—the trees felled; and the manse and the school-house, with a smithy and a wright's shop—the two last of modern erection—were all that remained.  Musing upon the mutability of such possessions, and the follies by which men, who had been comparatively rich, may become poor, I stumbled into the churchyard, where many of the former possessors of property in the place were lying silent: it alone seemed to have undergone no change.  Most of the graves, indeed, which were prominent when I was a schoolboy, had sunk to the level of the surrounding soil, but their places had been supplied by others, which were raised high by new tenants, and it looked still the same.  The monumental stones, too, were familiar to my eye, and I could not help scanning them with a strange interest—an interest to which those who are in high health are entire strangers.  But among them there was one whose diminutive size and modern appearance particularly attracted my attention.  It scarcely rose a foot above the grave which it protected; and after pressing down the long grass with which it was nearly covered, I was able to read the words "John Elliot," graven upon the plain stone, without date or ornament, or aught beside.  "*The poor illegitimate,*" said I to myself, as I looked upon it, "housed at last where his poverty is no crime;" and, full of melancholy reflections, I left the place.

For some time after I arrived at my new residence the only thing I could do was to walk a few miles every day upon the public road.  During the very first of these sanatory excursions my attention was arrested by one of the stonebreakers, of whom there were several in my way.  In passing and repassing I viewed him attentively, and on both occasions felt an inclination to speak; but there was a something in his manner which seemed to forbid this freedom.  It was neither haughtiness nor pride—there was nothing of the kind about him—but that peculiar expression which bespeaks a mind under the influence of some absorbing pursuit, and says at once, "my thoughts are not as your thoughts."  To appearance he might have seen some nineteen or twenty summers.  In stature he was not more than the middle size, but well formed and active.  His figure, however, was not one of those which are calculated to convey an idea of robust health and great personal strength, being in proportion rather slender than otherwise: but this might be partly owing to the scanty dress in which he pursued his laborious calling.  The only articles of clothing which he usually retained were his shirt and his trousers—his shirt collar being always thrown open, and his shirt sleeves folded upward and inward in such a manner as to leave the whole of the fore-arm bare. Though he was exactly at that time of life when men in general are most sedulous in cultivating any little charms which they may happen to possess, on his personal appearance, on his complexion, on his dress—the last of which was composed of the plainest and cheapest materials—he did not seem to bestow a single thought. When at work he wore no covering upon his head save his own dark brown hair, to the extremities of which constant exposure had imparted a lighter shade. From being thus exposed to the burning sun of that almost tropical summer his hands, arms, and face were so much sunburnt, or rather so completely tanned, that he might have been mistaken for a native of some more southern latitude; but upon those parts of the upper arm and neck, which were only seen when he assumed a new attitude, or stretched himself for some uncommon effort, the skin was of a delicate whiteness. His features were perfectly regular, well defined, and formed for giving expression to manly feeling. His complexion must have been naturally pale, though, from causes already noticed, it was impossible to say in what degree; but upon a close inspection something like a faint red might have been discovered upon his cheek: it was so faint, however, that the superincumbent tanning he had received from the sun nearly concealed it. His eye was of a hazel colour—not particularly dark—full, and of a thoughtful cast. It was not one of those which indicate "a heart of fire," or "a soul of flame," as poets have been accustomed to say: it rather seemed to tell of a spirit which could pursue a fixed purpose "through good report and through bad report"—heedless alike of the praise or the blame, the notice or the neglect, of the world. Still it was far from being the eye of a stoic; for it was lighted up with a glow of feeling, dashed with sadness, which told at once of warm affections, of imagination, and of care. This description can convey little to the mind of the reader; but there was a something about the subject to which it refers which does not admit of being described, and to this he seemed to owe much of that interest which he evidently excited in the bosoms of others: it was that modification which mind sometimes produces upon matter—that general expression which the character diffuses over the countenance, which the painter may catch in a particularly happy moment, but of which the commonplace scribbler can convey no idea. To complete this imperfect sketch, the ease and gracefulness of all his motions, and the dexterity with which he addressed himself to his work, showed at once that he was decidedly the best *breaker* upon the road.

After having made these observations, the individual upon whom they turned became to me at once a favourite subject of meditation. Thinking of him served for the time to divert my mind from more melancholy thoughts. Though inconsistent, and often contradictory, many were the conjectures which I formed concerning him; and to be satisfied as to the accuracy of these conjectures, on the following day I fairly introduced myself to him by an attempt at conversation.

In making this attempt, I found, as I had expected, that he was not one of those young men whose words run continually before their wits. In whatever he might excel, it was not as an everlasting talker. While he answered my little inquiries about places and things with the utmost ease and readiness, he at the same time pursued his work with a perseverance which is seldom equalled. It seemed as if nothing could divert his eye even for a moment from the stones, which appeared to crumble down by magic beneath his hammer. There was, moreover, a perplexing *explicitness* in his replies, which exhausted every subject of conversation almost as soon as it was introduced, and left the listener no alternative but silence, till he could contrive some new topic with which to assail him. All this he accomplished with the most perfect civility, and the greatest suavity of manner; and though he showed no wish for what is commonly called friendly or familiar conversation, as his silence was neither that of stupidity nor pride, whether he spoke, or spoke not, he was still interesting. It seemed as if something had preoccupied his mind, and stolen his thoughts from those common concerns about which others think, speak, and write, and in which they find a pleasure. Could that something be love? No; for from all the vagaries of that wayward passion he appeared to be perfectly free. Could it be enthusiastic piety? No; for he spoke not after the manner of a religious enthusiast. Could it be incipient madness? No; for his eye was uniformly calm, and his manner composed. What could it be then? The question was more easily asked than answered.

Upon this, and several other occasions, I had ample opportunity for observing the light in which he was regarded by others. Very few could pass him without turning to look back before they had gone far. This was more particularly the case with young females, more than one of whom seemed to be secretly delighted with the symmetry of his person, and the graceful ease of his motions; but upon them and their charms he never paused to look: indeed, it seldom seemed that he was aware of their presence.

For more than a week I had passed a portion of every day beside him; this course of idling, however, was now drawing to a close, and as I was anxious to learn something of his personal history, and believed, moreover, that he might be easily induced to satisfy my curiosity, I resolved, if possible, to turn the conversation in that direction the next time we met. But just as I had seated myself upon the grassy bank beside him, the stage coach came in sight, and my attention was called away to another object. That object was a lady, whose age might be somewhere between eighteen and twenty, sitting upon the front seat immediately behind the driver. Brief as was the time for observation, I remarked that her dress was of the finest materials, but made after the plainest fashion, as if she had scorned to be indebted to art for *setting off* a figure, which seemed to require no such aid. Her air appeared to be pensive, but not sad, and I soon discovered that her face was interesting in no ordinary degree. It appeared as if the sun had tried to stamp her complexion with the signet of a warmer clime, but had left an impression so faint, that the natural red and white—the blending of the lily and the rose— shone through. Beauty, however, depends oftener upon form and expression, than upon mere colour; and, though she was by no means deficient in the latter of these qualities, it was in the former that she principally excelled. In the words of a modern poet—

> Oh, black were her eyes—black intensely—and black
> Were the ringlets of jet which flow'd down her back.

Her raven locks, indeed, did not "flow down her back," as is the case, it seems, with Italian beauties, to which these lines allude; they were braided and curled after the fashion of these islands; but to ascertain their hue, enough of them was seen upon her snowy temples, where they contrasted strongly with the dazzling whiteness of the skin which they alternately shaded and revealed. As the coach advanced, her dark eyes became fixed upon my youthful companion; and by some curious coincidence, in turning to replace a stone which had started from under his hammer, he caught a glance of her nearly at the same time; and, contrary to his usual custom, he allowed the hammer to lie still, rested his arm on his knee, and continued to regard her for a time with a look of fixed and deep admiration. I had never seen him do the like before, though occasionally all but wooed by individuals of the softer sex, and to me the scene became doubly interesting. An event, however, was at hand, which was destined to break the spell.

As the coach drew near, it became evident that it would meet a cart heavily loaded with hay, nearly opposite the place where we were standing. The carter had somehow fallen behind his horses, and the animals still kept the middle of the road. The driver of the coach, as I afterwards understood, had overturned several carts before, without suffering any accident himself, and on the present occasion he evidently contemplated something of the same kind. Measuring the road carefully with his eye, he drove his cattle so close, that the fore-wheel struck, but slipped past without doing any serious injury. The sudden jerk, however, which it gave the cart, brought the *shaft horse*, who was a powerful animal, still nearer to that side of the road, while it made both him and the *tracer* lower their heads, and stretch their sinewy limbs, to overcome, by a determined effort, what they considered a permanent resistance. The result was what might have been expected. The hind-wheel of the coach, and the wheel of the cart, came fairly in contact, and the weight of the cart being greater than that of the coach, while the diameter of its wheel was somewhat less, the coach wheel began to rise over it; the horses in both vehicles made a desperate spring forward, and the next moment the coach lay on its side, with the passengers sprawling on the dusty road. The young lady already noticed had been jerked from her seat by the concussion of the meeting, and thrown among the horses, where, to a certainty, she would have been kicked and trampled to pieces in a few minutes, had she not been rescued from her perilous situation by the stonebreaker, who snatched her thence almost before she fell. Leaving myself, and such of the male passengers as were not stupified by their fall, to render what assistance we could to the other ladies, he raised her in his arms, placed her passive head upon his bosom, and fixed his eyes upon her seemingly lifeless face with an expression of deeper concern than could have been expected from a stranger. He evidently had not been accustomed to see people swoon, and it must have struck him that she was dead. The confusion, however, soon subsided; it was discovered that nobody else was seriously injured; and after a few drops of cold water, brought from a neighbouring spring, had been sprinkled upon her forehead, she opened her dazzlingly dark eyes and turned them full upon the face of the individual who still supported her. He was at the time regarding her with a look of mingled interest, admiration, and apprehension; and the sight which she there met seemed to operate like a charm in restoring her at once to consciousness and self-possession. With a graceful movement she extricated herself from his arms, drew back a few steps, and there they stood like two statues inspired with life, but at the same time destitute of the power of motion. As they stood thus they might have formed an excellent subject for a painter. It were, indeed, difficult to conceive an idea of two more interesting figures brought together in circumstances so entirely dissimilar. But notwithstanding the difference of sex, dress, and the widely different spheres in which they had been bred, I could not help imagining that I could trace a curious resemblance in some of their features. The upper lip of both, for instance, had the same slight curve, their foreheads were similarly formed, and though the eye of the soiled and sunburnt stone-breaker was smaller, lighter in colour, and less brilliant than that of the young lady, to me they seemed to have the same quick motion, and the same expressive glance. This, however, might be partly fancy, and partly owing to the circumstances of their being, at the time, actuated by the same feelings of respect and admiration, heightened by that degree of embarrassment which the first impression of these feelings is calculated to produce.

The time thus passed was necessarily short. A peculiar smile seemed struggling for existence on the young lady's countenance; she offered a large silver piece to her deliverer; and when she spoke, though her voice was set to no tune, it seemed in itself "Nature's music." He appeared to feel its full effect; but he drew back at the same time with a slight feeling of pride, which, if it did nothing else, restored him at once to a consciousness of his situation, and enabled him also to speak.

"Thank you, ma'am," he said; "but I never in my life took money before I had earned it."

When he had uttered these words he seemed to think he had said too much; while the lady looked as though she had detected herself in a serious mistake, glanced timidly at me to ascertain if I observed her; and then silence, accompanied by an evident increase of embarrassment on both sides, succeeded.

While this little side scene was going forward, a band of

rustics from the neighbouring fields and farms had assembled to satisfy their curiosity or offer their assistance. With their aid the coach was again placed upon its wheels; the injury it had sustained was not such as to unfit it for the road; and the guard and driver, having got their cattle in order, were now heard calling to the passengers to "take their seats," and swearing about being "behind their time." Though this summons was loudly repeated, the young female, of whom we have been speaking, still seemed to hesitate, and lingered as if she wished to say something more; but at that moment one of the functionaries offered her his hand to assist her to her place; thus pressed, she again took her seat upon the top of the coach, and the next minute it drove off. I remarked, however, that the stone-breaker followed the vehicle with his eye as long as it was in sight, and the young lady's head was several times so far turned to one side as to allow her to have a sweeping glance of the place we then occupied. But the time I had to spare was now more than spent, and wishing him a good day I also took my departure.

I now felt myself so much better as to be able to attend to a number of little concerns, which hitherto had devolved upon those friends with whom I sojourned; and as they were pleased to consider my presence as a favour, rather than a tax upon their friendship, the pride of poverty was lulled to sleep, and a wish to have my health fully re-established reconciled me to the idea of spending with them what remained of the season. But as I was now employed opportunities of seeing the stone-breaker seldom occurred, and when they did occur I could never muster resolution to make any direct inquiries concerning his name or story. It struck me, however, that his health was declining. At each successive meeting he appeared paler and thinner than he had done before; but this was easily accounted for by his extraordinary exertion, and the amazing quantity of work which he performed. Convinced that he was injuring himself, and that he would ultimately come to be a sufferer from this species of imprudence, I sometimes ventured to remonstrate on the necessity of relaxing his diligence, and satisfying himself with more moderate earnings; but upon these occasions, his uniform answer was a solemn assurance, that "it was impossible for him to do so;" and farther I did not consider that it would have been delicate in me to interfere.

Time passed on—autumn was merging into winter; and as my own health was now tolerably re-established, I had taken leave of my friends to follow my fortunes elsewhere. The stone-breaker lay in my way, and as I approached, I was surprised to see him *idling*. He stood leaning upon a low wall, with his forehead clasped in one of his hands, while the other, in which he still held his hammer, hung motionless by his side. His eyes being shaded, he did not notice my approach; I had thus an opportunity of seeing him unseen, and I was deeply struck with his altered appearance. Owing to the change of the season, the *sunburn* had nearly disappeared from his face, leaving it more ominously pale than I had ever seen it before. Whatever his original complexion had been, it was now painfully evident, that this was not a natural paleness, but one occasioned by some disease at the time preying upon his constitution. His hands, arms, and more particularly his fingers, appeared attenuated in no ordinary degree; and when he withdrew his palm from his forehead, I almost started to see the blue veins rising over it with a shadowy distinctness, which indicated anything but health.

"You look surprised," said he, "but it is only an old friend of mine—a headache, come to pay me a visit."

I said he was looking ill in other respects, and should unquestionably go home, and take rest for a day or two, till his health was restored.

"When these are broken," said he, pointing to a few stones, which were all that remained of the heap, "I *will* go home; but it is hard to leave them when so few." With these words, he again placed himself in an attitude to resume his work, and, endeavouring to collect all his energy, made several strokes, which, however, fell wide of the object for which they were intended. He now paused for a few seconds, sighed deeply, and then made a second attempt to no better purpose. Weakness and pain had evidently disordered his sight, and, finding that his most determined efforts were fruitless, he flung down his hammer, pressed his hand once more upon his forehead, moved a few steps to one side, and unable, as it appeared, to support himself longer, he again leaned over the wall.

"You *must* go home," said I, "or you will repent not having done so when it is too late."

"Yes," was his reply; "I must go home *now*, and the question is, how am I to get there?" I immediately offered to assist him; he accepted the offer, not without some reluctance; and when we were about to leave the place, he took up his hammers with a sigh, looked steadfastly at the heap of stones; and then speaking in a tone, which was solemn rather than sad, "I had hoped to be able to finish these," he said, "before it came to this; but with me it is all over now, and some one else must do what I am forced to leave undone."

I tried to cheer him with the hopes of soon being able to resume his work again, mentioning such instances as I could recollect of individuals who had been more seriously indisposed than he appeared to be, and yet a single day had been sufficient to restore them.

"No, no," said he, with an incredulous shake of the head; "I know the nature of my complaint, and it were in vain to deceive myself as to its termination. But it is kind in you," he added, after a short pause, "thus to try to persuade me that I shall soon recover." And as he spoke, he smiled after that sort which "makes not others smile again."

Finding him firmly fixed in this opinion, and fearing from what I saw that it was but too well founded, I made no farther attempt to shake it; but instead, begged to know what made him so certain as to the nature of his disease.

"Three years ago," said he, "when I was recovering from a severe illness, which the doctor called *inflammation of the lungs*, he took me aside, and warned me to be particularly careful of myself ever after, otherwise, I should run a great risk of falling into *consumption*. I heard him, and I knew well the fatal nature of the disease he named; but with a mother, two sisters, and a brother to provide for, and already deeply in debt, what care could I take? The very idea of it was folly. I must either work, or they must starve. That illness left a weakness in my chest, from which I never fairly recovered; and from that day forth, I looked upon myself as one on whom sentence of death had been already passed. Though I never spoke of the circumstances to any one, such was the impression which it made upon my own mind, that when my birth-day, or the longest day in the year, or any other particular day occurred, I have stood to watch the setting sun, and ere he disappeared, bade him a long farewell, thinking the while on the probability of being cold in my grave before the returning season brought that day again. But to me, who hitherto had been neglected, scorned, and despised by all save my mother, and, with little more than a boy's strength, obliged to drudge out the long, long day, in hard labour, death did not appear very terrible—only the grave seemed a gloomy place, and the thought of what I might have to suffer in dying sometimes made me sad. I had but one object in view, and one wish to accomplish; and these were, that I might be able to clear off my widowed mother's debts, and live till my little sisters were able to work for themselves. Had I been able to finish the few stones you saw me leave, the money in my master's hands would have been sufficient to pay the last farthing; and for my work"—here he paused for a little, sighed deeply, and then, in a low melancholy tone, added, "but it is in vain to speak of that now."

More deeply struck than ever with the extraordinary character of my youthful companion, eager to hear more of his sentiments, and anxious to improve the last opportunity which I was likely to have of seeing him, I inquired if the wish to live to old age had never mingled with his other wishes.

In answer to this question, "I must confess," he said, "that as my strength began to increase, as labour became less irksome, and new enjoyments presented themselves to my eye, I have wished to live; and sometimes, too, I have indulged the vain idea that I might live and be happy like others; but it is the province of the *grisly king* to dash the cup from the lips of those who are most eager to drink, and in his wonted mood he now comes to me. But see, yonder is my sister coming with my dinner: if I should grow suddenly worse she will be near, and as you may have other demands upon your time, it were unfair to detain you." I expressed my willingness to accompany him home. "But," continued he, "there is another reason for your leaving me. Though I have made free to tell you my sentiments, in the belief that we may never meet again, to my mother I have never spoken of the subject. From her I would gladly conceal the nature of my complaint as long as possible; and were she to see me assisted home by a stranger, it might alarm her fears, and give rise to questions which were better unasked. And now," he added, holding out his hand, "let me thank you for assisting a poor invalid so far, and let us part."

I took his hand, but was so deeply affected, that I could not return his salute.

"Do not distress yourself," he resumed: "you see I can be calm. I have now more reasons for wishing to live than ever, and yet I am resigned to die. Trust me, to those who have been long accustomed to think of the subject, there is nothing very appalling in the prospect of death.—But see, here is Mary: she must not hear me speak thus—farewell!"

And this is a hero, said I to myself, as I turned away, who has performed a task from which most of those heroes, whose fame has kept the world awake, would have shrunk. Without the prospect of fame or profit, or one applauding word, he has drudged out his short life in honourably discharging debts which he never contracted; he now falls a martyr to the stern integrity and affectionate warmth of his own character; and a widowed mother's tears, and a nameless grave, will be his sole reward. With these reflections, I lost sight of Locharrow— the place on which we had been advancing—but I could not so soon lose the recollection of the interesting individual from whom I had just parted; and after waiting a considerable time, without being able to obtain any information concerning him, I became impatient to learn his fate.

About the end of January, 1827, I had again crossed the country to Locharrow, and stood before the little inn, over which was the representation of a plough and harrow. The hostess, as I soon discovered, was no other than the daughter of my former pedagogue, now dignified with the name of Mrs. Jugster; and from her I learned, that the *poor Illegitimate*, and the stone-breaker who had interested me so much, were the same; and that the stone I had seen in the Kirkton churchyard had been erected to his father. As almost always happens in such cases, I had got the end of the story long before I had heard one word of the beginning; but by dint of much questioning and cross-questioning, I at last succeeded in getting something like an intelligible account of some events which had occurred both before and after my departure; and of that account, the following is a sort of confused abridgment.

In the course of the preceding summer, a good deal of surprise had been excited, and many conjectures set afloat in the village, by the arrival of a young woman, calling herself Margaret Morrison, who took a house, and tried to earn her own support, by performing the finer sorts of needlework. When she first came among them, she stated that she had once had some expectations; but having been deprived of her friends by death, and reduced to the necessity of doing something, she had resolved to seek her bread by her own industry. Farther she told not, and farther she seemed determined not to tell. But with this account the village dames were by no means satisfied; and in the lack of fuller information, the more charitable part of them said, that "she must have been some unfortunate gentleman's daughter, who, after her father's death, had come there to conceal her poverty;" while those who were inclined to judge harshly, asserted, that "she was only some light-headed lassie, who, having learned to speak English by accident, had taken up her residence among strangers, that she might be thought a lady." In the midst of these speculations, even the most envious were forced to acknowledge that she was beautiful; and her beauty soon drew around her a crowd of admirers, among whom were several, who, in the language of the place, might have been regarded as "good marriages." But whatever motives had induced her to settle there, the getting of a husband did not appear to be among them. There was a native dignity and reserve in her manner, which repelled their advances without a word on her part; and while the young men were thus forced to keep their distance, their mothers, piqued, as it appeared, by her unaccountable indifference, christened her *the nun*. Friends or acquaintances she sought none; and except an occasional call upon Catherine Elliot, she was seldom seen to enter a neighbour's house. But by and by it came to be observed, that wherever there was a case of extreme poverty or great distress, she was always ready with her assistance and her *mite*, the last of which was often larger than could have been expected; and—such is the effect of every thing like generosity or benevolence—even the mothers of her unsuccessful suitors began to speak of her with more respect. As the season advanced, it was also observed that her visits to Catherine Elliot became more frequent, and then the village maidens, who, with all their charms, had never been able to move the heart of the widow's imperturbable son, began to wonder if she had fallen in love with him, or if it were possible that he could fall in love with her. In this mood they speculated upon his "pale looks," and the probability of her soon being left a widow, even if he were to make her his wife; but no decisive evidence could be obtained, and all was mere conjecture as to the state of their affections, when an accident occurred which placed the matter beyond a doubt.

On the evening of the day on which I had assisted the stone-breaker so far on his way home, the carriage of an eminent physician from the county town, which was more than ten miles distant, drew up at the inn door, and while the coachman was preparing to unyoke his cattle, the doctor inquired for the house of Mrs. Elliot, and whether she had a son who was then complaining. Mrs. Jugster had already noticed the declining health of the young man; but why Dr. Overburn should have been brought so far to visit him, while their own doctor, who lived within half a mile of the place, had never been called, excited her surprise; and she proceeded forthwith to question the coachman. He in his turn appeared rather shy, and said that "he did't know much about it;" but after she had given him a glass of *double strong*, he became more communicative, and proceeded to tell her without reserve what he had himself heard from his master's little daughter. "The little girl," he said, "told him that her papa had received a letter without a name, enclosing twenty guineas, and requesting him to visit a young man living at Locharrow, who had been very poorly for some time. The letter mentioned Friday evening as the time at which the writer wished his first visit to be made, and at the same time enjoined him to call in whatever medical assistance he might think proper—to do everything in his power for the recovery of his patient, without any regard to cost—to prohibit him from working, if he thought it would tend in the slightest degree to his restoration—to give him money to support the family, for which he had been accustomed to provide, in comfortable circumstances; and finally, to send his accounts to a banker in London, where they would be promptly acknowledged." This information only served to excite Mrs. Jugster's curiosity still farther, and after ministering to the comfort of the underling she hastened over to the widow's to see if any unravelment of the mystery could be obtained there.

The young man, it seemed, had grown much worse after he got home: pain in the head, which amounted almost to agony, repeated vomiting, and other alarming symptoms had awakened the fears of his anxious mother, who was in the act of despatching her eldest girl for the medical man of the district when Dr. Overburn arrived. By his directions an opiate was to be administered about bed-time, and after enjoining the patient's mother to watch him for the first part of the night he proceeded to the house of a neighbouring gentleman, where he was to remain till next day. The effect of the opiate was such that the young man almost immediately fell into a profound sleep; and his mother, who had been up for the greater part of the previous night, set the candle down upon a table, on which lay a quantity of flax, at which she had been spinning, and, relieved in a great measure from her anxiety by the favourable opinion which she had heard the doctor express, she soon began to feel drowsy.

Mrs. Jugster, who had not been able to obtain any information beyond what has been stated, but who was, nevertheless, full of the important secret with which the coachman had intrusted her, now began to entertain some suspicions that Margaret Morrison might have been the writer of the letter; and with this idea in her head, before she went home, she determined on calling at her house "to see how she would look." The door, however, was locked, there was no appearance of light or fire within, and, though she craved admittance both by words and actions, nobody made answer. Convinced by this circumstance that Margaret was not at home, she concluded, from her absence on the very evening which had been named in the nameless letter, that she could have had no hand in the affair. Thus disappointed of every thing upon which even a feasible conjecture might be founded, she returned to her own house, and as there was no appearance of customers she went early to bed. But about the middle of the night she was awakened by the cry of *fire*, and after throwing on her garments in a hasty manner, slipping her feet into her *bauchels*, and opening the door, she saw over the top of the next house a bright appearance in the lower atmosphere, which was reflected far along the dark sky like the rising moon. She instantly hurried off in the direction whence it proceeded, and soon saw the widow's house, which was on the outskirts of the village, in flames. A crowd had already collected, and the widow herself, who was found sleeping by the fire, and her three younger children had been dragged out. But the moment after this was accomplished, a portion of the roof above the door fell in, and, by choking up the entrance with rubbish, smoke, and flame, prevented any farther attempt. The distracted mother was now wringing her hands, and crying: "My son—my son—oh my son! will none of you try to save him?" and in her eagerness to accomplish that which even the boldest of the other sex durst not venture to attempt, it was with the utmost difficulty she could be prevented from rushing on certain destruction. As her efforts grew more frantic, force was used to restrain her, and the scene in many respects became truly distressing. This had only continued for a very short time, when a female figure, closely wrapped up in a coarse brown cloak, was seen flitting round the crowd, and, upon it all eyes were turned. In the confusion which prevailed, and the fluctuating glare, which was now shaded, and now bright, as the dense smoke intervened, or the wind swayed the flames, it could only be seen indistinctly and by fits. Its face, with the exception of the eyes, which gleamed like balls of fire when the red light fell on them, was completely muffled up; it appeared to have shoes on its feet, but its snowy ankles were bare. Farther none could tell, and each looked in his fellow's face as if afraid to speak—even the wretched mother hushed for a moment the voice of her despair.

"A ghost!—a ghost!—or the great enemy himself come to look for his prey!" whispered half-a-dozen voices at once, the moment it had disappeared behind an angle of the wall.

At this ominous suggestion some trembled from head to foot, while others breathed short prayers for protection, and all were more or less amazed. The object of their terror, however, did not appear to heed them; it had made the circuit of the house, in a time incredibly short, and it now stood before the door for a moment, till the wind drove back the flames, and then rushed in as fearlessly as if the fire had been its own element.

"In God's name, run for the minister!" cried some one in a voice which was at once loud, tremulous, and indistinct. "Run—run, for Godsake!" repeated a second, and a third, in the same breath. But before any one could obey the mysterious figure was again seen forcing its way through suffocating smoke and scorching flame with what appeared to be a bundle of bed-clothes, which it could scarcely support in its arms. As soon as it had reached the free air it deposited its burden on a grassy bank with much caution, staggered forward a few steps, and then fell to the earth. The crowd at first started back, terrified by the idea—already partly expressed—that it was the devil carrying off the young man soul and body; for they had never imagined that anything earthly could have made the attempt and escaped with life: but his agonised mother was not to be scared by such apprehensions. The moment she saw the figure emerge from the burning ruin she burst from the grasp of the man who held her—sprang forward, and throwing aside the folds of the bed-clothes, discovered her son, still sleeping from the effects of the opiate, but to all appearance uninjured—the blankets having protected him from the terrible element through which he was borne.

"God bless his deliverer!" she exclaimed, "God bless him!" But for the present no such blessing seemed to be bestowed. As she spoke the wind threw aside the thick smoke, and the bright red glare fell full upon the supposed fiend, who was now divested of its cloak and one of its shoes—the last of which had stuck fast among the rubbish, with which the entrance was choked up—and lying full length upon the ground, with a portion of its clothes burning. The next moment Katherine Elliot was bending over it, extinguishing the fire with one hand, and turning its face to the light with the other.

"Margaret—Margaret," she once more exclaimed, "I thought it was you. May God bless and reward you!" But Margaret, who had swooned the moment she fell, heard her not.

The crowd, restored to their senses by these discoveries, now began to act like men. Some proceeded to take precautionary measures for preventing the fire from spreading to the rest of the houses, while others assisted in conveying the invalid to the spence of the inn, which had been readily offered for the accommodation of the family, till better could be procured. The women also performed their part by removing Margaret Morrison to her own house, and using such means as their limited skill suggested for restoring her to consciousness. This task was soon accomplished; but the moment she could speak, instead of uttering some complaint as they had expected, she startled them by inquiring in the most peremptory terms "at what time Dr. Overburn had left the village?" Some one who had heard him tell his coachman where to drive chanced to be present, and mentioned the circumstance, together with the hour of his departure. Margaret then offered a guinea, without the slightest hesitation, to the individual who should first reach him. "Tell him," she continued, "to hasten to his patient, who has met a severe accident, without delay; tell him also that if he can save his life, or mitigate his suffering, his own reward will be liberal, if I—if I—but I am unable to speak—go, despatch a messenger immediately."

As she spoke these words her manner was so unlike what it had formerly been that the good dames stood amazed. The prospect of the *guinea*, however, was sufficiently tempting to secure more than one messenger; and, after having called at the inn, and seen his patient safe, and as well as could be expected, the medical gentleman was hurried off to visit the intrepid maiden herself.

"Poor girl," said Dr. Overburn, in a kind and encouraging tone, as he approached the bedside, "I hope the injury you have sustained is not so serious as it has been represented."

"In what state have you left your patient?" said she, with a voice and manner which seemed to make him start. The doctor assured her that, though weak at present, his constitution was still good, and with proper care he was likely to do well.

"But the burning, doctor," inquired she eagerly, "what of it? Has he suffered much from the fire?"

"No," said the other. "Owing, as I suppose, to some current of air having carried the smoke away from the bed on which he lay, he does not seem to have sustained the slightest injury."

"Then I am satisfied," was her brief reply. She now allowed Dr. Overburn to examine her own case, and time it was; for besides her hands, which were fearfully scorched, one of her feet and a part of the leg had suffered so terribly that the flesh in some places seemed to be burned to a cinder. When everything had been done which medical skill at the time could suggest, and after she had intimated a wish that the rest of the company, with the exception of Katherine Elliot, should withdraw, "Doctor," said she, "is it common for fever and delirium to follow such accidents as the present?"

The doctor acknowledged that in very severe cases such a thing might happen.

"Well," said she, "I shall probably die, and farther concealment would be fatal to my purpose. It was *I* who wrote the letter, and for your prompt compliance with the request which it contained I owe you a deep debt. But I must now be your debtor in other respects. Here is a family left homeless and desolate by the fire—you know where to find money—make them comfortable, no matter at what cost, and the blessing of a friendless orphan will attend you, as you discharge the trust which she now commits to your care."

Having signified his willingness to execute her behests, and expressed a hope that she would yet be able to superintend her own charities, Dr. Overburn was proceeding to a delicate and somewhat embarrassed inquiry as to how the mistress of a fortune came to be in her present circumstances, when she laid her finger on her lip, as a sign that she did not want to be questioned; and he was about to retire.

"But hold!" cried she, as if some second thought had struck her; "I have some money—pardon my abruptness—and no relations that I know of—may I bequeath it to whom I please?" The doctor frankly acknowledged his ignorance of these matters, but professed his willingness to assist her in any way she could point out.

"Then," said she, "will you be so kind as take a few memoranda of my wishes, and employ any lawyer whom you can trust, to draw out the thing in a legal form?" The doctor took a note-book and pencil from his pocket, and she proceeded, "*I*, Julia Ruthven, wish to bequeath the money which was placed in the British Funds, and also that placed in the bank of Messrs. Glyn and Co. by my father, Francis Ruthven, to——"

Here she stopped, or rather was interrupted by Katherine Elliot, who seemed to start as she spoke, and now approached the bedside, repeating her words:—"Julia Ruthven—Francis Ruthven! it cannot be, and yet my own maiden name was Ruthven, and my only brother's name was Francis. Dear

Margaret, did you know him? but my brain is bewildered with long, long recollections."

Margaret, however, or Julia—the reader may now call her which he pleases, seeing she had assumed both names—answered not. The effort she had made, and the intolerable pain which she had all along been struggling to conceal, were too much for her strength, and she was once more in a state of insensibility. All farther questioning was now strictly forbidden by Dr. Overburn, who enjoined the widow to exclude all visitors, and keep her as quiet as possible. But, though these orders were obeyed to the letter, in the course of the morning fever came on, which was soon followed by delirium. In her ravings she spoke much of one of the West Indian Islands—of West Indian scenes, and flowers, and also of an aunt, of whom she had heard her father speak, with the bitterest sorrow, as having been driven from the shelter of a paternal roof, and afterwards drowned, through his unkindness. These ravings were mingled with others, about "being thrown from the stage-coach among the horses' feet, and having her life saved by a stone-breaker, whom she loved at first sight, and could never forget. But as he was sick," she said, "and could not marry her, she intended to bequeath her whole fortune to him, when she died." Deeply would she have blushed, had these disjointed sentences been repeated to her after she recovered—for, by the blessing of God on Dr. Overburn's exertions, she did recover—but they reached no ear save that of the widow, and to her they afforded a sort of clue, which seemed in some measure to establish their relationship.

When she was so well as to be able to talk of past events, the mystery was more fully cleared up. Her deceased father was indeed the widow's only brother, and as there was every reason for believing that she had been drowned, when the vessel in which she sailed was wrecked, he fancied that his unkindness had been the principal cause of her death, and consequently that he was little better than her murderer. This thought had made him so unhappy, that he could no longer endure his native country; and, to be free from those scenes which to him seemed haunted, he had sailed for the West Indies, where he soon after married the widow of a rich planter, who brought him a considerable fortune. Julia was their only child; and some time before his death her father had transmitted the greater part of his fortune to Britain, whither he advised her to follow as soon as possible. It was in endeavouring to comply with this advice, that she met John

Elliot, alias the poor *Illegitimate*, of whom it is almost needless to say that he was her cousin. As soon as they were both perfectly recovered, there being now no cause of delay, they were married, and that fortune which she had been unable to bequeath, she *gave* along with her hand; thus forming one of a very few instances in which humble merit, after unheard of struggles, is rewarded with unearned riches.

## THINGS AND THOUGHTS.

WIDELY different as things and thoughts at first may appear, there is often a very intimate connection between them; and as the former tend to soothe or ruffle the surface of the mind, to excite or depress its energies, so will the latter be either pleasing or painful. How often does the most trifling incident call up a train of associations involving the profoundest interest, or the deepest melancholy? and, on the contrary, a passing shadow, or the appearance of an inanimate object may, as it were, recreate the most ludicrous images from the very dust and ashes of scenes which we had witnessed long years ago — scenes which but one moment before were entirely forgotten — and once more summon up the whole of the mirthful feelings with which they were then beheld, till a smile plays unconsciously around the lips of the solitary muser, or till an involuntary laugh actually bursts from him, making him look around to see if he has not been observed by strangers who, not knowing the cause, might perhaps deem him insane. As the truth of these observations has doubtless been felt by others, so it was strikingly experienced by the present writer at a very recent period.

Last evening\* the necessity of soon removing from the room which I had previously occupied, set me to examine a parcel of old lumber, and half useless articles, which had been brought from a former dwelling, and which, owing to circumstances, had remained since then almost wholly untouched. But as the apartment which I was about to occupy afforded less space for such things, it had now become necessary to dispense with the whole of what was useless, and as much as possible of what

---

\* The evening here alluded to was that of the 2nd of March, 1841; and, if truth were any excuse for dulness, it might be stated that what follows is merely a narrative of what occurred on that evening.

was least useful; and when I emptied the repository which contained them, I accordingly felt fully determined to burn a large quantity of the materials before me; though, as the reader will shortly see, I was not very successful in following out this determination.

The first things which came under my notice were a boy's top and some marbles — technically called bowls, or rather *bools*—such as are used in the games of children. Both were completely useless, and the one might have been thrown on the fire, and the others to any distance over the fields, without the slightest loss being incurred; but they had once belonged to my brother, and to see them again after a succession of years, during which I had not been aware of their existence, called up a vision of early days, which, for the time, made me insensible to every other object. As I took them up, and turned them over, and eyed them with a look so intent that all around "grew vacancy," there was presented to my imagination —I had almost said *there was before me*—a fair-haired, bright-complexioned, blue-eyed boy, whose vivacity and buoyancy of spirit nothing could repress, to whom, as being several years his elder, my word had been a law; and who, through infancy and youth, had looked up to me for instruction and example, as well as protection. Alas! to think now how much more perfectly these might have been bestowed; but though older than him, I was then only a boy. There were but two of us: and passing over some little disagreements which were soon forgotten, we had become "all the world to each other." We had, moreover, been bred up on the shady side of Fortune's eminence, frequently subjected to all the privations incident to the children of poverty; and I could still recollect the time, almost as freshly as if it had been but a few weeks ago, when the toys were bought in a village market with some halfpence, which had been carefully hoarded for nearly a year before. When our circumstances were considered, it was, no doubt, misspent money; but, with the exception of the trifle which they cost, we had little of the kind to reflect upon. Utterly useless as they now were, and childish as the thing may seem, I could not destroy them; and after having dissipated I know not how long in gazing on them, and pondering over those happier scenes with which they were associated, I put them carefully aside, determining that they should still have house-room, if something else should want it.

The next thing which I took up was the remains of what had once been a sort of rude snuff-box. It was as useless as the others, and in the estimation of many the fire would have been the proper place for it; but like the top and the marbles it had once belonged to my brother; and, what was more, it had been constructed by himself, as a sort of trial of mechanical skill, in his early days.  The box itself had been scooped out of a piece of solid wood, with no other instrument than a pocket-knife, and now I could not help regarding it as a monument of what even boyish industry may accomplish. The lid, however, was lost, and for it I looked in vain; yet it was the most ingenious and curiously wrought part of the whole.  Upon the upper side of it, the wood had been cut away, and indented in such a manner as to prepare it for receiving a number of devices, such as a Scottish thistle, a crown, a heart, the initials of the maker, protected on either side by some warlike weapons, and several things beside. The materials of these, again, had been supplied by an old tin or pewter spoon, which was found in a potato field; and after being hammered out, cut into their proper shapes, and polished with much care, they had been fixed in the lid of the box, by the humble artist, in the manner already described.  Recent events had conspired to give a deep and permanent interest even to such trifles.  The remains of the snuff-box, as if by some incomprehensible spell, were at once associated with its juvenile maker; and again he seemed to stand before me as he then was—a growing youth, with health depicted in his well-formed countenance; still cheerful and full of hope, but with a something altogether different from the usual levity and thoughtlessness, which characterise the last stages of boyhood, in his look and manner.  By the time alluded to, he had, in fact, been broken to the yoke which Providence seems to have imposed upon nine-tenths of the human race: he had already bent to the severest drudgery for the simple fare which sustained life, and the few homely articles of dress which protected him from the storm; and he had brought to the dull and monotonous task a degree of patience and perseverance beyond his years.  This consideration alone, seemed to give the little fragment of wood a double claim upon my attention, and it was not only respited from the flames, but placed in what was considered safe keeping, with as much care as ever Catholic devotee locked up a piece of the *real cross*, or a *paring* of some of the apostles' nails.

When this was done, I took up an old book, which, from mould and damp, together with the ravages of moths, was nearly unreadable.  By this time, however, I had almost forgotten my original intention; and being exactly in that mood which delights to ponder over past events, and to collect all the minutiæ of circumstances connected with them—forgetful alike of the present and the future—I began to examine it with as much interest, perhaps, as an antiquary would feel in examining, for the first time, some newly discovered and important monument of antiquity. It was a collection of "Missionary Magazines," which had been printed as far back as 1797, and had been preserved by the parents of the individual who now writes, in their originally separate form, for more than a quarter of a century before it was thought worth while to unite them under the same cover. The *stitching* of the book had been done in a way altogether different from that followed by bookbinders, and plainly indicated the efforts of one wholly ignorant of the art. The edges, with infinite labour and pains, had been cut even with a knife, which must have been sharpened, it were difficult to say how often, in the course of the operation; paper, as is well known, being a substance which soon destroys the edge of any instrument. The boards, instead of pasteboard, had been taken from an old hat, over which a piece of paper had been pasted, so as to conceal the original. The back consisted of black glazed linen, such as is sometimes used for pockets to men's coats, and which was actually a fragment of cloth which had been thus applied; while the back title, which had evidently been printed with a pen, was a tolerably good imitation of type. The snuff-box, as may be easily guessed, and the binding of the old book, were the workmanship of the same individual. In early life, we had been eager to cultivate our minds by reading as often as we could spare money for the purchase of books. To preserve and keep together our little store, we had conjointly constructed a small book-case, which, small as it was, proved too large for our collection: he was anxious to have the empty spaces filled up, and not being at the time able either to buy more new books, or to employ a bookbinder upon the old materials which we already possessed, he undertook the task of putting them together himself, which will readily account for the unwonted manner in which it was done. The old book, like the articles already enumerated, was a memorial of the proverbial happy days of youth; and it, too, was preserved.

A few things I did commit to the flames, but they were few indeed; and then, after a long fit of abstraction, I took up five old numbers of a widely circulated and very popular periodical, which, when new, must have cost two shillings and sixpence each, though we had bought the whole for little more than that sum, being what is called "second handed," at the time the purchase was made. In the hurry and confusion of a former removal, they had been stowed away among the mass of heterogeneous articles which I had undertaken to examine: for years after, a continued struggle for bread, and, if possible, to better our circumstances, had left little time for reading; and thus they had remained unmissed and undiscovered till the present occasion. The first was for "May, 1830," and, though more than ten years of toil and care, with all their obliterating influences, had intervened, I had scarcely time to read the title page, when imagination had conjured up the whole succession of events connected with the evening on which they became ours.

As already said, we had been eager to increase our little library, and in the autumn of the year last mentioned—it might be near the 1st of November—we got notice of an auction of books, which was to take place in a village about three miles distant. Fortunately, as we then thought, we had saved about £2—it was nearly the first spare money which we had been able to command—but the vision of *cheap books*, and an abundant choice, was before us; and as soon as we came home, hands and faces were washed, a hasty supper despatched, and away we hied, happy in the anticipation of the good things which we were to bring back with us on our return. These consisted of the five numbers of the work already mentioned; Johnson's "Lives of the English Poets," in four volumes; Goldsmith's "Citizen of the World," two volumes; "Byron's Works," four volumes; a copy of "Burns' Works;" and some other trifles of comparatively little importance. Some of the books were not exactly what we most wanted; these, however, we could not obtain, and so we took what we could get, rather than bring home our money. But I am giving a history of the transaction from memory, rather than an account of the scene which was represented to my imagination. There was, in the first place, a cloudy and somewhat dark autumnal evening, with a slight breeze from the north, and a long streak of clear sky in the same quarter, indicating the approach of northern lights—a phenomenon which, for a number of years previous to 1830, so far as I recollect, was but rarely seen. Then the road, and the open country with its scattered trees, hedges, cottages, and farms, and the distant hills, scarcely visible to the straining eye amid the shadows which rested on them, were exchanged for the long, narrow street of a rather populous village, slippery from recent rain, with figures gliding to and fro, or hurrying past in perfect obscurity, save when they glanced occasionally into view for a few seconds in the light of a shop window. Anon, there was a large hall, dimly lighted at the farther end, where a large collection of books had been placed upon temporary shelves, with a motley crowd of variously dressed and careless looking people, sauntering through it, or resting on the seats along the wall. In the middle was the auctioneer, with a clerk at his side, and two candles burning before him—his eye evidently acquiring new lustre as it caught a glance of a supposed purchaser, while a broad grin of the most exalted satisfaction never failed to brighten up his whole countenance as often as any thing like a "competition" could be got up. But what interested me most was a young man—apparently older, but in reality under eighteen—with a thoughtful expression of countenance—hair which had gradually darkened as his years increased, till it was now almost black; and a complexion which was evidently paler than it had once been, from the combined effects of unremitting toil by day, late evening studies, and indifferent health: though several years my junior, he was taller than me by nearly the head. For a time he watched intently the progress of the sales; then he obtained permission to look over the books upon the shelves; and, finally, he requested the auctioneer, if it were agreeable, to "put up" one or two of the works which he wished to purchase. His request was at once granted; and then, with a straightforwardness of character but ill suited to the present state of society, and the very humble sphere in which he was destined to move, he "carried" them, regardless of the price. Again the hall and the books, the auctioneer, the candles, and the motley crowd, were exchanged for the slippery street, from the lateness of the hour now completely dark—the public road, and the open country; and once more the acquaintances whom we passed, or spoke with on our homeward way—the deep hush of night—the aspect of the distant mountains, and the bright aurora which, rising from the northern part of the horizon, streamed up to the zenith in long streaks of wavy flame, making the path before us almost as distinct as if it had been but the twilight of a summer's evening—the whole scene was again before me almost as vividly as if it had been reality.

As the concluding part of this panoramic view of the past, there was the misty walls and smoky rafters of a low damp cottage, faintly illuminated by the flame of a rushlight, which burned in an iron lamp, suspended from a nail driven into the rustic frame-work which supported the *clay vent*, and which had been kindled with some difficulty from the embers of a nearly burnt-out fire. Before that lamp sat the same young man, forgetful alike that he had to be abroad before six o'clock next morning, and that it was then considerably past midnight; so intent was he in scanning the contents of the books he had recently purchased.

This was the closing scene of that particular evening, from which, as already said, Imagination had shaken off the shadows of more than ten years. But she did not stop here: many painful recollections were inseparably interwoven with the intervening period; these, at her command, were carefully collected by memory, and, when they had been invested with her most vivid colouring, placed exactly in the array in which the corresponding events had occurred. After having yielded implicitly, for I know not how long, to the various emotions thus produced, I put aside the things which I had been vainly endeavouring to examine, extinguished the lamp by which I had pursued these musings, and went to bed. As the consequence of previously excited feelings, a sort of imperfect and broken slumber soon came on; and then my dreams were of that brother whom imagination had so recently placed before me in the various stages of his existence, from infancy up to manhood. If the *impression* in the one case had been vivid, what may be called the *perceptions* in the other seemed to participate in a still greater degree of reality. Methought it was a bright Sabbath in the very pride of summer—that we had been engaged in the service of the day, and had strayed, during the interval of public worship, to the ruins of the old church, and the parish burying ground which surrounded it—a favourite haunt of ours at such seasons. There, as fancy deemed, we were employed in deciphering the moss-covered inscriptions, and half obliterated names, engraved on the rude monuments which had been "erected to the memory" of individuals long ago forgotten, when he started off all at once, and, after running to a short distance, disappeared behind a tombstone, beckoning me to follow. I hastened to obey, but I had taken only a few steps, when I stumbled over an open grave, which I had not before observed, and fell; and the fall, imaginary as it was, served to awaken me to a full sense of the cold, and saddening realities by which I was surrounded—to a sense that *that* brother was no more!—that he had been remorselessly cut down by death in the very prime and flower of youth—that my few friends had sunk, in rapid succession, into their graves! and that I was alone in the world—the sole and solitary inhabitant of a home which had once contained a whole family, of whom, myself excepted, not a single individual was now alive! The dream was over: but the impression which it had left served effectually to banish sleep: and being too much excited to enjoy even waking repose, I got up, lighted the lamp which I had extinguished scarcely an hour before, and employed myself in noting down the various incidents which have been noticed in the preceding paragraphs, till the grey and sickly dawn of a morning, in early spring, called me to other pursuits.

Does the reader think the dream ominous? He may rest assured, that it was *not* mentioned for the purpose of leading to such a conclusion; but simply as a part of what *really* occurred. Dreams embrace a wide range of very disjointed subjects: in short, they may be tortured into almost any interpretation by those who allow their fancies to run wild in those regions of mist and uncertainty; but, as men die at all ages, and in every variety of circumstances, the event to which he would say it points may happen without the one having the slightest reference to the other: coincidence does not necessarily imply connection, and it may be fulfilled without being at all an omen. One word more, and I have done. Is the reader inclined to think that I have given too partial a view of the personal appearance, the character, or the talents of so near a relation; in other words, that I have spoken too favourably of an *only brother?* Let him recollect that it is of the dead, and not of the living, that I have been speaking, and he will, perhaps, be able to pardon the error, if such it should be deemed. My little tale is now told; and its *truth* is the only apology I can offer for its lack of interest.

## JONATHAN MOUDIWORT.

### Chapter I.

#### Indications of Character — Small Beginnings.

JONATHAN MOUDIWORT was born of very obscure and very poor parents. If our information is correct, his father was a weaver; and Jonathan himself was initiated, at a very early age, into all the mysteries of threads, reeds, haidles, and treadles. But this is anticipating: for it should first be told that the boy had a great deal of natural talent even in his earliest years; and, when at school, or rather before he was old enough to go there, that he frequently contrived to buy up nearly the whole of the toys of which his play-fellows were possessed. He would first give them something in exchange for a top, or a knife, or whatever they might chance to have; and then something else in exchange for that—always taking care to give an article of less value at every successive bargain, until he had fairly bartered them out of their last farthing's worth in the most fair and honourable way. When he found them particularly stubborn he sometimes tried another expedient: upon these occasions it was his custom first to try to get "a piece" from his mother: and, if he succeeded, his next step was to engage his refractory companion upon some long excursion a little before dinner-time. When he had brought matters thus far, he scarcely ever failed of success, by pushing onward as briskly as possible with the little commercialist, under pretence of some great sight which they were to see, or some fine things which they were to get, till he had got him to a considerable distance from home; and then, when the afternoon was well advanced, and the poor boy had begun to suffer from the extreme of hunger, with still a mile or two of road between him and the prospect of any supply, he, in general, found him willing to sell whatever he might have, as Esau did his birthright—not, however, for "a mess of pottage," but for a portion of *peas,* or *barley bannock,* as the case might be. We cannot afford space to narrate more of Jonathan's boyish proceedings; but the specimens already given, it must at once be acknowledged, afforded sure indications of a wise, bargain-making, prospering man when time should have matured his intellect: and Jonathan's riper years did not belie the promise of his youth. He had tact and talent—an enterprising disposition, and an abundance of ambition; and, with such qualifications, who ever failed to get forward in the world?

As yet, however, he was surrounded by what the poets have been pleased to call "the thick mists of poverty." By his connection with threads, reeds, haidles, and treadles he could earn a bare subsistence, and very little more; but then he knew that "money makes money, as poor Richard said;" and if he could only save, or in any other way get hold of a few pounds, or even a few shillings, these, in the course of time, might make a few more; and thus he might get forward on the road to fortune and respectability; for the two are always to be found together. He had, moreover, an uncle, the worthy Mr. Mungo Mondiwort, who, from having wriggled himself into a writer's office, as an errand boy, when he was a lad, had actually risen to be factor and law-agent for the estate of Lord Crippledonky. " Blood is thicker than water," even at the thinnest: his lordship lived constantly in London; a farm might fall vacant in the course of time; and Jonathan thought that he already saw through these same " mists of poverty."

Having saved a trifle by rising early and sitting up late— at least he had by some means or other got his hands upon a few pounds—his next proceeding was to take a *grass park*. It was a very small one, inasmuch as the rent for the season was only £9 : but, small as it was, there were people who thought he would never be able to *stock* it with cattle. Jonathan, however, thought more correctly, and saw farther than they did: and, thereupon, he went to work in the following highly commendable manner.

Duncan Toddleben, an old man, and his wife, an equally old woman, who had made their living for some time past by selling milk, had a cow to dispose of. The thing had become indispensable, from the cow not being *in calf*, as the dealers have it. Now this was the very kind of cow which Jonathan wanted. He accordingly attended two markets to which the creature was successively taken, and, by some judicious and well timed, as well as mysterious hints about " the health of animals," and " biting not being the only fault for which a cow was commonly brought to the market," he so influenced the sagacious cow-merchants, alias, cow-coupers, that not one of them would offer poor Duncan Toddleben a single penny for his cow.

The last of these unpropitious market-days was drawing to a close, and Duncan had no prospect save that of returning home with the " beast," for whose support he was in great want of fodder, when Jonathan, who appeared to be passing the place where he stood by accident, stopped for a little to condole with him upon his *ill luck;* and then begged his company to the nearest ale-house, to get a " single bottle of ale," as he phrased it, " for auld acquaintance' sake." This invitation was accepted; and the " bottle of ale," was followed by "a gill," which had a wonderful effect upon the old man's spirits. Another gill was called in: who would wish to do otherwise than make an old man happy? It was succeeded by a third, which made Duncan as *cheery* as if he had sold his cow for twice her value; and, in the end, he actually did sell her to his friend Jonathan for *three pounds and half a crown*, though, on the morning of the same day, he had confidently anticipated getting nearly three times that amount. Nor was this all; for it was stipulated that the *half-crown* should be returned as a *luck-penny!*

By such bargains as the foregoing, Jonathan soon succeeded in *stocking* his grass park to great advantage. The season was a favourable one for the graziers, there being a proper modicum of both warmth and moisture; and, when the animals were well fattened, he sold them to the butchers with a goodly "percentage" of profit upon the prices at which he had bought them. With this per-centage, it was an easy matter for him to "pay the rent, like a gentleman," as the factor said, and even deposit some *fifteen* or *twenty pounds*, in the Fiddlesticks' Bank.

"Maist things hae a sma' beginnin',"

says the poet: here was a beginning to Jonathan, and he did not fail to profit by it. On the following year, he took a larger grass park, for which he promised to pay £30; and, by attending regularly and carefully at a number of markets, and making the most fair and honourable bargains with all sorts of simpletons and old men, who had cows or other cattle to sell, he again stocked it in a manner as advantageous as he had done heretofore. When the proper season arrived, the butchers were once more fain to give him good prices for his "fat cattle;" and at the end of the year, besides "paying the rent, like a gentleman," as on the former occasion, he had between sixty and seventy pounds to deposit with the money changers at Fiddlesticks. Thus did Jonathan from year to year, increase in riches, even as he was increasing in knowledge.

But, to proceed chronologically with his history: on the year following that last noticed, the harvest was rather late; in the course of it a good deal of rain had fallen, while the weather was, at the same time, "warm and smoky," as the country people called it; and much of the grain had begun to grow again before it could be got into the barn-yard. During the earlier part of this period, a considerable rise in the price of corn had been anticipated; but as the weather had at last become dry, and it was supposed that the greater part of the crop had been "secured in excellent order," speculation upon the subject had in a great measure ceased. But Jonathan knew that when grain has once been allowed to *sprout*, however well dried it may afterwards be, it can never again be made to produce any thing like the ordinary quantity of meal, and upon this circumstance he founded his hopes. While the wet weather lasted, and even after the dry weather had come, day after day he might have been seen wending his way through the fields which had been lately reaped, thrusting his hands into the stooks, and "rubbing out" small quantities of the grain, which he winnowed with "the breath of his nostrils," or rather his *mouth*, and forthwith proceeded to examine carefully. At last his resolution appeared to be taken. As yet, from the farmers being busy in securing their potato-crop, and sowing their wheat, but little of any kind of grain had been thrashed or brought to the market, the deficiency of the season was not much suspected, nor had any rise of prices taken place; and Jonathan invested the whole of his £60 in the purchase of oats—selecting, as a matter of course, the heaviest and the best which he could find, and always buying them "reasonably cheap."

By and by, prices began to rise a little, and exactly in proportion as they rose, that degree of anxiety which, for some time past, had been visibly depicted in Jonathan's countenance, gradually disappeared. He now regretted that he had not more money to invest in the purchase of corn, and, at last, he fairly thought of availing himself of a little credit. Credit, he knew, was a desperately bad thing; but he knew also, that the danger lay principally in *giving*, not in taking it, and therefore his scruples were the less. It was known to all that Jonathan was a hard-working, industrious man, who rose early on every morning of the week, except Sunday; and, with a little cajoling, Mr. Flapabout, the cloth merchant, in the village of Aberdouf, consented to be his security with the Fiddlesticks' Bank for an additional £50—the whole of which was also invested in the purchase of corn as fast as possible.

This done, Jonathan's next operations were directed to the two meal-mongers of Aberdouf: by dint of argument and logical deduction, of both of which he was a great master, he succeeded in persuading one of them, that the beggar-making business was incomparably more profitable than meal-mongering. This individual, accordingly, emptied his sacks with all convenient speed, and, instead of filling them again as had been his wont, took up a beggar-maker's shop, otherwise called *a public-house*. The other meal-monger, from being rather a refractory character, did not come so readily into his measures; but, by buying up a debt of £20, which he had been long owing to a miller, and prosecuting for its recovery in the proper nick of time, he ruined him, and thus got quit of him also. No man could lament more deeply, or more sincerely, or more pathetically, for the unfortunate meal-monger, than Jonathan did. "But then the poor miller!" he said; "it was simply to save him from ruin, that he had advanced the money, and bought up the debt; and one man was all the same as another."

As soon as the field was thus scientifically cleared of all opposition, Jonathan commenced meal-monger himself in the village of Aberdouf; and scarcely had he done so when the farmers, who had now begun to thrash out a part of their crops, discovered that, in winnowing, at least a fourth part of the grain went away with the chaff, while that which remained was scarcely more than half the usual weight. This, though it had remained partly unknown till now, was what Jonathan had foreseen, as the legitimate consequence of its having begun to vegetate before it was brought home; and, as a farther proof of his far-seeing faculty, in a week or two after the real state of the crop was generally understood, prices rose from *eighty* to *one hundred per cent.* Great emergencies require great geniuses: Jonathan Moudiwort was a great genius, and here *he* prospered, while evil times appeared to have fallen upon many.

Having no "competition"—that everlasting pest to all speculators in the matter of money-making—wherewith to contend, Jonathan did not fail to make the most of it. "His meal," he said, "was better than other people's: and, therefore, he must have some additional profits to remunerate him for the very great risk which he had run in buying up so much good corn, and the very great price which he had paid therefore; and these additional profits he rigorously, or rather religiously charged. The people of Aberdouf, it is true, grumbled a little thereat; but he pacified them with an assurance, that there would have been not only a great scarcity, but an actual dearth, if he had not provided the necessary supply; and then he proceeded to draw a comparison between himself and the patriarch Joseph, who saved the whole land of Egypt, and half the world beside, from the scourge of famine, by the same sort of foresight. These, it must be allowed, were conclusive arguments, though the people to whom they were addressed, did not seem fully to comprehend their force, nor to be so ready as they should have been to thank Heaven for having sent a second Joseph among them.

How much he saved by this speculation was never exactly known; but, as Andrew Tetherend, the bellman of Aberdouf, observed, "it must have been a gey penny."

When the whole of the meal was sold, and a plentiful crop next year had brought down the prices to their ordinary level, it was said that Jonathan had serious thoughts of taking unto himself a wife, and *running* her in the meal-selling way, by which he supposed a little might still be made; while he was to attend to the grazing, and other *et ceteras*, as he had done before. But somehow, upon mature consideration, it had appeared to him that there were objections to this important step, which counterbalanced the advantages to be expected therefrom; and, to the great dismay of those who were most deeply interested in the "replenishing of the earth," the thing went no farther. What these objections were was not clearly explained; for Jonathan was a cautious man, and had the good sense, when it was necessary, to conceal his sentiments upon such subjects; but our friend, Andrew Tetherend, who, upon these occasions, sometimes served as a sort of guesser-master-general to the community, said, that "he believed the great obstacle to their being honoured with the presence of a Mrs. Moudiwort was the circumstance of there not being a *weel tochered lass* in the market at the time."

Shortly after the period at which we have now arrived, the lease of Fodderrigs, one of Lord Crippledonky's largest farms, expired. Does the reader suppose that Jonathan would immediately succeed to it? No such thing. Had he done so, it might have subjected Mr. Mungo Moudiwort, the factor, to the somewhat *scoury* charge of being more ready to consult the interest of his friends than that of his master—a charge which, in the case of such a gentleman, would have certainly been very unfounded. And here, be it remarked, that a great part of the character and respectability of a certain sort of honest gentlemen depends, in a great measure, upon their taking care not to give public grounds for bringing such charges against them.

At the end of the lease which had just expired, the whole of the lands of Fodderrigs had been "laid down in grass," which was forthwith to be let for pasture. The greater, however, and by far the most productive, part of the farm was almost perfectly level, having been, at a very considerable expense, reclaimed from a swamp by the previous tenant; and now, to quote from the advertisement, "Contractors" were "wanted to clear out the large drain into which the small ones emptied themselves." This sort of work was entirely out of Jonathan's way, inasmuch as he had never attempted anything of the kind before; yet he, too, "gave in his estimate," and, by offering to perform the work cheaper than any one else, strange to say he got the job. Early in the spring he commenced his labours; and the people of the neighbourhood were much amazed at the conscientious, or rather super-conscientious, manner in which he performed his work. He not only cleared out the large open drain, according to his agreement, but the mouths of the whole of the small ones, which, as is common in these cases, had been partly filled with stones, and then covered up with earth, so as to allow the plough to pass over them without interruption. The lower extremity of the whole of these, as already said, he opened up for a yard or two, apparently with the disinterested intention of taking out any mud which might have collected in their bottoms; and then, laying in the stones again, he left them, to all appearance, in a most efficient state for keeping the land perfectly dry. The whole of these operations he performed without any assistance; and, so great was his modesty, it was remarked, that he never interfered with any of the small drains, if any one chanced to be beside him.

The "large drain" was cleared out, and the whole of the work done before the season for "letting the grass parks" came on; but, notwithstanding this care on the part of the factor and Jonathan to improve the pasture by keeping it dry, the land appeared to be a thousand times wetter than it had been before. The moisture kept up to the very surface of the ground, in the furrows long pools of clear water were seen standing, and nothing like vegetation had made its appearance after the spring was far advanced. The day of auction, however, arrived, the graziers had been called together by advertisement, and the auctioneer bawled himself hoarse in calling out, "Gentlemen, don't deceive yourselves—once, twice—just agoing—who bids more? once, twice;" but, in consequence of there being no appearance of grass, none of the "gentlemen" would "bid" anything worth mentioning for any of the lower fields of Fodderriggs; and Jonathan might have had the whole of them for a mere trifle, had he been so minded. But he, like a prudent and cautious man, satisfied himself with one of the largest of them. Here, however, his far-sighted genius again manifested itself in a manner which might have well arrested the attention of the most unthinking; for, in a very few days after it became his, it was as dry as it had been for several years before, and shortly thereafter, it was clothed with the most luxuriant herbage; while the others remained wet, sour, and stunted throughout the season.

The plan of letting Fodderrigs, annually, in separate lots, for pasture, was soon discovered to be untenable, it having been found that, in this way, it would scarcely yield as much as would satisfy the respective claims of the dominie, the minister, and his majesty! and Lord Crippledonky accordingly instructed his factor to advertise the farm to be let again, as it had been before. The thing was done as his lordship desired; and a number of agriculturists from different parts of the country "looked over the grounds," with the intent of making up their minds as to what rent they could afford to give for Fodderrigs. One and all of them saw, however, that the whole of the lower fields, except that which had been tenanted by Jonathan, were "deluged with water!" and that they would require to be drained anew before anything could be expected from them. Formerly they had constituted the best part of the farm. The last occupant was known to have been very particular in the matter of drains, and had expended a very considerable sum of money in this species of improvement, to very little purpose, as it now appeared. Such being the case, some of the intended "offerers" seemed to think that the land was "undrainable," while they all agreed in the opinion that "it could not be effectually drained without an enormous additional outlay of capital." At the period to which we now allude, capitalists, whether agricultural or commercial, could not afford to throw away their money for nothing, any more than they can do now; and thus it came to pass that the rents which the whole of them proposed to give were of a most conveniently trifling description. This was a most favourable state of things for Jonathan, who, accordingly, stepped forward, and by offering *five pounds* more than "the highest bidder" was promoted to be farmer of Foderrigs. Should any reader be inclined to ask how the landlord deported himself anent these matters, we must confess that we cannot exactly tell; but perhaps the best answer to the question would be to say at once that he was *Lord Crippledonky*, and that he lived *constantly* in London.

Here we must digress a little to remark, that, but for "the superfluous moisture," Jonathan would have commenced his career under the most favourable auspices. When a tenant comes to a farm, which has been previously cropped in the ordinary manner, he must either purchase a great deal of manure, or a great deal of unthrashed corn, and likewise cattle wherewith to convert the straw into manure for the succeeding crop; but Jonathan had only to "till and sow," while there was every reason to expect that the ground, from having been previously "rested," would produce an abundant return.

The "superfluous moisture," however, and the draining of the lower fields, still rode, like a nightmare, if we may be allowed the metaphor, upon the neck of his prosperity; and many doubted if the new tenant would ever be able to get over these enormous stumbling-blocks, which lay in the way of his making a fortune. The blind goddess, however, it has been said, "favours the brave." Jonathan had already shown his bravery by the boldness of his speculations; and here the good lady stepped in to favour him, in a way which, to say the least of it, was altogether miraculous! Shortly after the bargain was concluded, the whole of those fields which, for the last two years, had been little better than a bog, became as dry as they had ever been before, without a single yard of new drain having been put into them! How was the thing to be accounted for? It was a perfect mystery, and a wonder to everybody except our old friend, Andrew Tetherend, who said that "doubtless it had been the work either of the brownies or the fairies!" In support of this theory, he told a story about his dog hunting a *rabbit* into the mouth of one of the drains, as he was returning home one evening with his spade on his shoulder; and thinking "that the creature might mak' a patfu' o' guid kail," he set about digging it out, when, to his utter surprise, he found only a few stones on the outside, and behind them a bank of earth, which kept the water as high as if no drain had ever been dug. To satisfy his own curiosity as to whether the whole of the drain had been filled up in the same manner, he bored a hole at the bottom of the bank with his staff, and presently the water issued from it in a jet, which he had much difficulty in stopping. He said farther that "he would cared little about stappin' up the hole had it no been that the fairies were kenned to be queer bodies! and, if he had destroyed ony o' their handiwarks, the least he could expect was, that they would stap his lum, if they didna rive up his early tatties, and his pickle cabbage-kail; and sae he thought it best aye to leave things as he fand them."

From this it would appear that Andrew did not consider himself a great favourite of Fortune, and that the "fairies," like everybody else, are under her direction; for had it been otherwise, that is to say, had he been on good terms with the blind lady, and had she instructed them so to do, these perverse creatures might have certainly done him a better turn than "riving up his early tatties and his cabbage-kail." In short, they might have "delved his yard" for him, or stolen seeds and manure for him from those who had these things to spare, or they might have made his crops grow without seed, or manure, or "delving," had they been so inclined; but it was evident that their tricky mistress, Fortune, had not commanded them to do any of these things, and as evident that Andrew did not expect to be benefited by their labours.

In descanting upon these matters, we had nearly forgotten to state the conclusion to which he came respecting the drains, which was simply this,—" That the fairies had stappit them up to be avenged on the laird for some ill he had done them ; and then *redd them out* again for some guid they expected to get from Jonathan Moudiwort." And with this sapient observation let us conclude our first chapter.

## Chapter II.

Ways and Means Indispensable to Rising in the World.

To an author, who is writing, not "against time," but against *paper*, the conclusion of one chapter, and the beginning of another, is frequently a matter of no small importance. The large capitals, together with the blank spaces which are usually left above and below them, are to him what the "return carriage" is to the toil-worn wayfarer, when the driver, for a small consideration, or it may be out of pure charity, takes him up, and conveys him rapidly over several miles of the road, without the necessity of moving his feet. Even thus, at the end of a chapter, the man of letters can pass over a part of his literary journey, without being obliged to tease his jaded intellect for thoughts and sentiments wherewith to mark the track which he leaves behind him. This seems to be the principal reason, if not the only one, for dividing so many works into "chapters," which, in most instances, are reasonably short ; and we trust the mention of it will be held as a sufficient excuse for the minute subdivision of this eventful history. Indeed, it is greatly to be regretted that the ancient manner of printing books has fallen into desuetude. In these days, according to a custom greatly to the advantage of the paper makers, as well as the scribbling gentry, the author, or rather the printer, always took care to conclude his chapters with two or three lines at the top of a page ; and, as the next chapter did not begin till about the middle of the following one, there was, in most instances, nearly a page and a half with nothing upon it ; and yet for this all parties were well paid, except the reader, who had to pay well for it, which was much the same—a *was* for a *had to* and an *ed*, being all that is awanting to make the cases the same. It should also be understood that, in the matter of book-making, the reader is to be considered as a person of very little importance, provided always that there is only a possibility of reaching his purse; and if this can be done by a good title-page, or a picture, or any thing else, it signifies nothing though the rest of the book should be wholly composed of the beginnings and the endings of chapters, with only blank leaves between them.

But not to proceed farther with this dissertation, it must be obvious to every sensible reader, that Jonathan had now the prospect of rising in the world, and attaining to respectability and importance in the eyes of his fellow-men. But still a great deal remained to be done before the end could be secured. There was yet a wide field for his talents and ingenuity to occupy, and the ways and means were not to be neglected. In this vile world, moreover, such individuals as he must always have a great many doubts and suspicions, apart from positive envy and ill will, in the minds of others, to overcome, before they can arrive at the summit of their glory.

In the first place, the less gifted portion of the community are always loth to think that a man of humble origin, whatever his talents may be, is really rising in the world; and when they see such a one advancing steadily to respectability and fortune, they naturally console themselves with the idea that he is only *speculating*, and that he will be shortly overtaken by ruin, corresponding in its depth to the extent of his vanity and ambition. Then there are those who are " well to do in the world "—those who have been born " with the silver spoon in their mouths," and who are always piqued at the idea of a " wooden-ladle " man aspiring to be on a footing of equality with themselves—these are always ready to doubt, and to depreciate, and to withhold the sunlight of their countenances from the individual who is struggling upward, until it has been fairly proved, beyond the possibility of farther dispute, that he is no less an ornament to human nature than they are themselves. With all these prejudices Jonathan had to contend, as will be seen presently: so that it was not altogether " Fortune," but his own talents and perseverance which, in the end, he had to thank for his prosperity.

After he had taken possession of the elegant, blue-slated farm house of Fodderrigs, he was frequently observed casting wistful glances toward the snug habitation of his neighbour, Mr. Evergreen of Feathercot. Mr. Evergreen, it may be remarked in passing, was in a very comfortable way, being worth some five or six hundred a year, which he derived from his own hereditary property; and when they met upon the boundaries of their respective fields, or at the markets in the neighbouring towns, Jonathan was fain to inquire after his health, and that of Mrs. Evergreen, and the Misses Adaline and Arabella Evergreen, in the blandest and kindest manner. But upon these occasions, the only answer which he could obtain was a formal "pretty well, sir, thank 'e," or a simple "thank 'e," followed by a "how d' ye do, sir?" during the latter part of which address, Mr. Evergreen, in general, walked off without waiting for a reply to his question. Jonathan knew both the cause and the cure of all this; and, instead of sitting down, as some silly people would have done, to make lamentations anent the "unfeelingness of the world," or to indite bitter things against the "exclusiveness" of the aristocracy, he set about making matters even in a scientific way, well knowing, that when he had succeeded in this great cardinal point, he was secure of success in every other.

He paid unremitting attention to the cultivation of his fields; and in the matter of bargains he was as careful that no one should have the advantage of him as he had been heretofore. It was even whispered that he had bought another cow from Duncan Todleben, as reasonably as upon the former occasion, albeit the latter was ashamed to acknowledge the circumstance. Even things which others would have been inclined to regard as disasters the genius of Jonathan enabled him to turn to his own advantage; and thus, in the matter of "servants' wages," he rarely failed to effect a considerable saving every year. But as his management in this respect deserves to be recorded for the benefit of those who would wish to rise in the world, the reader will, no doubt, be pleased to have an opportunity of contemplating it more in detail.

Here, it must be acknowledged, that in the choice of his servants he was sometimes a little unfortunate or so. He seldom engaged them till the stock in the market had been "o'er-waled" by others; but then, as in other cases of the same kind, the inferior article always sells cheap, and he got them for less money. The fellows, however, were not unfrequently such mixtures of stupidity and arrogance, that scarcely any other master could have known how to manage them. But, when it was for his own interest to do so, Jonathan could command the virtue of patience in as great perfection as ever it was exhibited by *Job*, or any of the other patriarchs. Whatever was to be done, he kept an eye upon the work constantly himself, and thus he was enabled to prevent the dunces from either idling or falling into serious blunders. At one time he stimulated them to do their duty by promising, if they behaved in an orderly and becoming manner, to give them such recommendations at the end of the year as would procure them the very best situations in the country; and at another, he terrified them into obedience by threatening to withhold these recommendations. Occasionally, by bestowing a little praise upon a vain young man, or rather by merely telling him that he was very strong, and very wise, and likely to attract general attention, if he could only regulate his conduct in such a manner as to give satisfaction to his employers, he secured his best exertions for a time; and when the "water began to wax light" upon the "motive wheel," and the oil to dry upon the machinery of his actions, he either repeated the dose or had recourse to some new expedient. In a number of ways, none of which would have occurred to any one except a true genius, he succeeded in getting his servants to do a great deal of hard work in the course of the season.

But then it is altogether contrary to the economy of Nature that crimes, or bad conduct, or stupidity, or arrogance—more particularly if the individual chances to be poor—should go unpunished; in short, the order of things is such that delinquencies of all kinds, when committed by serving-men and serving-maidens, must necessarily draw disagreeable circumstances after them; and Jonathan's mind was so constituted as to afford a beautiful illustration of this principle. Patient and forbearing as he certainly was, it generally happened that toward the end of the season—that is to say, after the crops of all kinds had been secured, and the greater part of the wheat for the succeeding year sown, the arrogance and presumption of one or more of these bumpkins became altogether unbearable, or it so happened that they were guilty of some misconduct which could not be pardoned; and, in both cases, it became a matter of conscience, and a duty owing to society at large, either to *turn them off* without their "wages," or to reprehend them so sharply as to make them glad to *run off*, without taking time to ask anything for their past services. The latter, it is believed, was the course most frequently adopted, and it was certainly that which best became a humane and honest man; for to *run off* at once implies a willingness to depart, and a consciousness of guilt upon the part of the fugitive servant; while *turning off* is always supposed—however erroneously— to convey the idea of harshness on the part of the employer.

A little experience, aided no doubt by extensive observation, had taught Jonathan the utility of trying to avoid, as much as possible, giving ground for this idea; and so prudently did he manage these matters, that when the dunderheads summoned him before the "Justices," for the fulfilment of his part of the bargain, he was almost always able to bring forward such evidences of their misconduct, and such good and substantial reasons for the course which he had adopted, that these "interpreters of the law," instead of sentencing him to pay "wages," not unfrequently awarded him "damages." Thus were these stupid clowns punished for their misdeeds and disobedience, with empty pockets and the loss of character, while Jonathan was rewarded for his patience and forbearance with as many pounds as he had promised to give them for their year's labour.

Apart from the tendency which they might have to increase his worldly possessions, these prudential measures were not without their effect in softening the hearts of his aristocratic neighbours. Even Mr. Evergreen and Mrs. Evergreen were not wholly uninfluenced by them. This worthy couple were strict disciplinarians: they were rigorous, with a wholesome rigour, in enforcing the duties of servants, as far as circumstances would permit; and they had frequently been heard lamenting most pathetically over the impotency of the law, and those imperfections in its administration, which allowed so many refractory servants to go unpunished; but when at last they saw Jonathan standing boldly forth as the champion of their rights, and successfully wielding the civil authority against disobedience, and all manner of misdeeds, they could not help regarding him with a sort of involuntary respect. By degrees this feeling ripened into an acknowledgment that he was certainly "a well disposed man," and that his firmness might, in time, be expected to work a great regeneration in the conduct of servants.

What cannot patience and perseverance in a good cause accomplish? Jonathan had now been five years in the farm of Fodderrigs, and every year he had reaped therefrom a more abundant crop than on the preceding one. During the whole of this period his respectability had been steadily increasing, and it was now observed that Mr. Evergreen had begun to eke out his wonted "pretty well, sir, thank'e," with the additional words, "I hope you're quite well, Mr. Mondiwort!" Here let the reader note the important revolution which had taken place in Mr. Evergreen's mind. But a few years ago and his neighbour was simply "Jonathan," or "the body Jonathan," or "that creature Jonathan!" But now, without a single cubit having been added to his stature, or a single hair of his head changed—through the sheer force of genius, and moral and intellectual enterprise—he had come to be *Mr. Moudiwort!* Surely there is an important moral in all this, which youthful aspirants after fame, would do well carefully to consider.

Contemporaneously with this change of sentiment, Mr. Evergreen had also begun to take Mr. Moudiwort's advice anent some matters of agricultural import, and to question him, in the most condescending manner, concerning the growth of his crops, and the best modes of cultivation. Nor were these the only triumphs which the latter had achieved; for by this time it was also remarked that Miss Adaline and Miss Arabella Evergreen, had begun occasionally to steal a most modest and maidenly glance towards his seat in the church, when he happened to occupy it on a Sunday. Some even went so far as to say, that he was most ready to return these glances with a look indicative of all true devotion. For the dignity of history, however, it must be stated, that the thing altogether, was perhaps no better than a mere surmise, originating in that disposition to indulge in scandal, which prevails in most towns, and in not a few countries. Or it might take its rise from the circumstance of the Misses Evergreen having discovered, that the side of the family seat in the church, upon which Mr. Evergreen was wont to sit, had now become so frail, that there was much risk of its giving way beneath his weight—in consequence whereof, like dutiful daughters, as they certainly were, they insisted upon resigning their own side of the seat—which by the way, fronted the wall—to their father, and encountering the whole of the danger which might result from a "break down," themselves! This, furthermore, was not the only disinterested sacrifice which they laid upon the alter of filial affection; for, as has been already hinted, the side of the seat which they were now to occupy, from being opposite to that which fronted the wall, must unavoidably front the whole congregation; and in taking possession of it, they incurred the very great inconvenience, not to mention the positive risk, of exposing their own most attractive countenances, which, during the singing of the psalms, and the reading of the text, were of necessity unveiled, to the vulgar gaze of all and sundry there assembled; or at least to that of as many of them as might happen to prefer those paragraphs which may sometimes be read in the eyes of young ladies, to the pages of their psalm books and bibles, or to the melody which the precentor was no doubt doing his best to make.

Had the congregation consisted exclusively of Mr. Moudiworts, or of young men, who, like him, though they had been once poor, were now rising rapidly in the world, the conduct of these young ladies would have hardly been worth mentioning; because the mere circumstance of accumulating money, has a wonderful effect in divesting even vulgar things of their vulgarity, and purifying and exalting them to a higher standard: so that any contamination which might have previously been about them, soon ceases to exist. But when it is known that the church of Aberdouf, like most other churches, was, to a great extent, filled with poor men, who had to throw off their coats every day and toil hard for their daily bread, without the prospect of ever being richer—and that the Misses Evergreen were the daughters of Geoffrey Evergreen, Esq. of Feathercot; who was the son of Mr. Abel Evergreen, a cow-doctor; who was the son of some other great man—an Evergreen no doubt—whose titles and distinctions were never distinctly understood,—then the filial affection of these young ladies, and the amount of the sacrifice which they were willing to make for the safety and comfort of their father, will be better comprehended.

We have been the more particular in noticing all the circumstances connected with this part of our history, lest the reader should fall into the same scandalous mistake with the people of Aberdouf, by supposing that the Misses Evergreen were making unmaidenly advances to the hand of Mr. Moudiwort; or that Mr. Moudiwort was anxious for a union with so distinguished a family, for selfish purposes. The truth seemed to be, that the young ladies, as yet, had nothing in view beyond a most commendable wish to improve their minds, by the friendship and conversation of so intelligent a man; while he, on his part, was willing to afford them the little advantages which they desired. Such being the case, it was hard indeed to have their disinterested care for the safety and comfort of their father misconstrued, in the manner already noticed. The blind goddess, however, if it were fair to judge from her conduct upon this occasion, must have had some little regard for her own father, and some little respect for those among her worshippers who entertained the same feeling; for she was now on the point of rewarding the Misses Evergreen, for their filial affection, with the full consummation of their wishes, as will be seen by and by.

After these things had supplied the people of Aberdouf, and the country thereabouts, with a subject of conversation for a time, an accident occurred, which at once placed Mr. Moudiwort high in the estimation of the whole family at Feathercot; and thus took away any awkwardness which there might have been in either party making advances to the other, in the absence of such an accident. It has been already said that the farm of Fodderrigs was bounded on one side by a large open drain: this drain separated it from the property of Mr. Evergreen; and it so happened that as Mr. Moudiwort was passing along upon its bank, engaged in deep meditation upon the luxuriance of the crops, with which his fields were crowned, he met Miss Adaline Evergreen, who, after the manner of romantic young ladies, had come forth to enjoy "the beauties of Nature" upon the other side of the drain. Had there been any of that bold and striking scenery, which Lord Byron has so majestically described—any "steeps and foaming falls," over which she could have "leaned," or any "trackless mountains," which she could have "climbed all unseen, with the wild flock which never needs a fold!" or any "forest's shadowy scene," which she could have "traced," she would have, doubtless, done all these sublime things! But neither "foaming falls," "trackless mountains," nor "forests," chanced to be within a convenient distance; of "flocks," whether "wild" or tame, none were within view—not even a single sheep; and thus it seemed that, on the present occasion, she had been forced to content herself with a walk by the side of a field of "blooming clover," which skirted "the Big Drain," as it was called.

Here, indeed, there was not much either of that "awful grandeur," or "enchanting loveliness," which has such incomprehensible charms for the whole race of poets, and poetesses, and romantic young persons of both sexes. The foresaid field of clover, which might yield, perhaps, about two hundred stones of hay per acre—another field of most unpoetical turnips—and a third of very promising oats, upon the opposite bank, with a lazy stream of water flowing over a dead level, which left its surface as smooth as that of glass, save where it was disturbed by a water rat, who had been basking on its side, "plumping in,"—these were the principal features of the landscape. But then the immaterial mind is not fettered by matter, or time, or place. It may soar away from coarse and vulgar things, and dwell in the regions of imagination and romance, and enjoy visions of all supposable sorts at pleasure! So, at least, the poets tell us, and we can do no less than believe them; for what could possibly be made by telling lies about such matters?

Thus it very probably was with Miss Adaline Evergreen, as she came slowly onward, musing, or endeavouring to muse, most romantically upon all that was, and all that was not around her. So absorbing, at last, were her musings, that she had forgotten to look up for some time; and it so happened that she was almost close upon Mr. Moudiwort, with only "the big drain" between them, before she observed him. Her delicacy, however, immediately took the alarm; but she was too late to think of flying in a contrary direction, which, moreover, might have looked a little silly, if not uncivil, as she was pleased to suppose. As a more becoming way of managing the matter, she endeavoured to make off, in pursuit of a butterfly—which came most opportunely to her assistance—through the field of clover; but she had only taken a few steps, when she discovered that there was dew, or moisture of some sort or other upon the grass, and that she would get her shoes and stockings, both of which were of a very fine texture, irreparably damaged if she persisted. Mr. Moudiwort, moreover, did not attempt to call after her; and, as a last resource, she returned to the footpath, and, casting her eyes on the ground in a very modest manner, walked slowly forward, indulging the hope, no doubt, that he might pass without noticing her.

Albeit it hath been said that "hopes beguile maidens," in this she was not so far wrong; for at the precise moment to which we now refer, he was so deeply engaged in computing the amount of money which every field might be expected to produce, that—unusual as the phenomenon would have been—an angel might have passed him on the wing, if the thing had been done noiselessly, without attracting any share of his attention! Save an unfortunate cough, which she could not suppress, but which, fortunately, he did not hear, Miss Adaline Evergreen passed him in silence and in safety; and thus far fortune favoured her up to the summit of her most maidenly wishes. The goddess, however, is almost as well known for her fickleness as her favours; and after having been blessed in no ordinary degree with the latter, it was perhaps but reasonable that Adaline should be left to learn a little of the former. At all events, she had only passed Mr. Moudiwort by a very few yards, when her foot slipped upon the grassy bank and she fell into the drain! uttering, as she did so, a very well bred and most lady-like scream, which had the effect of at once awakening him from his dream of bank notes and golden guineas; and, when he looked round, he saw her standing upon a place in the bottom of it, which the lessening stream had left nearly dry, and struggling violently, but without any appearance of success, to extricate her foot—with the shoe upon it as a matter of course—which was sticking about half an-inch deep in the mud.

It has been said that a momentary smile dawned upon Mr. Moudiwort's countenance at seeing this event. Perhaps it was the benevolent contemplation, of how much good he would be able to do at a small expense to himself, which gave it birth; or, it might be, some remote idea about young ladies with great fortunes always falling in love with the gentlemen who rescued them from robbers, or from drowning in tempestuous rivers, though the last is not very likely, on account of its being too sinister an idea to pass through the mind of so honourable a man, as well as from the circumstance of his seldom condescending to read any of the fashionable histories in which these events are principally recorded. Be the matter as it may, in a moment he had jumped over the "big drain," which might be about four or five feet wide, and had actually taken Miss Adaline Evergreen in his arms—a thing to which necessity compelled her to submit,—and had lifted her from this "Slough of Despond!" and set her down on terra-firma, with as much dexterity and courtesy, as if he had been the most valorous knight whose name ever graced the historic page.

The young lady, as might have been expected, felt a great deal of gratitude, but could not by any means find words sufficient to express it. She was, however, so much frightened, and so much out of breath, from her recent struggles to get out of the drain, that Mr. Moudiwort could do no less than offer to accompany her home—an offer which served both to increase her gratitude, and her difficulty of expressing it. Indeed, to have heard her straining her invention for fitting terms, wherein to thank him for his "unbounded generosity," one would have thought that Mr. Moudiwort had saved, not merely a single individual, but the whole world, from being drowned by a second Deluge! By the time they got home, however, she had so far recovered from the effects of her fright, as to be able to introduce her deliverer to her "papa" and her "mamma;" and to tell the whole story in so circumstantial a manner, that it appeared quite "an adventure;" while it also appeared pretty evident to all, that Mr. Moudiwort had been the means of saving her from being either drowned or devoured by the water-

20

rats! In short, the thing seemed to have been altogether providential; and Mr. Evergreen and Mrs. Evergreen at once acknowledged that it was such, while they expressed their unbounded thankfulness to their much respected neighbour for the kindly part which he had acted toward their beloved daughter; and hoped that he would honour them and the Misses Evergreen with his company as often as he could find a moment to spare.

Such thanks, and such an invitation, must have been highly gratifying to Mr. Moudiwort. Indeed, the whole occurrence was most favourable for him, inasmuch as he got nearly half his victuals at Feathercot for several years after; along with the still greater privilege of as much of the company of the young ladies as he might choose. For a time these seemed to vie with each other in their devotion to him; Adaline out of pure personal gratitude, and Arabella out of respect for the prompt assistance which he had rendered her beloved sister. Great, too, was the labour, and great the cost, bestowed upon every dinner, or tea-party, or other entertainment, at which Mr. Moudiwort was present, and these were not a few.

Chapter III.

Important discovery concerning the keeping of the Sabbath, and other matters, ending with a marriage.

To pursue our history systematically, it must be mentioned, that if the plain tea dishes had been set upon the table for the family repast at Feathercot, and it was afterwards discovered that Mr. Moudiwort was approaching, and likely to be present, the serving-maidens were drilled into the greatest possible despatch to get them removed, and their place occupied with the finest china which Mrs. Evergreen's cupboard could supply; and when, by dint of great exertion, everything had been got in proper order for the reception of so distinguished a guest, then would the good lady and her fair daughters wait with breathless attention till the step of Mr. Moudiwort was heard at the door, when all were up and ready to shake hands with him as he entered, and to give him the most cordial welcome; assuring him, at the same time, that they were so very happy to see him, and so very much honoured by his company.

The reader need scarcely be told, that upon these occasions he was uniformly invited to partake of their afternoon's repast, with many apologies for its "plainness," and the unfashionableness of their tea-equipage—the last of which, they assured him, they could have wished a thousand times more elegant for his sake. The whole, however, was, in general, concluded by Mrs. Evergreen, " hoping that he would excuse their homeliness, as they were just accustomed to regard him as one of the family " —whereat the Misses Evergreen would turn their bright eyes, in downcast thoughtfulness, upon the carpet, or fall to examining some figure in the table-cloth, with an air of the most interesting abstraction, and endeavouring the while to blush in the best manner they could.

After these young ladies had fully displayed their ingenuity, ability, and superior skill in the brewing and distributing of that most social beverage, *tea*, if it happened to be summer, and the evening a fine one, Mr. Moudiwort was invited to accompany them in a walk to the garden. This invitation he always accepted, giving his arm to one or both of the damsels as they went along, and endeavouring to admire, with all his might, those exotic plants and flowers, of which every fashionable Miss, who can command a few inches of ground, must have a reasonable collection, to ensure her being held up as a young lady of refined taste, and a devout worshipper of " the beauties of Nature." Sometimes, too, he would repose with them under the cool shade of the arbour—over which their own fair hands, with the help of those of old John Dibbletree, had trained the honeysuckle and the Ayrshire roses—and listen to them reading about " cupids," and " darts," and " unquenchable flames," or other wonderful things from their favourite poets—responding with a sigh, as in duty bound, to those sighs which occasionally heaved their fair bosoms when they came to any passage which was particularly powerful or pathetic. But if it chanced to rain, or to blow hard, or to do anything else which would have rendered it disagreeable for young ladies to be abroad, then he would remain in " the parlour " with them and their lady-mother, and talk of religious matters, and lament over the profligacy of " the lower orders "—Mrs. Evergreen being a very pious woman; or she would converse learnedly for his entertainment upon the " upsettingness " and " disobedientness " of servants, together with the " hardness of the times " and the difficulty of making money as fast as respectable people would wish to make it. To vary and give relief to these grave and somewhat solemn matters, the piano was sometimes brought into requisition; and at such seasons, while Miss Adaline or Miss Arabella played and sung most divinely, Mr.

Moudiwort would sit with his eyes, and occasionally with his mouth also, wide open, and stare at them in an attitude of the most ecstatic delight. True it was, indeed, that he sometimes made little misnomers in his efforts to praise their inimitable performances, and to seem skilled in musical technicalities; but then his grave counsel upon other subjects, and the wisdom and the riches which he was known to possess, were an abundant excuse for these trifling inaccuracies; and, what was more to the purpose, when he went wrong, the demure maidens were always ready to set him right again, and to make it appear that his mistakes were no mistakes at all. Finally, in the course of the winter season, Mr. Moudiwort's visits to Feathercot were very often terminated over a "bowl of toddy" with Mr. Evergreen; and, in the inspiration which it supplied, the probabilities of lowering "servants' wages" and raising the "price of grain" was frequently discussed in a manner which was both interesting and edifying. So interesting, indeed, were these discussions, that Mr. Moudiwort, who was said to have no particular dislike to a glass of toddy when it was supplied by a dear friend, often tarried till the night was far advanced.

Upon one of these occasions, Mr. Evergreen's toddy must either have been very good, or the charms and the music of the young ladies must have been uncommonly attractive, or perhaps it was only the conversation of their mother which was pious and interesting in no ordinary degree—our authorities do not warrant us to say exactly which—but it was Saturday night, and Mr. Moudiwort prolonged his stay till it was two o'clock on Sabbath morning; and when he went away he appeared to be so much *"in the spirit,"* or, speaking more correctly, to have so much of the spirit *in him,* that he paid little attention to the things of this sublunary and perishing world; and, as the natural consequence of this exalted state of mind, stumbled frequently over small stones and other trifling obstructions which happened to be in his way. There was nothing wrong in all this—nothing which even a Methodist could reprove; and surely nobody will venture to say so. Indeed, he might have sat in the house of so steady and so respectable a neighbour till the Sabbath sun on the following morning had enlightened the deepest recesses of the forest, and deserved nothing save the highest commendation for his conduct. Had he been a poor man, however, and sitting up in the alehouse and *getting drunk,* the case would have been widely different.

After his departure from Feathercot on this particular occasion, the shoes of the whole family were taken to the kitchen to be "cleaned," according to the established rules of the house, by the serving-maidens. There were also sundry glasses, tumblers, and dishes of other sorts, which required to be washed, together with several things besides, which could not be conveniently seen to till the gentle folks were on the point of going to bed. Formerly, however late or early the hour might be, all such matters had been regularly attended to—as, doubtless, they should be in every well ordered household. But on Sunday morning, when Mrs. Evergreen, after having lain a little too long in bed, entered the kitchen for the first time with a good set lecture upon the " carelessness of servants " and "the upsettingness, disobedientness, and wretchedness " of working people generally—a lecture which she had prepared for the especial benefit of those of her own household, exactly at her tongue's end, she was both thunderstruck and struck dumb by the sight which met her astonished eyes!

There!—in her own kitchen—were those very serving-maidens—for whose spiritual instruction she had laboured so zealously—and it half-past eight o'clock on the morning of the Sabbath day—the one busily engaged in "cleaning shoes," and the other washing glasses, dishes, tumblers, and the like! The thing was unspeakably awful! and, after a becoming pause of horror, having first prayed audibly that the Lord might have mercy upon her own soul, and the souls of all she loved, she lifted up both her hands, and exclaimed, " What do I see! Can I believe my own eyes, when they show me my own servants, whose hearts I have so laboured to impress with a due sense of their undone state by nature, profaning the Lord's holy day, and incurring eternal wrath and torment by doing work on this blessed morning, which any sensible and devout woman would have done last night; and which is only done now out of contempt to my orders, and the command of our Lord and Saviour!"

"No just that either," retorted one of the refractory handmaids. "It was twa o'clock this morning afore the things were brought to the kitchen, and, as we were baith perfectly worn out, I e'en said to Meg there, that we would gang to our bed, and clean the shoon and wash up the dishes when we raise ; for it was Sabbath morning at ony rate, and there could be little difference between doin' the wark wi' the licht o' the sun, and that o' a can'le."

This was, no doubt, a most preposterous idea, but it had got into the girl's head, and there was no getting it out again. Had her mistress been fully acquainted with the bearings of the case, and prepared to state that it was quite impossible for Sabbath morning to begin with working people, and more particularly with such of them as were servants in "gentle houses," till they had gone to bed on the previous night, perhaps something like conviction might have followed. This important view of the matter, however, did not seem to strike her; or it is possible that she might be at the moment puzzled with the indistinct wording of the statute, which refers to the commencement and termination of the Sabbath. At all events, she could only tell her unmannerly handmaid, that " she would not keep an upsetting cutty, like her, about her house longer than the first term"—a promise which she kept to the letter—and then retired to condole with Mr. Evergreen and her daughters upon the " profligacy of the present age!"

To return to Mr. Moudiwort, he went on prospering exceedingly. By prudent management, as has been already said, he always contrived to save the wages of one or more of his farm-servants every year. More recently, but in the most honourable and upright manner, as was always the case with him, he had succeeded in nearly ruining several stupid individuals, who had "contracted" to reap his crops upon different years. By these means, however, he had got the work done at a cheap rate, which enabled him to effect a considerable saving in the matter of "harvesting." On every successive year his farm yielded him a better increase; and, in the midst of all this prosperity, it was believed that a blessing rested upon the endeavours of so honourable and upright a man.

It was, indeed, true, that some individuals grumbled a little at what they called "his gripping disposition;" and said, that he did not stick to "grind the face of the poor," when an opportunity for so doing presented itself. But then these individuals were "poor" themselves, and this was enough to set their testimony at nought in the estimation of all sensible men—it being well known, that such people must always have somebody or something upon which to indulge their propensity for evil speaking.

Others there were, of the same class, who did not scruple to call Mr. Moudiwort a hypocrite—asserting that, if he were really sincere in all his professions, he would not allow the "profane swearing" and "barefaced profligacy" which daily passed under his eye, among the people whom he employed. In their spleen they said farther, that "if he could get his work done for little money, he would have no objection to the devil being the doer thereof!" In all this, however, his good was only evil spoken of: for here again the more respectable and discerning part of his acquaintance believed him to be a perfect paragon of unobtrusive piety. "Mrs. Evergreen," they said, "had been blessed to do him good by her pious counsels, inasmuch as she had awakened him to a just sense of the way wherein he should walk; and it was only the meekness of a recently regenerated man which prevented him from rebuking others sharply for their wickedness."

"Great, indeed, were the exertions which Mrs. Evergreen had made in his behalf, and great, too, the respect and attention which she had manifested toward him. Nay, it was even whispered among the well informed circles, that she would have been willing to give unto him one of her daughters, as a wife, that she might be continually beside him, to watch over, and strengthen, and lead him onward in the right path; and this consummation, so devoutly to be desired for the sake of all parties, really appeared to be approaching.

To go back a little for the *beginning* of this affair—a thing which should always be scrupulously attended to in matters of historic import—for a time Mr. Moudiwort's attentions and his affections seemed to be pretty equally divided between Miss Adaline and Miss Arabella; but by and by, as is quite natural in all such cases, he seemed to become more devoted to the former, who was the oldest of the two, and who, it was said by some gossipping individuals, would have a better "portion" than her sister by at least *two hundred pounds*. But people who knew better averred, that though her looks were not quite so good as those of Arabella, it was on account of her "stronger common sense," "greater experience," and, above all, "her superior piety," that Mr. Moudiwort preferred and loved her more than he preferred and loved her sister.

As soon as this preference was fully ascertained, Arabella, like a discreet damsel, who knew exactly the part she was to act in every emergency, began to "veil her own exquisite charms," and to afford the devoted pair every facility for cultivating each other's affections. When they chanced to walk by the side of "the big drain"—whereinto Adaline had formerly fallen, and in which, but for the well-timed exertions of Mr. Moudiwort, she would have probably been drowned—Arabella would stay behind, to contemplate the minnows darting to and fro in the lazy stream, with so much interest and sentimentalism that the others frequently lost sight of her, and then she would return home by a different road. If their steps were directed to the garden she would suddenly recollect that some of her plants or flowers required watering, and return to the house for the necessary utensils, where she would presently become so much engaged in some pressing domestic duty as entirely to forget that her company was expected elsewhere. On these occasions when her sister, at their return, chid her for her absence, she was frequently reduced to the necessity of pleading a great many excuses, such as her own forgetfulness—her anxiety to have things right in the house—the carelessness of the servants, and the like—the whole of which excuses were, in general, accepted with considerable reluctance, and only upon condition that she was never to forget herself again.

With respect to Miss Adaline, the reader will at once perceive, that necessary as the thing in a certain sense might be, it was a very trying situation for a young lady to be thus left with a young gentleman. In these cases, and in so far as the passing moment is concerned, there is nothing like having a third party always present. It sets the minds of the whole perfectly at ease. None of those explanations which are so painful to the feelings of young ladies can be even thought of in such society; and this of itself is a great safety, and a protection for the hearts of all concerned, besides being a wonderful promoter of cheerfulness, and good conversation, and all manner of clever sayings.

When left, as has been already hinted, with no other companion than Mr. Moudiwort, Miss Adaline felt sadly the want of this third party. On these occasions she frequently became very silent and very thoughtful, looking a good deal at the ground, and sighing at regular intervals: nor was it without some difficulty that Mr. Moudiwort could succeed in restoring her to her wonted animation. This was evidently a state of affairs which could not last long; and, what was more, the young gentleman, it was believed, now felt inclined to bring it to a conclusion.

Now it so happened that upon a certain very fine day in the month of June they had taken a long walk together; and freed, as it would seem, from former embarrassments, the conversation had flowed on harmoniously. The young lady had declared that she had no patience with those creatures of her own sex whose hearts were wholly set upon finery and vanity, while they utterly forgot the more important concerns of their friends; and the young gentleman had spoken of a wish, which he had long entertained, to have a true and faithful friend, with whom he could commune upon all weighty matters, and who could assist him in the management of his domestic concerns. This, it must be allowed, was coming pretty near *the question;* but Mr. Moudiwort showed an inclination to come still nearer it, by begging the fair damsel, at the termination of their walk, to show him into a room where he might speak with her *alone,* upon a subject in which he was most deeply interested.

With this odd conduct of his in preferring to speak of important subjects in a room, rather than under the glorious canopy of heaven, history has nothing to do. It may, however, be surmised that his never-failing friend, *Fortune,* had some hand in the matter ; for had he entered upon the said subject in the open air, it is probable that all would have been settled beyond the possibility of a recall before any other object could come to divert his attention. As it was, no sooner had Miss Evergreen, in an evident flutter, shown him into the parlour, so called, which chanced to be empty, than his eye fell upon "*The Fiddlesticks Gazette,*" and more particularly upon the word MARKETS. The temptation was irresistible : he saw at once that the prices of grain were rising, and he could not refrain from reading this department of the paper aloud ; while his fair auditor sat down at the opposite side of the room, in a state of feeling bordering upon " tremulous anxiety," to await his pleasure respecting those important communications which she now confidently expected. Alas, for "the love of woman !" which, some one has told us, "is a fearful thing !" But we must not grow sentimental, nor fall to making lamentation when we should be narrating facts. The dignity of history must be maintained inviolate. But, as it is one of the duties of the historian to bring the *moral* of everything he records before the reader, we may be permitted to say in passing, that what follows was certainly intended to convey a very important moral to the whole race of young ladies who are accustomed to see young gentlemen, namely, that they should never venture to "expect" anything upon earth.

No sooner had Mr. Moudiwort read the "markets," than his eyes fell upon " A STRANGE TRICK OF FORTUNE," and then he read the following paragraph to himself—

"Some of our readers will, perhaps, recollect a Mr. Andrew Meggins, a native of this county, going out to the West Indies some ten or twelve years ago. The account of his death has just reached us ; and we understand he has left money and property, to the amount of between *four and five thousand pounds*, to his fair nieces, the Misses Meggins, who are now inconsolable for the loss of so dear a relative!"

By this time, some of our readers may perhaps expect, that Mr. Moudiwort would now be prepared to proceed with the business which he seemed to have in hand, but this is only another instance of the vanity of all expectations, without exception. Mr. Moudiwort knew the Misses Meggins perfectly. Indeed, the youngest sister, who was the healthiest and the best looking—the other being deemed consumptive—had sometimes deigned to smile upon him most lovingly, in former years; and it is highly probable that her smiles would have kept pace with those of Fortune, had they been duly encouraged: but she was then only a dominie's daughter, and had nothing to expect. Matters, however, were widely different now, and Mr. Moudiwort perhaps saw the difference; or it might be, that the mere circumstance of seeing her name *in print* fanned up the embers of a former flame, and made it burn afresh. At all events, he seemed to think the thing deserving of some consideration; for, after having read the paragraph, and mused over its contents, in silence, for the space of a minute or so, instead of making any communication to Miss Evergreen, he all at once recollected that there was a breach in one of the fences, which he had neglected to have repaired that morning, and that, by this time, a number of his cattle would probably be among the corn! With this recollection, he bade his "expectant fair one" a hurried "good day," and hastened off to look after his fences and other affairs at Fodderrigs.

After this, Mr. Moudiwort did occasionally return to Feathercot, and at times, too, he still looked lovingly in the face of Miss Evergreen; but neither the fineness of the weather, nor those personal charms upon which she now bestowed a double share of her attention, nor her stronger common-sense, greater experience, or superior piety, could ever again tempt him to walk forth with her alone, or to solicit another private conference. If truth must be told, and, as we have already said, the dignity of history requires that it should be so—on the afternoon of the very day on which he left Feathercot to look after his "fences," some important business led Mr. Moudiwort to Aberdouf; and, as he was passing the door at anyrate, and had heard that Miss Marjory Meggins had been complaining of late rather more than was her usual, he thought that he could do no less than step in and inquire after her health. What were his words, or the exact purport of the inquiries which he made upon this occasion, history saith not: but "true it is and of verity," that Miss Matilda Meggins, the younger sister, smiled upon him so graciously, and appeared to be so deeply interested in his welfare, that he could do no less than call again in a few days thereafter. This second call led to a third: many old associations, and subjects of mutual interest sprung up between them; and, to cut off all unnecessary prolixity, Mr. Moudiwort succeeded better than he had himself ventured to anticipate in renewing his former acquaintance with Miss Matilda Meggins, whose elder sister died in a few months after, leaving her the sole inheritor of the "four or five thousand!"

In what follows, let not a sneering and scandalising world endeavour to pry into the motives of Mr. Moudiwort; or impute to him any sinister or selfish purpose. The thing was brought about as naturally and as honourably as a thing could be. He went, out of pure benevolence, to inquire after a distressed person: he saw her sister, and saw, at the same time, that she had become an exceedingly amiable young lady. This made him wish for a renewal of their former acquaintance; and with the renewal of that acquaintance, came still farther discoveries of her charms, mentally and bodily. It is natural for man, when he sees anything very desirable, to wish to possess it: it is, moreover, not good for man to be alone: Mr. Moudiwort had perhaps felt the inconvenience of being so; and thus *Miss Meggins* and *matrimony*, somehow or other, began to connect themselves in his head.

After having devoted a reasonable period to that sort of preliminary intercourse called "courtship," and with a most becoming degree of "embarrassment," "diffidence," and so forth, he made out to tell her that he was "desperately in love with her!" He told her farther, according to the most approved and scientific manner, that "should she refuse to marry him within a few weeks, if he did not die of despair, he must either go and drown himself, or hang himself, or break his neck, or do something else to rid him of an existence which would be altogether unendurable without her smiles and her society!"

What romantic young lady could have long resisted such a declaration when made by such a promising young gentleman? Miss Meggins did not attempt to resist it, and in a very short time thereafter she obligingly allowed herself to be "transmuted" into Mrs. Moudiwort.

This marriage, so fitting in all respects, seemed to give great atisfaction to everybody except Mrs. Evergreen, who sometimes whispered her fears for "the stability of Mr. Moudiwort's religious feelings," and "doubted if his fine young wife would do much to establish him should he waver." But not finding this sentiment properly responded to, she joined the rest of the world in commending the whole affair. The Misses Evergreen, and more particularly Miss Adaline, sometimes tossed their heads a little when they heard the bride's name mentioned, but that was neither here nor there. It was now as plain as truth or a travelling merchant could make it, that Mr. Moudiwort was fairly above the world—very far above it; and with this remark let us close the present chapter.

## CHAPTER IV.

Poetical Justice—Untoward Accidents, and the Conclusion.

IN this age of wonders, a most foolish idea has somehow or other gone abroad—namely, that such meritorious persons as Mr. Moudiwort are fitting subjects for what is called " poetical justice." That is to say, it would gratify certain fanciful individuals to hear that he had been visited with some terrible misfortune; because, forsooth, he did not give Duncan Todleben a great deal more money than was necessary for his cow; and did not keep his refractory servants and pay them their full wages when the law—the very fountain of justice—justified him in turning them off and giving them nothing; and, finally, because, after having walked and talked so much with Miss Evergreen, and actually gone so far as to solicit a private conference, he did not run through fire and water to marry her! The reader, however, may rest assured that in reality, and in all veracious history, as well as in the experience of every sensible man and woman throughout the length and the breadth of the land, there is no such thing as poetical justice. Indeed, poetical justice is to be found nowhere except in the *heads* of the poets, and unless some new invention in the sciences, or some new application of steam should enable the philosopher to expand these heads into *the world*, or rather to make a "new moral world" out of them, there can be no hopes of its ever being found anywhere else. Really the "Novelists" must begin to delineate "Nature," as the thing is called, in a more natural way, or nobody will believe a word of the histories which they send forth.

Accidents, however, sometimes do occur, which sadly derange

the plans even of the wisest men; and from these it were rather too much to expect that Mr. Moudiwort should be wholly exempted. Accordingly, we do find that the remaining part of his history presents some untoward occurrences; and to these we must now proceed with all convenient brevity; but first, in the true spirit of philosophy and history, we must give some account of the causes which led thereto.

Having now secured a wife with a fortune amounting to "between four and five thousand," together with sundry spare "thousands" of his own, and the stocking of a large farm, the produce of which was every year pouring into his pocket a shower of golden guineas, Mr. Moudiwort began to consider how he might best dispose of all this riches so as to ensure its due increase. Now it had so happened a good many years before that the gentlemen, together with the farmers, and the great men generally of the county of Fiddlesticks, had laid their heads together, and in the wisdom which sprung out of this combination of brains had established a concern called "The Fiddlesticks Bank"—the purpose whereof was to enable the tenants to borrow money wherewith to pay their rents without selling the produce of their lands until they had attained to a reasonable price, and also to enable the lairds to put any spare "bawbees" which they might possess, in the way of becoming profitable not only to themselves, but to the farmers and merchants, and more especially to the labouring portion of the community. The last proposition of this beautiful theory appeared rather a little misty or so to some individuals; but they succeeded in making it perfectly clear by looking at it in a logical way.

"By investing their *capital*," they said, "in the shares of a provincial bank, which would give accommodation to their tenants, they would enable these tenants to keep their grain till they got a high price for it; and when they got a high price for their grain, the natural conclusion was that they would be able to give high wages to their servants, and to employ more of the said servants, in improving their land,— which would be a great benefit to labouring people, inasmuch as it would be the means of giving them high wages, and bread for themselves and their families."

This was, no doubt, a most important truth, which has been too much overlooked by recent writers—seeing that it proves, in the most satisfactory manner, that the political economists babble sheer nonsense when they talk about "the omnipotent principle of *demand and supply* regulating the price of every thing;" and about "people always selling their grain, and whatever else they may have to dispose of, as *dear*—and purchasing *labour*, and whatever else they may require, as *cheap* as possible; without any regard to the interests of their neighbours." This vile, and sordid maxim, may indeed hold among an ignorant and selfish rabble; but the foregoing will show that it could have no place among the enlightened and philanthropic inhabitants of the county of Fiddlesticks.

To return from this digression, the Fiddlesticks bank was supposed to have prospered greatly, and to have done much good. Yet, nevertheless, some individuals, who hitherto had been the principal supports thereof, now wished to dispose of their *shares;* and as they said, and it was believed by others, that these shares had brought them a great many per cents., Mr. Moudiwort did not see how he could do better than buy them, and get a great many per cents. also for the "capital" which he should thus invest. He accordingly bought shares of the Fiddlesticks bank with the whole of Mrs. Moudiwort's "four or five thousand," and as many of his own thousands as he could conveniently spare—which thing being done, he began, with good reason, to suppose himself a very great man. To this sentiment his helpmate responded with the greatest cordiality: to account for which, it must be understood, that she entertained a very strong desire to be thought, and to become— not merely a lady, for she was that already, but—a *fine lady*, or a *great lady*, or something or other of that sort—this being an exaltation whereunto she had not previously attained, she, as already stated, having been originally only a dominie's daughter.

They accordingly laid their heads together, and, with the assistance of the factor, succeeded in persuading Lord Crippledonky to build a "new wing" to the house; after which they got a "gig," and hired sundry additional domestic servants. They also began to make festivities, and to invite gentle folks to come and eat bread and drink wine with them: and it was truly wonderful to see how these gentle folks came, and how they called their host and hostess, Mr. Moudiwort and Mrs. Moudiwort, as often as they had occasion to speak to them, and looked upon them with a great deal of respect, while they talked about the "pretensions" and "pride of vulgar upstarts" with a great deal of contempt—thus making it perfectly evident that they could not endure any thing except "genteel society."

While the greatest liberality and the greatest hospitality

was going on within doors, it was pleasing to see what strict economy was practised without, and how Mr. Moudiwort was still as careful to exact obedience, and a good day's work from his servants, and to turn them off without their wages if they disobeyed, as ever he had been at any former period. Mrs. Moudiwort, too, was sharp-eyed: and, notwithstanding her attention to the gentle folks, she looked well to the labour of her handmaids; and all things seemed to prosper exceedingly for a season.

Alas! that there should ever be a necessity for making "history change its tune." Among all the inventions of the present age, could nothing be devised for bringing people's affairs "to an anchor" when they are in a moderately prosperous condition? As yet science has done nothing in this respect, but let us hope that it may be able to do something by and by.

In the course of a few years after Mr. Moudiwort's marriage, the lease of Fodderrigs expired. In the interval his uncle, the factor, and the old Lord Crippledonky, had both died. The estate had consequently fallen to the management of a new factor, and into the hands of a new laird, who—if patronymics could be changed to make them suit the dispositions of those who bear them—might have been most appropriately called *Lord Suppledonky!* Mr. Moudiwort had thus no "friends" at "a court" which was beset with a whole host of offerers for the farm of Fodderrigs—each and all of whom had been tempted by the idea that they could hardly offer too much for a place in which such a splendid fortune had already been realized. His Lordship, moreover, had declared that he would prefer "the highest bidder;" and, in this untoward state of affairs, Mr. Moudiwort had no alternative but either to offer a very high rent for Fodderrigs, or to depart therefrom. His wife—Mrs. Moudiwort we should say—thought that it would be a pity to leave the place after they had got "a new wing" to the house, and a gig and a gig-house, and everything comfortable and convenient; and, influenced by these considerations, as it would seem, Mr. Moudiwort promised the high rent, and was preferred.

The farm, however, had been thoroughly *scourged*, as it is technically called, during the last years of the previous lease, and it now produced comparatively little. But instead of prosecuting new improvements, and purchasing materials wherewith to make the land again productive, Mr. Moudiwort was now obliged to lay out considerable sums of money in buying bread and wine for the gentle folks, who still continued to visit him in increasing numbers, and to talk about "vulgar things" and "vulgar people" with increasing complacency. Thus stuck upon the horns of more than one dilemma, in his heart he sometimes well nigh cursed Fodderrigs, the "new wing," the gig, the gentle folks, and the bread and the wine which they consumed, outright! but, upon these occasions, his loving wife comforted him with the prospect of " better times," and told him that they must "keep up their dignity." They did, accordingly, endeavour to keep up their dignity, and, that it might be kept up, a stricter system of economy was introduced into the kitchen: the domestic servants were made to work more *conscientiously*, and eat less *gluttonously*, than they had done heretofore; while the outdoor servants were deprived of all *extraficial* allowances, as Mrs. Moudiwort called them, and made to rise half an hour earlier than was their wont. In short, everything which human ingenuity could suggest was done to put things in a fair way again; and, had it not been for matters which must shortly be brought under the reader's notice, there is every reason to suppose that the attempt would have been eminently successful.

Other untoward occurrences, however, were now impending. By this time the reputation of the Fiddlesticks Bank had greatly declined; and, what was worse, the great many per cents., which it was supposed to have paid to its shareholders, were now reduced to no per cents. at all. In this state of affairs, to enable him to pay his rent, for which Lord Crippledonky had become a little clamorous, and also to ascertain what they might be worth, Mr. Moudiwort determined to sell several of his shares;. and, with a view thereto, he mentioned the thing to a certain Mr. Gledsclaw, who was understood to have some money for which he wished to find a profitable investment. This individual manifested no great reluctance to engage in the speculation; but, before he would advance the money, he determined to have some satisfactory evidence as to the solvency of the concern in which it was to be invested. He accordingly set his brains to work, and by operating upon the fears of some of the principal shareholders he induced them to call a "general meeting," and to issue orders for the "accounts" to be made up before the day on which it was to take place.

To this meeting Mr. Moudiwort had his own reasons for looking forward with considerable anxiety, not without some impatience; and there were seasons at which he almost wished that time would either get better wings or borrow a balloon to help him over the intervening space. The old rogue, however, kept on in his usual way without hastening his flight a bit on this account. But, notwithstanding this tardiness on his part, the day did at last arrive, and the parties concerned assembled, at the appointed hour, in the Black Lion Inn at Fiddlesticks. The hour at which business was to commence passed over, and still the cashier was not there. At last a messenger was sent to summon him, when it was found that he had been from home the whole of the preceding day. This looked suspicious; and, upon farther inquiry, it was discovered that nobody knew anything about where he had gone. This looked more suspicious still; and, after waiting for some hours more, without being able to learn anything of his whereabouts, it was at last determined to proceed with an examination of the books, aided by such information as could be procured from the underlings employed about the establishment.

Almost at the very commencement of this examination it was discovered that the accounts were in a most fearful state of disorder; but, in so far as they served to elucidate the subject, it appeared that the notes issued, and other liabilities of the bank, amounted to some *two hundred thousand pounds* or thereby—against which there was almost nothing to set as a balance.

On the following day it was farther discovered that the cashier had absconded, carrying the whole of the "specie" and the "types," or engraved plate, from which the *notes* had previously been taken, along with him. While the shareholders, and others concerned, were busily engaged in devising and putting in execution a number of schemes for capturing the fugitive—who, it was soon found, was beyond their reach on his way to America—the report of the insolvency of the bank spread like lightning; claims from all quarters came pouring in; and Mr. Moudiwort, or *Jonathan,* as we may again call him, instead of being able to sell his shares, soon found that the whole sum thus invested, and all he had in the world beside, would not suffice to clear off his liabilities. To add to this misfortune Lord Crippledonky, who wished to make sure of "the rent," placed the whole of his effects under sequestration; and Poor Jonathan was now a ruined man!

As soon as this was known the gentle folks at once forsook him, and soon after began to talk of him as "a vulgar upstart," who had met the fate which he deserved. Mrs. Evergreen lamented pathetically over his "backslidings," which, she said, had been evident to her ever since his marriage; and which, whatever a profane world might say to the contrary, had been the cause of his ruin! The Misses Evergreen tossed their heads, and "wondered what his useless thing of a wife would do now?" and Mr. Evergreen acted the most philosophic part of the whole by forgetting that such a creature was in existence all at once.

And what does the reader himself expect that Jonathan should do now? break his heart, perhaps, or die of disappointment, or that foolish feeling called *despair!* No such thing. He only scolded his helpmate a little for having led him astray, as he called it. This made her take to drinking in good earnest, which, fortunately for her husband—as her fortune was now gone, and she had no children—soon terminated her existence.

Thus freed from all encumbrances, Jonathan removed to a different part of the country, and commenced the world again in the capacity of a *cow-couper*. In following this vocation, it is said, that he speaks just as much truth as is indispensable, and, when more speaking is necessary, that he supplies the deficiency in the best manner he can from other sources. He has already made several bargains, which, for "tact," and a knowledge of business, fairly threw into shade that which he effected with Duncan Todleben. But, as it is the general opinion, that the world is now less favourably constituted for getting forward in it than it was at the commencement of his career, it still remains to be seen whether or not he will succeed in raising himself to eminence a second time.

## THE COUSINS.

WITHIN somewhat less than thirty miles of Edinburgh—in what direction it matters not—there was a small farm, which, about the time of the revolutionary war in America, was known as *Glenlochy*. The low, thatch-roofed dwelling-house, with its other appurtenances, stood upon a small eminence, in the middle of a sequestered valley, from which the outlets, forming a communication with the surrounding country, were so devious, that it appeared to be completely shut in by hills on every side. From the site which it occupied, the ground sloped gently downward to a small sheet of water, called the loch, or Glenlochy Loch; and so short was the distance between them, that in summer it served as a watering-place for the cattle, etc. At the time alluded to, the place was tenanted by an individual bearing the very commonplace name of Robert Langton. It was cultivated by himself, a young man, and a boy. At the period when our little narrative commences, his family consisted of two sons, William and Frederic, of whom the former might be about four, and the latter about two years of age.

Nearly at the same time, two of his sisters died of an infectious fever, which was then said to "run in the blood;" but which, in reality, had been *communicated* by the younger to the elder in the course of those visits which the illness of the former seemed to require. The two sisters left three infant daughters; and as the fathers of these children did not appear to have the means of providing for their immediate comfort, two of them, Grace and Eliza, were taken home by Robert Langton, to be reared along with his own family. From their being thus so early brought together, and from their being treated in every respect as if they had been born of the same parents, it may be easily conceived that the four children would grow up like brothers and sisters, rather than cousins, and this was actually the case.

Years, the ordinary details of which the reader can easily imagine, sped on: with them the seasons of infancy and boyhood passed away, and Robert Langton was at last enabled to cultivate the farm without any other assistance save that of his two sons. Grace and Eliza, too, were, by this time in the opening bloom of womanhood. They had reached that period at which, perhaps of all others, the female face and form is most engaging, and most likely to excite sentiments of admiration and regard in the bosoms of the other sex; and, being decidedly the best looking lasses for miles round, they had already become objects of pretty general attention with a certain class of persons in the neighbourhood. Some young men, who could occasionally spare a few hours for their own amusement, seemed all at once to have discovered that the little creek of Glenlochy Loch, immediately below the house, afforded the best place which was to be found in the whole parish for *curling:* through their exertions, stones, and people to use them, were collected; and in winter, while the ice lasted, from a dozen to twenty players might have been seen there every afternoon. Nor was the summer destitute of reasons for assembling near the same place. As that season advanced, it was found that the green level margin of the little lake afforded excellent accommodation for playing at *quoits* and other masculine sports; and to it the youth of the neighbourhood accordingly resorted for these purposes.

As the magnet invariably draws certain metals toward it, there is likewise a principle, or rather a charm in female beauty which has a strong tendency to draw the unthinking of the other sex within its circle, almost without their being aware of the influence by which they are attracted—in many instances, at least, without their having any definite purpose, or serious intention in view; and this alone can account for the proceedings just noticed. The moth, fluttering around the candle till it is singed by the flame, were, perhaps, an apt illustration of the manner in which such things not unfrequently terminate; and, in the present instance, this may have been the case with more than one individual, though it was never openly acknowledged. During these winter-afternoon and summer-evening amusements, however, many excuses were found or formed for calling at the "modest-looking mansion" above. If either of the old people chanced to have caught cold, their health was most carefully and perseveringly inquired after. If a cow or a horse happened to be taken ill, the inquiries, though of a nature somewhat different, were scarcely less numerous or less sincere. The very dogs and the cats about the place came in for a share in the general sympathy. If one of the former happened to have overfeasted himself upon a "rotten sheep," or if a rat had, unluckily, scratched the nose of one of the latter, they, too, were inquired after with much benevolent feeling, and many expressions of pity and commiseration. On these occasions, more than one individual held himself a happy man when he had succeeded in engaging one or other of the cousins in something like an exclusive conversation. This, however, was no easy task; for, "when strangers were within," the girls were, in general, busiest with their work—knitting, sewing, spinning, or whatever it might be. During the harvest season, too, numerous offers of assistance were made; and when "before the ripened fields the reapers *stood* in fair array," scarcely a day passed on which some one did not try "to mitigate, by nameless gentle offices, the toil" of one or other of the cousins. For a succession of years, this helpful disposition prevailed to such an extent, that Mr. Langton, who, though rather a stern character, was himself a humourist in his own way, was heard to remark, that, "to a certainty, the world had greatly improved in benevolence, since he commenced farming; for then, when he had a great deal more work to do, with fewer hands to accomplish it, he was left to struggle on without a single offer of assistance; but now, he verily believed, that he should get the greater part of his crops cut down, though he were not to hire a single reaper."

If Grace and Eliza were thus objects of attention with the neighbouring youth, William and Frederic seemed to occupy, at least, a fair share of the thoughts of the softer sex. Sometimes a fair damsel, on the point of emerging from her teens, would "step in in passing"—instructed by her friends at home, as she said—"to inquire for Mr. and Mrs. Langton;" and become, *unwittingly,* so much engaged in conversation upon sundry topics, as to "forget herself," till the increasing darkness of the evening made it a matter of common civility for some one to insist on being allowed to escort her on her homeward way. Occasionally the mother of one or two "marriageable daughters," would solicit their assistance at some little job, or their company for an evening; and then the "neat repast" —as neat, at least, as circumstances would permit—was served up by the girls themselves, who, with a profusion of smiles, and locks braided, and dresses arranged in the best style of the day, generally contrived to get seated, as if by accident, beside their guests. At these seasons, some little delicacies prepared by their own hands—such, for instance, as a cheese made in a particular way—were almost always placed on the table; and a number of articles, displaying considerable skill in the housewifery of these days, exhibited; while their various excellencies, and the numerous difficulties which had been overcome before they could be brought to their present state of perfection, were all descanted on, merely to *amuse* their visitors. Sometimes, too, as the brothers were on their way to or from the church, a thoughtful looking maiden might have been seen, who, in stooping to pick up her handkerchief or her Bible, which had, no doubt, dropped by *accident,* stole a wistful glance from under her arm, to see if she were particularly observed by either of the young men; and if she had any reason for surmising that such was the case—albeit the road might be free alike from mud and dust—she was almost certain to manifest a greater degree of care for the preservation of her under garments, by slightly tucking them up; and thereby, in the forgetfulness of the moment, exposing more prominently to view a very pretty foot and ankle—both of which she would have, perhaps, wished to conceal.

Nothing, however, can last always: and in this changeful world, most things are extremely evanescent. Eliza, who was the youngest of the cousins, had reached the mature age of twenty-three, while some of the others were nearly four years older; and still there was not the most distant prospect of any of them being married. Respecting the girls, it was even asserted, and with the greatest appearance of truth, that, among the whole of their admirers, not one had ever ventured to speak openly of love, or to make a direct proposal for their hands. William and Frederic were still occasionally invited to a New Year's or a harvest feast, by the mothers of grown up daughters; but among the daughters themselves, a feeling of hopelessness seemed to prevail; and, though they were still willing to honour their visitors with their presence and their conversation, their smiles were less bright, by many degrees, than they had once been. The *curlers* and *quoit players*, too, had discovered, by this time, that there were other places in the country which would suit their sports quite as well; the "benevolence" of the world had again somewhat declined; and if any accidental allusion was made to the younger members of the Glenlochy family, it was common enough to see individuals of either sex toss their heads, and make some sneering remarks about "bachelors" and "old maids."

One reason for the conduct of the parties thus sneeringly alluded to might be found in the circumstance of the family possessing within itself all the elements of happiness, and its members having no temptation to seek it elsewhere; but perhaps the reader will discover another reason, which, though unacknowledged, was not inoperative before the conclusion of the story. Be that as it may, the scene was indeed one which appeared too completely happy to be long enjoyed by mortals.

Coeval with these events, and in the early part of the year, Mrs. Langton sickened and died. It were almost trite to say that the death of a wife and a mother is always an irreparable loss to a family; but in the present instance, and to parties situated like the cousins, there was, perhaps, a something which made it more so than common. That minute attention which extends to the most trifling contingency—that intuitive knowledge of the workings of the human heart, in every varying situation, which is so natural to woman after she has arrived at a certain period of life; and above all, that gentle control which an experienced matron knows so well how to exercise while she does not appear to lay the slightest restraint upon the inclinations of those who are under her—these had gone to the grave with one of the heads of the domestic establishment;

and it is highly probable that this circumstance hastened on at least the consummation which followed.

The summer and harvest season passed over without anything remarkable occurring. But about the autumnal equinox, during a violent gale, the wind broke upon the roof of an old house which, though in a crazy condition, could not be well spared; and, as soon as it was discovered, both William and Frederic mounted to the ridge, while their father and cousins endeavoured to supply them with pieces of wood and other materials with which to secure the thatch. From age and other causes, the gables of the house already leaned so much to one side that a line drawn perpendicularly from the centre of gravity would have fallen without the base; and thus, upon scientific principles, but for the support which they derived from the roof, they must have fallen. They had, however, stood long in this position, and their insecure state gave no alarm. But the absence of apprehension is not always the absence of danger. They now began to yield before the pressure of the tempest, but so imperceptibly as not to be noticed till they fairly swung over, carrying the whole of the roof, the wood of which was so rotten that the greater part of it crumbled into short pieces before them, and burying both brothers in the ruin. A wild scream of terror burst from Grace, while Eliza appeared to have been struck motionless and dumb by despair. After a few seconds of inactivity, the former flew to that part of the ruins at which Frederic had been last seen, and displayed what was, for a woman, an almost superhuman degree of strength; but she evidently knew not what she was doing, and she only rolled about large stones and rafters, without advancing one inch towards her object. Aroused from a trance of speechless terror by her example, as it seemed, the other called on her uncle to assist her, and moved to the place at which the older brother had disappeared; but her strength was gone, and her feeble efforts could produce no effect. The one appeared to have strength without mind to direct it, and the other had mind without strength to do its behests—so differently may individuals be affected by the same cause.

Fortunately the accident had been seen from a distance, and a number of active hands soon arrived, and exerted themselves to better purpose in searching for the young men. On lifting up a rafter, which still supported a part of the fallen roof in such a manner as to leave a cavity below, William rose to his feet unhurt. The moment he was discovered, poor Eliza— who, with cheeks as pale as ashes, had never lifted her eye from the spot at which he disappeared—advanced hurriedly a few steps toward him, as if she would have clasped all she loved on earth to her bosom. But when she saw the look of deep interest which he bent in another direction, she checked herself abruptly before she reached him; while the blood which, with the first assurance of his safety, had again begun to mantle on her cheek—producing a faint tinge like the reflection of the evening clouds upon new fallen snow—once more receded and gave place to a second paleness almost as marked as the first. If these sudden changes were to be compared to aught, it must be to the colours of the pigeon's wing, which seem to vary in the twinkling of an eye when the light is thrown upon them in a new direction.

They were entirely unnoticed, however, by the individual who had occasioned them. He saw her not, nor seemed to be aware of her presence. With the first glimpse of daylight, his eye sought her cousin, and continued to follow her half frantic movements with intense interest for a time. Grace, on her part, took no notice of the circumstance, nor did she seem to heed in the smallest degree the words of those who told her he was safe. The whole of her distracted attention was fixed upon another quarter of the ruin, and, apart from that particular spot, the whole world beside was evidently nothing to her.

The joy at having found one brother had somewhat abated the activity of the search for the other; and it was not till William had recovered a little from the confusion of ideas incident to his late situation—or, rather, till he had roused himself from a momentary fit of deep musing into which he had been thrown by some unknown cause—and pronounced the words, "Frederic, where is he?" that it was resumed with full vigour. A very few minutes more served to bring him also to light. He had been stunned by the fall, while he had, at the same time, been protected from serious consequences by being thrown under a beam which still remained unbroken. The time which had elapsed since the accident, had, however, allowed him to recover his self-possession. But before he could utter a single word, Grace had him by the hand, reiterating, with an almost frantic earnestness, the words, "Are you hurt, Fred?—it's me—it's Grace—it's your cousin—are you hurt?" As she uttered the last interrogatory, their eyes met, and he said, rather faintly, but with a characteristic smile, "I only feel a slight pain in one of my legs." As these accents fell upon her ear, she seemed with great difficulty to suppress a scream of ecstasy. Her feelings, however, found vent in a sort of half hysterical laugh, which was several times repeated, along with all the other demonstrations of irrepressible joy.

With his first attempt to rise, it was found that Frederic's ankle had been dislocated, and that he could not walk. When this was known, Grace, in the excitement of the moment, would have carried him to the house in her arms. Indeed, she was almost on the point of making the attempt, when William and Eliza, both of whom were silent spectators of the scene, stepped forward and offered their assistance—the one with a degree of embarrassment and restraint, which contrasted strongly with the former ease and freedom of his manners, and the other with that affectionate timidity which was natural to her disposition. With their aid he was removed to the house. The dislocation was soon after reduced; but, from the limb having been bruised as well as disjointed, he was confined to the house for several weeks. During this interval Grace seldom left him. His comfort and his recovery seemed to be her only care; and, while she found a thousand opportunities for making tender inquiries, and bestowing unnumbered nameless offices of kindness, he did not seem to be greatly distressed at the accident which gave him so much of her company.

"Throw up a straw—'twill show the way the wind blows;" and an occurrence as trifling will sometimes show the current of human passions. From the time at which the old house fell, a marked change seemed to have come over Eliza. Her eye no longer met William's with that free, joyous expression which it was wont to display. If he spoke to her, she would answer him without venturing to look him in the face; and when he retired she would follow him with an intent gaze, and sigh deeply, and appear to be absorbed in melancholy reflection as he disappeared from her view. Sometimes she seemed willing to eschew his company as much as possible; at others she manifested an unwonted degree of cheerfulness as often as he was present: and, when both these moods had passed away, there was an unaccountable confusion in her manner as she approached him, and a strange tremulousness in her voice, as she tried to ask him some unmeaning question, or to answer some question of his which was almost as meaningless as her own. Altered as she had become, gentleness, and an ill-concealed melancholy, were still the predominating features in her character. Yet nobody seemed to be aware of the change which had come over her except Grace, who occasionally asked, "When she expected her wits to return from their wool-gathering?" or some such question.

The intercourse between the brothers appeared to have undergone a similar revolution. It was no longer of that unreserved and all-confiding kind which it had formerly been. Some subject now seemed to lie near the heart of each, about which he felt that he could not speak to the other. In short, the very demon of discord was now between them! and, but for the restraint imposed by early training and strong fraternal affection, their future histories might have served to darken the annals of crime. Of the whole family, Grace alone appeared to be perfectly happy. The only thing which seemed to give her the slightest uneasiness was, when she chanced to meet William alone; and then it only manifested itself in a distant, and rather pettish demeanour, till she could make her escape.

In this manner the winter months passed on, and, with the revolution of the seasons, spring approached. The little lake had been long frozen; but repeated thaws, alternating with returning frost, had rendered the ice of very uncertain and very unequal strength. Upon some parts of it, boys might have still been seen at their sports, while there were others which they carefully avoided.

"It will not do for the plough this morning," said William Langton to his brother, as they stood looking down upon the frozen lake, glittering in the first beams of the sun. "The frost has been too hard last night," he continued, in a thoughtful voice, not without a shade of embarrassment; "and I believe—I think I may take this opportunity to speak to you about something—for we are not *now* as we were *wont to be*."

"Well, well," said the other—affecting to laugh, though the confused blood mounting to his cheek, and the unsteadiness of his voice, told of other emotions than mirth:—"You look so serious," he continued, "that really I cannot help from laughing, but I will hear what you have to say some other time— only, just now, I must run down to the loch and take a *last slide*." With these words he ran hurriedly down the sloping bank, while the other retired slowly to the barn, and mechanically took up a flail.

Frederic's mind appeared to be in that tremulous state which does not admit of calculating consequences; and, without pausing to try the strength of the ice as had been his wont, he took a long run from the shore, and, with the force which he had thus obtained, placing himself upright upon the smooth surface of the frost-bound element, where it joined the land, he glided over it toward the middle of the lake. He had only proceeded a few yards, however, when the ice began to crack and bend under him. Still the rapid motion with which he passed along did not afford time for its going down. But, with the progressive diminution of that motion, the cracking and bending of the treacherous floor which now supported him became every moment more alarming, and ere the first had fairly ceased to operate, the latter gave way, and down he went, at a place where there was perhaps three or four fathom water, and at a distance of nearly fifty yards from the shore.

Although at the moment unnoticed by his friends, he was seen going down from some houses at the other side of the lake; and, in less than ten minutes, nearly a dozen of men and women were on the spot, with ropes in their hands, and all eager to lend assistance. The noise which they made alarmed his brother and his two cousins, who, pale and breathless, joined the others in a few minutes more. But what could they all do? After being repeatedly plunged below, and rising again to the surface, he had at last succeeded in grasping the ice in such a manner as to keep himself afloat, with no more than his head above water; so that, but for the cold, which had already weakened his voice to such an extent that he could scarcely be heard, and was fast benumbing every other faculty—there was still a prospect of saving him. Nobody, however, could throw the rope more than half the distance, while nobody could venture more than a few yards upon the ice without the certainty of going down also; and thus it seemed that he must inevitably perish!

In this dreadful dilemma, Grace threw herself before the elder brother—throwing back at the same time a profusion of shining auburn hair, which she had been in the act of arranging for the day when the alarm arose, from her countenance—and addressing him with desperate energy: "Oh, William!" she said, "you can save him!—You can swim, though he cannot—only save him and I will give you all I possess—my life, or whatever you may ask!" and in her eagerness she threw her arms about his neck, and clung around him as if she would not be denied.

Beautiful at all times, beyond the most of her sex, she was now superlatively so; and, even at that fearful moment, his eye turned from his drowning brother to look on her as she gazed in his face, with the flush of hope, fear, and a thousand mingled feelings beside, brightening her expressive countenance till it almost seemed inspired with the intelligence of other worlds. It was a trying scene; and, as he afterwards confessed, while he returned her ardent and inquiring look, the thought, "If *he* perish, *she* may yet be mine!" passed through his mind. He pressed his hand upon his eyes, as if by shutting out the light from them he could have shut out the demon from his heart; and in another moment his resolution was formed.

"Yes," he said, as he unclasped her arms and shook her off, with a look approaching even to sternness, "he is *my* brother, and I *will* either save him or perish with him!" He then proceeded with what appeared to be more than mortal despatch to tie the whole of the ropes together; after which he coiled them up, and reserving only the two ends, he threw the rest as far as he was able upon the ice. His next step was to fix one of these ends around his own body, thus making his purpose apparent. But, while he did so, Eliza approached him, and holding up her hands imploringly, "For Godsake, and your poor cousin's," she said, "do not venture on the ice!—I could not live—I mean, what would become of your father, and the rest of us, if you were drowned too!"

He heeded her not. Indeed, he did not seem to hear her. "Hold that till I bid you pull," he said, giving the other end of the rope to the man who stood nearest him.

"Oh God!" Eliza was heard to ejaculate, and, summoning all her energy, she grasped his hand to detain him from his desperate purpose. As little moved by her second, as he had been by her first attempt, he twisted his hand out of her grasp, pushed her hurriedly aside, and, while she staggered, dizzily, to the stump of a broken tree for support, he retired to some distance from the shore, to give himself the necessary momentum; and then doing as his brother had done, he shot along the ice exactly in his tract.

There was now a dead silence among the spectators, who seemed to suspend their very breathing till they could ascertain the result. Eliza alone raised her hands and lifted her eyes to heaven, for a moment, as if she had implored a higher power to save him from the death which she supposed he had planned for himself; and then she turned a steadfast—almost a frozen gaze upon that form beneath which the ice was every moment bending and cracking more fearfully. Notwithstanding appearances, it continued to support him till within little more than a yard of the place where his brother first sunk; and then it gave way at once, and down he went! For a moment he was lost to the spectators, and Eliza clasped her hands in an agony of hopeless feeling; but, with the next, he reappeared like a daring swimmer, as he was; and, pushing aside the floating fragments of broken ice, with a few vigorous strokes he succeeded in laying hold of Frederic at the very moment when his benumbed hands could hold on no longer, and he was sinking for the last time. "Pull on now," he shouted, as he threw himself upon his back, placing his body at such an angle as that his head and shoulders might rise over the edge of the ice; and thus the two were dragged toward the shore, till the frozen crust became strong enough to carry them.

A scene which it takes a length of time to describe, may frequently pass under the eye in a few minutes; and thus it was in the present instance. The praises and congratulations which were offered were numerous and loud, and the scene which followed was an interesting one; but lack of space forbids any attempt to describe it. Suffice it to say that the accident produced no permanent bad effects; only Frederic seemed to labour under a sort of depression of spirits throughout the day, as if he had incurred a debt, which he could neither discharge nor forget, and which, in the event of its being brought against him, would for ever mar his happiness.

On the following morning Mr. Langton took his sons aside, and told them that Grace's father, who, as they knew, was dead some time ago, had left about thirty acres of land, of which he had been the sole proprietor, to her younger sister, who latterly had kept his house; while to Grace herself he had left only a small portion—that of late he had entertained a wish to see them settled in the world—that he was now determined his youngest son should marry the heiress, a union which he conceived would be easily brought about, as he had himself been nominated the sole manager of her property—and that William should marry Grace, and succeed to the farm of Glenlochy at his own decease.

Both the young men knew that their father's disposition was unbending, and that it was utterly in vain to argue with him; but they appeared to be very differently affected by what they had heard. The younger blushed and stammered, but could make no intelligible reply; while the elder, with a half bitter, half melancholy smile, which seemed to spread slowly over a calm concentrated paleness of countenance, only remarked that,—"These were matters of some importance, and might crave at least *one day* for consideration."

"Hitherto you have been dutiful children," said the father, "and I do not expect that you will disobey me in this. I go off immediately," he continued, addressing his youngest son, "to break the ice about your marriage to your cousin; and, recollect, you are to follow me to-morrow, that she may have an opportunity of seeing you." With these words he left them, to prosecute his journey.

Shortly after he was gone, William, too, departed. At another time he might have found it difficult to get away without some explanation; but at present no one appeared to question him. Having travelled in a contrary direction till he lost sight of the place, he took the direct road for the shores of the Forth, intending there to try if he could find a passage to America; and, if that should fail him, he had determined to enlist rather than return home. In this respect, however, fortune seemed to favour him. In the harbour of the first coast town which he reached, he found a vessel bound for the western hemisphere, which was to sail in two days; and having engaged for his passage, he had only to lie by till she was ready for the voyage. As one of the thoroughfares to the metropolis passed through the place, he kept himself rather retired for what remained of the day. But on the following forenoon, as he ventured to look abroad, he saw a horse at full speed, with the cart to which it was attached, turn the corner of a street, and dash forward, without a driver; while a man, who quitted the arm of a woman, and tried to intercept it, was thrown down. Something like a shriek was heard, and a crowd instantly collected behind the cart; but William Langton paid little attention to these matters, being himself meditating an attempt to stop the animal. Having accomplished his purpose, he next hastened to see what was the nature of the accident which had drawn the crowd together. The first thing which attracted his notice was a woman, whose face he instantly knew, standing with her hands clasped together, and her eyes fixed in a glassy stare upon some object which he could not see. His first impulse was to start back, and leave the place without speaking; but there was a something in the look and attitude of the female, which dashed that idea almost before it was formed; and pressing forward, and touching her on the shoulder, "Grace," he said in a rather stern voice, "what brought *you* here?"

As if only half awakened, by that touch and that voice, from some horrid dream, she pronounced the word, "Frederic," and then sunk to the earth, leaving an opening toward the centre of the crowd; and, while such expressions as, "Poor man!"— "ay, ay—nae mair o' him,"—"it's a' ower noo!" and the like, were uttered by various voices, William saw the body of a man prostrate on the street—his head literally crushed to pieces by the cart wheel, with the warm blood welling up from among the brains and fractured bones. The arms and the upper part of the body were already motionless, but the limbs continued to quiver for a few seconds longer. Face, or feature by which to recognise its owner, none were left; but the proportions of the body, and some parts of the dress, told too truly that it was his brother.

What remains of the story must be told in a few words. Instead of going to America, William returned to Glenlochy, with that brother for whose happiness he had generously determined to forego his home and his native country, a mangled corpse; and the woman whom, in spite of himself, he still loved, a poor maniac. How they came to be in the situation where he found them, could never be exactly ascertained; for one was not, and the other could tell nothing distinctly. "Where is Frederic?" she would say. "He should come and see me. I am his wife now. We were married at Edinburgh at the *Half-mark*. My uncle thought to prevent us, but we took the opportunity of his being from home. Can't you tell him, William, that I am ill? I would do as much for you. I'm sure I always loved you like a brother; but perhaps you are angry because I did not love you as I loved Fred, but it would have been wrong to love you both. Only tell him that I am ill, and he will come and see me." Ill she was in body, as well as mind; and, notwithstanding all the care and tenderness which could be lavished on her, in a few weeks she followed her fancied husband to the grave. The old man did not long survive the death of his son, the suddenness of which gave such a shock to his feelings and his constitution, that he never recovered it. But in the midst of these severe trials, William Langton learned to appreciate the real worth of Eliza. In her presence he felt that he could indulge his sorrows, unrestrained. Her deep sympathy, and unobtrusive affection, won gradually upon his heart; and, in due time, they were rewarded with his hand.

---

## AULD PETER AND HIS FOSTER SON.

PASSING over that endless diversity of disposition which, in every day life, distinguishes one individual from another, without being so marked as to excite much attention, one does occasionally meet an oddity which stands out in prominent relief from the plain surface of society—a something original, which does not seem to be under the control of those principles which regulate the conduct of others. In these instances, the peculiarities may be the most amiable, or the most pitiable, or the most disgusting, or they may be simply ludicrous; or, as it sometimes happens, the lights and shadows of the individual's character may be so strongly contrasted as to excite a strange mixture of feelings in the bosoms of those who contemplate it. At times a man may be met with who seems to be seriously impressed with the importance of religion, and who, apparently, takes a deep interest in its ordinances and outward observances; while he cannot refrain from cheating and oppressing his fellow-creatures, as often as an opportunity for doing so, without incurring public odium, or the dread of positive punishment, presents itself. Such a man may be chargeable with the most sordid meanness, and the vilest duplicity, and yet, if a judgment were to be formed from his conversation, he would be taken as a perfect model of piety and resignation to the will of his Maker. On the other hand, there are not wanting instances of individuals who give themselves little concern about these matters, who regard with comparative indifference the religious institutions and observances of the country, and of whom it might almost be said, that " they cared for none of these things;" yet, nevertheless, they may be strictly conscientious in their dealings with others; they may also be generous to their friends, benevolent to the poor, and in every other respect highly useful members of society. These anomalous characters have long been sad puzzles in mental science: nor does it appear that they could be accounted for upon anything like rational grounds till a comparatively recent date, when it was discovered that the brain was the apparatus, so to speak, with which mind must work to produce an impression on matter—that this apparatus consists of a number of different organs, the particular development of any one of which, from the increased power which it gives to the mind in that direction, will give a decided turn to the character, in the same manner as a man can travel faster on a full-sized horse than on a small pony; and farther, that each of these organs, under certain circumstances and conditions, may act, in a great measure, independently of the others. Upon this principle the eccentricities of, at least, one of the characters about to be noticed in the following story may be easily explained. As to the story itself, the incidents which it embraces were communicated to its present narrator, several years ago, by an acquaintance, who had himself been an eye-witness to some of them. There being thus in it more of truth than fiction, the reader need hardly expect to find there the plot, and that regular succession of events, all combining to bring about some unlooked for result, which constitutes the great charm of a work of fancy. But to it, such as it is, we must now proceed.

"Auld Peter," as he was commonly designated, once lived, and, for any thing which is known to the contrary, may be still living in B—— Lane, in the city of Glasgow. Though well advanced in years, as late as 1835, he was stout and healthy; and, without being an extraordinary, he was in some respects a peculiar, character. In youth, he had been bred a gardener. This occupation he had followed through life, but, not being very fortunate in procuring situations, for a number of years past he had ceased to seek after them, and satisfied himself with cultivating the gardens of a number of wealthy citizens who lived in his neighbourhood, at so much per day, or per hour, according to the length of his job.

Three or four times every season, Peter might have been seen swaggering home with "a sheet too much in the wind"—that is to say, he carried more sail than accorded exactly with his ballast, and thus he sometimes lost the power of steering himself in the proper direction. Just as he had come about to the starboard tack, he would sheer off again to the larboard, and run upon it till he was fairly aground in the quicksands of some gutter at the road side; or, if he chanced to be in the country, till he stuck fast, not upon a rock, but in a thorn hedge, or something else of the same kind, which impeded his farther progress. On these occasions his "leeway" always made a considerable item in the reckoning; and sometimes, after "lying to" for more than a minute, instead of advancing to his destined port, he would go "right astern!" In this respect, Peter resembled a steamboat, which, by merely reversing the motion of her paddle-wheels, can go either way, rather than a ship which can progress only with her head first.

Among other plans which Peter had tried to enable him to meet this extra expenditure, and, if possible, to better his fortune, one was the keeping of lodgers. These consisted exclusively of trades' people, masons, wrights, etc. To them he was a kind landlord; and from his wife being unremitting in her care for their comfort, his beds were seldom empty. In general matters he was remarkably indulgent: the little faults and failings of those who sojourned with him he passed over without notice, but in two particulars he was inclined to be rather strict; and, inconsistent as it may seem, these were, that none of them should *get drunk*, and that the whole should attend regularly every night at family worship, or *the reading*, as he termed it. Whether he was himself drunk or sober, he could never rest satisfied unless a portion of Scripture had been read, part of a psalm sung, and what he considered an appropriate prayer offered up. When he chanced to be in the former of these conditions, as might have been expected, rather odd scenes sometimes occurred. While some verses of the chapter which had been selected were read three or four times, others were passed over with a long yawn. The singing was in general managed with tolerable decorum, from being under the direction of another; but the prayer, though offered up in tones which were really intended to be solemn, was frequently like anything save what an address to the Omnipotent and Omnipresent Ruler of the Universe should be.

Another of Peter's foibles was card-playing: a pack of cards was kept almost constantly lying on the table, and, as soon as he came in from his day's work, it was his custom to get engaged in a game with as many of his lodgers as could be persuaded to join in this sort of dissipation. He made it a point, however, never to play for money, in which, according to his idea of the matter, lay the whole of the sin of card-playing: yet he was as zealous in his play as if the winning or losing of a whole world had depended upon every game; and when he chanced to be successful, he would have played on and on till next morning without showing the slightest symptom of getting tired; but when the tide of fortune happened to flow in a contrary direction, the cards were thrown by at an early hour, and the Scriptures were called for.

"D'ye hear," was his usual exclamation on these occasions; "hand me the Bible that I may read and mak' preparation for gaun to our beds in a reasonable time, like ither Christians."

With all these inconsistencies, Peter was not a hypocrite. He believed in the truth of the religion which he professed; and, though it could not restrain him from certain pieces of folly, in other respects it had a considerable influence on his character and manners. As already hinted, he was a laborious and hard working man; and what was still more extraordinary, he possessed no inconsiderable share of benevolence, and was ever ready to assist, as far as he possibly could, those who were in distress.

Having thus described Auld Peter as he was about the year 1835, we must now go back for the beginning of our story to an earlier period of his history. While residing in the country, previous to his marriage, he had become acquainted with a young woman, whom the reader, for the present, must be pleased to call Susan Anderson. There was nothing particular in their intimacy beyond what may be expected in common intimacies of the kind—that is to say, Peter never spoke of love to her in a direct form, though, perhaps, he might have been justly charged with certain of those gallantries which some unmarried men consider themselves called upon to display in the presence of every female between the ages of fifteen and five-and-thirty. For several years, however, he had not seen her: he was now married, had settled in Glasgow, and his wife had brought him several children, when Susan one day called on him with a child in her arms and tears in her eyes. Peter welcomed her with all his natural kindness of disposition, and soon began to inquire the cause of her distress.

Her story, which is only a counterpart to that of thousands, was soon told. A sawyer, by name John, or, as he was more commonly called, Jock Dempster, had pretended to be desperately in love with her, and promised to make her his wife as soon as he could make the necessary arrangements for their future comfort. She returned his supposed affection with unsuspecting simplicity; but only a few months had elapsed when he began to relax in his attentions, and to exhibit evident symptoms of being tired of her company. Nor did matters long remain thus: his next step was to collect those trifling sums of money which were owing him for work in the neighbourhood, and set off privately for Glasgow, where he no doubt expected to be free from any farther annoyance which she might think of giving him. The reader need scarcely be told that he was the father of her child—that she had traced him with some difficulty to the above mentioned city, and that she had now come to try if she could obtain that justice which the law awards in cases like her own. Success as yet depended entirely on circumstances. Among such an immense mass of human beings, innumerable difficulties remained to be encountered in the way of discovering and securing him. To obviate these, Peter did everything in his power, by giving his advice and assistance almost unasked. He instructed her, in the best manner he could, how to proceed, while his wife undertook to keep the child till she could make the necessary inquiries. Thus befriended, she commenced her search, and after a considerable time spent in questioning the people about the timber yards, etc., she succeeded in procuring what she deemed certain information concerning him. She had been previously instructed by Peter not to make him aware of her presence till she had provided herself with the means of preventing his flight; and her next care was to procure two officers. With these she entered the room where he was making merry with some boon companions, and, heedless alike of his promises, entreaties, and threatenings, got him conveyed straight to the gaol.

To all appearance, she had him now fairly in her power: the evidence was too clear to admit of his denying the charge which she brought against him, and the authorities of the place seemed willing to enforce the law in her behalf, as far as that was practicable. But with his confinement, aided, perhaps, by a conviction, that the cause was one in which he was likely to be worsted, the obduracy of his heart began to melt; he appeared once more to entertain a sense of right and wrong, and to be willing to do justice to the victim of his previous misconduct. This change of sentiment was carefully paraded before Susan, who still continued to visit him in the prison, and to try, with feminine feeling, to make him more comfortable in his solitude, while she herself lodged with Peter, whose wife kept her child when she was abroad upon these expeditions. The thing had, if we may so speak, its desired effect: won over by these signs of contrition, which he was so careful to exhibit, and his promises to make ample restitution for the evil he had done, she consented to his liberation, and immediately put a stop to all farther proceedings against him.

For one day she had the pleasure of enjoying her triumph, and lived in the hope that he would deal honourably with her at last. But, in the language of the inspired penman, "If the Ethiopian change his skin, and the leopard his spots, then may they that are accustomed to do evil learn to do well." When evening came, he pretended some business with a former master which would detain him for half an hour; she had now no suspicion as to the integrity of his intentions, and he was permitted to go without a word. But his resolution had been already taken: at the end of two days he had not returned, and Susan was once more left to lament the facility with which she had listened to his vows of repentance, and believed his faithless promises.

After several days more spent in what at first appeared to be fruitless inquiries, she ascertained, that on the morning after leaving her, he had been seen on the road to Edinburgh, in which place, or in Leith, it was supposed he again intended to seek a concealment from the woman he had wronged. She had already spent nearly the whole of the little money she could command in paying officers' fees, etc., to get him arrested, and in treating him after he was set at liberty; but she still entertained the idea, that if she could discover him once more, she would profit by the lessons she had previously received, and not let him go so easily again. Peter and his wife were still willing to befriend her, and leaving her child to their care, and taking with her a small sum of money, which she had borrowed from them, she set off a second time in pursuit of the fugitive.

There are some individuals, whose ideas of gratitude and propriety will stand the test for a length of time, and, in moderately favourable circumstances, they may maintain a fair reputation for consistency and good conduct through life; but when severe trials come, and temptations follow each other in close succession, they lack that stern and unbending principle which prompts to virtuous perseverance, even in the midst of the most gloomy prospects; and it is no uncommon thing to see them giving way to expediency, or what they are pleased to think necessity, and yielding in the end to profligacy and ruin. To this class Susan seems to have belonged; for she never returned.

The boy, thus left without father or mother to care for him, was named Jock Dempster, after the first mentioned parent. During the helpless years of infancy, Peter's wife nursed him with almost as much care as she did her own children; and as he grew up, for a length of time, he experienced from Peter himself nearly the same treatment as if he had been a legitimate member of the family. At the proper age he was sent to school, and from the time which he spent there, he *might* have been a tolerable proficient in reading, writing, and arithmetic; but he would not learn, and in his eleventh or twelfth year he was, at best, but a sorry dabbler in the whole of these sciences. About this time he was also encouraged to try various sorts of common labour, by which, had he been so inclined, he might have afterwards earned his bread. To sum up the matter in a few words, he was, in most respects, treated more like a son than the son of a stranger; but somehow, there was from the beginning a marked difference between him and the other children of the family.

Common experience teaches us, that the parents often communicate a very considerable share of their looks and personal appearance to their offspring; and a closer scrutiny would almost lead to the belief, that along with these, in some instances, they also transmit many of their habits and propensities. Be this as it may, Jock showed a decided aversion to everything like close employment, in which respect he exactly resembled his father, who never wrought steadily, but only when he was driven to it by necessity. Almost from infancy he had been noted for smooth-tongued falsehood, and a very great proficiency at framing excuses for all sorts of errors and misdemeanors; and here again the reader need not be reminded how much of the same disgraceful qualities one of his parents had exhibited in his conduct toward the other. As he advanced in life, and began to earn trifling sums for little jobs which he was occasionally compelled to perform, he always manifested a greater inclination to steal away and spend them in the taverns and ale-houses, than to supply them to any useful purpose. Numbers of little things were also, from time to time, amissing in the neighbourhood, and could never afterwards be discovered. At first, some doubts were entertained as to what could have become of them; but by and by evidence began to appear of Jock's being *tarry-fingered* as well as *slippery-tongued*. As these habits became better known, he began to acquire a very bad fame in the immediate vicinity of his foster-father's dwelling; very few cared for being much in his company, and this compelled him to seek his associates at a greater distance.

Among other places which he frequented, there were some houses on the outskirts of the town, in one of which lived a woman called Margaret Thompson, who had been lately married. For her he had, somehow or other, performed some little services, and, though she had heard rumours of his character, and did not greatly like him, she still considered herself bound to receive him with common civility. Among her neighbours, there was a girl named Jenny Stewart, who, when very young had learned the art of weaving with her father, after which she had spent several years in the country at service; but that parent having died some time ago, she had returned, and now supported herself and her widowed mother by her exertions at the loom. With her Jock had frequent opportunities of meeting in his visits to Margaret Thompson; and being both about the same age, and having arrived at that period when young persons of different sexes are apt to contract a sort of regard for each other, which, though not exactly love, is nevertheless nearly akin to it, they soon seemed to become mutually attached. Jock's real sentiments it was impossible to fathom; but Jenny was, at least, sincere in her friendship, and while almost every one else looked upon him as "a ne'er-do-weel," she still continued to regard him with pity, if not with affection.

Jock, however, did not seem destined to reign over the heart of the orphan girl without a rival. Shortly after their acquaintance commenced, a young lad called Robert Thompson, who was a cousin of Margaret's, after having spent some years with a farmer in the country, returned to the place of his nativity for the purpose of learning the art of weaving. As was natural, he became a visitor at his relation's, and there he, too, saw, and soon seemed to like, Jenny Stewart. This circumstance produced a sort of rivalry between the men, or boys, whichever the reader chooses to call them; and, as might have been expected, increased the attentions of both as often as they could find an opportunity of bestowing them apart. It also made Jock more careful, for the time, to conceal his misdeeds, and more assiduous in his endeavours to appear amiable in her eyes. Had the object of these attentions been one of those mixtures of littleness and levity, who can never be in love with anything save admiration, such an occurrence would have only increased her vanity, and, perhaps, made her alike indifferent to both. But, young as she was, she had a heart already formed for an exclusive attachment; and, unfortunately for herself, in the present instance, the kindness and attention of her last come admirer only made her cling more closely to the first, who was, unquestionably, by far the most worthless of the two.

Matters stood thus when Jock had reached his seventeenth year, and Peter, who hitherto had afforded him a home, as well as a considerable portion of his victuals, insisted on his betaking himself to some regular employment, by which he might provide honourably for his own wants; and, to stimulate him onward in the path of duty, fairly refused to shelter him any longer unless he did so. Jock pleaded hard for another week to consider as to what line he would adopt, and this was granted. But, instead of improving it by making preparations for active exertion, he continued to lounge idly from place to place as he had done before, and when the last days of his reprieve from toil were drawing to an end, he began to dream of going to America, where he had heard of people making large fortunes, and where he expected no doubt to do the same. This, however, he intended to keep a profound secret till he was on the point of sailing, or, perhaps, till he had sailed altogether for that country; and to raise money to pay his passage was now the prime object of his cogitations. As a first step on the road to realising the necessary sum, he contrived to obtain an interview with Jenny Stewart, and by telling her a long and pathetic story about the ill-usage he had received from Peter, and his determination to leave the house of that individual immediately, if he could only procure as much as would purchase a few tools with which to work for himself, and something over to support him till he could earn a fortnight's wages, he easily persuaded her to go to the master for whom she wrought and take up the price of the web upon which she was then employed for the purpose of giving it to him. In this speculation he was completely successful: he was now master of £1 8s., and with £1 12s. more he expected to be able to effectuate his purpose. His next attempt was, if possible, of a still less honourable kind. Margaret Thompson had a favourite game cock, for which, if he could lay his hands on him quietly, he believed he would make certain of from eight to ten shillings; and with the intention of trying to "wrest the proud bird from his perch," he continued to linger about the premises till the whole of the neighbours were in bed, and, as he fancied, fast asleep. His movements, however, had, unknown to him, been observed by his rival, who, judging that Jenny Stewart was the object of them, determined to watch him; and, just as he had brought chanticleer forth from a hole in the thatch, which he had made for the purpose— grasping the feathered prey firmly around the neck to prevent noise—he found himself in the hands of Robert Thompson, who, in personal strength, was more than a match for him.

"Sae, this is the way ye contrive to mak your living," said the captor; "but as ye dinna seem inclined to work, I maun try if I can lessen your expenses by getting free lodgings for ye." As he spoke these words, he gave him a slap on the face with his open hand, and a severe shake, neither of which boded any good will; but in performing the last mentioned operation, his foot slipped, and, to prevent himself from falling, he was compelled to let go his grasp. Jock, when at liberty, was as much an overmatch for his antagonist in speed, as his antagonist would have been an overmatch for him in strength; and, once free, he did not fail to make the best use of his heels. He was, however, perfectly aware, that he had now committed a crime—namely, that of housebreaking and theft—which would subject him to public odium, and that the fact of his being thus guilty was known to one who would make no secret of it. His plan of raising money, with which to pay his passage to America, was, moreover, at an end; he had no reason to suppose that his former benefactor would again take him in; and such was the impression made upon his mind by these comfortless reflections, that he went, hot foot, to the quarters of a recruiting sergeant, and immediately enlisted.

He had now engaged with masters who had the power of enforcing obedience to their wishes, and from their employment, however hard or disagreeable it might be, there was no escaping. We have no intention, however, of following him through his drillings and drubbings for awkwardness, or of giving a history of his soldiership. Suffice it to say, that several years passed quietly away, and the neighbours, who at first considered themselves well quit of him, had begun to forget that such a creature had ever been among them, when, in 1835, he again made his appearance, in all the pride of a military costume, and with all the airs of a finished soldier.

"By having done some services for the *Curnal*," he said, "he had got a *furlo*, and he didn't know how he could spend it better than by coming down to see his father and mother, and all them people who had been so kind to him when he was a lad."

Auld Peter, to whose habitation he went directly, and who had now forgotten the greater part of his former misconduct, was once more ready to receive him with open arms, and to treat him with the best the house could afford. Upon his former benefactor he bestowed the parental appellation with almost every alternate sentence: it even seemed that he paraded the words *father* and *mother* more frequently than the occasion required, and, indeed, a great deal oftener than a real relationship would have warranted. But at this piece of ostentation Peter did not appear to be at all offended: he saw that his outward man was greatly improved, he hoped that a corresponding change had been effected in his conduct, and he was willing to believe him when he asserted that he was perfectly reformed.

"I have entirely given up drinking, and all them low things," said he. "I never tastes a single *glass* now; and I can assure you, the *Curnal* is anxious to have me made a non-commissioned officer as soon as possible, but somehow the thought of it doesn't agree with me."

As he began to feel moderately certain of being once more established in their good graces, Jock amused the family with a great many accounts of his escapes and exploits since he became a soldier, some of which bordered on the miraculous, if not on the incredible; but they all did their best to believe them, and that evening was a happy one with Auld Peter. The following day was Sunday, and to grace the stranger, some extras had been provided for the *tea*, which, on these occasions, formed the usual family breakfast. The bread, in particular, was to be toasted and buttered, and Jock at once volunteered his service to cut it into slices of a fashionable thickness. At first he proceeded with his self-imposed task in perfect silence, appearing to display great dexterity, but ever and anon casting a glance on either side to see if he was observed. He was evidently fishing for a little praise, but somehow no one thought of taking the bait, and when he could contain himself no longer, he stopped work, and looking toward the family, "Don't you see," he said, "how neatly I can do them things now?"

"Whatten things?" was Peter's brief reply, couched in words which made it also a question.

"Cutting the *brade*, I mean," said Jock: "don't you think I can do it better now, than when I went away? We're *larned* to do all them things neatly in the *ragement* you know."

"Unco right," rejoined Peter; "but I guess, if onybody would learn me the way to get siller to buy bread, I could e'en cut it as I've done afore, without muckle learnin!" This settled the matter for the present, and Jock soon after gave evidence that he was, at least, as great a proficient at *eating* bread, as he was at cutting it.

Notwithstanding his previous professions of perfect reformation, on the Monday following he contrived to persuade one of Peter's sons to accompany him to a public-house, where they spent the greater part of the day; and when they returned in the afternoon, it was evident that they had both imbibed more proof spirits than prudence. Auld Peter, as the reader will recollect, was sometimes inclined to judge less charitably of the failings of others than of his own; in particular, he disliked to see any inmate of the dwelling—himself always excepted—in a state of intoxication; and at this piece of conduct he appeared to be rather offended. Albeit he had no objection to a dram himself, he could not brook the idea of any of his sons becoming drunkards; and when he considered how a very small beginning may sometimes lead to a fatal ending, he began to look coldly on his red-coated guest. The latter appeared to have some notion of what was passing within him, and more than half maudlin as he was, he strove with great assiduity to obliterate the unfavourable impression which his misconduct had made on the heart of his entertainer.

"I would be very sorry to do any of them things which you don't agree with, my dear father," said he. "But I only meant to give my brother here a *glaas* out of pure respect. Had it not been out of respect to him, and to the house where he was born, and out of love to yourself, my dear father, I wouldn't have never set my foot in one of them publics; for I doesn't like them at all."

"Ye had better gi'en him some ither thing than a glass," said Peter shortly, "or keepit your respect for him, an' your love for me to yoursel', till a better opportunity for showing them came round."

Jock did not drop the matter here; as the effects of the liquor wore off, he made repeated attempts to establish himself again in the good opinion of his host; but from the thoughtful expression which his countenance at times assumed, it was evident he had begun to fear that his reign in the affections of Peter, and the time which he could saddle himself upon his hospitality were both drawing to a close.

Next morning he did not appear at the usual hour, and when breakfast was ready, thinking that he had lain too long in bed, some of the family went to tell him that it was time to rise. The bed, however, was empty, and the bed-clothes cold; but this excited little surprise, and no alarm. It was simply concluded that he had risen and gone out before the other members of the family were astir. Had they ever suffered from the visits of "the nightly thief," this circumstance might have caused some suspicion, or it might have produced an immediate examination to see that all was safe; but hitherto their property had been providentially protected from all attempts of the kind; long security has a tendency to lay vigilance asleep; and, to make them yet more secure, they knew that the whole of the chests, drawers, etc., in the house were locked, and they saw the keys hanging safely, where they had hung for many a year in the corner of one of the beds. Not a single thought ever crossed their minds of anything being wrong, and when, at breakfast time, one of the lodgers asked "What had become of Jock?"

"If Jock do weel for himsel', I care unco little what becomes o' him," was Peter's reply.

The forenoon passed, and the dinner hour was approaching, when Peter, finding that he must call upon some individuals belonging to the better class, came home to dress himself in a manner befitting the occasion. But what was his surprise when on going to his chest to take out his clothes, he found it swept of everything valuable, and left with only a few half-worn garments lying at the bottom! A farther search was made, the other repositories of the house were instantly examined, and, to the utter dismay of Peter and his wife, they found them in the same condition. Chests, drawers, and all, had been ransacked—nothing had escaped either the eye or the ingenuity of the depredator; and scarcely a single article of wearing apparel, which was at all respectable, had been left within the door. Peter himself was in what has been called *a peck of troubles*, and when the lodgers returned to their dinners, his wife was wringing her hands in the bitterest distress.

"What's the matter now?" inquired one of them.

"Matter enough," was her reply. "That villain—that scoundrel—that sodger Jock—the foul fiend rive the heart out o' him!—if *he* hasna robbit the house o' every rag worth carrying awa', either last night or this morning. No ae steek has he left Peter or the laddies to pit on their backs—deil gae wi' him, and may he break ilka bane in his bouk, and his neck to the bargain the first time he gangs out-ower the door—Lord forgi'e me; for I dinna ken what I'm sayin'. But surely he's the greatest blackguard that ever set a croun to the lift, to come an' rob them wha had done sae muckle for him!"

From such an examination and valuation as could be made at the moment, it appeared that he had carried off clothes and other articles, equal in worth to between six and seven pounds. To people in easy circumstances, this might have been a small matter, but to those who could only provide for their daily wants, in the natural order in which they occurred, by their daily earnings, it involved something nearly akin to ruin. Still no one knew what to do for the recovery of the lost property, or where to look for the thief. So secretly and so ingeniously had he managed his nocturnal operations, that he had left no trace behind him; and not the slightest hope of a discovery could be indulged, till one of Peter's lodgers, more acute than the rest, happened to think of an attempt to waylay him at the coach-offices.

"If he had disposed of the property," this individual argued, "he must have waited till the brokers' shops were open, in which case he could not leave the town till the day was considerably advanced; while, on the other hand, if he intended to take it along with him, some time for packing would be necessary, and some conveyance would be required to carry it to its destination; so that in either way there was a chance of finding him among the passengers of the afternoon coaches."

This idea was acted upon without delay: inquiries were made at the various coach offices, and it was soon ascertained that an individual, answering exactly to his description, had paid for a seat in one of these vehicles running between Glasgow and Edinburgh. The necessary steps for having him arrested were immediately taken: a strict watch was kept, and it was expected that he must now fall into the snare which was laid for him; but, from having understood, as was supposed, that his person was in request, he never came to occupy the seat for which he had paid, and the coach started at the appointed time without him. The circumstance, however, gave evidence that he was still in the town; a close search was instituted, and next morning he was apprehended, in the company of a female of indifferent fame, in one of those dens of prostitution and crime, of which, sad to say, there are but too many in our country. It is almost superfluous to say that he was forthwith conveyed to prison; but still not the slightest evidence could be found by which to criminate him. The property had indeed been stolen—that was clearly proved—but beyond the mere circumstance of his having left the house clandestinely, at an early hour in the morning, there was not even a presumption of his being the thief; and, though no one seemed to doubt his guilt, the chances appeared to be as a hundred to one that he would escape after all.

It is hard, however, for the evil doer to elude at every turn the consequences of his crimes; in one way or other punishment generally finds him out. The supposed culprit appeared to have plenty of money in his pocket, and, thus provided, he easily found means to procure a supply of spirits, with which, during the time that elapsed between his being taken into custody, and his being brought forward to answer for his conduct, he made so free that, when his examination came on, he was completely drunk; and the magistrate, before whom he appeared, ordered him to be remanded to prison till the following day. While staggering through the passages of the jail, to the apartment in which he had been previously confined, his bonnet fell off, and, as it rolled on the floor, a pair of braces fell out! Had he been sober, or if he had known that his examination would come on so soon, these were articles which he would have, no doubt, been more careful to conceal; but his love of liquor, and consequent intoxication, had prevented him from managing this part of the matter with his usual circumspection. Drunk as he was, he tried to recover the braces, however, and to thrust them into his bonnet again, with an eagerness which excited the suspicions of his conductors. By these they were immediately secured, and sent to Peter's family to see if they had been among the articles which were amissing; and thus the means of convicting a profligate and unprincipled villain of one crime were supplied by his indulgence in another. The braces were instantly identified, and sworn to as having belonged to Peter. A farther search was made, and before the infatuated soldier had recovered from the effects of his potations, some other articles were found upon his person, which served as incontestable proofs of his guilt. These, as it appeared, he had reserved from the spoil for his own particular use, and in so doing, with that infatuation which not unfrequently clings to evil doers, he had kept about him the silent witnesses of his crime.

When they were produced on the following day as so many evidences of the charge brought against him, and he was asked what he had to offer in his own defence, "I can offer nothing," was his reply, "but as how I was insulted the night before, and as I didn't like to take them sort of things without showing that I had some spirit, 1 went off next morning, and I picked up them articles in the dark, instead of some of my own, which were worth twice as much."

When asked how he could account for the door being opened, when the key was on the inside, and so much property removed by one who was unacquainted with the house: "Please your honour," said he, with a degree of cool effrontery which seemed to surprise even the Judge, "when as how it happens that a theft is committed, all the innocent men in the country are not called upon to account for them things; and I cannot account for it, but as how the thief might have come after I went away." When told that the circumstance of his going away, and leaving the door of the house open under night, was in itself a crime punishable by law, he appeared for the first time rather at a loss what to say.

Without following him farther the foregoing may serve as a specimen of his manner of pleading, which was such a mixture of evasive impudence and cunning as to show that he was by no means new to the trade. All would not do, however; the examination was patiently and impartially conducted to an end, and when it concluded he was sentenced to sixty days' imprisonment, with the usual fare, bread and water; and the punishment of his past crimes seemed at last to have found him out. But at first he had money in his pocket, and with this auxiliary his natural disposition for trick enabled him to devise the means of mitigating, in various ways, the rigour of his sentence. His finances, however, at last failed, and then he was completely miserable; but to the no small surprise of his fellow-prisoners, who knew no means which he could have for obtaining it, before the term of his confinement expired, he again appeared to be in possession of the *wherewithal*; and when liberated he was able to get drunk before leaving Glasgow to join his regiment, which was then lying in Edinburgh.

While he went on his way "glorying in his shame," Jenny Stewart was seen returning to her home with a look of thoughtful sadness strongly depicted on her countenance.

"Ye'r looking ill the day, Jenny," said Margaret Thompson, who chanced to come up to her.

"Maybe I am," was Jenny's brief reply.

"I've been vext for you aye since I heard it," rejoined the other; "for it's a sad thing for a weel doing lass to tak up her head wi' the like o' him."

"The like o' wha?" inquired the young woman, with an evident increase of anxiety, but without blushing.

"Dinna, be angry," said the other, "for I'm only saying what I've heard ither folk say; and dinna think," she added with a degree of unaffected sympathy in her voice, which did not escape the notice of her listener—"dinna think that I want to laugh at your misfortunes, or triumph ower you in your distress; for e'en when ye was a lassie, I didna like to see that ne'er-do-weel Jock Dempster come sae muckle about you; and since he came back wi' his red coat, an' his fool's cap, to steal Auld Peter's claes, and folk began to notice that ye was concerned about him, and to say that ye was in love wi' him, I've felt mair on your account than I can tell."

"I'm no in love wi' him," said Jenny emphatically, and still no blush crossed her cheek,—"I'm no in love wi' him: we had only some acquaintance when we were baith young."

"Ah Jenny, Jenny!" rejoined the other, "ye'r just acting the part I've acted mysel'; but if ye would only tell me the cause o' your present distress, I would never mention it to anither, and it would maybe lighten your heart."

Jenny was at once won over by the deep sympathy which her friend thus evinced, and, without farther hesitation, though not without a good deal of embarrassment, she went on to make a candid confession of her own feelings and motives.

"I'm no in love with him noo," she began; but I maun confess I likeit his company better than ony ither body's afore he gaed to the sodgers. In spite o' a' the ill things I heard about him, I aye thought he had a wark wi' me, and that I would be able to persuade him to do better some time, sooner or later. And when he came to me wi' a story about the ill usage Auld Peter had gi'en him, and said that he meant to do for himsel' noo, I canna tell ye how happy I felt; for I thought the time had come when he would gi'e ower his wierdless ways, and, to encourage him, I e'en gied him siller that I should hae keepit to provide for my poor frail mither. But a' wouldna do, and aff he gaed an' left me. And even after he was awa', it aye pleased me, somehow, to mind about the hours we had spent thegither; and mony a time I've stown out my lane to think upon him. Aweel, he came back, and he never thought o' coming to speer for me, though my mither was dead, and I was left maist without a freend. And then he stealt Auld Peter's claes, and I saw that it was a' ower wi' him; but still when he sent word to me that he was starvin', and sought siller to help to keep him leevin', I couldna refuse him a' I had. But what was war than a' that, and what mak's my heart sair to think on't, noo when it is past, he persuaded me to meet him, and to gie him the last shilling I had in the world after he was set free,—no that I regard the siller, but the shame o' bein' seen in sic company."

"Aweel," rejoined the other, "I can hardly blame ye, when I consider the regard ye ance had for him. But I hope ye've now gi'en ower a' thoughts o' keepin' up a correspondence wi' him, or ever bein' sibber to him than ye are."

"May God, wha kens my heart, keep me frae ever bein' conneckit wi' sic a man!" ejaculated Jenny. "And, so far from having ony thoughts o' the kind, I'm sae ashamed o' my ain simplicity, and the cracks it has occasioned, that, if I could get a place, I would gang whaur I was never seen on earth afore, to be out o' the gait!"

"I'm glad to see you that way mindit," said Margaret; "and I think I can maybe help you a little to the accomplishment o' your wishes. My cousin Rob, wha, as ye ken, was at farm-service afore he learned the weaver-trade, has grown tired o' the loom, an' he's gaun to a place ca'd Double Dykes, mair than twenty miles frae this. But that's no what I was gaun to tell ye. The foreman—a freend o' his mither's—when he greed him, bade him send word if he could hear o' a steady lass, wha would engage for a year to work i' the house. Now, ye've been at service already, and ken a' about it, and ye've only to say that ye'll tak the place, and I'se warrant it's yours."

Jenny sighed deeply, and almost seemed as if she would have said, "I've been insensible to the merits, and the kindness o' your cousin ower lang." She did not say so, however, but she seemed well pleased with the prospect of obtaining a situation at a distance from her present residence, in the neighbourhood of which, as she said, she was now ashamed to be seen.

While these things were going on, the conduct of Jock Dempster had become so consistently and uniformly bad as to attract in a particular manner the notice of his officers. After having pardoned many of his minor offences, and tried in vain to reclaim him, by flogging and other expedients, it was at last resolved, in a court-martial, to inflict on him the last and most degrading punishment which can be offered to a soldier; and he was accordingly, with due formality, *drummed out of his regiment!* This to him would have been a light matter had he been acquainted with any means by which he could support himself without labour. Labour of all sorts he mortally hated, and, to avoid the distressing alternative of adopting it, he began to look around for those upon whose simplicity he might successfully prey—in other words, he began to look about for individuals whom he might dupe into the belief that he was a legitimate object of charity, and thus extort from them the means of living in idleness as long as possible. His first plan was to pretend that he was a deserter, and that a party of soldiers were close upon his heels to capture and convey him back to his regiment again, where, he said, he would have to undergo so many lashes, that he would a thousand times rather be shot than fall into their hands. To give an appearance of truth to this story, he had contrived to daub the letter D upon his breast, with some sort of black, or rather brown colouring, so as to resemble the burnt mark which is commonly bestowed on individuals thus disgraced for their first offence—his, as he pretended, being the second. Another method by which he frequently tried to extort charity was to secrete his clothes at some distance from a village or farm, dressing himself the while in a parcel of rags, which he carried for the purpose, and when he came to the place, by affirming that his habiliments had been nearly torn from his back while running through plantations and among rocks to escape his pursuers, he often succeeded in inducing benevolent individuals to give him a complete supply of such garments as came first to hand. These again he never failed to dispose of for what they would bring with the first favourable opportunity. It were almost an endless task to give an account of all the devices to which he had recourse.

Suffice it to say that by such arts he contrived to live like a gentleman for several weeks, making the most of the road wherever he went; and proceeding slowly the while toward Glasgow, where he no doubt expected to be able to dupe some of his former acquaintances more effectually than he had hitherto done.

A few hours after he reached the scene of his early exploits, he met his earliest benefactor on one of the bridges, and one might have thought he would have been ashamed to look him in the face. But, no!—he hesitated not a moment to address him with the greatest familiarity, and the greatest apparent ease. "My dear father," said he, "I am glad I have seen you! I trust we shall yet be friends, in spite of all them things which are past, and if my misfortunes were over, I am sure I could show you how dearly I love you." He was on the point of beginning to tell the story of his feigned misfortunes, but he already saw that it would be in vain. Auld Peter was not one of those who could be twice taken in the same snare, and he passed on without once appearing to notice the individual who thus addressed him, or even to be aware of his presence. The other cast a rather rueful look after him, and then sheered off in a different direction. This was the last meeting of Auld Peter and his foster son—as such we have mentioned it—and, so far as is known, he never heard of him afterwards. Heard of, however, he was, and in what manner it must now be our task to tell.

Shortly after the above mentioned occurrence, Robert Thompson, whose going to Double Dykes has been already noticed, accompanied Jenny Stewart as she went to the cowhouse in the evening to milk the cows; and almost as soon as they were safely housed beside these animals, "My heart," said he, "has boded some mischief a' this afternoon."

"I'm sorry to hear that," rejoined Jenny; "but what reason can ye ha'e for boding mischief this afternoon mair than ony ither time?"

"I'll tell ye that enoo," was his reply. "We were but a short time yokit, when that ill-looking sinner, Peter Hepburn, as he ca's himsel', came to me pretending that he wantit to see the master; and, when I tell'd him he wasna at hame, he speer'd a' about him—whaur he was, and whether we expectit him hame the night?—Now, I'm far cheatit if he dinna ha'e an e'e after the siller the master gat by his aunty. They say he has keys about him that will open ony lock in a' the parish; and, if that be true, how easy might he find his way to the master's writing desk, and pouch the siller, when you and the mistress are fast asleep, and no ane ken what time he did it, or whether it was him or no!"

"That's terrible!" said Jenny, rising up from the cow she had just begun to milk, "that's terrible," she repeated; "but do you really think Peter Hepburn is a character o' that kind?"

"If a' be true that's said, he has done as ill already," was the answer. "And forbye, they say the woman he lives wi', though she has had twa or three bairns to him, is no his wife; and that doesna look very like an honest man."

"No like an honest man indeed!" said Jenny, with a feminine sense of delicacy, and the treatment which her sex had a right to look for in these connections. "Na, na—that settles the matter, and after that he is fit for onything! But what can we dae noo?"

"That's no a' yet," continued her companion: "a short time after he left us, wha d'ye think comes across the field but your auld acquaintance Jock Dempster! He didna come to me, however, but gaed to the hauflin when I was tillin' a headrig on the tither side o' the hedge, and tell'd him a lang story about desertin' frae the sodgers, and the sodgers being' after him to tak' him again. And then he speer'd if he could get a nicht's lodgin's about the toun, and when the hauflin tell'd him that the master was frae hame lookin' after his aunty's effects, and that the mistress never quartered gangrels, he said he couldna help it. And then he speer'd a' about you, and about the house, and whether there was a wa' between it and the auld *hay-loft;* and when the hauflin tell'd him that it was just plaistered, he said the house would surely be cauld. I keepit out o' his sight as weel as I could; I'm maist sure he disna ken that I'm here. But what think ye o' a' this?"

"I dinna ken what to think," was Jenny's reply. "But I hope he'll never come back."

"Dinna trust ower muckle to that," rejoined her companion. "It's maybe shootin' at far marks, but, if I'm no mista'en again, him and Peter Hepburn are either to work to ane anither's hands, or else, ilka ane for himsel', about the siller; and I wou'dna wonder if they were baith back the nicht; for Jock is as fit for takin' a purse as preachin' a sermon, and as likely to fill a halter as an honest man's bannet!"

Though it was not without some reason that the young man had hazarded these conjectures, besides his care for his master's property, he had perhaps a secondary object in view—namely, that of establishing his own sagacity and penetration in Jenny's eyes, together with the concern which he felt for her safety. Whatever had been his intention, the starting nerves and terrified looks of the maiden, along with the hints which she gave, that she would not remain another hour at Double Dykes unless the whole of the men about the place kept her company, gave evidence of extreme agitation; and it was now his task to soothe rather than to excite her fears.

"Dinna terrify yoursel', Jenny," he said tenderly, and as he spoke he pressed her shoulder with his hand, which, as if instinctively, began, by slow degrees, to "slip round her neck," till, in the words of Burns, "his loof" was fairly "upon her bosom." "Dinna terrify yoursel'," he again repeated, "and ye may trust to a' the assistance I can gi'e ye. But ye ken the mistress is nervous, and, in her present state, if we were to raise an alarm it might be as muckle as her life is worth. Sae never ye *leet* a word about the matter, and I'll keep watch mysel' and warn the rest o' the men to the bargain; and, if the rogues come, they'll maybe no win sae easily awa' as they reckon on."

With some farther persuasion Jenny consented to adopt this plan; and though she started several times when the kitten made a noise by running across the floor, and, oftener than once, when the wind made a hollow moaning sound in the branches of the old tree at the end of the house, listened attentively to make certain that it was not human voices, nothing occurred to disturb the quiet till toward bed time, when she thought she heard a foot at the kitchen window, which chanced to be uncovered, and then a gentle rap at the door. With trembling limbs and a beating heart she went to ask who was there, and her more serious apprehensions were soon dissipated by the well known voice of Jock Dempster, which now saluted her ear in "the softest, sweetest tones," not unmixed with a degree of pathos which seemed well calculated to excite pity.

Men and women, with all their boasted powers of memory, understanding, and reflection, are very often guided by the impulse of the moment. Young persons, moreover, and more particularly those of the fair sex, can rarely return courtesy with coldness, or apparent kindness with harsh words; and thus it was with Jenny. Though she could have wished to bid her visitor go hence, she could not resist his appeal when he asked leave to come in and warm himself; and, foolish as it may seem, she opened the door.

It would be tiresome to narrate particularly the conversation which followed. Jenny was not again to be cajoled into giving him money, and, when he saw that his endeavours in this way were fruitless, he asked her for a drink of water. With this she readily supplied him, but the moment he had tasted it he declared it was not good.

"It is quite warm, I assure you," he said. "Now, Jenny, couldn't you take one of them jugs and bring me a drink of good fresh water from the well! It may be the last good turn you may ever be able to do me in your life; for I may be catched and taken to *hade*-quarters and tied up, like one of them cows of yours, to a stake, and shot in a day or two!"

Jenny disliked the idea of leaving him alone in the house even for a moment, but she could not resist the piteous appeal which he had made; the well, moreover, was but a step from the door, and, taking a jug from the wall, she hastened to comply with his request. Scarcely had she disappeared, however, when Jock started up with the quickness, and almost with the noiselessness, of the lightning which flashes harmlessly on an autumnal evening, and snatching a bunch of keys from a nail on which they hung, he concealed them in his bosom. When he had slaked his thirst, he pretended that he must travel a great many miles before morning, and immediately betook himself to his journey with all possible speed. He proceeded no farther, however, than a small plantation at the distance of about a quarter of a mile from the place; here he lay till the middle of the night was passed, and then cautiously returned. As he approached the house, he took off his shoes and carried them in his hand, treading as softly as if the road had been paved with glass. When he had proceeded a little farther, he lay down, and, by an ambiguous sort of motion, which he appeared to have practised before, drew himself along, something after the manner of the serpent. By the same process he ascended the stair of the auld *hay-loft*, and stopped before the door to take from his bosom the bunch of keys with which he had provided himself in the kitchen. He soon found one to answer the lock, and checking the *throw* of the bolt so as not to produce the slightest noise, he found ready admittance. To find a passage through the slender partition which separated the place he now occupied from the house, was an easy task; but even after this had been effected, it were difficult to say in what manner he proposed to avail himself of the advantage he had gained. Other doors, with the keys of which he was not provided, were to open before he could lay his hands on any valuable property; and, after all he had done, it is probable the thing might have turned out only one of those *intended burglaries* which are discovered next morning by certain unsuccessful attempts upon locks, windows, etc., without anything being a-missing.

Here, however, fortune seemed to favour the depredator; the door of the apartment which he now occupied stood open. This led him to another, and groping his way noiselessly along the wall, he came to a second door, which was also unlocked. Here he began to think it time to try if he could discover something which he could conveniently carry away. Fortunately, as he thought, his hand touched a writing desk, the lid of which appeared to be already open, and his heart bounded at the expectation of a rich prize. But on going round to the other end of it, what was his surprise, when, instead of money, his hand laid hold of the arm of a man, who instantly grappled with him, and tried to throw him down! Jock was neither very brave nor very daring, but he struggled manfully to overcome his opponent, without which he had no hopes of being able to get away. A desperate strife followed, in which both parties rolled on the floor, while chairs and tables crashed around them. At last a pistol was fired, which did no harm; and the first intruder had drawn a large knife from some concealment about his clothes, with the intent of inflicting a mortal wound on his antagonist; but before he could effect his purpose, the united screams of Jenny and her mistress had brought three or four men to the house, who instantly flew to the scene of strife with lighted candles, and Jock Dempster and Peter Hepburn were both easily secured.

Next morning the Sheriff-substitute was busily engaged in examinations as to the nature of the intended robbery, the names, occupations, and character of the offenders, and in endeavouring to procure evidence upon which to commit them for trial. When the ci-devant soldier was questioned concerning his name, from a conviction that it was already known to at least one of the witnesses, he gave it readily; and when questioned farther as to the place of his nativity and his parents, "I can't say as how I ever knew any of them relations," said he, "but if you go to Glasgow, Peter —— can tell you all about them, for he has seen them both."

"Ay, ay—it's just as I thought it would be!" screamed a half-frenzied female voice among the crowd of spectators who had gathered to witness the scene; and a meanly dressed and squalid-looking woman, apparently beyond the meridian of life, was seen elbowing her way to a position where she could have a clearer view of the prisoner. When she had gained her point, "Peter ——" she said, throwing aside a portion of her grizzled hair which had escaped from under a dirty cap, and raising her voice to a pitch which seemed to indicate a certain degree of insanity, "Peter ——, that's the man's name I left him wi', and now the son has been sent by the hand of God to condemn the father.—You need not send them to Glasgow for your parents," she added, addressing the prisoner, "I am your mother, and it is to that wretched man you owe your birth—Peter Hepburn, as they call him; but that is not his name, for he called himself Jock Dempster when ye were born."

Need we say more? The father and son were both convicted upon the clearest evidence, and both were sentenced to transportation. Susan Anderson, who had lived with the former in the capacity, without the name, of a wife, and whose reason had been rather affected by the ill usage and privations which she had already borne, stunned by the last blow, went deranged, and was afterwards supported by the parish. Jenny Stewart and Robert Thompson were married some months after; to their care the poor maniac was committed by the kirk-session; and with them she continued to live till Providence saw meet to take her away by death. And from her fate it is to be hoped the young will learn to beware how they form intimacies with dissolute characters, or with those whose characters are unknown.

THE END.

www.ingramcontent.com/pod-product-compliance
Lightning Source LLC
Chambersburg PA
CBHW030309240426
43673CB00040B/1108